Feminist Challenges in the Information Age

Schriftenreihe der Internationalen Frauenuniversität
»Technik und Kultur«

Band 5

Christiane Floyd et al. (Ed.)

Feminist Challenges in the Information Age

Information as a Social Resource

Leske + Budrich, Opladen 2002

Die Schriftenreihe der Internationalen Frauenuniversität „Technik und Kultur"
wird gefördert durch das Niedersächsische Vorab der VW-Stiftung.

Der vorliegende Band wurde durch die Universität Hamburg gefördert.

Gedruckt auf säurefreiem und alterungsbeständigem Papier.

Die Deutsche Bibliothek – CIP-Einheitsaufnahme
Ein Titeldatensatz für die Publikation ist bei
Der Deutschen Bibliothek erhältlich

ISBN 978-3-8100-3255-3   ISBN 978-3-322-94954-7 (eBook)
DOI 10.1007/978-3-322-94954-7

© 2002 Leske + Budrich, Opladen

Einband: design agenten, Hannover
Satz: Berthold Druck und Direktwerbunrg, Offenbach

Contents

Contents

Preface

In the last three decades, women's intervention in the social and natural sciences, in medicine and technology has introduced new paradigms. We have to admit that it takes time and energy to influence these fields in a feministic way. Women do not only work for the growth of knowledge, but also for the transformation of knowledge systems. This book is about using knowledge for action in an interdisciplinary effort focussing on information as a social resource.

Women's approach to the information age is different, as becomes visible in this book: Women's scholarly explorations include not only developing technology, but also improving communication and networking, as well as supporting democratic processes by taking advantage of the tremendous technological options. I am convinced that this approach is vital for living the information society, and that it will also make fields relating to information technology more attractive to women.

This book is the outcome of the Project Area INFORMATION of the International Women's University (*ifu*) held at the University of Hamburg in the summer 2000. As the Deputy Minister for Science and Research of the Free and Hanseatic City of Hamburg I was responsible for promoting this study program. The international gathering of 150 participants was a most exciting event. The experience of *ifu* has enriched me as a scientist, as a feminist and as a politician.

Events like *ifu* are politically encouraging. In Hamburg alone, *ifu* brought together – counting both faculty and students – women scientists and professionals from more than 60 countries all over the world. We obtained a realistic and vivid vision of international relations, which has of course always been most important for the development of science and technology. At the same time we recognized that the international dimension does also affect this positive vision adversely, since the broad consequences of economic globalization are going to benefit only a few nations and multinational companies of the North. The meeting of women scientists at *ifu* proved that another international world is possible, one which includes the interests of women and the participation of the South.

The realization of the *ifu* vision requires financial support. This was made easier for *ifu* 2000 by the fortunate circumstance that the responsible ministers on the federal and regional level were women. Since then the political situation and direction in Hamburg and elsewhere have changed. I hope that the now governing (mostly male) politicians will also understand the value of the *ifu* experiment and open the way for its continuation in the future.

This book presents and reflects some of the scholarly works, project designs, strategies and life experiences of the participants during the *ifu* period and makes it possible to share them with others. I hope it will be a milestone for a new beginning.

Hamburg, March 2002
Prof. Dr. Marlis Dürkop

Foreword

It was an honor and a pleasure for me to have the opportunity to participate in the *ifu* (International Women's University) pilot project in Hanover, Hamburg and Kassel. I learned much from my faculty colleagues and students.

Three aspects of the ifu courses and programs were especially valuable for me. One was the focus on interdisciplinarity and on what we could call 'counter-disciplinarity'. The resources of the multiple disciplines were brought to bear on the *ifu* topics. Moreover, the courses revealed the limitations of the ways in which the traditional social science, natural science and humanities disciplines could approach these topics. A second valuable aspect was the way in which the courses were designed to focus on concrete, practical 'problems' that shaped women's lives around such topics as water, cities, migration, work, bodies, and information. Here interdisciplinary and counter-disciplinary theoretical perspectives could enrich understanding of the conditions of women's daily lives. Third, *ifu* insisted on internationalizing its curricula, faculty, and students. The visions of higher education for women and the kinds of knowledge shared at *ifu* benefitted immensely from the resources provided by these kinds of internationalization.

Ifu provided resources and a model which can inspire transformations of women's higher education around the globe. A motto popular in the early days of the women's movements of the 1970's proclaimed that no woman could be liberated until every woman was liberated. Ifu has made it possible for us all to imagine more clearly how to approach this goal.

University of California at Los Angeles, June 2002
Sandra Harding

Introduction

This is a book resulting from a historic event. Its chapters present some of the scholarship that comes from our participation in the event, our reflections on the event, and our current research.

In 2000, nearly a thousand post-graduate women gathered in Germany to help construct and participate in a new International Women's University (called *ifu* throughout this book) that offered an experimental study program from mid-July to mid-October. The program was subdivided into six Project Areas – BODY, CITY, INFORMATION, MIGRATION, WATER, and WORK – distributed over several locations at different Northern German universities.

While other books in the *ifu* series are devoted to the scholarship in other Project Areas, this book reflects the research and experience in the Project Area INFORMATION held at the University of Hamburg. Here about 150 women spent three months working closely together and organize inclusive ways of creating and discussing knowledge about *Information as a Social Resource*. The women included teachers, graduate students, journalists, doctors, lawyers, politicians, businesswomen, representatives from non-government organizations, and more.

Readers need to imagine women from many languages and nations organizing themselves into twelve (sub-)projects: Community Development through Information; Cultural Modes, Self-Expression and New Media; Curiosity, Intuition and Information Technology; Future of Education; Health Care Information; Identities and Globalization; Information Kiosks; Knowledge Architectures; Media Industries and Democracy; Reconstructing Gender on the Internet; Virtual Communities and Visions of Citizenship. These projects provided an environment for goal-oriented cooperation across disciplinary and cultural boundaries throughout the *ifu* period.

In addition the participants attended and organized lectures and short courses on a variety of topics, such as Feminism, Multiculturalism and Postcolonialism; Intercultural Communication; Knowledge Management and Information Technology; Theoretical Approaches to Autonomy; Indigenous Knowledge and Technology; Participation in Decision-Making and Design, as well as art workshops enabling creative ways of dealing with information technology and the new media.

Each of the project groups produced one or more 'final results' presented both in Hamburg and at a large scholarship fair held at the main *ifu* campus in Hanover as women from the six Project Areas met to share some of their work of the summer.

They have all benefited from the intellectual freedom that women experienced at *ifu* – a chance to consider their own lives as relevant to their studies of science and art. We had the very unusual chance to listen to women from many cultures as experts in their fields.

The actual lived *ifu* was not always smooth, of course. We were faced with a new educational institute, shaped by a central organizing committee that had spent several years and thousands of women-hours working out the logistics of such an historic enterprise, defining the curricula, contacting lecturers and facilitators, raising money for scholarships and housing, building up the local organization, and so on. Once the women arrived on campus and had the chance to create their own intellectual space, we had many and sometimes quite differing ideas about how best to use our limited time. But certainly the experience changed all of our ideas about what could happen in this world if many thousand women more were given the freedom to create their own intellectual spaces.

An important part of *ifu* was the Virtual International Women's University that enabled communication through and around the website http://www.vifu.de, where the results of the Project Area INFORMATION have also been integrated. At the end of *ifu*, most of the women went back to often heavy responsibilities in their home countries, incorporating their *ifu* experiences in quite different ways in their everyday lives – even while maintaining *ifu* contact, and in some cases project work, online.

All chapters in this book are related to the Project Area INFORMATION. The contents are in part drawing directly on the experience in the projects, courses and art workshops and others presenting theoretical approaches, analyses and case studies that were brought into *ifu*'s lectures and courses to stimulate project work. The chapters do not necessarily represent the viewpoints of all the participants. They do, however, give an indication of the strong analyses that can result when women are specifically encouraged to consider themselves knowledge makers (and not only supporters and modifiers of men's knowledge) and to consider their own experiences as relevant to the creation of knowledge. In this way these articles offer important challenges to Information Science and related fields.

The book is structured into six sections, the first one reflecting *ifu* itself, and the other five focusing on topics that are largely derived from the areas of concerns associated with the idea of *Information as a Social Resource*. Based on a unifying organization principle, each topical section starts with an account of one of the *ifu* (sub-)projects, bringing out the interdisciplinary and intercultural process in the group, the working methods adopted as well as some of the results. In subsequent chapters of each section the emphasis shifts to other experiences at *ifu* and is gradually opened toward more general issues dealing with theoretical analyses and practical implications worldwide.

Above all, this book is about women entering the information age. It reflects the objectives of *ifu*, Project Area INFORMATION: finding ways in which information as a social resource can be made available to all those who need it in order to keep and assure their human rights; identifying roles that women want to fulfill in the emerging and changing fields of activity related to information technology, and ways to overcome structural obstacles; exploring interactive and creative ways to co-construct knowledge supported by information technology; enabling women to take constructive steps for improving their situation with respect to information.

Producing this book was only possible due to the continuing commitment of the authors, now back in their home countries all over the globe and engaged in different tasks and responsibilities, to the visions created and lived at *ifu*. Moreover, we would like to express our sincere thanks to Gudrun Parsons and Bettina von Stockfleth for their invaluable contributions in the final editing of the manuscripts.

May this book provide you with insights and orientation for your own work and studies in this time of technical revolution and social transformation.

Christiane Floyd (Hamburg, Germany)
Govind Kelkar (New Delhi, India)
Silvie Klein-Franke (Bovenden, Germany)
Cheris Kramarae (Eugene, Oregon, USA)
Cirila P. Limpangog (Manila, Philippines)
March 2002

Part 1:
Building International Learning Communities

This part of the book is devoted to the International Women's University (*ifu*) as a model for international learning communities. Focussing on the Project Area Information, held at the University of Hamburg, it tells the story of building up, realizing and living through this study program from the subjective viewpoints of the editors. It also gives voice to the participants, bringing out their expectations before *ifu* and highlighting from different angles issues of identity and communication in connection with affinity and solidarity as well as with difficulties of dealing with diversity during *ifu*. The resulting picture is a very lively one, telling about the energy and enthusiasm, the efforts and achievements of many women cooperating, but also of the limitations and shortcomings, some of which were due to the specifics here, while others seem inherent in any such effort.

The first chapter by Christiane Floyd and Silvie Klein-Franke, written by two of the organizers, aims to acquaint the reader with the concepts of *ifu* and the main challenges in developing *ifu*'s Project Area Information. It emphasizes key activities such as building the international faculty through networking, developing an interdisciplinary curriculum, selecting the students from all over the world and setting up the study program in Hamburg.

The second chapter authored by Christiane Floyd embeds a number of personal statements by participants, quoted from their applications as students in the Project Area Information, that were used in the opening lecture to show the rich diversity of individual standpoints and expectations. 'Students' at *ifu* in many cases were scientists, professionals and NGO members with a seniority comparable to that of the faculty.

The actual experience of living through the study program is described by Govind Kelkar, Cheris Kramarae and Cirila P. Limpangog, all members of the *ifu* faculty in various roles. The questions addressed here include the challenges and difficulties involved in forming and leading group work, the issue of feminism(s) in this study program, and the cultural issues arising in a community comprising women from well over 50 countries.

In her thorough analysis of identity ascriptions and identity formation, Sabina Mihelj deals with *ifu* as a whole. She points out how *ifu*, by calling itself a university, international, and for women only, made a distinct identification offer that included certain aspects, while excluding (omitting) others. But then the actual identification process during the study program brought about a more differentiated picture of affiliations leading to affinity between different groups rather than to unity.

Dorcas Mofoluwake Akande takes a linguistic stance in bringing out how even in international feministic settings such as *ifu*, the actual expressions used tend to reinforce patriarchic structures of hierarchy between women from dominant cultures and indigenous women, leading to marginalization and showing clearly the limits of universal sisterhood. Focussing on expressions used in the Information Age, she argues for including a linguistically transformative perspective in the curriculum of a possible continuation of *ifu*.

How can we generalize from this experience to other efforts of international learning communities? Each such effort will be situated, much like *ifu*: unique in aims and hopes, in conditions and constraints, and shaped by the women engaged in bringing it about and realizing it. How the *ifu*-experience can become an inspiration for others, is left for the reader to decide.

Christiane Floyd

Christiane Floyd & Silvie Klein-Franke

The Challenges of Building *ifu*

Abstract

This chapter tells the story of planning and organizing the Project Area INFORMATION of the International Women's University (*ifu*) from the subjective points of view of two members of the Hamburg local team. It explains the origin and the key ideas of *ifu* as a whole and recalls the different work steps necessary for making this vision come true in this project area. Important issues include: co-operating in the international curricular working group; designing the interdisciplinary, project-oriented curriculum on 'Information as a Social Resource;' building up the faculty and selecting the students from all over the world; preparing the setting for forming the *ifu* community at the University of Hamburg. The work reported here was an effort of worldwide cooperation in co-constructing knowledge, networking and community development supported by information technologies and thus exemplifies the concerns of this study program.

1 Opening up the *ifu* Space

Christiane: When I first met you, Silvie, in May, 1998 I had already accepted the challenge to build up the Project Area INFORMATION of the International Women's University at the University of Hamburg.

Aylâ Neusel, the president and main promoter of the whole undertaking had called me in early April and explained the key ideas to me. I had learned that the International Women's University was not going to be a permanent institution, but rather a three-month experimental study program to be held once during the summer of 2000. Although it was to be in English, it was referred to as *ifu*, abbreviating its German name 'Internationale Frauen-Universität.' *ifu* would be a study program designed by women for women graduates from all over the world. Centered in Hanover and integrated in the general framework of EXPO, it would consist of several project areas hosted by different Northern German Universities[1].

Aylâ went on to assure me that she had the support of the Senate of the City of Hamburg, so there would be funds for us. Moreover, the president of the university had promised to welcome *ifu* on his premises. And, indeed, although the funds available were strictly limited, *ifu* enjoyed the unfailing support of the Hamburg authorities, represented by deputy minister Marlis Dürkop, and the generous hospitality of the University, ensured by its president Jürgen Lüthje, in terms of rooms and infrastructure.

My task, Aylâ said, would be to design a scientific program around the topic 'Information' that should at once be interdisciplinary and intercultural. She made it sound so easy. It seemed to be in keeping with what I could do, with my informatics department's interdisciplinary outlook and the overall concern for promoting women's issues at my university. So I said Yes rather spontaneously. Later on, I often wondered whether my spontaneity had been wise.

Joining *ifu* was like being invited to a mountain hike into unknown territory for me. First, it seems, that it is just about climbing a hill. Only when you have reached the top do you see the much higher mountain behind and the valley you will have to cross to get there. And only when you reach the top of that mountain you get a glimpse at the yet much higher peak behind it (and the valley you will have to cross to get there), and so on. At the end, building *ifu* turned out to be a mountain hike that was spectacular and memorable, but took me as well as the whole Hamburg team to the limits of our energy and endurance.

You, Silvie, in particular, have performed a great many miracles that were essential for this effort to succeed. To begin with, you were my guide into the world of *ifu*.

Silvie: At that time, I was working at the central *ifu* office in Hanover.
The whole *ifu* effort originated from an investigation into the situation of women in the natural and technical sciences in Germany, conducted in the beginning of the 90s at the request of Helga Schuchardt, then Minister for Science and Arts in Lower Saxony. Led by Aylâ, an interdisciplinary group of women professors had analyzed the situation in a depth previously unknown, focussing on restricting factors for women's success. This survey revealed the reasons for Germany being one of the world's least advanced countries, as far as integration of the other half of the population's intelligence into science is concerned.

One of Aylâ's recommendations in this survey was to initiate a worldwide university off the shores of any existing institution. *ifu*'s basic principles –interdisciplinarity, internationality, synthesis between arts and science, practice-orientation, gender-perspective and virtuality – were also derived from this sur-

---

1   The concept of *ifu* as a whole is described in Neusel (2000), the results are collected in Neusel & Poppenhusen (2002), both available in German only.

vey. The idea was strongly supported by Helga Schuchardt, who eventually became the co-leader of *ifu* and was, in particular, associated with our project area. The framework of EXPO 2000 made it easier to find political support for realizing *ifu*.

During the first year of *ifu*'s existence my task had been to help initiate curricular working groups (CWGs), entrusted with building up project areas on BODY, CITY, INFORMATION, INTELLIGENCE, WATER, MIGRATION, WORK. I was responsible for INFORMATION, INTELLIGENCE and WATER (INTELLIGENCE was dropped later on). In the course of the year, I had moderated or taken part in each of the CWGs. From the very start I could thus realize how very different the approaches to cooperate amongst each other and to metabolize *ifu*'s principles turned out to be in the individual project areas.

Christiane: I was very intrigued by the idea of a problem-centered 'project area' as opposed to the customary subdivision of scientific work according to disciplines.

However, the topic 'Information' was too broad for me to handle. I could not envisage a coherent study program around this notion as a whole. At our first meeting I argued for the topical orientation around 'Information as a Social Resource' that we eventually adopted. To my relief, you went along with this, although narrowing down the topic in this way must have seemed a loss to you, considering your own scientific background as biologist.

But, I guess, you identified more with the ideas of *ifu* at that time than with your home discipline.

Silvie: I was fascinated by Aylâ's idea to conduct an educational experiment generating friction between disciplines, cultures, sciences and art, practice and theory – and, as it turned out, generations – transcending all borders restricting scientific thinking, and doing so with women, who have to fight for their role and involvement in science. I was convinced that this would be a most fruitful and rewarding experiment that would leave no-one emotionally untouched – in my eyes a prerequisite for in-depth learning.

I treasure similar experiences in my own life as pivotal for shaping my personality. I have struggled to cross disciplinary boundaries, which was not welcomed in scientific Germany in the 1980s. And I have spent some time in such different cultures as Japan and Thailand. The latter left me with a deeply felt responsibility to help stop my own country from exporting its problems to other countries – problems that are manifested in sex tourism, in the exploitation of women and children, for example in the textile industry, in protectionism in the agricultural sector, in imposing doubtful Northern values through the media, and so on.

I would rather contribute to worldwide dialogue on equal grounds, sharing visions and strategic considerations on how to achieve these visions for a peaceful future of our children. *ifu* seemed to me an opportunity to understand all this more deeply and to involve others in a process of understanding with the heart.

Christiane: I certainly agree with your basic values, and no doubt, they were the solid foundation for the cooperation between you and me. But, of course, I had other experiences to bring into play.

One of my motivations was to continue the interdisciplinary work I had embarked on in software engineering, when I started to shift my attention from formal and technical aspects of software to the processes of communication and cooperation amongst the people involved in developing and using it. This took me to participatory design, epistemological foundations of software development and knowledge co-construction. And this, in turn, was my starting point for designing the *ifu* curriculum.

At least as important was my experience with foreign students at my former university, the Technical University of Berlin. In several years of counseling I had become aware that our study programs implicitly assumed an industrialized society and prepared students for their roles as scientists or professionals in Germany. This was of limited relevance to students from other continents. They had to adapt completely to a German way of seeing the world. And the better they succeeded in doing so, the more they would be attracted to stay. This did not seem a fruitful paradigm for cross-cultural learning and interchange. By contrast, I saw the chance for *ifu* to design a study program that would take seriously the needs and perspectives of students from different cultures and help to promote an exchange in a spirit of mutual respect.

Entering *ifu* was also my chance to learn about feminism, which was overdue, since I have been a woman in science for a long time. At *ifu*, it became clear that we need to think in terms of 'feminisms' varying considerably according to regions, political situations and women's orientations.

I initially partly agreed because my friend Heidi Schelhowe, who has a strong feminist background, was also involved. To my dismay, she could not stay with us in the long run, because she took responsibility for the virtual *ifu*.

The core group meetings in Hanover and Hamburg in spring and summer 1998 consisted of just you, Heidi and me. We were supposed to assemble an interdisciplinary and intercultural CWG within a few weeks and draw up a first conceptual paper until October. You were responsible for coordination, moderation and networking.

2 Establishing the Curricular Working Group

Silvie: 'Finding' committees, consisting of women in leadership positions in science, politics and organizations, had been established to propose key members of the CWGs in the different project areas. They were invited by Aylâ to an initial meeting to set up a list of names, a rough concept on which disciplines should be involved, and what the regional focus would be.

Then I established contacts to the proposed candidates. Beyond that we looked for certain profiles leading to women from all over the world who were interesting on grounds of their scientific standing or their political activities. And I needed to invite them to join the CWG in a way they would not reject!

Thus, the selection was highly personalized. This was strongly criticized from outside *ifu*. I understand the criticism, but the task was enormous, and the realization of *ifu* – given limited time and resources – only feasible through the use of existing networks.

Christiane: The first members of our CWG were also found through personal contacts. I knew Tone Bratteteig at the University of Oslo through our common interest in participatory design. Heidi was friendly with Marsha Woodbury at the University of Illinois. Through a friend who had worked in Brazil we came in contact with Edla Maria Faust-Ramos at the University of Santa Catarina.

The meeting in September 1998 was our first opportunity for cross-cultural cooperation with Heidi, Tone, and Edla. Some of us did not know any of the others before the meeting and our agenda was staggering. We had just three days for drawing up a conceptual paper giving the topical orientation, the curricular structure, and the projects to be conducted by the students.

It was then that I became aware of the quality of cooperation between you and me. We took on complementary roles in moderating: You kept track of the process and thus allowed me to facilitate a conversation that integrated a variety of individual perspectives into a shared vision.

Silvie: Curricular development had to reach a convincing state by October 1998 to enable *ifu* to apply for more funds, to anticipate the organization of the project areas, and to advertise the programs in cooperation with the German Academic Exchange Service (DAAD), which fortunately had decided to support *ifu* with its worldwide structures and expertise.

The first international meeting of our CWG was quite exciting for me. I had a double obligation: I was responsible for all organizational aspects but also for preparing the agenda in detail and for making sure that all *ifu*'s principles would be addressed in the discussion.

The disposition in our group was just perfect, as all had at least a double scientific qualification and quite different backgrounds. I felt attracted by the contents, some of which had been and even more became essential parts of my life: participation, democratic processes, networking, usage of media, technology *for* and not *against* women, and so on. I was relieved that our group was completely devoted to goal-oriented work without the least bit of fighting for positions. And

I felt accepted as an equal member, welcome to contribute my own set of intercultural and interdisciplinary experiences.

3 Defining the Curriculum

Christiane: The motto 'Information as a Social Resource' proved helpful in forming our community. We formulated some key lines of our program description together during the September 1998 meeting in order to be sure that we agreed on basic ideas[2]:

- *Viewing information as a resource for individual and community concerns*: "It aims to bring out women's perspectives on understanding information, on achieving autonomous use of information, and on exploring how to develop information for human needs."
- *Being sensitive to cultural differences*: "The way in which information is handled as a social resource varies in different cultures. We see the need for focussing on how modern information and communication technologies interact with and radically change traditional ways of dealing with information, thus giving rise to what we call the information society."
- *Aiming at women's empowerment*: "The information society offers new challenges and opportunities for women. It is important, therefore, to assess technology and make it our own by conceiving and trying out meaningful ways of using it."
- *Establishing a forum between the disciplines*: "This requires an interdisciplinary cooperation among specialists in computer, cultural, educational, gender, information, media and social sciences."

Silvie: One of the decisions was to internalize the gender perspective as an overall issue in all themes. Another, that we would stick rather close to information and communication technologies and concentrate on what we, as women scientists, would like to discuss about and achieve with them. And we wanted to involve as many regions as possible and thus aimed for a curriculum relevant for all this world.

Christiane: An important contribution initiated by Edla was to draw up general objectives for our curriculum. These were:

---

2   All quotations are from the *Program Description* of the Project Area INFORMATION, issued by the International Women's University in Hamburg, July 2000, available at: http://www.vifu.de

- to develop planetary citizenship consciousness with respect to the information networks of the world;
- to be more able to recognize the conditions needed for the development of women's autonomy and liberty;
- to develop an intercultural feeling of mutual respect and solidarity.

Silvie: In order to make the idea of information as a social resource concrete, we thought of five areas of concern that would be reflected in the curriculum: *Organization and Availability of Knowledge*; *Democracy, Privacy and Public Sphere*; *Identity and Communication*; *Cooperative, Interactive Learning*; *Community Development and Participatory Design*. They eventually became very important for us in building up the study program.

Christiane: We also worked out the basics of the study structure, distinguishing two kinds of learning periods. *Grounding Time* (two weeks at the beginning, one week after the mid-term vacation and the closing period) served to establish and nurture the cross-cultural dialogue, to make basic knowledge available and reflect on the experiences at *ifu*. *Project Time* (two stages of four weeks each) was devoted to acquiring specialized knowledge and for the project groups to work together towards a common goal. Following a suggestion by Tone, this allowed the combination of different forms of learning: lectures, class room instruction, and group work.

I proposed to form *home groups* already in grounding time, for students to find a meeting place with others, to open up to cooperative work and to reflect on their experience. Much later, I learned from Mona Dahms that home groups were well established as a way for women to get to know each other in international conferences on gender, technology and development.

Silvie: The projects were to be the main and rather autonomous working form of our curriculum. We envisaged that they would be enriched by courses and lectures contributing specific and relevant scientific perspectives as an introduction.

Christiane: We only had one afternoon left to come up with project ideas. I had no hope that this could possibly work. Then we encouraged all CWG members to make suggestions and went into a break. When we returned, sixteen project themes had been proposed within twenty minutes. These formed the basis of our curricular work and eventually were condensed into the twelve curricular projects held at *ifu*.

Silvie: So we ended the meeting with discussing guidelines for specifying the projects: What are relevant ideas, situations, problems? What is the relation to gender issues? What are the goals, objectives, possible results to head for, methods, disciplines involved, supporting media? What is the connection to the virtual *ifu*? The intention was to form virtual project groups already before *ifu*. However, due to pragmatic considerations we had to give up this plan and set up the project groups in the first week of the study program.

I was overwhelmed by the intensity and smoothness of our cooperation and by what we achieved in such a short time. This extraordinary atmosphere of cooperation, openness and equality in the CWG was part of the special flair in the whole project area later on.

And I saw my hope fulfilled that the friction between cultures and disciplines would lead to new ways of thinking about knowledge.

4 Re-thinking Knowledge

Christiane: The way we conceived of 'knowledge' was remarkably similar in the curricular group, and this, in turn, showed the confluence of different discussions into a radically transformed view of knowledge.

One source of insight shared by some CWG members was participatory design and development, where the idea is to build up knowledge anchored in the experience and needs of various groups of people, and related, for example, to the deployment of a proposed technology in a community.

Another avenue of similar insights was experience with adult education, in particular with indigenous groups, in a spirit of autonomy that emphasizes that knowledge cannot be implanted on someone else's terms, but needs to be developed on one's own terms.

And there was the feminist discussion relating knowledge to standpoints. In the *ifu* setting, different perspectives according to both academic disciplines and cultures were important, and, of course, the gender-perspective was adopted throughout.

Rather than referring to general, objective knowledge only, as in science, we were interested in knowledge projects, where general knowledge is appropriated as needed in the situation and new knowledge is built in the group's interaction. This knowledge co-construction unfolded mainly in the *ifu* projects, where situated knowledge was built up by the project groups in unique ways[3].

---

3   See the chapters by El Tobgui & Gregory; Link et al; Kerr & Mätschke; Keskitalo & Limpangog and Weber on individual projects, as well as the chapter by Floyd on knowledge co-construction, in this volume.

Silvie: Through my interdisciplinary and intercultural experiences I had been reflecting on ways of arranging knowledge in terms of 'knowledge houses' (inspired by the German word *Gedankengebäude*), consistent throughout as long as you stay in, but surprisingly different from one another, as soon as you step out and compare different houses. The various scientific disciplines share a similar Western scientific setting, but differ in language, paradigms, ways of reasoning and methods of deduction. But, as a real house does, each kind of knowledge excludes people even from adjacent (knowledge) houses without much care about the needs of neighbors.

As a student, I had initiated seminars on borderline themes between the natural and social sciences. Later, the gap between science and the needs of society was one of the reasons which kept me from pursuing my original scientific career in biology. So my reflections on knowledge came from a more practical end, but I felt that I could live my ideals in a very authentic manner in our work at *ifu*.

Every one of us went into many 'houses' during *ifu*, experiencing other perspectives, getting an idea of different ways of life and other meaningful approaches. Thus we were enlarging our coping-strategies enormously.

Christiane: This started already in the CWG. The most important issue in the winter of 1998/99 was to gain a clearer idea of the contents of our curriculum. We did this by specifying the areas of concern which had already been drawn up roughly during the first meeting.

Silvie: Our second meeting was in Hamburg in February 1999. At that time Marsha could be with us, and Irma Avila Pietrasanta from the University of Mexico City, whom we got to know through the emerging *ifu* network, had joined our CWG.

To me, the areas of concern really span the whole field. The cooperative way they were specified in the CWG was a deeply felt experience. Never again did we take the time to work so intensely as a group on agreeing and integrating all articulated views. We fought for each word trying to really fulfill the presumptuous claim of creating a curriculum relevant for women all over the world. I remember, for example, Irma's indignation at our Northern assumption of information being freely available – this is not so for most people in the world (maybe even including ourselves), living under conditions where the media are monopolized and under political control.

I treasured this work because it stood for a serious effort at mutual understanding and putting this in words – raising our awareness for the process each project group would have to go through later. At the same time this was an implementation of our motto 'Information as a Social Resource,' and it was very satisfying to live what we had proclaimed.

Christiane: And we were so happy at the end, when Marsha was kind enough to produce a polished version of our text!

I became increasingly concerned, however, with how to realize what we had planned. The project areas were about to be founded. I knew that you were in the position of choosing the project area you would join. And I very much wanted you as a partner.

Silvie: To me, the Project Area INFORMATION seemed to have the greatest potential for intercultural and interdisciplinary experience. This seemed a challenge worth any effort. In view of the fact that I have small children, it took some energy to decide to join you in Hamburg, 267 km from my home. But the authenticity I sensed in your work and life, a truly multidisciplinary and international approach and openness for new perspectives – and maybe some of your flattering words – finally made me try it.

5 Building Up the Project Area INFORMATION

Christiane: I was certainly most grateful that you joined us. Also, we got a chance to experiment with new forms of cooperation. In keeping with the ideas of our project area, you spent much of your time working at home using your personal computer.

In spring 1999 we set up the *ifu* office in Hamburg. One by one, we built up the Hamburg local team.

We had the good fortune of finding Dorit Heinsohn, who took on the responsibility of being the head of the Hamburg *ifu* office. Combining great effectiveness with an unusual gift for networking and communication, Dorit managed the negotiations with the university, made all resources for the study program available and handled our public relations. At the same time, she was involved in curricular work and in the selection of students.

We hired Tina Bach to build up the service center, designed to help students with housing, arrival and departure, health insurance, child care, and many other practical matters during their stay. Because of the geographical separation from the main campus, she built up our service center entirely on her own, instructed a whole team of student assistants and managed the affairs of all our students in summer 2000. It is hardly possible to describe her outstanding devotion and contribution.

Wolf-Gideon Bleek, a member of my research group in software engineering, was in charge of software support for our project area. He made sure that the more than sixty computers that *ifu* would use provided a uniform interface to the *vifu* server in Berlin. He also made available the community system Comm-Sy[4] for supporting the group work of the projects. Because of complex technical interfaces and compatibility problems, maintaining the infrastructure proved to be a very difficult task indeed.

So a community was formed in Hamburg. Regrettably, we had a lot of fluctuation with respect to secretarial help. But the cohesion of the core team and the cooperation with our temporary helpers in summer 2000 was quite remarkable and held up even in times of extreme pressure.

Silvie: You had your share in this through your empathic and participatory moderation of the team. You gave us acknowledgement of our engagement and work. And you took responsibility and gave support for the project as a whole.

Christiane: Your main task in 1999 was to build up a worldwide network in recruiting the faculty.

Silvie: Finding the 'right' faculty members was impossible on the basis of written materials alone. So I went to the Women's World Conference in Tromsø. This was a real breakthrough. I got approval right away from Govind Kelkar, at that time with the Asian Institute of Technology in Thailand, to join the CWG, and initiated the contact with Esther Williams from the University of South Pacific, Fiji, who became a virtual CWG member. I also found suitable candidates for being lecturers.

And we continued to draw on your friends. Through personal connections we found Cheris Kramarae from the University of Oregon, U.S., who took over the role of international dean.

Christiane: One idea of *ifu* was to have a local and an international dean for each project area. How these would share responsibilities was left for us to invent. To welcome Cheris, we had a special meeting with her in July 1999. We went through the work that the CWG had already prepared and planned the first two weeks of the study program in detail. We also discussed how to expand the faculty. Fortunately, Cheris had many promising contacts that we could follow up on.

ifu made a distinction between 'professors' and 'tutors'. All our CWG members would become *ifu* professors. We also realized that we would be needing guest lecturers for plenary talks and courses.

The tutors were supposed to be at students' level and would be hired only when the study program started. For us, this was problematic, since the curricular projects required expert guidance. Therefore, some of the women we had in

---

4 See http://www.commsy.de

mind as 'tutors' were themselves professors at their home universities. This unwanted hierarchy eventually gave rise to considerable tensions, which we were
never able to fully resolve. Though we renamed the tutors 'facilitators' and tried
to treat them as being of equal rank, their contracts and their status at *ifu* remained different. And since we were not able to include them in the preparation,
they were faced with a study program designed by others.

We did not quite foresee these difficulties when making the curriculum concrete.

6 Consolidating the Curriculum

Silvie: In the fourth CWG meeting in October 1999 we finished the outline of the
curriculum with details on projects, courses and lectures. We decided whom to
invite as a lecturer or facilitator and set up teams of directors and facilitators for
all projects. These project directors were CWG members, and each had a CWG associate for discussion.

Christiane: We also clarified the educational goals we would follow and how
we would frame the project work (for example through feedback and mutual
evaluation). I think, it was at that meeting that we made the mistake of simply
aiming for too much. Everyone had ideas for courses, all topics seemed so important, we wanted to be sure to 'offer something relevant' to the students.

In addition, *ifu* requested us to integrate art workshops into our program.
Since the artists were found and invited by a separate committee, we had difficulties getting to know them and scheduling the various curricular events in a
convenient way. Eventually the art workshops turned out to be a great gain[5], but
our study program became so full that students, teachers and organizers alike
were overworked.

Silvie: My next task was to integrate the CWG members, the facilitators and the
guest lecturers into a faculty – another major challenge.

I did not even know all of our faculty members personally and all of them
were very busy. I had to ensure that everyone received the important information
in time. I had to develop strategies to remind our lecturers personally in a way
they could accept – and still let me have their comments, plans, requirements,
abstracts, papers, and many other things in time. Networking at this stage was
difficult, had to be done most politely and with constant readiness to clarify
misunderstandings. Only later, while we were together, did networking become

---

5   See the chapters by Eske & Beer and by Biemann & Jottar in this volume.

a source of mutual understanding, of reliable information and of power to create new ideas.

The greatest uncertainty of our curricular work was that we had to do it without knowing who the students would be.

7 Selecting the 'Students'

Christiane: Selecting the students for *ifu* was a quite unique experience in my life. According to the procedure proposed by DAAD, each applicant was to get two independent reviews from scientists associated with the project areas, as well as one from central *ifu*. Since the applications were slow in coming, the deadline was extended, and the original plan to involve the CWG in the reviewing process had to be dropped. This meant that Dorit and myself had just three weeks around the Millennium New Year to read and review 360 applications! We had to assess every one of them to prepare the final selection in a very strenuous meeting with the DAAD.

We had indeed received applications from all over the world, only about a quarter from Germany (one third was allowed by *ifu* policy!), of the Northern applicants many came from Central and Eastern Europe, and we had many applications from the South, including strong groups from India and the Black African countries.

Reading all applications was not only an incredible work load, it also meant getting involved with as many individual cases and personal stories. I treasured this experience.

We quickly learned that only a part of the applications came from actual students. The idea of an International Women's University was met with great interest around the globe. Although the only way to sign up was as a 'student', we received applications from teachers, doctors, lawyers, government and NGO officials and so on, ranging in age from 23 to well over 50 years!

Silvie: The intergenerational character of *ifu* had not been planned for and was not really accommodated in our curriculum. Though we came to talk about 'participants' rather than 'students,' our program was designed to be offered by 'teachers' to 'students.' Fortunately, the major part of the time in our project area was spent in projects that allowed experienced participants to bring in their competencies.

Christiane: It also became clear that we had a great many applications from women who were dependent on a grant.

Silvie: This was in January 2000 and it presented us with a real crisis. We had planned our study program for 150 students. We had selected 172 out of 360 applicants, but due to the lack of grants we feared that we could only have 80 actual participants!

On one hand, this meant that we joined central *ifu* in a desperate effort for acquiring more funds for grants. On the other, we were left with great uncertainty until the very end as to the actual number of participants.

Christiane: There was a severe clash between our need of getting ready to start the study program and the continuing uncertainties and changes we had to cope with. We only knew the actual number of students when they arrived in July. It turned out to be 126.

8 Setting up the Study Program

Silvie: Our last meeting before *ifu* in February 2000 was the first meeting with facilitators, though, due to financial restrictions, we could only invite the European ones.

We had found some facilitators through personal contacts in Hamburg: Tatjana Beer and Katja Fischer, artists, Yvonne Dittrich and Heike Winschiers, computer scientists, and Monika Pater, a journalist, all from Germany. Others were recommended by CWG members: Alleida Calleja, a journalist from Mexico, by Irma, Judith Gregory, a social scientist from the U.S. by Tone, Zhang Wei, an educationalist from China, by Cheris. Yet others were among our highly qualified students: Dorcas Akande, a linguist from Nigeria, and Cirila Lilac Limpangog, an administration manager from the Philippines. Mona Dahms, a professor of electrical engineering from Denmark, as well as Jutta Weber, a philosopher from Germany, had applied for participation.

At that time the situation was very unclear, leading to a difficult meeting with quite some tension between the two of us. I felt we should cut it short and stick to our previous decisions at a time when you were still willing to accommodate substantial changes. The most important change was to reduce the number of projects from originally sixteen to twelve. To rearrange the teams of project directors and project facilitators was a trying experience.

Yet we managed to set up course schedules and recommendations for projects, we discussed the infrastructure in Hamburg, the Internet training and many other things.

Christiane: In the months before *ifu* the local team in Hamburg worked with very high intensity.

Perhaps it was worst for Tina: the organization of living accommodations for an unknown number of students, childcare, shuttle services, information leaflets, sports, travel organization for the participation in some Hanover events and much more was left to her. And she needed to build up and instruct a team of helpers. Fortunately, Tamara Rollocks, an expert on intercultural communication, joined her team and provided an intercultural training for the whole faculty. She proved invaluable in handling difficult situations and conflicts arising during *ifu*.

The rest of us tried to concentrate on getting the study program ready: a lot of energy went into the creation of the infrastructure and into getting the equipment and the necessary agreements from each part of the university. The 're- quired reading' list had to be done and the recommended books to be made available. Only very late did we learn about *ifu*'s decision to assign credit points according to the ECTS standard, which meant a lot of extra work for us. We had to maintain attendance records for all curricular events. It also was a strange ex- perience for us to assign credit points to participants, many of whom were be- yond the status of students.

Silvie: In between everything else we had to write up political justifications for the senate of Hamburg's financing of *ifu*. We also tried to get more funds and needed to inform and integrate the sponsors we had gained.

In spite of my flexibility regarding short-term changes I now and then felt the need for more security and pragmatism instead of reorganizing again and again. But this was a question of differing priorities, and the true wonder is how harmonious the team got along most of the time!

Christiane: And in this hectic atmosphere we had to prepare the two weeks of faculty training. In retrospect, I have to admit that this was our weakest point. We just did not have the time and leisure to think about it carefully. And when the facilitators arrived, it became clear that we had not really anticipated their needs, there was too much work waiting for them and the conditions were very hard. For these and other reasons it was difficult to integrate the faculty into a team and we had to cope with a great many tensions throughout *ifu*.

Silvie: We could perhaps have used some of our time more efficiently, if we had taken time beforehand to imagine how things would be and during *ifu* to reflect – but we were too exhausted already when this would have been due.

9 Coming Together at *ifu*

Christiane: All the attention of the faculty and the organizers focussed on the arrival of the students between July 15 and 17. We had planned it very carefully. The students coming from abroad were met at the airport or at the train station and helped in finding their accommodations. Their visa matters and police registrations were taken care of. Tina did not get much sleep during these days.

On Sunday, July 16, we met for an informal welcoming ceremony. It started with an intercultural flower ritual in silence, prepared by Baliboo Naur with Dorcas Akande and Cirila Lilac Limpangog. Then the home groups were formed and joined for a plentiful meal. Everyone tried to make first contacts, for me it was my opportunity to connect faces to the stories I had read.

Silvie: This and other informalities such as cooking together during CWG meetings and a few times with the faculty during *ifu*, balanced the otherwise tough program a bit.

Christiane: I remember the first *ifu* week as if I had been in a kind of trance. The welcoming on Sunday, the official opening in Hamburg and the treasure hunt organized for the participants to find their way on Monday, the plenary lectures in the other mornings, all of which I chaired, the project fair in the afternoons, the gradual settling down of the participants, the choosing of the projects on Friday, the beginning of the Internet training...

Many unforeseen difficulties arose on the technical level. And in the midst of trying to help everyone to start their work, Wolf-Gideon had a bicycle accident and broke his arm!

The hours of overtime each team member had to put in were counted by the hundreds already. But I understand that it was also a very strenuous week for the faculty and the participants.

Silvie: In working together in the faculty, we learned about different working styles, both at the individual and the cultural levels (e.g. German = endless critical discussions with action only hours later!) and there was the feeling that we had been misunderstood several times. I learned a lot from interacting with the faculty: Edla assured me that we had planned too much time for structured studying. Govind criticized some expressions, such as 'Bridging the gap,' as it regards indigenous ways of knowing as inferior. The facilitators confronted me with their criticism of being too much control-oriented, and so on. Even so, we tried to maintain flexibility and willingness to change, and to live what we proposed. In most respects I think we succeeded.

Christiane: I found myself in the combination of three roles: the head of the Hamburg local team, the local dean of the project area and the head of the group responsible for the infrastructure.

Regrettably, this left only little time for me to be active as a teacher. Together with the other members of the Hamburg local team, I was essentially engaged in 'enabling work,' creating conditions, providing resources and giving orientation so as to allow the intricate web of learning networks that we had initiated to unfold. It was, at times, a lonely job. I could not be part of any community for any length of time, found myself as the object of criticism whenever something went wrong, and had no leisure to enjoy the global view from my solitary peak. On the other hand, I had the unique experience to get involved in *ifu* activities at many different levels and to perceive them as interconnected.

And I did get the opportunity to learn from others, to communicate personally and to become very friendly with quite a few of the lecturers and participants.

Silvie: You have this gorgeous memory, how you knew each participant, by name and with her with life-story and interest. And you had the warmth and at least the willingness to lend an ear to everyone's concerns on whatsoever.

Christiane: Yes, in principle. But in practice there were contradictions that I could not resolve. It was impossible to please all participants, since the community was so heterogeneous, so when I was accepted by some, this implied being rejected by others. Also, I was given to understand ever so often that I was not primarily perceived as an individual but as representing an hierarchical position, very much against my own wishes. I learned about the limits of what I could do. Even the criticism became a valuable source of insight.

Important for me was to see the self-organization unfolding in the learning community. It was clear that I needed to step back, to let go and allow the processes to emerge. So the positive experience prevailed at all times.

Silvie: How great it was, seeing the women assembled here: full of power and energy in spite of hardest fates! I dislike the term 'empowerment' since then, because to me it mediates a passiveness I just could not connect with any of the women I have met. I felt awe for the participants as well as for the teachers. There was at times the sensation of facing some insurmountable barriers in communication, some impossibilities to be understood, regardless of what words were used. But knowing someone in each corner of the world now makes an enormous difference when listening to elections here, war there, famine in a third place...

Christiane: The forming of an intercultural community where we all joined for three months was generally considered the most important learning process at *ifu*. The situation in Hamburg was special. Due to the geographic distance from the main campus in Hanover we could not participate much in the events at central *ifu*, which caused quite a bit of regret. On the other hand, the sense of community in our project area was particularly strong and the Wing Building West of Hamburg University, nicknamed 'Mamma's Big House' by Mona El-Tobgui, where many of our activities and all our celebrations were located, became something like our home.

The degree of intercultural interaction became manifest in a creative way in the final performance of the project *Identities and Globalization*. One after the other, they appeared on the stage: a Polish woman wearing a sari, an Indian woman with a miniskirt, a woman from Bosnia in African gear, and so on. In plenary meetings I was touched to observe how participants from far away countries hugged one another. Now they had a friend wherever they would go.

Beyond the personal encounter, the insights gained in working together were remarkable.

Silvie: It was marvelous to see how the themes the CWG had generated were reflected in the projects – in their extension, but also in their deviation from our anticipations. What a proud feast the presentation was! Even more precious than the results was the process of opening up and crossing some of the many borders, as was the participants' willingness to try out different perspectives and gaining a new awareness. I had a true feeling of success in spite of criticism and exhaustion in the end.

My conviction remains that *ifu*, its principle and aims, are right steps on the way to have a slight chance for lasting peace. In addition 'Information As a Social Resource' became a motto that holds great relevance for my own daily life. I also see it as essential for the future in general.

References

Neusel, Aylâ (ed.) (2000). *Die eigene Hochschule*. Opladen: Leske + Budrich.
Neusel, Aylâ & Poppenhusen, Margot (eds.) (2002). *Universität neu denken*. Opladen: Leske + Budrich.

Christiane Floyd

Students' Motivations for Joining *ifu*

When applying for participation at *ifu*, each potential student had to submit together with her official data a personal statement explaining her motivation. As described in more detail in the chapter by Floyd & Klein-Franke in this volume, one of my responsibilities was to read all of 360 submitted applications for *ifu*'s Project Area INFORMATION and decide on who was to be admitted in cooperation with other *ifu* experts and the German Academic Exchange Service (DAAD). The personal statements were particularly important for making this selection. The actual participation of the 126 students was, in many cases, determined by the availability of grants.

One of the distinct features of *ifu* was that only some of the women applying to be *ifu*-'students' were students in their home settings. Many of them were scientists in various fields, professionals (including doctors, nurses, lawyers, teachers, and so on), or representatives of government and non-government organizations.

To bring out the diversity of participants' expectations, I showed the following quotations from a number of successful applications in my lecture *Opening ifu*, on July 17, 2000. The order was chosen so as to group statements with related concerns.

> "I am interested in developing strategies how to bring the information and Internet fever back to the ground, demystify it and realistically develop useful applications." (Germany)

> "My research experience reinforces my conviction that the development and the promotion of health care are influenced by the quality and quantity of available information." (Togo)

> "It is important to assess technology in an interdisciplinary cooperation and to make it work for us, to serve our needs and to enhance our democracy, especially in countries where all of these issues are so new." (Romania)

> "I would like to take part in a profound research on how women from poor urban or remote rural areas could get access to health care information and education." (Germany)

"Women in their social roles have to be prepared to face transformation, and need access to information, need to be educated to communicate, cooperate and demand their right, because information is somehow the license to live." (Romania)

"I am interested in women's representation in and use of New Media, in particular, the Internet to find, strengthen and channel their voices – politically, socially and on a personal level – and create real and virtual networks." (Jamaica)

"My particular interest is how traditional images and conceptions are being used in these New Media – either identically or transformed, disassembled and put together in a new form." (Germany)

"I specifically want to be in an environment to discuss and clarify the sociopolitical issues for women around the use and the exchange of information and women's input and control in information technology." (Australia)

"The Women's University offers a unique possibility to approach the field of information in an inter- and transdisciplinary as well as intercultural way." (Austria)

"All existing studies (on management information systems) are male-oriented... However, women should not be shunned in upcoming information society and knowledge society any more." (Korea)

"As technology continues to develop, communications transcend national boundaries, create social change, impact the unity and governance of nations, undermine or exacerbate language differences, and expand educational opportunities." (India)

"I believe lacking awareness of cultures is a main hinder for communicating: If you are communicating on different assumptions, you are not able to explain how to access information and include people in decision-making." (Sweden)

"In the field of information, one would know how to 'deconstruct' the language to suit women in the new millennium. This would mean taking into reflection things like culture and art, and the role they've played in keeping women down." (Uganda)

"If I am selected for this course, I aim to use whatever tools and methodologies I learn to improve resource management skills of the women in the community activities." (Sudan)

"What I really want is to reinvigorate my motivation to continue working in public sphere with a much more deep knowledge of the new challenges and opportunities that women nowadays have." (Argentinia)

"The information society could be a population increasingly responsible for its own informed choices, but one has to find one's way to the information and the information has to settle in as knowledge." (United States)

"Upon hearing about and reading the materials related to *ifu* course, I came to the conclusion that the course would offer me a good opportunity to engage in studies in my field of interest, i.e. women." (Iran)

"By participating in this post-graduate course and obtaining knowledge thereby I hope to construct a library classification system which involves a collection of all literature about women." (Sri Lanka)

"For me the question stays that though becoming more and more globalized and using the same language, mainly English, how can we preserve and transfer our culture, and how much our attitude changes." (Hungary)

"So to participate at the *ifu* project is for me a moment to rationalize and organize methodologies and categories that I already used in different context and with different media." (Italy)

"What is also relevant of this experiment is what will take place afterwards. Women attending will go back to their cultures, they will go back with a vision of something in mind and with strength." (Mexico)

"What I am particularly interested in, is the gender studies which consider the women's position in contemporary cinema and the new media." (Poland)

"I may be an independent thinker, but I am fully involved in the global information society that I am immersed in. Therefore, I wish to play an active and informed role in articulating visions and developing the passion to engage others..." (Canada)

"I would like to examine in the future how local/indigenous knowledge can be captured in a knowledge system." (South Africa)

"I simply want to take part in this huge project which, by directing more public attention towards the question of a permanent women's university, brings the women's movement another step forward in its quest for more equality." (Germany)

"Since the human being constructs himself ... such that the rules of social living are the support of the construction of his own intelligence, the technology that is a product of this intelligence must be made by the same criteria and sharing them." (Brazil)

"My aim is to question the information technologies taking the newly introduced medium Internet into consideration ... I will try to conceptualize how women initiate themselves to these technologies both as receivers and participants." (Turkey)

"Information is an imperative empowerment in any society but it is much more so where illiteracy and poverty cannot be addressed without the effective use of information." (India)

"Currently it seems that from a data security, data safety and data amount point of view we might create a lot of problems for the future. ... What about our responsibility as computer scientists in that subject?" (Germany)

Some of the women quoted here appear as participants in projects and courses or as authors of individual chapters in this book. I hope that their statements give you a better feeling for the richness of perspectives brought to *ifu*.

Govind Kelkar, Cheris Kramarae, Cirila P. Limpangog

The Experience of Living *ifu*

Abstract
The authors of this chapter were faculty members at the International Women's University (*ifu*), Project Area INFORMATION, acting in various roles: Cheris Kramarae was international dean; she and Govind Kelkar were members of the curricular working group, lecturers and project directors; Cirila P. Limpangog (Lilac) was a home group leader and a project facilitator. Drawing on their subjective experience and on comments by *ifu*-participants they deal with questions that might help other faculty and students at other universities, including those at a possible continuation of ifu. Among them are the relation between own motivation in joining *ifu* and the framework offered by the institution; the role of feminism in a women's university; the way that groups were formed and learning activities unfolded given organizational constraints and technical difficulties; and the intercultural issues arising in a community of more than 150 women from all over the world working and living together for three months.

1 Introduction

Christiane and Silvie have written about some of the challenges and specifics of planning *ifu* (see Floyd & Klein-Franke, this volume). Here, we talk briefly about *living* the months of *ifu*. Given that every participant of *ifu* helped with the continuation of the building of *ifu* during her on-campus months, and given that each of us came with her own expectations, resources and limitations, we need to say quickly that our stories and analyses can not be considered representative. However, in discussing our experiences and in thinking about what might help other faculty and students at other universities, including our successors at other international women's university sessions, we found that we could isolate a few questions and responses that highlight some of our new perspectives about working together at an international women's university.

2 What Attracted You to *ifu*?

Lilac: In 1998-2000, I led in evaluating the Philippine government accomplishments on the Beijing Platform for Action – an assignment that influenced me to devote my doctorate research on women in decision-making. I learned about *ifu* through the Goethe Institute in Manila, where I took the language course in preparation for another fellowship. But the notion of learning together with women of various disciplines, colors, and stand-points, and of having the rare chance to attend lectures by renowned feminist scholars, tempted me to come to Germany one year in advance. I was doubly lucky to be admitted as participant, (meaning I could earn credit points) as well as to be offered the post of project facilitator. Dr. Esther Williams of Fiji and I moderated the curricular project *Visions of Citizenship*.

Cheris: When I first heard about *ifu*, I recognized it as a dream come true. Several years ago, a group of us in the field of communication studies published a series of articles about our dreams for a feminist university. We wrote, for example, about the possibility of new subject topics more closely related to the challenges of women's lives, about new methods of cooperative learning, about ways of making closer links between university and community, and about scholarships that would enable more women to take advantage of the university-level study. We thought that making our dreams explicit was a valuable exercise as we worked toward what small changes might be made in a quite rigid institution, but I had no illusions that I would have the chance to participate in a program set up to actually encourage the educational visions of hundreds of women from around the world. Needless to say, I immediately accepted the invitation to be an *ifu* international dean and project director.

Govind: Why was I attracted to *ifu*? Well, in my case, during the *Women's World Conference* in June 1999 in Tromsø, Norway, Silvie gave me details of concerns and potential efforts in making *ifu* an international university of women across all cultures and regions. My reaction was yes, certainly I would like to be part of such an important initiative for women's training/education or development of capabilities in the area of gender and information technology. For me, being in Germany was not a concern at all. The *ifu* was for the women across all cultures and regions. We all knew the financial remuneration and the living conditions during the *ifu* days would be very, very modest. What really drew me to *ifu* was an inner force to say "Yes, I want to be part of the effort to found an international women's university, particularly a part of our project area with its focus on technology and gender relations."

3   Would You Call this International Women's University 'Feminist'?

Lilac: Interestingly, feminism was a concept many participants were very out-spoken about. But I also met women who were hesitant to use such a label for themselves. The ambiguity and the growing tension when *feminism* was taken up in classes was more ignited day by day; however, it was not necessarily addressed. In one forum, I took courage in explaining 'gender equality' and met opposition from a colleague who was advocating a 'gender-less' society. Because we were each coming from our own socio-cultural and sexual orientation we couldn't assume agreement, so the participants organized a forum to discuss this issue in length. We felt that the different brands of feminism associated with those presented in the lectures of Sandra Harding and Govind needed to be discussed.

Govind: Some of the *ifu* participants felt that there seemed a divide on the concept of feminism. I did and do not think so. What appeared as a divide was a result of some misinterpretation and misconstruction of the concept, and of feminists being seen by some as only those who have 'nothing to do with the men' and those who prefer to live in the same-sex relationships. During debates and discussions that followed my plenary presentation (and also that of Sandra's), two concepts emerged as major components of feminism: elimination of women-specific inequalities in socio-cultural economic and political spheres, and extension of human dignity and rights to women. Feminism is, of course, historical in character. The new wave of feminism swept across Asia, Africa, and other parts of the industrializing world in the 1970s.

We have begun to see some achievements: patriarchy is being challenged, gender relations are being transformed, and it is acknowledged that globally women have played a key role in building the civil society. These transformations have been very limited. Nevertheless, there is an ongoing global feminist movement to bring about change both in North and South as human rights and human dignity are extended to women.

These issues became the subject of discussion in informal and formal circles of *ifu*. In the words of one participant:

> [Concern for feminism] was evident in the informal chats. The participants wanted some lectures zeroing down on the term feminist ideology, maybe considering/covering the entire world ...There were valid reasons for such a demand. Not just the concept was different; the commitment to the issue was of various degrees among the participants and teaching faculty as well. There were women who openly claimed having nothing to do with feminism but were devoted to the area of communication only. Some of the participants were in my opinion totally naive (ignorant) and insensitive. I cannot say whether

they were sufficiently sensitized during the *ifu* term. However, they had started giving thought to the idea but for sure did not receive enough input to clarify their stand.

Cheris: The feminism label wasn't an official part of the title of the university: Some of us who have been working for years with the particular difficulties women face with traditional structures and curricula of academe just assumed that this very special university planned by, for, and about women would be feminist. After all, we were asking new questions and using gender analyses to come up with new answers. We were interested in the ways that women's perspectives were affecting the world politically, educationally, culturally, economically, and spiritually. We were looking at new models for education that considered sex-equality a basic principle. Feminist, certainly. However, the words feminist and feminism continue to worry some employers and others who have control or influence over the jobs and educational opportunities of some of the women attending *ifu*. So while feminism was always there, the label wasn't always used by all the women.

4 How Were the Home Groups Organized?

Lilac: There were no models, no blue-prints, no detailed guidelines in implementing a participatory process for *ifu*. Every member of the faculty was armed with her home-grown – and to some extent, cross-cultural – competencies. At the commencement of *ifu*, participants were divided into Home Groups[1], "safe" spaces where we could initially 'go home to' to gain mutual support, both emotional and practical. Our concerns would be varied – from how to open a local bank account, how to deal with anxieties about inter-personal communication, how to buy groceries and cook our meals in new places, how to organize field trips – to discussions about the relevance of *ifu* to our respective engagements back home. As lectures and project work occupied most of our time, the Home Group met only on emergencies, and on flexible schedules.

5 How Were the Curricular Projects Planned?

Cheris: The project directors and the other faculty members were assigned to each other in the early planning days of *ifu* (see Floyd & Klein-Franke, this vol-

---

1   Home Groups were established to provide the students with a forum for informal meetings with others, to encourage opening up to intercultural communication and to enable reflection on the experiences at *ifu* (see Floyd & Klein-Franke, this volume).

ume). Although they would be working very closely during *ifu*, most teaching team members did not know each other before *ifu*. (The same was true, of course, for all the participants of each project, as few of the women arriving at *ifu* knew anyone else in their chosen working group.)

I felt enormously fortunate to be working with Jutta Weber for the *Reconstructing Gender on the Internet*, and Zhang Wei for the *Future of Education* project. I met Jutta only once before the *ifu* summer began, but after we were assigned to our project, we immediately began sharing, via email, ideas and references for our project. I had briefly met Wei in China, where she is a university teacher and I had been a visiting university teacher. They are both very wise women, each with a great sense of humor and responsibility. So planning was always enjoyable.

The email attachments flew back and forth during the pre-*ifu* months as we worked on syllabi for each of these projects. The plan for these (and for the other projects in Hamburg) was to offer participants a working syllabus (including readings and some possible class collaborative plans) at the beginning of *ifu*, and course participants could/ should make revisions – including tossing out much of the syllabus if they decided on other plans.

As it turned out, some faculty continued with their suggested structures. Most, however, asked participants to use the syllabi as initial plans, as they worked out their own final arrangements for the duration of *ifu*. After all, even though some participants joined online discussion groups before *ifu*, until they got together the women could not really know all their background strengths and their expectations for *ifu*. This plan for providing only an initial 'working' syllabus, to be revised or discarded by class members, was not eagerly accepted by all. One woman in the *Future of Education* project told Wei and me at the end of our first sessions (when we were, in effect, turning the future planning over to the members of the project) that she had come a long way to Hamburg and *ifu* to get the advice of 'experts.' What sense, she seemed to ask, did it make for the people who had been working for a year on a program to so quickly turn all further decisions regarding the course over to the participants from a dozen countries, who had only recently met each other? It seemed especially strange to her to be doing this without suggestions, other than the tentative syllabus, about how future decisions should be made.

The process worked more easily and quickly in the *Reconstructing Gender on the Internet* project, probably because many of the women (although certainly not all) were from European countries and perhaps share more conversation / interaction conventions. Also, their topic, while a stated interest and project choice for them all, was the specialty of none, so they may have had less fear that in suggesting plans they might violate another's sense of how the topic should be treated.

Lilac: I found that the greater challenge in planning the course units was on installing mechanisms for participatory group work. Esther came prepared with a thorough project outline, complete with recommended readings and possible outputs. But we had to step back in order for the women to express their ideas, and in so doing, clarify their expectations. How Esther smiled and took gracefully the changes, was something that still stands in my memory. Alas, the magnitude of topics to be covered was just too much. As facilitator, I took caution in reaching consensus decisions because the out-spoken women from the north would tend to dominate the discussion. We resorted to other communication modes, such as the use of meta-cards (see the chapter by Link et al, this volume), and taking turns in moderating. Creative, participatory designing was both fun and challenging as we conceptualized, and later, staged a street theater dubbed 'Citizenship through Her Lenses'. Defying the primacy of computers, our group opted for something more ingenious: to illustrate the skewed impact of globalization on democracy and on women through a skit.

As lectures competed for project time, we met some snags and hitches here and there. There were times that boredom, homesickness, and severe exhaustion crept in. But we were sustained to the very end by the strong teamwork and spirit of 'fun-work'.

6 What Were the Days Like?

Cheris: To do everything for the first time took much more time than we anticipated. We had difficulty finding campus computers and printers that would respond to our English-requests (even though careful plans had been made to have machines reserved just for *ifu* participants). Participants sometimes had unanticipated difficulties because they still had some home responsibilities even though most of them were far from home. However, except for a few cases, all the participants were firmly committed to the process of *ifu* and to the work they were doing with the others.

I served as project director for two projects, which met at the same time in the afternoons. (Each participant chose one project throughout her stay at *ifu*.) I would attend one group meeting at the beginning of the three-hour segment, then during the coffee break I would jump on a bike rented for this purpose, to quickly get to another classroom to meet with the members of the other project for the remainder of the afternoon. Splitting my time this way I was never sure I knew what was really going on in either project. Most of the project directors were involved with two groups and had this problem. Fortunately, most facilitators were assigned to only one project so there was always a faculty member meeting full time with each project group. I was envious of the chances the facilitators I worked with, Wei and Jutta, had for long regular meetings with project participants.

7   What Were the Special Technology Issues in this Information Project Area?

Lilac: First of all, we had different experiences and skills with the new technologies. While many had advanced computer skills, some had little exposure. We were introduced to CommSy (a cool name for Communication System), an innovation by Wolf-Gideon Bleek and his group[2]. There was a mixture of resistance and curiosity as participants manipulated CommSy. Some projects, such as mine, used it in keeping diaries, participating in discussions, sharing files, and so on. I have witnessed how our research work gave birth to an academic article, through participatory writing and editing of the manuscript through CommSy. Some projects made use of the chat room (see Weber in this volume), while the others opted not to use it at all.

Inability to access computer programs due to problematic passwords, and occasional system breakdowns caused some short-lived irritation. Yet I was awed at how the women after having received lessons on various equipment, produced exceptional results. Many groups developed web-pages, while others produced videos as well as radio talk shows. Art and creativity, although subdued in many respects by some traditional ideas about academe, found expression in various forms: painting, theater, photography, games, poetry, live presentations using PowerPoint. Many realized that art should not be taken only as a form, but also as a process that defies logic and completeness. Much more, we were introduced to activities in which art – in contradiction to general understanding – can be shaped through group work. (See for instance, Wagner, and Eske & Beer in this volume). Through this work, cross-cultural and intergenerational communication was better facilitated.

In each encounter with information technologies, we were confronted with the blatant reality that arts remained more subsumed in science than the other way around, in spite the careful planning for integration. In like manner, the use of Internet was given more emphasis above traditional media and ways of expressions, thus, pushing to the periphery the relevance of oral and 'silent' communication, the so-called alternative media. The tension between technology and culture was even more pronounced and invited critiques in workshops that questioned common spaces and borders, such as the one held by Ursula Biemann and Berta Jottar (see in this volume).

---

2   See the chapter by Floyd, this volume.

Govind: I never saw issues of technology excluded from cultural questions. For the past 15 years, I have been working in this field as well as editing the journal: *Gender, Technology and Development.* However, in recent years I have been interested in exploring the information and communication technologies in particular. (We know that India has made some significant progress in this field, including the development of software.) My major interest has been to examine: Does women's participation in the ICTs change their position in the home and in the community? To what extent has the ICT sector changed participation of women? Where and in what fields do we find that patriarchal structures are being challenged, largely as a result of women's participation in industry, and in particular information technology? Some of these issues I have addressed in my chapter in this volume.

8 What Were Some of the Cross-cultural Issues?

Cheris: We knew that we would be speaking not English but Englishes, with different histories, intonations, meanings, and non-verbal characteristics. We knew that we would be coming from different places – geographical, cultural, spiritual, and sexual, from different disciplines and life experiences, and with varied ideas about what constitutes research practices, social justice, and just about everything else. We also knew that most of us wanted to participate in *ifu* precisely because of these differences. We wanted to expand our understandings about other ways of thinking, planning, and studying together.

In the week before the official beginning of *ifu*, the faculty and staff members had some special training in cross-cultural communication and during *ifu* some participants took part in a short course on cross-cultural communication. These few hours could not, of course, really deepen our understanding about the linguistic and cultural norms from many cultures let alone the various histories of the *ifu* and other social and political topics. At the most, in the exercises we learned a few details about a few cultures, and tried for a general openness to the knowledges and concerns of others.

Some participants wanted a list of the rules for talking politely to people from each of the countries and cultures represented at *ifu*. This is an understandable if unreasonable request. As we know from the complexity of our interactions in our own cultures, the 'rules' are changing all the time as our cultures change, and the implementation of the 'rules' always requires some understanding of the context of the talk.

After talking with many others about this issue, I now think that in addition to more structural attention to cross-cultural communication characteristics and potential problems, we could have also collectively worked out a set of principles, general and practical, from which to conduct our day-to-day sessions, as we learned from each other about specific conversational norms and expectations. For example, we could have decided about how we at *ifu* were going to try to listen without resistance, share responsibilities as well as leadership, and to be inclusive without forcing others into unwanted discussions—if those were determined to be some of our goals. In their chapter, Lisa Link, Therona Moodley, Heike Pienkoss, Sara Sanchez Mera, and Birgit Thies write about some of these issues. Christiane Floyd (see her chapter in this volume) talked at *ifu* about the process of knowledge co-construction. In our courses, we could have expanded and revised some of those principles into working *Ifu Guides to Cross-Cultural Interaction and Decision Making*. Such a process would itself alert us to diverse perspectives about communication and group interaction.

Govind: Since my initial days in the women's movement in India, say the mid-70s, I have internalized a critique of the cultural systems, since these systems tend to sanction inferiorized social position of women, with all their work reduced to duties to the family. However, it was a different experience in directing the *ifu* project group *Cultural Modes, Self-expression and New Media*. All the 5 project participants (in addition to two facilitators, Dorcas from Nigeria and Heike from Germany) were feminist in their own ways – both in thought and actions. I was surprised to notice the keen interest women (particularly from Europe) had in the clothing, hairstyles, and jewelry that women (particularly from the Asian and African countries) used to express acceptance and resistance to various social stereotypes. There were two major strands in the theoretical framework of the project participants: 1) a cross-cultural perspective and criticism of western representational regimes to denaturalize specific representation of gender; and 2) utilization of the new media to construct new selves of women. The latter came up in various discussions related to 'body politics' in different societies and interviews with *ifu* women. I found some responses around women's hair very interesting. A few examples:

- The decision of a woman not to process her hair chemically was explained by a woman as a refusal of European standards of beauty and as an acknowledgement of the 'black is beauti*ful*' ideal.
- Hair color was cited by some women as a means of negotiating gender stereotypes, in particular a refusal of the 'dumb blonde' stereotype and an affirmation of the red-haired witch stereotype.
- The decision to cover or not cover hair was discussed by women with respect to religion, but with quite different approaches to the subject: some saw it as a positive mandate, granting them protection from the male gaze in

public and affording them a means to express identity; others refused it as a patriarchal intrusion into their self-presentation.

Two other subjects that drew our attention in the Information Project area of 130 women from 55 countries were: same-sex relations (gays/lesbians) and 'the bias against the developing countries', in the words of one participant from India. A number of participants acknowledged that Afro-Asian cultures have 'very strict measures for women and their sexuality'. These societies do not tolerate deviations from the presented norms of heterosexuality. There are women and men in same sex relationships, but they exist underground. However, in the cross-cultural setting of *ifu*, participants began to understand these cultural prejudices against same sex relations. One Indian participant[3] stated:

> The realization came quickly ..our opinion about them was strong to hurt their feelings. However, this encounter forces us to think more sympathetically and learn more about them. ..The women from Australia, USA and Germany were our guides. They confessed that lesbians are not accepted in their society as well. They normally end up hiding the relationship from their parents and other elders. ..[Later] All of us were of the consensus that the life of lesbians is even more full of struggle than the heterosexual women in any given society.

With regard to dealing with differences related to color and the way of life, there were some unpleasant experiences as related by participants and faculty members from African and Asian countries. A Nigerian professor at *ifu* told me that one morning when she was walking towards campus, a young child pointedly called her a 'nigger'. When we discussed this matter with some participants in the *Cultural Modes* project, it caused embarrassment. One German woman explained that the word 'Neger' (which sounds much like 'nigger') is not a derogatory term in the German language, it only means 'black' or 'dark'. There were, however, others who objected that 'Neger' is often used in a derogatory sense.

Such instances drove many participants to hang around in the coffee shops and corridors in clusters of color – black, brown and white. Some of them described their 'fear of physical assault' and being 'uncomfortable with the staring eyes of the strangers.' Several women from Asia told me that their illusion of knowing the other cultures in *ifu* vanished within no time. Let me again quote the same participant from India:

> One of the Asian participants and her son had to go through a nightmare by breaking a law, which they were not aware of. The police were rough and biased. The organizers blamed the police but did not help the victims of racism. She had a complaint against the organizers who failed to understand them as well. She was even described as a weird lady by a white participant since she continued wearing traditional look. The life was

---

3   See *Bridging the Gap by Informal Communication*, a report on *ifu* by Ila Joshi at http://www.orbicom.uqam.ca/en/column/may01.html; accessed April 9, 2002

even more difficult for her son, who was labeled as retarded, because in the emotional moments he manifested the Indian custom of touching the feet of elders.

I used to take myself as smart and lucky both for not having such accidents. But this did not last long. I stayed in a dorm along with two other Asian women. We were always concerned about being blamed for the dirt in washrooms and kitchen by other white occupants. We were extra cautious about such things. In fact three of us were housewives and had low expectations of young [*ifu*] students around in this respect. Without many objections, we used to contribute more in cleaning and arranging things. However, three of us realized that we were easy targets for putting blame on. The experience was not very different for those who had accommodation with the families [in the city].

This does not mean I did not come in contact with kind people. In fact there are many occasions when I received help from the Germans and specially ladies within *ifu* and outside too. We received help and special consideration because we had a different look and the label of 'poor country'.

Our interactions in our groups and in the city were often full of difficulties, challenges, and, sometimes, great enjoyment, although in varying degrees for all participants. We hope that this brief discussion of intercultural communication issues helps alert us all to some of the ways that global politics enter our local interactions.

Lilac: Animating the maiden *ifu* in the brief period of 2000 summer semester, notwithstanding the limitations and shortcomings, had been a source of great learning as women were enriched in their academic and professional pursuits. The thirst for re-living the experience, if not, sustaining the gains is seen in the vibrant networks of *ifu* alumnae, concretely, through the virtual *ifu* that thankfully continue to connect us up until now. *Ifu* was, in the end, an ambition partially fulfilled in three months – just enough time to sow the seeds of an international university for, by and of women, but insufficient to witness the entire harvest. As we are again entrenched in our respective duties back home, *ifu* remains a legacy that inspire the women to enlarge the space for cooperation by using holistic approaches, and hopefully, bestows a meaningful grounding for those who will carry on the task of institutionalizing *ifu*.

Please read on. The other chapters, while focussing on the topics of study, also have a lot to say about how we succeeded in working collectively.

Sabina Mihelj

Revising Sisterhood: from Unity to Affinity
The Case of the *International Women's University*

What became also crucially clear is, that it is not enough from our side to expect an institution to give us the most emancipatory, democratic place (...) It is we – respectively each of us – who have to have (or just have) interests, goals and aspirations, we who have to fight, engage in conflicts over the ways we make sense of the world, we who have to see the 'differences,' complex systems of hierarchies, and the different positions amongst us and consequently the limits to an easy 'global feminism'; it is we who have to find and fight for the conditions of collaborative ways of establishing and shaping our social lives and the world around us without ever assuming a given unity, a sameness in regard to our interests and desires.   *Corinna Genschel*

Abstract
The main aim of this chapter is to analyze the International Women's University (*ifu*) from the point of view of the identification process in a global context, with a special focus on gender identity, taking into account also the role of different forms of communication inside which these processes took place: from virtual (based on Internet) to personal and face-to-face communication. The condensation of cultural, religious, political and other differences makes *ifu* an excellent case study to reflect on specific transformations in the conception of 'women' in a global context, especially transformations in the way individual women construct their relation to (or identification with) the group of women. Could an idea of sisterhood, of women unified by the universality of male dominance, still function in such a setting, or should it be totally replaced by a coalitional politics organized around affinities of interests and values ('affinity, not identity')?

1 Introduction

One of the most important traits of the initial representation of the International Women's University (*ifu*) as discernable in information booklets and other materials published before *ifu* started (for example Bauschke, Bradatsch & Kreutzner, 1999) was its inclusiveness. Surely, each new institution contains a certain level of openness simply because the future of it is yet to be defined.

However, *ifu* was not inclusive just because of being new, but also because the initial definition of *ifu* was constructed in a very specific way. Two important strategies of this construction were to hide controversies that *ifu* was provoking even before it started, and to avoid any explicit positioning of *ifu* with regard to highly contested issues. The result was a very open and relatively non-exclusive first definition, which can be read as an offer or framework of identification, inside which various identifications, various ways to construct a relation to the group, could take place.

Inside such a framework, some divisions remained under cover and were not visible – but they surfaced immediately after *ifu* started. It is important to note which differences were (at the official level) given priority and which remained unmentioned or surfaced only occasionally, as well as how all these differences were dealt with. Owing to the variety of differences apparent at *ifu*, the traditional conception of sisterhood – as a unity of women 'naturally' unified by a common feminine identity and by male dominance – could not function easily, and therefore also the exclusion of men was not easily employed as a basis of identification. Rather, the encounter with diversity required a rethinking of one's own positions and presumed normalities or anomalies and supported selective affiliation on the basis of common interests. Instead of developing affiliations along recognizable unifying traits such as gender, race, nationality, religion, the everyday exposure to diversity helped to overcome initial stereotyping and supported more individualized contacts.

Another important aspect to consider when approaching the process of identification at *ifu* is the shift from communication based on printed materials and Internet-based communication practices (those offered by *vifu*, the Virtual International Women's University) to personal and face-to-face communication in the specific project area. In general, this shift provoked a further diversification of the process of identification.

2 Conceptual Framework

In order to capture as many different attitudes and issues appearing at *ifu* as possible, the identification and group-forming processes were approached using a two-level analysis. One was the level of the official, pre-planned understanding of *ifu* as it was embodied in the initial presentation materials (web pages, brochures etc.). I will refer to this level as the *proposed identity* or *the identification offer* framed by the organizers of *ifu* (i.e. 'official *ifu*'), and I will talk about *identitary prescriptions* as elements of this proposed identity. The other level was the level of the actual *identification processes* as they took place among the participants during *ifu* (Project Area INFORMATION), and can be traced in texts produced by the participants, in the internal e-mail communication among them etc. Here I will talk about *self-ascriptions* as elements of identity as constructed by participants, based on their previous experiences and on their own interpretation and selection of identitary prescriptions.

Another important strategic decision taken when framing an appropriate conceptual approach was to focus on the second level of analysis – the level of identification processes. Thus, the main aim was to see how the affiliation to the group 'women' (and more specifically '*ifu* women') was actually constructed once the participants came into play – both before the semester started (in communications mediated by printed materials and the Internet) as well as afterwards (in mostly personal, face-to-face communication). Although the identification offer as presented by the organizers of *ifu* was the general framework guiding these processes, it did not necessarily determine them. The actual affiliations sometimes followed quite unexpected paths, broadening the possibilities expected.

However, such a stance should not lead to a too optimistic view of the identification process. Although it was a multidimensional process stemming from different points, it should be noted that different actors in this process were not equally influential, neither did they all have the same amount of power to influence the official presentation of the overall *ifu* identity. Again and again, identity formation proves to be a product of different (small and big) elites (be it those having symbolic, economic, or political power). A controversy well known to anthropologists dealing with ethnic identity might be at work here: the most vocal champions of cultural revivals are almost always the educated elites, while the most traditional, often physically isolated members of the group, are the ones least concerned with self-conscious and self-defined identity (Fitzgerald, 1991:199-200).

It could be said that concerns about one's identity come along with increased social status and economic security. Maximizing identity thus usually goes hand in hand with maximizing resources and achieving power. Therefore, besides searching for different ways of affiliation to the group, it is also important to weight the relative distribution of power and thus the possibility to affect the identification processes and impose one's definition on the overall *ifu* identity.

3 The Identification Offer: Inclusiveness Produced by Strategic Omissions

Which were those identitary prescriptions composing the identification offer produced by the organizers of *ifu* and discernable in initial information materials? The main identitary prescriptions can be inferred from the name: *ifu* was a *university*, it was *international* and it was by and for *women*. These three points open up a whole range of questions, for example: What is the relationship of *ifu* to other universities? What are the intercultural and interdisciplinary aspects? Why is it only for women? What is its link to feminism? Let me consider them one by one.

3.1 University

Although named 'university,' *ifu* was, from the very beginning, an attempt to subvert and rethink traditional universities, as well as traditional ways of doing science. The main aims of *ifu* – namely to achieve an intercultural, international, and interdisciplinary setting, to integrate theory and practice, art and science, and to implement women and gender studies as well as promote women inside academia – can be interpreted as a challenge to traditional universities. These are (still, mostly) male-dominated, predominantly monocultural or mononational or at least euro-centric, split into a number of disciplines which rarely communicate with each other, heavily theory-oriented and disregardful of practitioners, and, last but not least, they place great value on 'objective' science and exclude 'subjective' art practices. It is important to note that by challenging the traditional university and traditional scientific practices *ifu* was also questioning the basic premises upon which such a university and such practices are built.[1]

One of the most important strategies employed to rethink these questions was the introduction and promotion of 'new subjects' in science and academia: practitioners, artists, different cultures (particularly those from former colonies) and, above all, women. All these subjects can be said to share at least one point: generally speaking, they are in a different social position from the prevailing subject(s) of science: theorists, 'pure' scientists, Western, white, male. The distinct social location is expected to provide these subjects with a distinctive basis for developing their own ways of doing science and producing knowledge.

But to grasp the full implications of *ifu* being positioned as an alternative to traditional university and scientific practice it is important to reflect on a seemingly unimportant detail: namely the fact that *ifu* was, despite clearly countering traditional university structures, named 'university.' Both before and during *ifu*,

---

1   These premises include a variety of basic epistemological as well as ontological questions such as: what are the distinct characteristics of scientific practices, in what ways does scientific reasoning differ from commonsense, how objective can a science be, and what does objectivity actually mean; what is the relation between so-called pure and applied sciences, what is the role and value of reason, the senses and emotions in scientific work, what are the appropriate procedures for 'doing science' and what is the relation of science (and universities) to society, to economy, to culture, and to politics.

there were numerous attempts to show *ifu* should not be named 'university,' nor should it be allowed to issue official documents and credit points (following the European Credit Transfer System). For example, in an article published on July 27 in one of the biggest German newspapers, *Die Welt*, a journalist argues that *ifu* should not be named a university: "You cannot study any of the 'classic subjects' here, nor will any teaching authority award academic titles or any other degrees. Instead, what is taking place bears the less promising name 'project' and, as so often when something concerns projects, it is hard to imagine what is meant by it and what the outcome will be" (cf. Assent, 2000). Finally, the journalist claims that for *ifu* to become a university, university contents should be incorporated under the title 'university.'

This article is a perfect example of the controversies *ifu* provoked simply by being a university and at the same time obviously not being a 'proper' university –i.e. a traditional university. *ifu* should not be read simply as a negation of the traditional university, but rather as an attempt to rethink it by adding some new elements and not necessarily erasing everything connected to traditional universities. Such a positioning towards traditional university structures can be understood as one of the many aspects of inclusiveness typical of the initial identification offer of *ifu*. If the organizers had not wished to maintain their position and let *ifu* be named a project, controversies around the term 'university' would probably not have arisen. Being 'only' a project, *ifu* would be more clearly positioned as different from the traditional university and science, and it would not be so irritating since it would remain enclosed in a space outside academic structures, as just an experiment not necessarily affecting their normality.

3.2 International and Intercultural Aspects

From the point of view of at least some of the organizers, the stress on the international and intercultural aspects of *ifu* was associated with very specific interests and based on postcolonial critique of science and on mainstream feminism.[2]

---

2   This is particularly evident in the transcription of a discussion on *ifu* held in April 2000 (before *ifu* started), published in a German art magazine *Texte zur Kunst* (cf. 100 Days of Feminism 2000). Despite holding different attitudes towards *ifu*, all discussants agreed that an intercultural environment as a springboard for overcoming present hegemonic positions in science was crucial to *ifu*. For example, one of the discussants, Vathsala Aithal, argues: "The presence of women, of feminists, of scholars, of students from countries of the South can help – even if only for a short while – to break open this state of imbalance concerning the ownership and the 'object' of knowing. Their very presence also means that the women of the South can win control over content and process of theorizing." Similarly, Encarnación Gutiérrez Rodríguez (also a lecturer at *ifu*) claims to see "the identity of this year's *ifu* as a project that can destabilize the hegemonic position of west-

However, this linkage was not made explicit in the initial identification offer. Rather, prescriptions laid down in official materials and in the selection criteria for grants were fairly loose and allowed different interpretations of what is international and intercultural. In this way, *ifu* satisfied some specific requirements of the political and economic environment that defined the possibilities for financing, while at the same time avoiding the conflicts that were surfacing in Germany even before *ifu* started.

These conflicts can be traced in some newspaper articles, in the critical statement given out by a German student organization, at the virtual forums at *vifu* (those were already activated some months before the participants arrived in Germany) and elsewhere. An analysis of these materials can give some insights into different expectations vested in *ifu* and make evident that *ifu* was not uncontested for its organizational structure and political orientation. One of the main points of criticism was *ifu*'s association with EXPO 2000 and that there was a subtle form of neo-colonialism (exoticization and objectification of cultures) related to it. The other neuralgic point was the participation fee and the admissions policy (a first degree and a good command of English were required), owing to which *ifu* was accused of being neoliberal and elitist. One further criticism addressed the organizational structure – the fact that *ifu* was an institution – as another element supporting elitism. The opponents of *ifu* argued that *ifu* "will not result in a fundamental critique of capitalism, nor of racist and discriminating asylum practice, nor of the state and the economy" (quoted in Förster, 2000; Puczs, 2000).

What is important from the point of view of the identification processes is that this conflictive context and the whole history of *ifu* remained largely unknown to its participants until *ifu* started. The identification offer included only those elements that were less controversial or that appealed (at least superficially) to some commonsense values shared by political groupings and capital owners supporting *ifu*.

3.3 *ifu* as a Women-Only University, Its Relation to Feminism and Non-Heterosexual Orientations

Finally, it should not be overlooked that even such an open-ended first definition of *ifu* was not totally inclusive. The first and most evident exclusion characteristic of *ifu* is the exclusion of men: *ifu* was a women-only university. In the initial information materials, this exclusion was not problematized; rather, the fact that *ifu* was limited to women was presented simply as a fact. Although one may ar-

ern white feminism. *ifu* offers another chance to deconstruct the knowledge power base of the West" (100 Days of Feminism 2000).

gue that such a way of introducing women-only spaces might support unreflected prejudices and stereotyping attached to women's initiatives in general, it
is also important to stress possible positive outcomes of such a strategy. First,
establishing a women-only space without from the very beginning trying to defend the legitimacy of such a space might help to contribute to a perception of
such spaces being normal (having a similar effect as the fact of naming *ifu* a
university). Secondly, because of being presented without disputing, the women-
only space of *ifu* was not so explicitly pictured as an institution excluding men;
thus, although the exclusion of men was present, it could not so easily become a
basis for identification.

Another, probably much stronger element preventing the straightforward
identification of *ifu* as a women-only space was the very open-ended definition
of women implicit in the initial identification offer: it explicitly appealed to different subgroups of women and underlined the intent to overcome different divides and barriers. One further important element of the identification offer that
added to its inclusiveness was the ambiguous relation of *ifu* to feminism. There
was no explicit mention of feminism in the information booklets distributed
worldwide, and even once *ifu* had started, references to feminism were (at the
level of organizers, faculty members etc.) very scarce, broad and almost never
explicitly grounded *ifu* in a certain historically or socially located feminism.

Besides the blurred relation to feminism, another crucial omission has to be
noted: the omission of the issue of sexual orientation(s). While in the official
representation the aim to cross all political borders as well as ethnic and religious divides was explicitly mentioned in the very first lines, there was no explicitly mentioned aim to overcome divides on the basis of sexual orientation.

4 The Identification Processes: Affiliations and Solidarity Instead of Unity[3]

As soon as the identification offer outlined above (presented in various information materials) began circulating among potential applicants around the world, it
started to lose its provisional consistency. Already in the context of communication mediated by printed materials and the Internet, it was disintegrating into a
variety of different interpretations, arousing a whole range of different expectations among participants. Internet-based communication allowed a two-way interaction between the participants and the university staff, as well as establishing

---

3   This part of the analysis is much more bound to specific experience inside Project Area
    INFORMATION, and only partly to *ifu* as a whole. However, this should not mean generali-
    zations are not possible.

first personal contacts among participants themselves. This already diversified possible ways to relate to the group of '*ifu* women' and made the process more multi-layered, including interpersonal relations, relations to certain subgroups according to some common interests, as well as relations to the group of *ifu* women as a whole.

An even bigger change occurred with the shift to face-to-face communication once the semester started. The identification processes were now also affected by contexts that did not appear in Internet-mediated communication: different accents of English, visual differences, differences in paralinguistic communication etc. Furthermore, personal and physical contact also allowed a much wider range of different ways of establishing interpersonal relations and relations to the group, since it included a variety of activities not predominantly centered on language.

During these processes, various prescriptions included in the identification offer were appropriated and transformed into self-ascriptions. Owing to the open-ended identification offer, different self-ascriptions could be developed from the same prescription, and the issues raised and affiliations formed among participants sometimes went beyond the range anticipated by the organizers. I will outline the various self-ascriptions and new issues arising inside the identification processes following roughly the same topics as in the previous chapter, but with some changes in ordering.

4.1 The Understanding of Women at *ifu*: Sisterhood Revised

The open-ended and non-exclusive understanding of 'women' implicit in official *ifu* presentation materials appealed to a very diverse audience, and this resulted in a variety of different women attending *ifu*. Diversity itself was one of the central issues already present in the Internet-based communication before *ifu* and in the speeches presented by participants at the official opening of *ifu* in July (Chahal; Mwingi; Faculo, 2000). Rather than picturing *ifu* as a place of harmony, consent and unity, participants explicitly praised differences and expected *ifu* to be a place where it would be possible to know persons and their stories beyond the stereotypes. This is also evident in the speech by Mweru Mwingi:

> I came to *ifu* to see my sister and also to tell her of things that we need to unlearn and relearn, I came so that she might see me and know of the real issues that concern me. I came so that she sees me beyond the victim, the statistic that I am meant to be, to make her understand that there are no easy answers to the social decay and degeneration, to disease and poverty, HIV/AIDS, the violence and abuse that afflicts me and my kind (Mwingi, 2000).

I would like to point here to the uncommon use of the notion of 'sister.' First, the use of the term 'sister' does not imply any presupposed common base or a mystical common feminine essence naturally unifying women. Rather, a sister is a person categorized as a woman and a person who was made a woman – but the specific ways in which this was done could have been very different (see also Akande, in this volume). Although the common ground of *having been made a woman* could allow for some similar experiences, views of the world, values etc., it is rather the differences that should, according to such an understanding of sisterhood, be in focus. And secondly, these differences should not be those stemming from stereotypes, but those stemming from specific issues that concern individual women in their life-situations. To put it differently, the 'sisterhood' here acquires a rather pragmatic, non-essentialist sense, suggesting solidarity, but not unity.[4]

4.2 Attitude to Feminism

Another set of internal differences that became evident only after *ifu* had started, i.e. during the identification processes, was the set of differences arising around the issue of feminism. For example, among participants attending *ifu* one could find women with very different understandings of and attitudes to feminism(s). Taking into consideration the concept of *ifu* and all the controversies arising around *ifu* before its start, *ifu* can be seen as a condensation of most of the internal conflicts and ruptures within women's movements and various strains of feminism. For example, tensions between lesbians and heterosexual feminists, tensions between feminists from the so-called First World and feminists from the so-called Third World, between feminists from the West and feminists from former communist countries, and between feminist activists and feminist theorists. Even more, *ifu* was also a condensation of a variety of different attitudes towards feminism itself: from those overtly identifying with feminism and labeling themselves 'feminist' to those opposing feminism (for various reasons)

---

4 However, this was certainly not the only way 'sisterhood' was employed at *ifu*. A telling example of a more essentialist understanding can be found in one of the mails that appeared at the forum, where a woman sees *ifu* as "a chance to search for new ways to add the lost feminine way back, to enlarge our world vision." Here, talking about a supposed future, enlarged world vision, two contradictory ideas converge: the enlarged vision is presented as both the utopia yet to come and the golden age buried in the past (the lost feminine way). This can be regarded as an example of an essentialist approach to gender identity, one that projects the essence of an identity or its pure state both into the past and into the future, conflating the old and the new and suggesting a cyclic and thus mythical vision of history.

and terming themselves 'humanists.'[5] Although the diversity of attitudes was in itself an illuminating experience, it tended to remain an end in itself, without explicit attempts at taking the ever-recurring discussions any further.

4.3 Multicultural or Intercultural?

Listing sets of differences that appeared at *ifu* might give an impression of *ifu* as a site of harmonious coexistence of diversity. The wish to 'celebrate diversity' was indeed sometimes unreflected and to a certain extent fuelled by romantic notions of a joyful equality (a phenomenon characteristic of EXPO 2000). The negative consequence of these notions is a tendency to overlook the unequal conditions of communication which go along with this diversity. At *ifu*, this tendency was very persistent also because the open-ended identification offer was so open to different interpretations that it left some social mechanisms of exclusion – e.g. some elements of neo-colonial relationships – undiscussed. For example, the terms 'international' and 'multicultural' were too easily taken to be synonymous. This apparently simple substitution activates an understanding of cultures and identities that can actually only perpetuate and not counteract existing divisions, because it tends to see individuals exclusively in terms of their cultural origins – and such a reduction was common enough also at *ifu* (Genschel, 2000: 13). In an atmosphere dominated by the ideal of cultural diversity it can be very difficult to counter such a reduction even on the level of self-ascriptions, since one may feel obliged to identify with the offered/prescribed position of 'representative of one's own culture' simply in order to fight the alleged cultural homogenization and dominance of 'the West.'

4.4 Heterosexuality Tacitly Taken for Granted

Besides the persistence of subtler forms of neo-colonial divisions, racist and nationalist arguments, one of the critical issues that became evident only during the identification process was the clash of different attitudes towards certain sexual orientations. Again – as in the case of feminism – the position of *ifu* with regard to these questions was not clear; in the initial identification offer there was no reference to sexuality at all, nor were these questions extensively present in the curriculum. Even in Project Area BODY, where one would have expected such issues

---

5   This variety became clearly visible at a discussion of feminism organized by the participants of Project Area INFORMATION in Hamburg, where at the opening everyone presented her understanding of feminism. The first conclusion that one could have drawn from the wide range of different answers was the impossibility of any all-encompassing definition.

to be raised, sexuality was, according to the report on reflection activities of this project area, introduced as regulated by institutions of power: state, medicine, technology, law. Its conceptualization as heterosexuality was not questioned and a strong bond between sexuality and reproduction was kept in place. No effort was made to discuss (hetero-) sexuality as a key structure organizing societies, knowledges, practices and institutions (Genschel, 2000: 8). Such an omission of issues resulted in heterosexuality being tacitly taken for granted, naturally occurring, unquestioned, and positioned at the center (Genschel, 2000: 8).

4.5 Countering Traditional Forms of University Structures

Conflicts arising around issues related to the organizational structure of *ifu*, the specific ways it supported of producing and exchanging knowledge, are of paramount importance to an analysis of the identification processes at *ifu*. Following different ways of understanding the term 'women' and '*ifu* women' and different ways to relate to the group(s) of women at *ifu* is undoubtedly necessary in order to grasp the diversity and the way it was dealt with at a more conceptual level. However, it is when taking into account the institutional context that the various tensions, agreements and disagreements take on a more concrete form. Since *ifu* was, after all, a university, it was around issues relating to university structure, institutional relationships, schedule, and content of lectures that the main discussions were centered. It is here that the different understandings of university, knowledge, women etc., and the different expectations towards *ifu*, came into play, and it is here that the differences among *ifu* women became apparent and affected identification processes and group formation.

One of the contexts where these dynamics can be demonstrated is the question of the content and the appropriate level of lectures at *ifu*, which was one of the most persistent issues at Project Area INFORMATION in Hamburg (but also in other Project Areas). The attitudes towards this issue were by no means uniform, and it soon became clear that this question could function as a means of identification and establishing relations to very different groups. First, criticizing the lectures as generally too basic was employed as a means of confrontation between the participants and the organizers, raising questions regarding how much participants can affect the university structure, ask for a higher level of lectures or a different format that allows more space for discussion. Secondly, the critiques also raised questions related to North/South and East/West divisions: the lectures, and the whole curriculum, were criticized (even more so in some other project areas than in INFORMATION) for being too eurocentric, relying on theoretical references typical of Western academic circles and focussing on topics relevant to the West or at least framed from a Western point of view. Finally, when discussing different critiques, the participants themselves took very different positions. Therefore, criticizing the curriculum was not only an issue that divided participants and organizers (along the lines of hierarchical divisions typical of traditional universities), but also participants themselves: some of them agreed that the lectures were too basic, others argued they were of an appropriate level. And even when agreeing that the level was too low, participants suggested different ways of reacting to this: some supported a more passive stance, others an open confrontation. Here, another range of differences came into play, namely differences stemming from the fact of *ifu* being strongly interdisciplinary and thus participants sharing different levels of insight into certain topics, as well as different understandings of science.

However, for a full understanding of the dynamics of identification processes into which these discussions were embedded it is not enough just to note the diversity of attitudes. It is also necessary to ask who supported what attitude, what was the relative weight and influence of certain voices, etc. But assessing this relative distribution is not easy and can lead to oversimplification if relying strictly on quantitative measures of, for example, proportions of women of different colors taking the leading roles. As far as Project Area INFORMATION is concerned, it could be noticed that in certain groups of women even a wish to be critical sometimes did not appear, or the strategies of how to deal with conflicting views were defensive rather than offensive. This certainly prevented easy solutions in terms of 'quotas' or a simplistic view of 'political correctness,' and showed how difficult it is to develop a democratic university structure.

5 Conclusion

As has (hopefully) become apparent in the text, the analysis of the identification processes at *ifu* was not an end in itself. Rather, it was a way of approaching a range of issues that are crucial to the concept of the International Women's University and constitute the pillars of its identity: the conception of women and feminism, the role of knowledge production and of different forms of communication in a globalized, yet highly diversified world. By taking into account the processes of identification and group formation inside *ifu* it is possible to get an insight into some of the crucial experiences *ifu* provided and identify some of the strong points and the shortcomings of the organizational structure of the first semester of *ifu*.

Although it is difficult to establish a hierarchy among the multitude of experiences *ifu* provided, I would argue that the most important ones are related to the question of coexistence of diversity and how to deal with it. For the most part, the background *ifu* provided was one that encouraged rejecting simplified explanations, smashing stereotypes and preventing people from one-sided judgements and critiques (sometimes, however, even to such an extent that it hindered any judgement at all), and disencouraging easy conclusions about common traits of women. Because of an open-ended first definition of *ifu* a wide range of identifications was allowed. Furthermore, naming *ifu* a university and making it *women-only* without much discussion had positive outcomes. However, as is evident from the analysis of the identification process, such open-endedness and the strategy of avoiding heated issues and clear-cut positions also had some negative consequences because it allowed some exclusions to pass unnoticed. As became evident during the first semester of *ifu*, some mechanisms of exclusion tend to be more persistent than others, and these should in future be given more attention. Following the results of the analysis, the most important among these issues ought to be sexuality (sexual orientation), feminism(s) and subtle forms of nationalism and racism disguised by ideals of cultural diversity and a multicultural outlook. Therefore, the omission of heated questions and use of open-ended definitions is a good strategy for a start, but the differences should be addressed and exclusions discussed once the selection of participants is finished. Otherwise, the result might be getting stuck in celebrating diversity, repeating how overwhelming and enriching it is – which might lead straight to a reinforcement and naturalization of differences and consequently hinder cooperation.

As one could infer from the analysis of identification and group-forming processes during the first *ifu*, Internet-based communication has potentials to support individualized communication beyond cultural and other differences (though not erasing them). In contrast to communication based on print-materials, some forms of Internet-based communication allow a two-way interaction between individuals or smaller groups, which can function as a relatively good substitute when face-to-face communication is limited. However, for technology to fulfill such a role, Internet-based communication should be more strategically incorporated into the entire study process, and not just remain an optional form of communication (since it then remains limited mostly to those who are already familiar with and have access to it).

Another important conclusion to be drawn on the basis of the analysis of identification processes and group-formation at *ifu* is that it is not enough to expect an institution to provide even the most emancipatory, democratic place, but that a large part of the burden is on the participants. It was mainly through group-forming and identification processes among participants, in connection with various issues arising throughout the semester, that it became clear how difficult it is to develop a democratic university structure on a global scale. Furthermore, through seeing the differences and acknowledging complex systems of hierarchies it became evident that establishing a 'global feminism' is not an easy task, and that it certainly requires giving up any *a priori* judgements about sameness with regard to women's interests, needs and desires (cf. Genschel, 2000).

Acknowledgement

An earlier version of this chapter was presented at the international course *On Divided Societies: Citizenship and 'Globalization'* in Dubrovnik (Croatia) in April 2001. I would like to thank all the *ifu* women who contributed their comments to the chapter, especially Mara Kuhl, who was following the development of the main ideas from the very beginning.

References

Assent, Ira (2000). First women's university still only a project. Article by Kathrin Spoerr in *Die Welt*, translated by Ira Assent. In: *ifu Future Forum*. Source: http://www.vifu.de/w-agora; accessed July 31, 2000.

Bauschke, Carola; Bradatsch, Christiane & Kreutzner, Gabriele (eds.) (1999). *International Women's University "Technology and Culture"*. Hanover: International Women's University.

Chahal, Tania (2000). *Speech delivered at the ifu Opening Ceremony on July 28*. Source: http://www.vifu.de/os/tainachahal_ok.html; accessed March 20, 2001.

Faculo, Stephanie (2000). *Speech delivered at the ifu Opening Ceremony on July 28*. Source: http://www.vifu.de/os/stephaniefaculo_ok.html; accessed March 20, 2001.

Fitzgerald, Thomas K. (1991). Media and Changing Metaphors of Ethnicity and Identity. *Media, Culture and Society*, 13, pp. 193-214.

Förster, Birte (2000). *ifu* accused of being neoliberal and exclusive by German student association. In: *ifu Future Forum*. Source: http://www.vifu.de/w-agora; accessed April 12, 2000.

Genschel, Corinna (2000). *Report on the Reflection Activities of the Project Area BODY*. Source: http://www.vifu.de/tmp/body_reflection.rtf; accessed March 15, 2001.

Mwingi, Mweru (2000). *Speech delivered at the ifu Opening Ceremony on July 28*. Source: http://www.vifu.de/os/mwerumwingi.html; accessed March 20, 2001.

100 Days of Feminism (2000). A discussion with Beate Gonitzki, Vathsala Aithal, Parwaneh Bokah, Katharina Pueh and Encarnación Gutiérrez Rodriguez, moderated by Sabeth Buchmann), translated by Emma Ferreira, Ulrike Brisson, Parwaneh Bokah, Brenda A. Risch, posted by Encarnación Gutiérrez Rodriguez to the the *ifu* participants' e-mail list <students@vifu.de> on September 30, 2000. Original in German published in: *Texte zur Kunst* 10, no. 38, pp. 86-97.

Puczs, Nicole (2000). Re: *ifu* elite? In: *ifu Future Forum*. Source: http://www.vifu.de/w-agora; accessed April 13, 2000.

vifu – Virtual International Women's University. http://www.vifu.de; especially the *Future Forum* and the *International Women's University Forum*. Source: http://www.vifu.de/w-agora; regularly accessed from May 2000 to April 2001.

Dorcas Mofoluwake Akande

Linguistic Expressions Connecting Women Across Cultures

> Sometimes what is required to communicate – to establish a reciprocal 'we' – is rupture and break – a refusal to accept the common ground laid down by the 'other'
>
> Richard J. Bernstein (1986: 206)

Abstract

Language is an instrument of communication. It is a powerful tool of self – as well as collective expression within a class, race, culture, and gender. It may be used effectively to construct or deconstruct. Within an ideology, language is the index of movement to achieving goals of awareness, reconstruction and reformation. This chapter seeks to reflect some of the linguistic expressions commonly used by feminists in the new information age and the implications of the linguistic expressions in terms of building a tightly knit coalition of sisterhood or conversely further dividing women in the developed and developing worlds, paying attention to indigenous ways of perception and integration within global schemes of 'villagizing.' Furthermore, this reflection will be contextualized within the *ifu* experience in order to see how it manifested itself, to possibly provoke a consciousness of creating a reformative linguistic inclusiveness in the *ifu* future agenda.

1 Introduction

The stylistic analysis of linguistic impressions attempted in this chapter was partly motivated by the experience at *ifu* (International Women's University, here: *ifu*'s Project Area INFORMATION) where the author was involved as a facilitator for the project group *Cultural Modes, Self Expression and New Media.* Though *ifu* was a positively unique experience, it also exemplified the problems of communicating in the context of feminism and indigenous cultures in the information age.

The reality of existence is framed in hierarchies and the control of power in all spheres of social, political, economic and, to a significant degree, religious interactions. Thus, it would be euphoric to postulate a future of total equality amongst all peoples of different cultures, gender, race and religions whether intra- or inter-nationally, in the domestic or public domain. However, the vision of (re-)creating an enabling global environment where every individual, people and culture is at liberty to express their distinctly unique human and spiritual essence in whichever manner, mode or method needed, desired or found comfortable, in so far as it does not result in the subversion of basic universally accepted law and understanding of peaceable and harmonious co-existence, is achievable.

This then brings to the fore how the gender issue is being addressed among feminists of various persuasions and cultures such that the questions posed against patriarchal tenets will not boomerang. Looking at the perspective of sisterhood between women in industrialized countries and those from countries with strong indigenous traditions, the following observations can be made:

• The heritage of women from the dominant cultures has hitherto interfered with their ability to understand other cultures in their full difference from their own (Fishburn, 1986: 21).
• Women from Western intellectual traditions tend to underestimate the importance of cultural differences alien to theirs (Marcus & Fischer, 1986: 38).

Such Western perceptions arise from the concepts of the self as nuclear, autonomous, and originating prior to social formations. This is further underlined by what Iris Marion Young (1990b: 45) refers to as "illusory... metaphysics of a unified self-making subjectivity."

Indeed, there are contradictions in the Western feminists' approach, which aim at affirming an international sisterhood and eradicating sexism on the assumption that women live in the same or similar conditions in all cultures. Thus, the full realization of this vision is far-fetched, most especially as the fundamental issue is still questionable, one of which is perception as reflected in the language of reference. I will examine this linguistic phenomenon, which is marked by a distinct dichotomy: the leader and the follower, the powerful and the powerless, the initiator and the initiated, the developed and the underdeveloped.

Fishburn (1986: 17-18) stressed the need for those in the position of power and control to be more sincere in their claim of the desire to understand the beliefs of 'other' or alien cultures by "extending their [own] categories of thought." She goes on to explain that this extension must also include the modification or even outright rejection of old models of interpretation even if only for the sake of cultural and intellectual humility. It is believed that doing so would allow the 'powerful' to learn how other cultures organize and explain the world, such that it leads to a better understanding of their own epistemology, which should be seen as one of many systems of knowledge (this comes up in several chapters of this volume, in particular in those by Floyd and by Floyd & Klein-Franke).

2 A Sense of Attempt

Steps to address the problem of the gender gap, bias and stereotyping have been considered and implemented in recent times. Donor agents from the developed world have committed themselves to financial backups to NGOs to promote various agendas, particularly in the developing nations. Despite this, however, little or no attention has been paid to the issue of the promotion of self-expression and elevation of the knowledge of indigenous women, which should be regarded as an integral part of who they are and what they are, without any apology. For how can feminist leaders, advocating empowerment of 'sisters' all over the globe, claim to be credible when they do not question the labels of inferiority and inconsequentiality for their counterparts in indigenous cultures (see also the chapters by Calleja and Mihelj in this volume, in particular the *ifu* opening speech by Mweru Mwingi quoted by Mihelj). Research paradigms, questions and analysis within feminist movement and discourse have ignored or marginalized such issues. In short, women from indigenous cultures have been sorely marginalized in the areas that matter most for the empowerment of women, and thereby reinforcing the masculine culture.

The implications of this are aptly foregrounded by Sandra Harding (1998: 148-150) in what she refers to as a heavy construct or "ruling group interest." The ruling group owns the language and creates the expressions which aid in the maintenance of their interests, perspective and theory. The ruling group ascribes power and relevance to some and powerlessness and irrelevance to others. It takes a critical linguistic consciousness to see beneath the surface of social life to the realities that structure it.

The need to be more perceptive in all issues of identity, democracy and empowerment cannot be over-emphasized, particularly in this era of new information and technology. For if indeed the world must become one village, and a harmonious one to boot, where women constitute over 50 % of the key players, then the role women are playing to promote and accommodate each other's unique and diverse equal participation is a challenge that must be embraced. Contributions based on other-than-dominant cultural awareness and knowledge formation should not be subverted.

3 The Language Question

The continuation of a culture of domination that has historically marked the interaction between the developed and the developing world has been strengthened by the language used by the dominant culture as a defining tool in the location of peoples and their cultures. This has been incorporated into feminist dynamics, in an inevitable manner that will ultimately corrode the fundamental core of the 'sisterhood' principle. Gadamer (1989: 227) surmises that what is brought along into an expression are 'prejudices', which need to be examined similar to the way one examines a foreign text. In order to achieve understanding whenever an 'other' is encountered, there must be a preparation to accept that others are 'potentially right' and allow them to prevail (Gadamer, 1987: 87).

The perspectives from which style has been defined and analyzed include that of the writer's point of view (in this case, the dominant culture's point of view), the characteristics of the text being analyzed (in this case expressions created to ascribe identity by the dominant culture), and the impression of the reader (interpreters of words of reference from developed and developing worlds). Style has also been described as the shell of thought, the choice between alternative expressions, a set of individual characteristics, amongst others. Crystal & Davy (1969: 9-10) attempt an all-encompassing listing when they relate style to the distinctive language habits of an individual, a group, or a period, and also in a restricted sense to the effectiveness or otherwise of an expression. Oloruntoba-Oju (1998: vi) says that significance, recurrence, and art are what should constitute a stylistic study. For the purposes of this chapter, however, only the first two perspectives are relevant.

The early classical perspective of a stylistic enquiry was moralistic and prescriptive. The old classical rhetoric was not only a technique of art, but a teaching, an ethic, and a strictly regulated social practice (Barthes 1970, in 1988: 13-14). The analysis of a text therefore followed the prescriptions of style as the right way of putting the right thing. For our purposes, the expressions chosen by scholars from the dominant culture (i.e. Western feminists) to describe their 'other' from indigenous cultures are observed to be constant both at the level of denotative as well as connotative interpretation; they conform to the classical perspective of a regulated, socially prescribed description of one particular group by another particular group.

The operative principle is that there is the involvement of a selection in the choice of lexis or phrase for a particular group of people, suggestive of a functional purpose and a desired communicative effect (Lucas 1955: 9). Furthermore, Lucas stresses that through the concept of style as 'the man' (dominant group, their paradigm, methodology and theory), there is the implication of the means by which one personality moves others (1955: 48) or (from the angle of this chapter) limits or controls others in the process of relating.

4 Analysis of Some Expressions

How does one begin to describe a people as 'information poor', a phrase used by the *ifu* working group for pre-*ifu* publicity? Is it possible for a people with a culture and a history to lack information about who they are and what they are? We need to clarify whose information and what information is being referred to, so as to dispel ambiguity and to restore their own respectability. Undoubtedly, 'information poor' implies backwardness and a lack of understanding, but does not specify the direction, so as to make overt the fact that 'information poor' is meant in terms of what another group considers to be information – their information, their viewpoint, their methodology. A graphic linguistic analogy is shown below:

noun phrase (i)	information rich people
noun phrase (ii)	information poor people

These noun phrases also perform the function of actors, who are either portrayed as doing or not doing something. Hence, the focus of attention has been placed on the phrases to project a qualifier that ascribes quality to a people. The word 'poor' reinforces the concept of a people deprived and lacking in something considered essential or fundamental to qualify them for the ascription of an identity of high value. Certainly, when 'information rich' is juxtaposed with 'information poor' there comes to life the dichotomy of two distinct calibers of people; one who has something of worth in abundance, and another who has not. The hyperbolic antithetical references -> 'rich' versus 'poor' <- sustain a divide.

The following examples, to mention a few more, also engender consideration along these lines:

Noun phrase (iii)	colored people
Noun Phrase (iv)	native people
Noun phrase (v)	tribal people
Noun phrase (vi)	other people

According to Linda Smith, when research in indigenous contexts is mentioned, there is a stir of silence, and a conjuring up bad memories, a rise of smiles that is knowing and distrustful (Smith, 1999: 1). For it is within the paradigm of Western research that such a catalogue of words as those focussed above were created, symptomatic of European imperialism and colonialism.

As an academic with an indigenous heritage, I ask myself why the Aborigines of Australia, the Maoris of New Zealand, or the Khasi people of north-east India are called by their self-chosen name tags or identity markers, while some others are referred to as 'colored'. Then again, the collective diminishing tag of reference for us all is 'natives' or 'tribes' (not 'ethnic groups'). Therein lies the evidence that words are not created in innocence of political and social ideology.

One can project along this line of thought the identity attributes of 'Third World', 'under-developed', and even 'indigenous.' The denotative as well as connotative end points reek of long-term divisions and restrictions on who determines the starting point of research on issues that affect all groups as well as where to start. Invariably, the conclusions of such processes will be rather more subjective than objective and inclusive (Harding, 1991: 268).

5 Connecting Women in the *ifu* Context

The *ifu* experience was positively unique. It was a collage of colorful women from a myriad of socio-cultural, political, economic, disciplinary and professional backgrounds. The result of the teaching and sharing of lives of women within marginalized boundaries globally, was to evolve a vibrant network which will possibly pioneer new projects to re-address the anomaly of their marginalization by using the new technology as a tool of reconstruction. To a large extent, much was achieved, but more is needed to be explored and considered for inclusion in its future agenda.

- *ifu* should make efforts to include a linguistically transformative perspective into its future curriculum. Since words have created and create a disempowering 'essence' about and for women worldwide, particularly those in indigenous cultures, it stands to reason that we must consider re-creating ourselves by determining our own identity markers. Until feminist discourse addresses the language question also, it will not have been holistic in its approach to resolving the gender crisis at large, or, more importantly, the marginalization flavor in the sisterhood recipe.
- One way to come to terms with this problematic issue is to involve 'conscious' researchers from indigenous worlds in *all* the stages and conceptualizing processes of tabling, planning and effecting the agenda and curriculum of the future of *ifu*. By 'conscious' I mean women who have experienced the yoke of colonization of their lands and cultures. Their participa-

tion will ensure that the indigenous women's voices are as loud and clear in the global feminist chorus as any other, so that their issues will not constitute an *ad hoc* or token input in the collective struggle of women. Be that as it may, researchers from indigenous cultures still managed to impart the indigenous spirit to the *ifu* atmosphere in the summer of 2000 in Hamburg. Undoubtedly, it made a difference.

6 Conclusion

The challenge for feminists from the dominant culture who propound the theories that define us all in the quest to resolve the women question is to beware of entrenching further the divide created by patriarchy. It must be borne in mind that, in the fields of science and technology, developing worlds are tied hand and foot to the strings moved by the West.

Hountondji reflects that the degree of this dependence is one we are sometimes only hazily aware of (1997: 1). We fail to recognize that all cultures have an indigenous base, and the fact that some still operate largely within this milieu does not relegate them to a diminished level of identity and knowledge value simply because great industrial centers create the complex criteria for global relevance and leadership participation.

Once we approach the issue from this standpoint, it becomes clear that the differences between scientific and technological work in the industrialized world and the vast knowledge of indigenous information from developing worlds should be re-addressed from both qualitative and quantitative angles. One of the areas to start, then, is with the reinvention of linguistic labels of inclusiveness, democracy, equality and motivation.

References

Barthes, Roland (1970). The Old Rhetoric: An Aide Memoire. In: Barthes, Roland (1988). *The Semiotic Challenge.* London: Blackwell, pp. 13-14.

Bernstein, Richard J. (1986). The Rage Against Reason. In: *Philosophy and Literature*, vol. 10, no. 2, pp. 206-208.

Crystal, David & Davy, Derek (1969). *Investigating English Style.* London: Longman.

Fishburn, Katherine (1986). Questioning Liberalism and Liberal Feminism. In: Fishburn, Katherine. *Reading Buchi Emecheta: Cross-Cultural Conversations.* West Port, Connecticut: Greenwood Press, pp. 19-22.

Gadamer, Hans-Georg (1987). The Problem of Historical Consciousness. In: Rabinow, Paul & Sullivan, W.M. (eds.). *Interpretive Social Science: A Second Look.* Berkeley: University of California Press, pp. 82-140.

Gadamer, Hans-Georg (1989). *Truth and Method*. (Weinsheimer J. & Marshall, rev. and eds.). New York: Crossroad.

Harding, Sandra (1991). Reinventing Ourselves as Other: More New Agents of History and Knowledge. In: *Whose Science? Whose Knowledge? Thinking from Women's Lives*. Ithaca & London: Cornell University Press, pp. 268-279.

Harding, Sandra (1998). Borderlands Epistemologies. In: *Is Science Multicultural: Post Colonialism, Feminisms, and Epistemologies*. Bloomington and Indianapolis: Indiana University Press, pp. 148-150.

Hountondji, Paulin J. (1997). Recentering Africa. In: Hountondji, Paulin (ed.). *Endogenous knowledge: Research Trails*. Dakar: CODESRIA, pp. 1-2.

Lucas, Frank Laurence (1955). *Style*. London: Cassell and Coy.

Marcus, George E. & Fisher, Michael M. J. (1986). *Anthropology as Cultural Critique: An Experimental Moment in the Human Sciences*. Chicago: University of Chicago Press.

Oloruntoba-Oju, Taiwo (1988). *Language and Style in Nigerian Drama and Theatre*. Ibadan: Ben-El Books.

Smith, Linda T. (1999). *Decolonizing Methodologies: Research and Indigenous peoples*. London & New York: University of Otago Press

Young, Idris M. (1990). *Justice and the Politics of Difference*. Princeton, NJ: Princeton University Press.

Part 2: Gendering Information Technology

Connecting gender and information technologies was one of the key issues at *ifu*, Project Area Information. Rather than making it explicit in the curriculum, the idea was that adopting a gender perspective would be implicit in all areas of concern and thus pervasive in all learning forums. But during the study program it became clear that this issue needed to be brought out explicitly as a challenge for women to meet in the information age. The chapters in this part of the book bring out different dimensions of this relationship: the gendered nature of technical, in particular computer artifacts, and thus, the importance of informing design; the gendered environment for computer professionals and the obstacles women encounter in entering the profession; the way that technological change affects gender roles and gender relations in different cultures.

Mona El Tobgui and Judith Gregory tell of information resource design in *ifu*'s *Health Care Information* Project. Health professionals with a great diversity of backgrounds used participatory design techniques to establish nutrition and reproductive medicine as their common focal points, and set out to develop a prototype for an interactive website informing adolescents on these topics. Drawing on inspiration from the art workshops they came up with aesthetically pleasing designs and provided the means for the website to be adaptable to different cultures.

Discussing gender issues in technology design, Tone Bratteteig looks at both the product and the process sides. Design products – artifacts – are not only characterized by functionality but also by cultural meaning and communication, the latter being clearly related to gender. Gender impacts the design process in subtle ways: the ideas guiding design, the visions of artifacts in use are made by someone with gender in a design context which is gendered.

Marsha Woodbury looks at the challenge for women to engage as computer professionals. Though they have been involved from the beginning, they remain a minority. An important issue in some countries is access, not only to technology but even to education. Where access is easy, women entering the profession have to struggle with a male-dominated environment and a one-sided orientation of curricula to technical and formal issues. Possible solutions may be women oriented study programs and professional societies strengthening women's positions.

Focussing on South East Asia, Govind Kelkar analyzes the societal changes brought about through information technologies for women in different cultures. New professional options bringing independent income change the status of women in their families and affect gender relations. Gender knowledge, as provided in some study programs, introduces new analytical frameworks to bring out women's contributions in various spheres of work. Information technology, if localized and made available to communities, becomes a promoter of development.

Taken together, these papers show an interesting dynamics of women affected, but also become effective actors in the field of information technology in various ways. Making these issues explicit allows to become more aware of them and to work together for positive changes relating to the situation of women in this field.

Christiane Floyd

Mona El Tobgui & Judith Gregory
With: Djesika Amendah, Zubeeda Banu Quraishy, Tone Brat-
teteig, Khatuna Dzotsenidze, Emebet Hassen, Hoda Zaki
Helmy, Lunna Hemed-Kyungu, Veronika Schulze, Luiza de
Mello e Souza, and Kwartarini Yuniarti

Cross-Cultural Cooperation in Designing Information Resources

Abstract
In this chapter, we analyze experiences in the *Health Care Information* Project at *ifu*. In doing so, we discuss a number of broad themes: information as a social resource, participatory
design and participatory community development, gender analysis as being critically constitutive of human rights and democracy (including rights to health care and autonomy), and the
integration of art and science in conceptualizing and creating information resources that take
advantage of new information and communication technologies. Discussion and analysis of
the distinctively participatory ways of working in the *Health Care Information* Project make
use of materials from the project portfolio and documentation of working group discussions.
Experiences in the project highlight values and relations in design.

1 Introduction

This chapter is based on the work of twelve women from eleven countries, a
multi-disciplinary group of women in the health professions and health informatics from Brazil, Egypt, Ethiopia, Georgia, Germany, India, Indonesia, Norway, Tanzania, Togo, and the United States, in the project *Health Care Information* of *ifu* (Project Area INFORMATION of the International Women's University), hereafter the '*Health Information* project,' during the summer of 2000.
Our discussion incorporates the reflections of project members in individual essays about how experiences in *ifu* may be integrated into their on-going practices as health care professionals and activists in non-governmental organizations (NGOs) promoting women's rights and participation (see reflective essays,
ifu Health Information Project 2000). The project work made use of participatory design principles and methods in beginning to create conceptual and material prototypes for health information resources. Project team members also
drew on inspirations from concepts and ways of working in the arts (sketching,
narrative, montage, multi-media representations) and architecture (mock-ups,
portfolios, models), and gender research methods and principles.

The team included three physicians, a health economist, a demographer working in family health services, a journalist and nurse reporting on women's health issues, a nutritionist, a clinical psychologist, a social anthropologist working in health sector reform, a biologist and biology teacher, a computer scientist, and a social scientist working in health informatics.

Work in the *Health Information* project raised challenging questions for ongoing development of the proposed website as a health information resource. Among these are:

- How can distribution of health care information be designed for culturally diverse and multilingual communities?
- How may information resources be designed to reach out to and engage the interest of vulnerable populations of adolescents in need of health care information?
- How may health information resources counteract gender biases that contribute to problems in the health and quality of life of girls and young women and health-related problems women experience later in life?
- How can information on preventive health care, common diseases and possibilities for treatment be provided for the general public, including people who cannot read and write?
- What conceptual insights and pragmatic learnings about information as a social resource and autonomous use of information can help us to design and communicate health care information in differing cultural and community contexts?
- How may we design information resources that promote autonomy, given global and local contexts of concurrent (co-existing) cultural traditions and new influences that shape identities and social practices, especially as these are implicated in gender differences?
- How will we 'translate' between languages, especially between clinical languages and teenage vernaculars, in creating an interactive website for diverse communities?

2 An Interactive Website for Health Information

At its outset, the *Health Information* project had two interrelated goals: First, to teach participants about how to design IT support for spreading information about health care and second, to make such a design meet real needs of different communities in different cultures (Bratteteig & Gregory 2000). Project members decided to focus on the development of health information resources for adolescents, both girls and boys, aged from thirteen to nineteen living in urban and in rural areas from different socioeconomic categories in developed and in developing countries. The information resources – interactive websites for adolescents – were conceptualized to fit into primary health care areas with emphasis on preventive health and lifestyle perspectives across and amongst diverse cultures and socioeconomic contexts, and to be adaptable to other media to reach communities without Internet access and adolescents who do not read and write. The websites were also conceptualized to go beyond biological aspects of health by offering other types of information for interactive learning and exploration, and to stimulate reflection and self-evaluation (reflective essay by Souza, *ifu Health Information* Project 2000).

The United Nations, the World Health Organization (WHO), and the German organization Gesellschaft für Technische Zusammenarbeit (GTZ) have recently identified adolescents as a vulnerable neglected group in need of special attention in health care policy, outreach, and action in the form of life skills training for youth regarding health, especially regarding nutrition and HIV/AIDS. Almost 30% of the world's population is accounted for by adolescents and youth between 10 and 24 years of age. The period of adolescence represents a crucial period in teenagers' lives as they are easily exposed to and influenced by peer pressures and media of various kinds including mass media messages that contribute to globalizing lifestyles.

An interactive website can provide anonymous access for young people to information about adolescence, menstrual cycle, pregnancy, parenthood, contraception, sexually transmitted diseases (STDs), and abortion. Teenage girls and boys need information about safe sexual habits – but many cultures do not openly accept the reality that adolescents engage in sexual practices, so that discussion is difficult. On one hand, sexual education is perceived by adolescents to be one of the most interesting topics related to health education (see, e.g. Candeias, 1984; and Souza, 2001). On the other hand, in school settings, students – and teachers – may be shy about discussing issues of sexual and reproductive health, and it is not easy to discuss these issues across generations.

Research studies suggest that there are serious repercussions for adolescent health, and for girls and young women in particular, as consequences of unhealthy and non-balanced diet typically consumed by adolescents in both urban and in rural areas, coupled with stress, poor physical surrounding and inadequate care-giving environment, and combined with the gender bias that exists in many societies. Gender biases exacerbate risks to lifelong health and quality of life for girls and young women. Problems experienced in adolescence manifest in poor health and nutrition-related diseases later in life, including diabetes, hypertension, coronary heart disease, osteoporosis, and gout. Better information is needed on the extent to which adolescent populations living in both urban and rural areas have access to and are consuming nutritious foods and balanced diets. Where nutrition among teenagers is poor, better understandings through active participation of teenagers, families, and communities are needed in order to promote change.

3 Integrating Art and Science in Information Design

In the experience of conceptualizing the design of the interactive websites, the health professionals in the project were 'becoming designers.' At the heart of project members' work together were conceptualizations of initial designs and learning how to articulate shared design visions in words, in concepts, and in visual representations (Figure 1).

Figure 1: Several members of the Reproductive Health working group discuss design ideas for interactive features of the website prototype.

The period of in-person collaboration created important preconditions for ongoing participation, not only in the imaginative co-construction of design artifacts amongst team members, but also in ways that the team of women health professionals began to learn how to communicate and work with technical designers and artists, and vice versa (see Floyd, this volume, for a general discussion of knowledge co-construction at *ifu*). Introductory technical skills gained in *ifu* courses and art-workshops as well as in the *Health Information* project provide a basis of familiarity with information technology that can enable collaborations with professional designers working with interactive multi-media in computer science, communication, and the arts.

Art played an important role at *ifu* in general and in particular in the conceptualization of health information resources. The *Health Information* project group decided to create a figure, a 'logo' to symbolize and communicate the project's themes: a neutral figure reflecting youth, happiness and balanced life, represented in Figure 2. It was important that all participants agreed that it bears the same meaning in all cultures. This figure was an outcome of the art workshops, collaborations with art facilitators, and discussions between project group members and artists who participated in the *ifu* summer in Hamburg.

The logo is meant to be the symbol for both the *Nutrition* and *Reproductive Health* working groups. The figure was used in the website prototypes. It was used in several combinations according to the subject and mode of presentation. For example, for Reproductive Health, the figure is doubled to represent the two sexes with the heading 'Teenage Sexual Life,' whereas for Nutrition, the figure is combined with healthy food items under the motto 'You are what you eat.'

Figure 2: 'You Are What You Eat'

4 Participatory Design: Values and Relations in Design

Participatory design concepts and methods in the *Health Information* project included information mapping, 'rich pictures' (Checkland & Scholes, 1990) exploring tensions between medical and social perspectives and between differing cultural contexts and situations, brainstorming possible modes of communication, participatory community development perspectives for primary health care, and open planning. (This technique is described in more detail by Wagner, in this volume.) In reflective discussions at the end of every other week, the team members discussed their individual development, interests and needs, as well as group processes and inspirations for the design of information resources from *ifu*'s program of lectures and courses. The individual 'reflective essays' (*ifu Health Information* Project 2000) represent another kind of result of the project.

This project illustrates how participatory design facilitates the development of people in relation to social change projects, and thus highlights themes of values in design and working relations in design (for discussions of values and relations in design practices, see e.g. Bratteteig & Gregory, 2001; Gregory, 2001; Moser & Aas, 1997; Suchman, 2000; Dahms & Faust-Ramos, this volume). Social interaction and in-person collaboration are key to creating resilient working relations and engendering mutual learning in group work that must be based on trust and mutual respect, including respect for situated knowledge and for different knowledges (Haraway, 1991; Suchman, 1987).

> Through the project group I have learned that without group work very little is accomplished. I also learned that in order for it to be successful, the group members must be flexible, in other words, open to change, and must respect each other. (Reflective essay by Hemed-Kyungu, *ifu Health Information* Project 2000).

> Restricting my words to interdisciplinary cooperation is actually unfair to the program, as there are two other important aspects to be highlighted. (...) These are the intercultural and the inter-generational cooperation. For me this is *ifu*: multi-cultural, multi-disciplinary, and multi-age or multi-generation. (El Tobgui, 2000).

5 Constructing Common Ground, Respecting Difference

Participants gained experience in jointly formulating problems related to health information and communication. To do so requires establishing common ground while respecting difference and diversity. Information mapping and 'rich pictures' (Checkland & Scholes, 1990) were among the participatory design methods for information systems design employed by the group during the first two weeks of the project.

Information mapping began with brainstorming about problem areas, modes of communication, target populations, and possible strategies, using a wall graph to represent these visually. Subsequently, the members of the team reorganized these informational elements into clusters of associated ideas, for example associating 'social medicine' and 'environmental health' with 'primary care,' to define the problem areas 'nutrition' and 'reproductive health,' thereby beginning to construct a common framework.

> In the beginning I was worried about the diversity of health professions of members of the project group. ..The only issue we had in common was that we were all interested in the primary health care system. ..So with that in mind, we started by mapping out the primary health care system. But then the primary health care system is such a huge topic, and again I doubted whether we could come up with a common topic. But through re-mapping and grouping concepts and interests in primary health areas, we narrowed our focus and came into common ground. It turned out that we had two common grounds. In the beginning I was not pleased at all with having two groups. I wanted us all to focus on

one topic – nutrition, of course! Looking back now I realize that I was a bit selfish there. I wanted to force everybody to work on what I am interested in. This would not have given effective results at the end. Instead it would have created conflict within the group. (Reflective essay by Hemed-Kyungu, *ifu Health Information* Project 2000).

Rich pictures, following the soft dialectics approach to computer systems design (Checkland & Scholes, 1990; see also Smørdal, 1998), were used to express and explore understandings of problems in specific cultural and socio-economic situations in different contexts. Soft dialectics comprises three activities: (1) Drawing *rich pictures*: drawings without any formal syntax depicting problem situations from different perspectives by individuals or a group (Figure 3); (2) Writing *root definitions*: written descriptions of the perspectives in the rich pictures (Figures 4 and 5); and (3) Identifying *contradictions*: descriptions of conflicts of interest or conflicting views on the problem. "These rich pictures are not a product to be constructed, but a means of gaining a discussible appreciation of a problem situation. They record relationships and connections better than linear prose ..." (Reflective essay by Souza, *ifu Health Information* Project 2000).

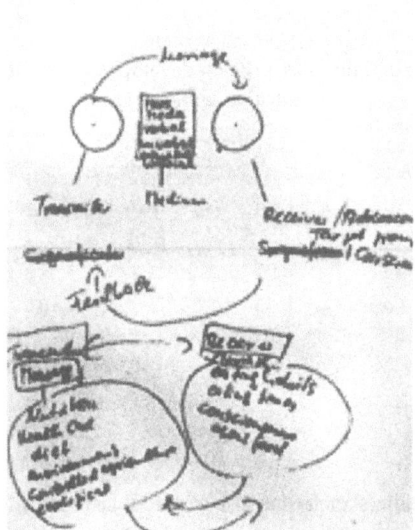

Figures 3: Rich picture developed by members of the Nutrition working group

Such informal 'low tech' techniques have the advantage that they can be used almost anywhere. It is essential in such a project to "bring out and accommodate diversity (acknowledge differences, allow for alternative proposals and aim for common understanding)" (Floyd, in this volume). As one member of the team commented: "I gained valuable knowledge as to how group project work can be planned and processed efficiently in a participatory way particularly when participants are non-homogeneous in terms of discipline, culture and interests but work on a common problem." (Reflective essay by Hassen, *ifu Health Information* Project 2000).

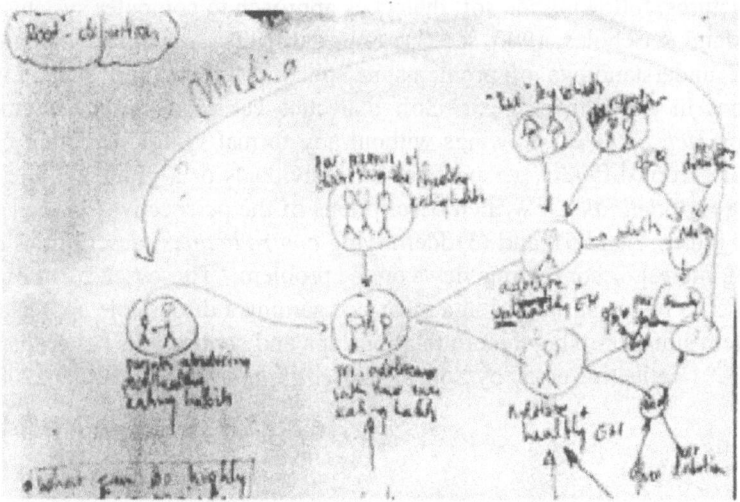

Figures 4: Root definition as a sketch developed by members of the Nutrition working group

Figure 5: Root definition (sketch) drawn by Reproductive Health working group

The use of rich pictures helped *Health Information* team members to understand each other's perspectives. As Amendah wrote: "It helped a lot in understanding the perspectives of the other members of the project team." (Reflective essay by Amendah, *ifu Health Information* Project 2000.) Hemed-Kyungu summarized the values gained in the project work and for her on-going use: "Through participatory design approaches, which included the use of 'rich pictures,' we came up with the conceptual framework as a guiding tool for our work. ... Mapping and participatory design approaches and the use of rich pictures were new to me and so I had just learned new tools to use in my working life." (Reflective essay by Hemed-Kyungu, *ifu Health Information* Project 2000). As a 'low tech' method for participation in problem formulation, rich pictures are both conceptual and practical tools for information design that can be readily used almost anywhere. By making use of images and visual representation, they are not necessarily reliant on the textual literacy of participants.

6 Using the Old and the New Media Side by Side

Midway through this project, an important and unexpected design juncture occurred, when both the Nutrition and Reproductive Health working groups decided to focus on designing interactive websites, thereby deferring design of parallel information resources that do not rely on on-line communication.

The decision to turn towards development of interactive websites was surprising, given the preponderance of traditional and non-ICT-based modes of communication identified in early brainstorming discussions. The orientation towards websites can be interpreted as representing new ways of thinking about combinations of traditional and new media, as a result of experiences in *ifu*. For example, Hassen writes about "Using the Old and the New Media Side by Side" in her reflective essay at the end of our project in Hamburg:

> At present more widely accessible and effective modes of information and communication, particularly for local communication in the developing world are the old media, i.e. print materials, radio, television and interpersonal communication, among others. And therefore expanding and improving the use of the old media ..could come as a priority while considering the improvement of modes of information and communication.

> On the other hand, in the spirit of globalization ..it would be to our advantage to introduce and expand modern ICTs, particularly making more use of the Internet side by side. While that segment of the community and organizations who can easily get access to the Internet benefit largely, the other segments of society will also benefit from indirect access to information on the web as it is possible to reproduce and adopt the latter to the old media (through print materials, radio and television programs).

Reflecting on Project Area INFORMATION of *ifu* in the context of her home country, Ethiopia, Hassen notes that "the use of the Internet as a social information resource for communities in many African countries including Ethiopia is extremely limited." She points to the need to consider both the use and prospect of modern information communication technology, and also traditional communication media, particularly in a developing country.

> While this phenomenon of virtual societies flourishes worldwide, ..the remarkable progress and use of the new information technology in the developed world is hardly felt in

some of the less developed countries mainly due to the near-absence or extremely limited access to Internet facilities. Economic barriers and power relations with regard to Internet ownership are the major factors that hinder the expansion of Internet services in these countries. (Reflective essay by Hassen, *ifu Health Information* Project 2000).

The orientation towards web design was also influenced by *ifu* course offerings in computer science and systems design concepts, uses of the Internet for networking and distance learning, and technical skills development for women's empowerment (see also Wetzel and Woodbury, both in this volume). These were of keen interest to participants, not only for personal development in relation to professional work but also as they suggest possibilities for action in NGOs and governmentally based women's councils.

> In the NGO that I am working with, the ICT aspect is totally non-existent. We do not even have our name on any Internet site. This is a pity since we are the most important women's association and NGO in Togo. We have a clear grip on traditional modes of information and communication but we are ... left behind by the lack of knowledge and lack of clear assessment of modern ICTs' importance in networking. I would like to help sensitize others and try to catch up with this lag. (Reflective essay by Amendah, *ifu Health Information* Project 2000).

> In Tanzania, there is very little use of the Internet in networking. There are very few groups of women's organizations able to use it. Through [*ifu* courses] as well as in *ifu* in general, I have come to realize its potential. I learned that through creating a women's network, or women's cyber-culture as Fatma Alloo refers to it, we can interact and produce our analyses to create news and views and feed it into the global community, therefore creating a positive change. (Reflective essay by Hemed-Kyungu, *ifu Health Information* Project 2000).

7 Health Education Information Systems

Differences in approaches to health education exemplify different underlying concepts regarding health and education and relations between citizens, patients and students and health management planners, clinical practitioners, and health educators. Writing about contrasting paradigms in health education, Souza emphasized different standpoints towards the autonomy of individuals and medical versus social concepts in health.

> In fact, health educators do not necessarily have a common value system, and they face controversies not only due to the nebulous notion of health, but also related to education itself. For example, one of such polemics is concerned with the degree to which health should be seen from a medical perspective or not – nowadays there is a growing demand for *demedicalization*, which aims to empower individuals over their own health, and to understand health in a broad perspective. (Reflective essay by Souza, *ifu Health Information* Project 2000).

Three broad approaches or paradigms in health education can be distinguished (see Tones et al, 1990), cited by Souza in her reflective essay *ifu Health Information* Project 2000, as follows: the *preventive model*, the *radical political model*, and the *self-empowerment model*. The *preventive model* "aims to persuade the individual to take responsible decisions in regards to her/his health. This is the traditional approach, and it has been much criticized because it ignores the real socio-political roots of ill health, dealing with health in an individual manner only (each person should be responsible for his/her own health)." The *radical political model* bears a relationship to Paulo Freire's pedagogy of the oppressed (Freire, 1972). In health education, this model is not fundamentally concerned with individual development but rather with political action that can lead to social and environmental change. The *self-empowerment model*, Souza writes, "has the goal of informed choice… [I]t is not only concerned with providing knowledge, but also with clarification of values and practice decision-making, attempting to promote personal growth of the individual." Central to this model is "respect [for] the individual's perspective, and therefore … change by choice, not by coercion." (Reflective essay by Souza, *ifu Health Information* Project 2000).

Thinking about design of an interactive website for teenagers, Souza suggests that the self-empowerment model "better suits the issue of sexual health [which] requires individual decision-making, for which reflection, assertiveness, ability to communicate, self-esteem … are necessary." (Reflective essay by Souza, *ifu Health Information* Project 2000.) The initial prototype for the *Health Information* web pages, 'Teenage Sexual Life' (Reproductive Health) and 'You Are What You Eat' (Nutrition) were designed to encourage such autonomy and self-realization among young people.

Further questions are raised: What kinds of relationships do we wish to have with young designer-users of the interactive website? Are 'users' (designer-users) conceived as 'co-designers' participating in iterative IS design? How are health information resources conceptualized in relation to contrasting models of health, education, information and communication? The *Health Information* project will need to work through all of these considerations.

8 Expanding Resources for Intercultural Relationships

In addition to learning from courses, lectures, art workshops and project work, the *Health Information* project team learned from other projects in formal joint meetings and through informal networks and autonomous activities organized by participants:

Another opportunity I was given at *ifu* was to meet people from different parts of the world with different backgrounds. That alone was a unique, unforgettable experience, as well as knowledge attainment. Besides learning about their cultures, through exchanging experience I learned a lot of things that will help me in my professional, academic as well as day-to-day life. I met women from war torn places, who still have hopes and dreams and determinations to go on. I met women from places where human rights and especially women's rights are a dream they never had, but still are very strong women who are not afraid to fight for their rights, and some for their survival. From all these women I was inspired by their strength, determination, confidence and willingness to continue with their lives. (Reflective essay by Hemed-Kyungu, *ifu Health Information Project* 2000).

Most importantly, we believe the experiences of intercultural and multi-disciplinary understandings, generative conceptualizations of information as a social resource, integration of art and science, and participatory design all expand resources for working creatively with cultural differences.

Acknowledgements

We wish to acknowledge the organizers of *ifu*, all of the members of the *ifu* team, staff, volunteers, IT support and technology advisors, resident and visiting faculty and art facilitators, and most of all, the participants in *ifu*'s Project Area INFORMATION from all over the world. We especially wish to thank Tatjana Beer, Katja Fischer, Adrienne Goehler, Wendy Harcourt, Magdalena Juma, Govind Kelkar, Roshini Kempadoo, and Silvie Klein-Franke for their encouragement to continue this project beyond the *ifu* summer.

References

Bratteteig, Tone and Gregory, Judith (2000). *Spreading Health Information (1.1). Project Description*. Hamburg: *ifu*, Project Area INFORMATION.
Bratteteig, Tone & Gregory, Judith (2001). Understanding Design. In: Solveig, Bjørnestad, Moe, Richard E., Mørch, Anders I. And Opdahl, Andreas L. (eds.): *Proceedings of the 24th Information Systems Research Seminar in Scandinavia (IRIS 24), Volume III*. Bergen: University of Bergen.
Candeias, Nelly Martins Ferreira (1984). Ensino de saúde: interesses na área de saúde de escolares adolescentes. In: *Cadernos de pesquisa*, 50, pp. 40-52.
Checkland, Peter and Scholes, Jim (1990). *Soft Systems Methodology in Action*. New York: John Wiley & Sons.
El Tobgui, Mona (2000). *Speech for Closing Plenary Session of ifu Project Area INFORMATION*. Hamburg: *ifu*, Project Area INFORMATION. Unpublished.
Freire, Paulo (1972). *Pedagogy of the Oppressed*, trans. M. B. Ramos. London: Penguin.

Gregory, Judith (2001). Scandinavian Approaches to Participatory Design. In: Dym, C. L. and Winner, L. (eds.): *Proceedings of Mudd Design Workshop III: Social Dimensions of Engineering Design.* Claremont, CA: Center for Design Education, Harvey Mudd College.

Haraway, Donna J. (1991). Situated Knowledges: The Science Question in Feminism and the Privilege of Partial Perspective. In: Haraway, Donna J.. *Simians, Cyborgs, and Women: The Reinvention of Nature.* New York: Routledge.

ifu Health Information Project (2000). Reflective essays by individual members of the *Health Information* project, Project Area INFORMATION, *ifu*, Hamburg, Germany. Unpublished.

ifu Project Area INFORMATION: See websites for the International Women's University (*ifu*) and for Project Area INFORMATION. Sources: http://www.vifu.de and http://www.ifu.uni-hamburg.de.

Moser, Ina and Aas, Gro Hannah (eds.) (1997*). Technology and Democracy: Gender, Technology and Politics in Transition?* Oslo: TMV Skriftserie Nr. 29, Senter for Teknologi og Menneskelige Verfier (TMV), Universitet I Oslo.

Smørdal, Ole (1998). *Work Oriented Objects: Object Oriented Modeling of Computer Mediated Cooperative Activities: An Activity Theoretical Perspective.* Dr. of Science thesis. Department of Informatics, University of Oslo.

Souza, Maria Luiza de Mello e (2001). *Das Tecnicas aos Fins: Educacao em Saude em Duas Escolas do Ensino Fundamental.* Masters thesis. Rio de Janeiro: Nucleus of Education Technology for Health, Federal University of Rio de Janeiro.

Suchman, Lucy A. (2002). Practice-based Design of Information Systems: Notes from the Hyper-developed World. Plenary address at the Conference on Information Flows, Local Improvisations, and Work Practices. In: *The Information Society,* 18, pp. 1-6.

Suchman, Lucy A. (1987). *Plans and Situated Actions, The Problem of Human Machine Communication.* Cambridge: Cambridge University Press.

Tones, Keith; Tilford, Sylvia and Robinson, Yvonne K. (1990). *Health Education: Effectiveness and Efficiency.* London: Chapman and Hall.

Tone Bratteteig

Bringing Gender Issues to Technology Design

Abstract
This chapter discusses gender issues in design of information technology: are there gender issues, and what could they be? It is relatively easy to apply a gender perspective to the result
of design: the artifact. Artifacts are designed to communicate with gender stereotypes in contemporary society (including stereotypes of work). Applying gender perspectives to artifacts
is not very different from other kinds of social analysis of use activities or artifacts in context.
Applying a gender perspective to the design process is more difficult. Some aspects of design
can, however, benefit from such analysis: the ideas and visions that guide the design process
come from someone who has gender. I do not claim that women software designers always
design different software from their male colleagues. However, the design process will benefit from having different sets of experiences as a basis for ideas and visions. These ideas were
presented in a plenary lecture at *ifu*.

1 Background: Issues in Technology Design

Design of technology is often presented and conceived as a mysterious process.
Most people conceive technology as a 'black box': it works or it does not – its
inner workings remain unknown for all except the technicians. As a computer
scientist I am trained in building technology, and for me technology is not a
'black box.' I find it important to use my knowledge to reveal the inner workings of 'black boxes': the invisibility and inaccessibility of how technology
works makes it difficult to question and criticize the problem definitions and basic assumptions underlying technical solutions. This chapter aims to point to
ways to 'open up' technology to enable a more open discussion of its role in
human activity and society. Technology is not neutral: it is designed by someone
for someone. I find it particularly interesting to discuss the bias in technological
solutions in relation to global and cultural heterogeneity. I specifically address
gender aspects in the design of information technology (IT), as I did in my plenary lecture at *ifu* (International Women's University, here: *ifu's* Project Area

INFORMATION), where I was involved as the director of the *Health Care Information* Project (see El Tobgui & Gregory, this volume). However, I will illustrate my points with everyday technologies; I want to draw attention to the fact that everyday technology is technology even if women seldom recognize their washing machines, stoves, or cars as technology (Mörtberg, 1997).

The notion of design means to give form and meaning to some material: to create an artifact, as well as making plans and specifications for the production of the artifact (e.g. Cross et al, 1997). The concept of 'design' is used to speak about the process of creating an artifact and about the artifact itself: the result or product of the design process. Literature about design often emphasizes either process or product: I want to include both in my discussion. Discussions about gender and design normally address the product side only: the artifacts or the use of artifacts. I also want to discuss gender aspects of the design process.

1.1 Design as Product: the Artifact

We are surrounded by artifacts designed with the aim to support human activity (or rather the designers' vision of human activity). I find it useful to characterize artifacts by their:

- function: their usefulness (or 'toolness') with respect to human activity;
- meaning: their symbolic value within a particular culture and society; and
- communication: how function and meaning are presented in form and structure.

We understand how a concrete, material artifact is part of human activities by analyzing its function and meaning. The function of an artifact is related to the activities it is designed to be used in, the activities "carry with them an intention of what those objects will do and how they will be perceived and used." (Winograd, 1996: p. xv). Their functions and the way these are communicated are often referred to as 'affordances' of the artifact: the 'reading' of an artifact (how to use it) should be easy for all – within the culture of a particular target group. For accidental users who are not members of the target group, the cultural codes may not communicate the functionality well: even if most technology aims to enable human beings and reduce disabilities by extending our muscular or memory powers, some artifacts contribute to further disabling some social groups.

The meaning of an artifact can be found if we interpret its form (or its very existence) as a sign within a particular culture. In Western societies consumers choose between a range of very similar products that do approximately the same thing, but give different cultural signals. The reason for choosing one brand rather than another has more to do with the cultural meaning of the artifact than with its functionality.

Neither the function nor the meaning of an artifact can be understood outside of the use context. Use happens as purposeful activity: in work, learning, everyday life, and the artifact contributes to – and receives – function and meaning through being made part of human activity. And human activity takes place in a larger context, in a group, an organization, a society/culture, and as part of societal change and technology development. Social science analyses of technology would include use at various societal levels: individual, group, organization, society/culture; and with various analytical perspectives: power (decisions), meaning (symbolic communication), activities (usefulness), change processes (use over time), etc. A feminist perspective on (computer-based) artifacts would address many of the same dimensions and levels.

1.2 Design as Creative Process

Design can be seen as a process that works with the relation between ideas and materials (Bratteteig, forthcoming). Design work is carried out by someone: a designer who has an idea and knows the material. Design work is carried out in a context: in a group, organization, society/culture, as part of global and local technology development. Both the design process and the design product are influenced by the situation and context.

The process of creating an artifact includes a series of stages on the road from an idea to a finished artifact. A common view is that design processes involve the making of visions, sketches, and specifications, seen as levels of abstraction and detail worked on in parallel during the design process (Bratteteig & Stolterman, 1997) – the vision may need re-vision after some sketching work, the specification may need some extra sketching. The vision that guides the design is created by the individual designers involved in the process, on the basis of their knowledge and skills in design and of their professional and cultural values and ideas. Visions are created when ideas and materials are set to meet (Bratteteig, forthcoming). Visioning is a situated activity to a large extent determined by what the designers know about design materials and future use situations. Sketching aims to make visions more concrete; sketches are used as tools for thinking as well as for communication.

Design processes are decision processes. Decisions in design concern the resources for the design process and the design result (see also Floyd, this volume, discussing design and decision-making as knowledge co-construction). Visions of system usage – the new way of doing things, the change – are constructed in negotiations between people with various roles, responsibilities, and power, between people from different organizations, i.e. design and use organizations.

Existing power structures are normally strengthened in a new system (Wajkman, 1991). Design is a work process that can be analyzed in the same way as other social processes, as referring to various societal levels (individual, group, organization, society) and analytical perspectives (power, meaning, activities, change processes, etc.).

In this chapter I focus on the design process because that makes it possible to question the material results of the design process, the technical artifact as such. I want to 'open up the black box' for the non-technical reader. In order to do this, I need to discuss the 'materiality' of process and product. I do this by discussing software as a design material. As a design material, software is a symbolic representation of parts of the world, and only technically skilled people are able to envision the model that the symbols refer to. Numbers in the bank's computer symbolize money in my bank account. The symbolic representation is materialized in a running computer, and the representation becomes a part of the world – it is really 'a difference that makes a difference' (to use Bateson's famous phrase). We can shop with the money we have in the bank by using our credit cards. I may never see or touch a single cent of this money as coins or bills, I just get calculations performed on the numbers that represent my bank account.

Software is different from other symbolic representations (e.g. architects' drawings) by being the basis for program executions (processes in a machine): the architect makes drawings that the carpenter realizes in wood, stone, brick, glass, metal, but in information systems both the 'drawings' and the realizations are the same kind of symbolic representations. Computers are machines, and this implies that the artifact is not finished until the program(s) can be executed. Before the program is executable it only exists as static textual and graphical representations of the program execution (i.e. as representations of representations). Interpreting the representations means envisioning the running program execution, and requires knowledge about system description languages (including programming languages) and computers (that make program descriptions become automatic processes) (Bratteteig, forthcoming).

2 Do Artifacts Have Gender?

Seemingly objective and factual things like railroad tracks, road tunnel sizes, or medical diagnostic categories can be interpreted as expressions of politics, power structures, cultural attitudes – and therefore not neutral at all (Bowker & Star, 1999; Suchman, 1994). By deciding that the gauge of the Paris metro should be narrower than that of the surrounding railroad system, a union of the two systems was prevented (Latour, 1996). The decision to make a tunnel too small for public transport materialized a political decision to disable public transport – and thus the people who rely on it – on those roads. Diagnostic categories change through time and space but are often presented as context-free and general. Bowker & Star (1999) use the – still topical – discussion about the definition of life (when does life start – is it at the moment of conception, is it when a child is baptized and given a name?) to illustrate this.

In the following sections I argue that artifacts are not neutral, and that applying a feminist perspective would help us understand this.

2.1 Use in Activities

Use is a relation between a human being – situated within a context, usually some activity – and an artifact (Bratteteig, forthcoming). The relation is personal, but the personal is shaped by – and shapes – the environment: the group or community of people of which the person is part. People behave with reference to socio-cultural roles and economic-political reasons while using artifacts. Seen as relations between a human being and an artifact, use activities can be discussed in a number of ways: in informatics the two best known are Human-Computer Interaction (HCI) and Participatory Design (PD). Basically, HCI looks at interface design in product development and thus focusses on general aspects of human beings (their 'bodies'), while PD addresses the development of an information system within an organizational context, and emphasizes the user as a worker.

A different perspective is found in social theories on human action in context, where the context at the same time delimits and enables human action. One of these is Actor-Network Theory (see Latour, 1996), where human beings and artifacts mutually influence each other and are seen together in heterogeneous networks of human and non-human 'actants.' Non-human actants (rules, procedures, technologies) have particular interests 'inscribed.'

> If we are interested in technical objects ... we have to go back and forth continually between the designer and the user, between the designer's projected user and the real user, between *the world inscribed in the object* and *the world described by its displacement*. For it is in this incessant variation that we obtain access to the crucial relationships: the user's reaction that give body to the designers project, and the way in which the user's real environment is in part specified by the introduction of a new piece of equipment. (Akrich, 1992: 208-209)

To move between 'the technical and the social,' and 'the inside and the outside' helps us see that the relation between human actants (users) and non-human actants (artifacts) is mutually constituting: it is in the use situation that use is enacted. It helps us describe the artifacts' meaning in use (Akrich, 1992). The relation between actants influences – and is influenced by – the surrounding network.

Use can be understood and analyzed in a number of ways. An example from my Norwegian everyday experience is that a bag of flour comes in 1 or 2 ½ kilograms, a bag of cement in 50 kilograms. The flour bag looks clean and white; the cement bag does not have to seem clean in the same way. The bags are designed to fit different use contexts, different activities and use environments: the kitchen at home, where we make bread and cakes for our families, or a building site where the cement can be used to build a wall or a fireplace. A similar discussion can be made comparing a kitchen mixer and a drill. A feminist perspective on product wrappings refers to assumptions about who are involved in which activities, i.e. to the segregation of the work life (Wajkman, 1991; Cockburn & Ormrod, 1994; Waldén, 1994).

Use of computers does not normally refer this openly to the gendered division of labor. However, when the use situation is seen in a larger, political and cultural context, gender can play a significant role in understanding the reasons for designing an artifact in a particular way. A well-known example is the introduction of the QWERTY keyboard to graphical work when typesetting replaced lead with electronic equipment (Cockburn, 1985). The typesetting keyboard was replaced by a typewriter-oriented keyboard: the QWERTY keyboard, hence favoring female, unorganized, cheap labor instead of the graphical workers, who were male, unionized, and skilled craftsmen.

2.2 Cultural Meaning

The meaning of an artifact relates to its symbolic value within a particular culture: the meaning of an artifact is always interpreted within a culture and thus has to 'speak' the language of the culture in an easily recognizable way. In order to speak to women, artifacts must communicate through symbols related to the contemporary cultural identity of women. The neat white bags of flour and the white and clean kitchen mixers both refer to clean kitchens and kitchen activities. The pink and the black steel razors are made for the same kind of activity but designed with different appearances to refer to gender stereotypes. Product wrappings are often designed with reference to cultural stereotypes and images of their target groups (which by this get reconstituted).

Cultural identity is a key to understanding how we design our environment by choosing among artifacts. We prefer the artifact that fits with or signals how we see or want to see ourselves – or rather want to be seen by others! In the same way language is used to signal social belonging to both insiders and outsiders, see, for example, in professional languages and sociolects. We design our identity. Artifacts visually signal social and cultural values: the Le Corbusier chair LC4 is not just a beautiful and comfortable chair, it is also a cultural signal.

The famous kitchen equipment designer and manufacturer Alessi talks about his vision of making beautiful products for the home that everybody could afford: he 'brings poetry to the kitchen.' It is the aspects of 'art and poetry' of an artifact that makes us prefer one product to another: when deciding to buy a car, its horsepower or safety program or cost plays a role – but its form, its colors, the feeling, or the trust in the brand are just as important (especially when most cars have quite similar characteristics).

Artifacts are cultural expressions that contribute to defining gender. In some countries pink has become the symbol for girls – and every time we use pink in order to 'speak' to girls, we strengthen this meaning of pink. When artifacts are made for a large market, clichés are used to reach as many as possible of the target group. This obviously reinforces cultural stereotypes.

3 Gendered Design?

Design is an individual process but carried out in the context of a group in an organization – it is a social process as well. Design processes are influenced both by the individual designers and by the design group and group process. Design processes are also influenced by external factors such as external agendas, goals, time limits, available people, resources, and power games beyond the control of the group.

Designers do have gender – but is gender an issue in software design? Some women systems development researchers claim that women make different choices in design and take on different roles in systems development processes from many of their male colleagues. Do female systems developers think more about the solution as a whole than about technical details? Do they show more responsibility for finishing a project on time? Some of these characteristics fit very well with gender stereotypes (always having an overview, tidying up and being responsible) and I think it may very well be that many women developers have developed such skills as part of being female citizens. Taking such roles at work may be a way of combining being female and a professional systems developer (Mörtberg, 1997). I have myself been part of a research project where we made a deliberate decision to come up with a simple and down-to-earth technical solution and experienced our choice as conflicting with computing culture, which emphasizes novel and 'fancy' technology (Bjerknes & Bratteteig, 1988). The experience also demonstrated that technical expertise can be challenged just as much by working to implement user requirements made by users who do not feel committed to think about how to realize the solution, and do not let well-known or easy design possibilities guide their needs.

I find it more useful to discuss whether gender influences work processes in the design process. I argue that it is possible to apply a gender perspective in design because designers have gender, their experience in life has gender aspects to it, and they act as part of a gendered society.

3.1 Visions and Ideas

Design is oriented toward use: it is based on a vision of how the artifact will be used (e.g. Winograd, 1996). The functionality of the artifact is designed with respect to a set of tasks and, consequently, assumptions about the needs of a user performing these tasks – both as imagined by the designer(s). In order to make the artifact useful, the designer takes care to communicate the functionality in ways that are easy to understand for the intended user group. Intentions of use are built into the artifact: some use activities are encouraged, while some are made difficult or impossible. Most information systems include procedures that do not fit every user's work perfectly, thus many users have to include system work-arounds as part of their everyday work routines.

Some information systems are based on visions about the work-and-use activity that are very far from the users' experience of their everyday activities. Studies of the introduction of groupware have concluded that groupware, which is based on the idea that people like to share information with other people in an organization by making all documents available to all people, who do not work in organizations where there are good reasons for not sharing all information – e.g. individual career patterns (Orlikowski, 1992). In a global network of biology researchers, PhD. students who were conducting lab tests as a part of their dissertation work did not want to make the results available to the project network before their theses were published – or else the basis for their PhD. might disappear (Star & Ruhleder 1994). They did not use the system as intended.

Design visions are both a product of the ideas that we have – from our lived lives, from the use we make of artifacts – and the knowledge about the material that we gain through education and work, theory and practice, and as users of artifacts. The ideas we have are based on our experiences – to a certain extent we reproduce existing artifacts and existing routines. It is very difficult to make technology that does not mimic current technology – see for example the way many computer systems mimic paper technology. A simple example to illustrate this point is sewing machines: designing a needle with its hole in the end rather than in the head revolutionized sewing machines as they stopped mimicking sewing by hand and started utilizing what machines can do (Waldén, 1994).

An experiment that engaged software designers to build educational software for boys, girls, and students, respectively, showed that gender stereotypes in designers' and programmers' minds made them design different software for the three categories (Huff & Cooper, 1987). Interestingly, the design for boys and students were very similar, while the design for the girls category used girlish activities as a basis (dolls and the like). The vision about usage guides the design all the way through.

3.2 Design Context

The context of design usually sets limits as to what can be made. Limited resources (time and people), are the most obvious way of controlling the design process. In addition, more subtle ways of power can be exercised in the decision process: control of the agenda, the problem definition and the range of possible solutions (Wajcman, 1991). In modern software development, which includes Internet and intranet solutions, time is very limited. When time is too limited, the designer needs to reuse earlier solutions to a greater extent, adjusting them just enough to appear tailored to the current customer.

In a larger context, technical solutions are not necessarily decided upon by technical arguments. Abbate (1994) analyzes the process that led to TCP/IP becoming the standard Internet protocol instead of the competing X.25. Her telling of the complex process shows that technical arguments were used to legitimate political and social positions. Development of software products aimed at a mass market is decided upon by market analyses of potential users' needs. Development of software tailored to a particular organization differs by the fact that the designers can get to know their users and even collaborate with them and discuss their needs for computer support. In these cases there will also be limits to what can be made, and these limitations may influence what the users experience and present as their needs.

A feminist perspective on the design context aims to identify actors and their interests, their resources and strategies for exercising power with a particular focus on gender. It will therefore be relevant to discuss the lack of women in computing: do women design differently? Do women decision makers decide differently? Whether or not women behave differently – and for whatever reasons – is perhaps less interesting than the fact that many women are not included in these processes (see also Woodbury, in this volume). The lack of balance and privilege, the different opportunities for access to technological resources in society, the injustice of not including women, make a basis for an argument for changing the current state of affairs based on fairness and principles of equal rights.

4 Software as a Design Material

How far into the material of design is it useful to apply a gender perspective?

I start with a set of examples that I find particularly interesting: games and web sites designed for girls and boys. We can easily interpret the very pink web pages of Barbie dolls[1]. The *Barbie* web pages also include games for girls where they can design clothes for their Barbie doll or dress her up in different costumes (but not at all as innovative as girls' play with real dolls can be!). An appealing introduction to the Internet for girls – or does this just contribute to reinforcing gender stereotypes? (Bratteteig & Verne, 1997). A different approach has been used by Brenda Laurel in making the game site *Purple Moon*[2] for girls aged between the ages of twelve and fifteen. Laurel and her colleagues interviewed 2,000 girls about games and hobbies before they designed Purple Moon (Laurel, 2001). The idea of Purple Moon is different: a young girl (Rockett) comes to a new school, and the game is about her introduction and interaction with her social environment. As 'tools' you get to read other girls' diaries or listen to their secrets, to assist Rockett in handling difficult social situations. The game awards utilizing and practicing social and emotional competences rather than training manual dexterity skills like speed and precision, it is about understanding human beings and making choices in ambiguous situations rather than killing dragons or monsters. Purple Moon utilizes game and Internet technology to offer a game to girls about things they are interested in, and in ways that they are interested in doing them in a more profound way than dressing pink Barbie dolls. The 'things girls do' also constitute what girls do: what girls should do and should be interested in, and encourage seeing 'girls' as a homogeneous target group. Nevertheless, I think Purple Moon realizes a new genre of games, and through this makes gender valid as an analytical perspective of games. Games 'as such' are not altered by introducing a gender dimension.

4.1 Technology as Material

Software can be characterized as symbolic representations of parts of the world (e.g. money in the bank) that become part of the world (e.g. we shop with the money we have 'stored' in the bank by using our credit cards). Software is different from other symbolic representations (e.g. architects' drawings) by being executable programs: processes in a machine – computers are machines. This also implies that the artifact, the product, is not finished until the programs can be executed – before that, only static, textual and graphical representations of

---

1   See http://www.barbi.com/ (Actually, the dominant website color ist violet).
2   See http://www.purple-moon.com/

the process in the machine can be represented. A 'correct' interpretation of the representations thus requires knowledge about computers and system description languages, among them programming languages (Bratteteig, forthcoming).

A program is a 'prescription,' a structure, of a generalized process in a computer system. To build structures in computers (data structures, program structures, programs) includes abstracting and simplifying. The common way to abstract in computing is to construct patterns that cover more than one instance of a phenomenon. We want to automate routine processes. We simplify in order to find or create properties common to several processes or properties that vary in predictable, limited ways.

The basic process of building computer systems is abstraction. We abstract from details and concrete materials, and construct levels of abstraction and detail as a way of handling complexity. The command 'print' hides the inner workings of the computer, it hides the complexity of making the computer actually send the text and format information of a document to a printer and get it printed. "The act of systems design is the creation and manipulation of abstractions" (Dourish & Button, 1998: p. 414). Abstractions are means to manage complexity and act as 'black boxes.' Abstractions can be used to hide complexity and to work with different levels of detail and complexity.

But not even abstractions are neutral: there are always different ways of representing what you have in mind. Choices can be due to personal preferences, e.g. do you prefer computational speed or minimal code, or to external requirements, e.g. particular hardware or environmental constraints: speed or minimal code can be a constraint and not subject to personal preference – or due to (limited) knowledge. Design is decisions – all the way down to the program code.

A study of computer science students revealed that there are different ways of thinking about computer programs: the abstract, mathematical way that emphasizes abstract logic, or a very concrete way, envisioning the program execution (Turkle & Papert, 1990). According to the students, only the first way of thinking was accepted in their environment, thus the students originally thinking in the concrete way had to learn how to explain their programs in the acceptable, abstract way. The authors claim that most of the 'concrete thinkers' among the students were women. I find the study interesting not because of the claim that one sex thinks differently about computer programs than the other (which I find hard to believe), but rather because it demonstrates that there are different ways to understand computers yet the established culture only 'allows' one of them. Not accepting heterogeneous ways of knowing may encourage an impression of neutrality and thus make it very difficult to articulate and accept differences.

4.2 Design of Software

Software design means making abstract models that have an internal logic and that relate to activities in the real world in a formal, specified way. Real world activities are both starting and end point of the abstract model. Modelling thus departs from some real world problems, and modelling is about finding ways to identify and formally describe the relevant aspects so that the desired routines are automated. The notion of 'relevant' is worth discussing because relevance is defined with respect to a particular definition of problems. In object-oriented modelling, the basic idea is to decide on which objects to include, which characteristics are relevant and what procedures the objects should carry out. The model is supposed to 1) portray all important and relevant characteristics of some part of the world, and 2) be a basis for constructing a computer system whose internal logic is without errors and works in a predictable, controllable way. This double aim may not be easy to achieve, as the two goals may have different priorities and different logics: the logic of the real world, the work, may differ from the logic of the computer. Formal systems development methodologies tend to encourage extending the logic of the computer as a perspective on the real world: describing the world in concepts that facilitate the kind of abstraction needed to build a computer makes systems analysis easier but does not ensure that the logic of the world is taken into consideration.

Models are described in ways that support communication between people performing different parts of systems development: 'systems analysts' communicate with 'systems designers,' interface designers, programmers, usability people etc. Systems description languages at all levels (i.e. programming, overall design etc.) are made for communication between people about the production of the artifact, and represent different levels of abstraction in the making of the system.

5 Gender Aspects in Technology Design

Concluding the discussion, I would claim that: yes, there are interesting insights to be gained from looking for gender in design of technology. Easiest to see – and do – and best documented are gender perspectives on the communicative or presentation aspects of design of artifacts: the wrapping of artifacts to fit with gender stereotypes in society. I include here stereotypes in society that make some artifacts designed to be used by women and some by men. Applying gender perspectives to artifacts – design products – is not very different from other kinds of social analysis of use activities or artifacts in context.

A more difficult task is to apply gender perspectives to the design process. Some aspects of design benefit from such an analysis: the idea that guides the design process comes from somebody: a designer, an employer, a customer. The idea is the basis for a vision of the artifact in use – and the vision is made by someone: the vision guides the design by suggesting the roles of the artifact in some activity, how the artifact can be shaped to fit the envisioned situation, how the design material (be it software or clay) can be pushed so that the needs of the user are better taken care of. Software design is about making formal representations of parts of the world: even if (!) the internal logic of the representation is gender-neutral, the act of representing, of choosing what to describe and how, expresses a particular understanding of the world – held by someone. The 'someone' – the designer or designers – should always be analyzed with respect to gender; gender may be significant in characterizing how we understand and envision the world.

I do not by this claim that women software designers necessarily design different software from their male colleagues. This may be the case. But it is also possible that professional culture sometimes overrules other cultural characteristics such as gender. I do not want women computer scientists to be given responsibility for being a different kind of computer scientists. I claim that the design process itself would benefit from having different sets of experiences as bases for ideas and visions, which is a reason for advocating participatory design (see Floyd and El Tobgui & Gregory, both this volume).

In a gendered society, gender would be a significant characteristic of how we experience and act in the world. Gender aspects of technology are particularly visible when we study the relations between design and use (e.g. Haraway, 1991). Design of gendered technology reinforces a gendered culture, which is the basis for designing gendered technology. Bringing gender issues to design may contribute to a more open attitude within technical cultures towards different ways of thinking about computers and software (Bratteteig & Verne, 1997), as well as towards different evaluation criteria for what makes a system successful.

Acknowledgements

For many years I have had the great pleasure of discussing many of the issues in this chapter with Guri Verne, Christina Mörtberg, Judith Gregory, and Joan Greenbaum. All have contributed to the arguments presented here: thank you! I also want to thank Heidi Schelhowe and Mona Dahms on the *ifu* faculty and the editors for helpful comments.

References

Abbate, Janet (1994). The Internet Challenge. In: Summerton, Jane (ed.): *Changing Large Technical Systems*. Boulder, Colo.: Westview Press, pp. 193-210.

Akrich, Madeleine (1992). The De-Scription of Technical Objects, In: Bijker, Wiebe E. & Law, John (eds). *Shaping Technology/Building Society*. Cambridge, Mass: MIT Press.

Bjerknes, Gro & Bratteteig, Tone (1988). Computers – Utensils or Epaulets? The Application Perspective Revisited. In: *AI and Society,* vol. 2, no. 3, pp. 258-266.

Bratteteig, Tone (forthcoming). *Making change. Working in and between design and use in systems development*. Thesis, Department of Informatics, University of Oslo.

Bratteteig, Tone & Stolterman, Erik (1997). Design in groups – and all that jazz. In: Kyng, Morten & Mathiassen, Lars (eds). *Computers and Design in Context*. Cambridge, Mass: MIT Press, pp. 289-316.

Bratteteig, Tone & Verne, Guri (1997). Feminist or merely critical? In search of a Gender Perspective in Informatics. In: Moser, Ingunn & Aas, Gro Hanne (eds.) *Technology and Democracy – Comparative Perspectives*. Workshop on "Gender, Technology and politics in transition?", Jan. 17-19, Oslo: TMV, pp. 59-74.

Bowker, Geoffrey C. & Star, S. Leigh (1999). *Sorting Things Out: Classification and Its Consequences*. Cambridge, Mass: MIT Press.

Cockburn, Cynthia (1985). *Machinery of Dominance: Women, Men and Technical Know-how*. London: Pluto Press.

Cockburn, Cynthia & Ormrod, Sue (1994). *Masculinity and Technology – Making Meaning, Giving Value, Achieving Dominance*. In: Gunnarson, Ewa & Trojer, Lena (eds.). Feminist Voices on Gender, Technology and Ethics. Luleå: Centre of Women's Studies, Luleå University of Technology, Sweden, pp. 122-131.

Cross, Nigel; Christiaans, Henri & Dorst, Kees (1997). *Analysing Design Activity*. Chichester: John Wiley & Sons.

Dourish, Paul & Button, Graham (1998). Technomethodology: Paradoxes and Possibilities. *Proceedings of CHI'96*. ACM SIGCHI, New York, pp. 19-26.

Haraway, Donna J. (1991): A Cyborg Manifesto. In: Haraway, Donna J.: *Simians, Cyborgs, and Women. The Reinvention of Nature*. London: Free Assoc. Books.

Huff, Charles W. & Cooper, Joel (1987): Sex Bias in Educational Software: The Effect of Designers' Stereotypes on the Software They Design. In: *Journal of Applied Social Psychology*, 17:6, pp. 519-532.

Latour, Bruno (1996): *Aramis, or the Love of Technology*. Cambridge, MA: Harvard University Press.

Laurel, Brenda (2001): *Utopian Entrepreneur*, Cambridge. MA: MIT Press.

Mörtberg, Christina (1997): *"Det beror på att man är kvinna ..." Gränsvandrerskor formas och formar informationsteknologi* ("It's because one is a woman ..." Transgressors are shaped and shape information technology), PhD. Thesis, Department of Work Science: Gender and Technique, University of Luleå.

Orlikowski, Wanda J. (1992): Learning from Notes. In: *Proceedings of CSCW'92* ACM, pp. 362-369.

Star, S. Leigh & Ruhleder, Karen (1994): Steps Towards an Ecology of Infrastructure: Complex Problems in Design and Access for Large-Scale Collaborative Systems. In: *Proceedings of the CSCW '94*, ACM, pp. 253-264.

Suchman, Lucy A. (1994): Do Categories Have Politics? The Language/Action Perspective Reconsidered. *Computer Supported Cooperative Work: The Journal of Collaborative Computing*, vol. 2 no 3, pp. 177-190.

Turkle, Sherry & Papert, Seymour (1990): Epistemological Pluralism: Styles and Voices within the Computer Culture. *Sign*, Autumn 1990.

Wajcman, Judy (1991): *Feminism Confronts Technology*. Cambridge, UK: Polity Press.

Waldén, Louise (1994): "Those living sewing machines..." or Is Male to Female as Technology to Humanism. In: Gunnarson, Ewa & Trojer, Lena (eds): *Feminist Voices on Gender, Technology and Ethics*. Centre of Women's Studies, Luleå University of Technology, Sweden, pp. 32-42.

Winograd, Terry (ed.) (1996): *Bringing Design to Software*. Reading, MA: Addison-Wesley.

Marsha Woodbury

Women in Computing

Women must take on science and technology, develop it, direct it, and use it, for to do otherwise can only leave us behind, out of touch, and out of power.

Anita Borg

Abstract
Based on experiences in a technology course at *ifu*, this chapter looks at women in computing, with a focus on their access problems. For those of us who want to actively engage in computing, the road to and through this technology can be filled with barriers and potholes that prevent our entry, impede our learning, or cause us to make a sharp turn and head elsewhere. The solutions to the dearth of women in computing are diverse, as no one path will work for any one group. While there are no global fixes, we can confidently state that drawing more of us into computing would be facilitated by improving access to technology and instruction, educating men and women about our current status and power in computing and describing the value of our contribution, and working collectively to overcome discrimination, provide mentors, and redesign computer courses.

1 What Do We Mean by 'Computing' and Why Is It Important?

The present discussion is anchored in the author's experience at *ifu* (International Women's University, here: *ifu*'s Project Area INFORMATION), where she was the director of the curricular project on *Knowledge Architectures* and taught a two weeks course on *The Who What Where When How and Why of the Internet* that attracted about forty women from all over the world. While their disciplinary background varied, they shared a serious commitment to acquiring advanced skills in computing so as to be able to become actively engaged on the Internet.

With the increasing pervasiveness of computers and computer chips in everything from cell phones to global positioning systems, from wristwatches to radios, from animal tracking tags to database management systems, the age of computing has been announced, at least by Western media. Women in many countries have seized the opportunity to shape society through our work with computers and information technology. We also realize that if we do not engage in this evolving area, or are prevented from entering it, the digital domain will continue to be largely shaped by men.

Before discussing the current situation in more depth, let us define our terms. Electronic computing is a relatively young area of study, with the first working prototype dating from 1937. We have been involved from the start. For example, in the 1940s, six women designed and built the trajectory program for ENIAC, the first general-purpose electronic digital computer (cf. Past Notable Women of Computing, 2002). Today, 'computing' includes everything from designing and constructing the machines, to programming, artificial intelligence and robotics, computer graphics, and web design, to computer networks, database design and implementation, and recycling machines. Further, computing also includes the study of the social and societal impact of computers, the structure, behavior, and interactions of natural and artificial computational systems, and the emerging field of computer law and Internet governance. With miniaturization and nanotechnology (computers made of molecules, manufactured atom by atom), computing has involved chemists and molecular biologists and physicists and medical scientists. Finally, computing includes the passing on of knowledge, creating tools for teaching, and teaching others about all of the above.

At present we find a dearth of women in computing. We thus have a serious feminist issue, because this under-representation leaves the control and construction of computers and their programs – and the heart of information technology – in the hands of men. As scholars such as Donna J. Haraway (1991) and Susan Leigh Star (1991) have pointed out, women become marginalized by the language and artifacts of computing, and as the practices of the modern computer information infrastructure are made more permanent, it will be harder to transform them.

2 The *ifu* Participants and Computing

As we learned at *ifu*, our technology courses were highly popular. We taught the courses in a supportive, question-driven manner, and as far as we could, we solicited from the participants their input on what they wanted to learn, and how. In order to encourage the participants who were hesitant or afraid to ask questions, we provided cards on which they could write their questions, promising we would try to answer them in class the next day.

As a tool for illustrating some of the issues before us, I will include entries from the diaries of *ifu* participants who took a computer course that I taught in Hamburg. Their comments underline some of the broader statements presented here. (They have given their permission to be quoted.) For example, in talking about the construction of the language of computing, two participants wrote:

> I remember when I first encountered UNIX commands like 'kill' and 'mount' and felt somewhat uncomfortable with it but never said a word because there were 6 girls in a class of 80 in Comp Sci. It's nice to know that [other] women felt this too. (*ifu* participant)

> I still believe that the interfaces could and should be designed much more user-friendly, and that it is therefore essential that numerous women take part in the design. A funny experience was to watch an American using a German PC (I am used to a North American PC at work and a German at home by the way). Since I and the other German-speaking women wanted to help out I realized that the German translation of a lot of the buttons is very misleading. (*ifu* participant)

Technology is not gender- or culturally neutral, and the computer technology that surrounds us is limited by not having more women involved in the conception and execution of the product (Huff & Cooper, 1987; Bratteteig, in this volume).

> In the beginning, among other useful tips, the instructor suggested to the participants to have their passwords changed. I didn't dare to do that. I'm afraid of a collapse in the system and I would be excluded from my personal universe. (*ifu* participant)

Feminist literature abounds on how computer and information technology have served and changed the women's movement, particularly as represented at the world conference in Beijing. Scholars have examined the power of computer-aided communication to forge and change relationships and daily life, to mold the content of a movement via the computing technology it employs (Scott, 2001). The Internet has the potential to improve our communication, if we can be inclusive in its development and governance.

For example, we now cannot imagine organizing an *ifu* without using computing, nor can we clearly discern the subtle ways that computing perhaps molded *ifu*, education, and technical expertise. We also learn from the positive experiences we had during the *ifu* months, when women learned about computers and computing in a very nurturing, sharing community. We do not wish to gloss over the problems that we encountered at *ifu*, such as unfamiliar language and interfaces, keyboards, and software, and a varying degree of computer and server access. Yet, we had far more advances than frustrations (see the chapters by El Tobgui & Gregory; Kerr & Mätschke; Link et al; and Weber, all in this volume).

In order to foresee and overcome the obstacles, grasp the opportunities, and understand more subtle discrimination, we can draw on research by people concerned about the status and condition of women. To contrast the *ifu* experience with life outside of that unique cooperative spirit, we start with issues of access and barriers to entry and work.

3   The Problem of Access for Women – Some Examples

> "If information systems are to meet the needs of all people, then all people must be en-
> gaged in the creation of information systems." *Edward D. Lazowska (1999)*

The cost of Internet access at all levels makes it inaccessible for the majority of the African population. The need to import computers and modems, and the fault-ridden, erratic telephone and electrical systems cause many problems. Most people lack access to training, have very limited technical information, less access to computer parts and repair, and watch their technology becoming obsolete even before it is running properly.

Here, as in many other places, language is also a hurdle for many native speakers, because most training packages, software, and electronic conferences and journals are in English (Huyer, 1997). These barriers to technology are worse for women because of "their lower economic and social status, their lack of training and literacy, their concentration in lower-level and entry-level employment, their lack of autonomy, and their lack of time" (Huyer, 1997). As one *ifu* participant wrote,

> Within this two weeks, I have learnt so many things which I have not had the chance to
> do in my country. I have learnt how the ftp and the telnet works and MUDs and so many
> things. (*ifu* participant)

Not only do men dominate computing, but when women do gain a foothold, we tend to work in the low-paying and less prestigious positions. Because of our lower social status, women often do not gain access to computer equipment even if we have more computer ability and need for it (Huyer, 1997). The majority of African women are involved in the informal economy, and often do not enjoy equal opportunity with men (see the chapter by Dahms & Faust-Ramos in this volume for a detailed account on gender and development). The attitudes towards women have often suppressed the development or advancement of women, restricting girls' and women's access to education, training and employment. Similar trends occur in most other cultures, where barriers to entry exist through cultural stereotypes and norms.

African governments, the largest employers in Africa, usually pay low wages, and have done little to promote women's participation in technical education, training, and employment. Women receive poor grounding in mathematics and science subjects at primary level, and this lack of exposure to technical subjects limits our performance in these subjects at secondary school and our access to technical programs at the tertiary level (cf. Odedra-Straub, 1995).

However, Africa is experiencing change. The growing number of Internet sites created and used by African women attests to their online presence. As we saw at *ifu*, community cyber centers can introduce women to computer technology. Several projects highlight that African women are innovative, entrepreneurial and courageous in engaging information and communications technologies, in spite of limited access to resources and infrastructure (cf. APPC 2001, March 14).

In addition, data processing work is growing, providing technology employment for hundreds of women. In Ghana, where the average income is about $ 380 a year, the best data processors make $ 300 a month. An employer in Accra said, "In Africa, if you give decent employment to one person, you are feeding 15 in the urban areas and 30 to 35 in rural areas. Also, 90% of my employees are female, and this sort of job makes them self-dependent." One female employee said, "I studied computers at the polytechnic. If this weren't here I would have been a secretary for a lot less pay. Most of my friends are trying to get a job here" (Friedman, 2001: A31).

From this first step into technology work could come many more gains and societal transformations. However, it would be women's direct participation in government, technical education, training, and employment that might provide some local determination about whether gender and culture sensitive changes occur (this is described in more detail by Kelkar in this volume, in particular for women from Asia).

Computer-centered careers are providing many Indian women with economic alternatives and more independence. In addition, the high salaries in the information technology field enable some women to become the primary wage earners in their families, giving women more control over decisions such as household finances. The technology industry is also spearheading a shift in India's work culture toward increased gender equality, as other industries follow the technology companies' lead in offering paternity leave and telecommuting (cf. Yee, 2000).

Indian women may account for nearly half of India's technology workforce within 10 years (although not likely in the more prestigious, well-paying fields). Women should play a major role in helping the Indian software industry grow from a $ 5 billion-a-year industry in 2000 to an $ 87 billion industry by 2008 (Yee, 2000). Although women now account for 14% of India's high-tech workforce, this figure is expected to jump to 45% by 2010. Half of the participants at various technology trade schools are women, and some of the engineering colleges in India also report that women represent 50% of their student population (Yee, 2000).

As a result of the economic slowdown of early 2001, thousands of Indian programmers working on short-term contracts in the United States may be heading back home. The return of these workers might augment the technology workforce in India, as some predict, and make it an even more desirable location for computer projects in the future. However, the return might result in the un-employment or 'downgrading' of many. More women and men are becoming 'migrant' workers even in their own countries, as transnational companies in-creasingly govern the employment and treatment of millions.

In China, jobs involving computers are especially attractive to young women because they can work in an office or with machines instead of doing manual labor (cf. Didier, 1993). In Malaysia, national policies have encouraged partici-pants to enter information technology. A number of universities offer degree courses in computing programs. Women in China and Malaysia are finding the same problems that women face everywhere, including the balancing of work and family obligations, particularly when employers are not sensitive or caring about local standards, and values.

In Brazil, women are nearly half of the information processing employees, although they tend to work at the lowest-paying jobs and miss promotion op-portunities. Few women do software development work. Nonetheless, women doing programming have fared far better than in the traditional professional jobs, such as engineering.

4 Women's Gains Are Not Without Cost

Women of the Third World might look forward to an equitable distribution of jobs in information technology. However, women's gains are not without cost. Some practitioners who survive in these highly paid jobs find that some of their basic behavior changes (Gaio, 2000).

> After thinking about it as a career and talking to people I know, I don't think I want to do it forever. It's very much about one person and a computer and mental masturbation, and the problems you are solving are in a very small, well-defined area that has little to do with real life. (Stanford University graduate, 2001)

In countries where access is not such a barrier, and women have begun to share more job and wage equality, women are not always choosing to study comput-ing. Of all scientific and engineering fields, computing in the United States has perhaps made the least progress in increasing the participation of women and minorities in the past decade. In *The Incredible Shrinking Pipeline,* Tracy Camp (1997) describes how in the United States, the discipline of computing loses women at all stages of the educational pipeline including elementary, middle, and high schools, college, graduate school and beyond.

Camp points to a shrinking supply of female computing undergraduates. As a consequence, there are disproportionately low numbers of women in academic computing and the computer industry. In contrast, other science and engineering fields show larger gains in attracting and retaining women, especially in physics and engineering. The pattern is not unique to the United States, for in the United Kingdom, the decline of women in computing is also noticeable. There, women's representation in higher education computing courses continues to run at around 10%, a significant decrease from the figures of the late 1970s and early 1980s (Frenkel, 1990), and shows little likelihood of improving.

The situation for minorities in computing in higher education shows a scant representation. The situation may be perpetuated for several generations, because research tells us that girls from grade school to high school are losing interest in computing (Grossman, 1998).

According to a survey of Association for Computing Machinery (ACM) members, factors that may have contributed to the shrinking supply of women computer scientists include: less prior experience playing computer games as children, the long work hours common in many programming jobs, gender discrimination, the lack of role models, and the antisocial image of the typical computer hacker (Grossman, 1998).

A new study by the Annenberg Public Policy Center examined the top executives and board members of major media, telecommunications and e-companies to determine if women are in a leadership role. Their conclusion found a lack of women, and particularly women with 'clout' (APPC 2001, 14 March).

Girls in the United States complain of 'tedious and dull' computer courses. A reason that only one-fifth of high technology jobs there are held by women is not that girls in middle school and high school are afraid of technology, but, in part, that they are bored by it. When asked, girls and women are concerned that devoting themselves to computing will stunt their diverse range of intellectual pursuits and interests. "Girls tend to imagine that computer professionals live in a solitary, anti-social and sedentary world" (Mollison, 2000, A9).

A student of computers (under the umbrella of 'infomatics' or the narrower 'computer science') may be concerned about the basic attitude of the culture in how the courses are taught. In many courses, there is little nurturing, and much 'survival of the fittest' mentality. The emphasis is on individual programming, not on teamwork, the major skill that employers look for today, and that women often excel in (Wetzel, this volume, gives a detailed account of what a women's learning culture around computer skills might be like).

Philip Greenspun (1995) suggests that anyone who is smart enough to succeed as a computer scientist could succeed with less work and risk by choosing to be a doctor, lawyer, or manager. The powerful film *Minerva's Machine* (Frenkel, 1995) probes the role of women in computing from historical role models such as Grace Hopper, to young girls who dislike computers. One memorable profile shows the emotional side of being a woman in computing, including sexual harassment, late night endurance contests with other programmers, raising a family while going to school and holding down a job, and managing a group of male employees who have genuine problems working for a woman.

Because women are a minority in the upper levels of the computing profession, men sometimes mistreat women through ignorance or malice. The ethical problem is not with men or computers, but with power imbalances. Some men post pornographic pictures in their offices or use pornographic screen savers at work. Either they are unaware that many women find these images offensive, they do not care, or they are intentionally trying to make women feel ill at ease or 'outsiders.' However, if women were the majority of powerful people at work, then men would quickly have their consciousness raised. The same phenomenon exists at *Wired*, a magazine that is written largely by men and for men (Borsook, 1996).

5 Conclusion

> I have been working on email and the internet since 1991 or so but never really had the
> chance to look at some of the social, political, and economic implications of things I use
> all the time like search engines, signature files, etc. (*ifu* participant)

As became clear at *ifu*, beyond the sphere of inter-personal communication, we have to make informed decisions about all sorts of computing issues, such as nanomedicine or implanting chips in people, and we ought to understand the limits and implications of technology. How can we keep up with the swiftly growing computing arena? No standardized practices and priorities involving plans to increase the number of women in computing will work for all places, and we do not propose a 'one-size-fits-all' solution here. The power and potential of computing contrasts with what surrounds us in the physical world: crowding, widespread poverty, and increasing differences in our income.

Perhaps one generalization we can make about women and computing is that local conditions deeply affect whether and how we might be left behind, and out of power. Even in the most technologically-committed countries, where women participate in computing, we remain a minority in the upper levels of the profession, and even in pivotal positions, women are subtly harassed.

Our experiences at *ifu* impressed upon many of us the importance of learning about historical contexts, culturally defined relations, and the realities of globalizing forces. Projects such as *ifu* give women time, space, and access to learn computing skills and the underlying assumptions behind the technology, an issue that is also treated by Wetzel in this volume.

At the very basic level, trying to lure women into computing without changing the atmosphere and basic assumptions of the trade will not work. We should push for wages and power, healthy working conditions and quality of life issues. If we want to become an integral part of computing and the technology infrastructure, and insure that women's concerns are met, we ought to increase our knowledge to make informed decisions, guarantee our income, and assure our ability to take an active part in economic and public policy decisions that involve technology.

As we learned in the *ifu* experience, many of us thirst for reliable access, and for information about computer technology – information presented in a cooperative manner, at a reasonable pace in a setting where we are not 'outsiders.' Once the basic problems of access are overcome, and the female students are in programs to learn about computers, we need also to immediately work on overcoming classroom discrimination, find positive mentors, and work from within to encourage more women to join our ranks.

In Germany, the *Informatica Feminale* project at Bremen University has operated since 1998, bringing together women students and women professors from German departments of informatics to work on new definitions of informatics curricula from women's viewpoints, creation of test-fields for new educational concepts mainly in the context of summer courses, and further education of women university staff in informatics (Vosseberg & Oechtering, 2002).

Women in the United States can join a group like the Association for Women in Computing (AWC), a not-for-profit, professional organization dedicated to the advancement of women in the computing fields. In New Zealand, Australia, Canada, and elsewhere organizations exist to encourage women in mathematics, science, space programs, education, and so on. Women in all parts of the world might form such groups.[1] Above joining together, we who are already in computing ought to enlighten our colleagues who make prejudicial or inappropriate remarks about women students, and increase sensitivity to women as professionals. Instead of trying to make girls fit into the existing computer culture, the computer culture must become more sensitive to girls.[2] One solution lies in making computing courses less 'tedious and dull,' redesigning computer games for girls, and reshaping the image of computer workers. (Eske & Beer in this volume report on a beautiful experience with computer-supported conversational games held at an art workshop at *ifu*). Another lies in supporting one an-

---

1   Profiles of women in computing are available at: http://www.sdsc.edu/CRAW/
     women.html and from other sources.
2   American Association of University Women Educational Foundation 2000.

other, encouraging and cooperating, and transforming the world of computing into one we care to live in.

Women, locally and globally, need to be deeply involved in planning if there are to be any deep changes. Offering the strongest possibilities for long lasting changes in the low numbers and status of women in computer science and computer work are: emphasis on (large) social changes, collective action from local, national and international women's groups, redesigning of computer courses, and further involvement from university programs (such as *ifu*) focussed on gender issues.

> Today was my first day in Internet class...I know nothing about Internet and am not so familiar with computer and its different programs. I found out how easy we can get different information through internet and I decided to obtain Internet when I go back to my country. (*ifu* participant)

References

APPC (2001). Annenberg Public Policy Center. *Progress or No Room at the Top? The Role of Women in Telecommunications, Media and E-Companie*s. Reports, March 14. Source: http://www.appcpenn.org/internet/publicpolicy/progress-report.pdf; accessed February 10, 2002.

American Association of University Women Educational Foundation. (2000). *Tech-Savvy: Educating Girls in the New Computer Age*. Source: http://www.aauw.org/2000/techsavvy.html/; accessed February 10, 2002.

Borsook, Paulina (1996). The Memoirs of a Token: an Aging Berkeley Feminist Examines *Wired*. In: Cherny, Lynn & Weise, Elizabeth Reba (eds.). *Wired Women: Gender and New Realities in Cyberspace*. Seattle: Seal Press, pp. 24-41.

Camp, Tracy (1997). The Incredible Shrinking Pipeline. *Communications of the ACM*. 40 (10), pp.103-110.

Didier, Michele (1993). *Impressions of The People's Republic of China: A Technological Sleeping Giant*. Source: http://www.awc-hq.org/publications/source93FW.html; accessed February 10, 2002.

Frenkel, Karen (1995). *Minerva's Machine: Women in Computing*. Video. Available from ACM. Source: http://store.acm.org/acmstore/

Frenkel, Karen (1990). Women and Computing. In: *Communications of the ACM*. 33 (11), p. 34.

Friedman, Thomas (2001). It Takes a Satellite. In: *The New York Times*. May 8, p. A31.

Gaio, Fatima Janine (1995). *Women in software programming*. Source: http://www.unu.edu/unupress/unupbooks/uu37we/uu37we0o.htm; accessed February 10, 2002.

Greenspun, Philip (1995). Women in Computing, *Communications of the ACM*. Source: http://philip.greenspun.com/careers/acm-women-in-computing.html; accessed February 10, 2002.

Grossman, Wendy M. (1998). Access Denied. In: *Scientific American*. Source: http://www.sciam.com/1998/0898issue/0898cyber.html; accessed February 10, 2002.

Haraway, Donna J. (1991). A Cyborg Manifesto. In: Haraway, Donna J.. *Simians, Cyborgs, and Women. The Reinvention of Nature*. New York: Routledge.

Huff, Chuck & Cooper, J. (1987). Sex Bias in Educational Software: The Effects of Designers' Stereotypes on the Software They Design. In: *Journal of Applied Social Psychology* 17, pp. 519-532.

Huyer, Sophia (1997). Supporting Women's Use of Information Technologies for Sustainable Development. Source: http://www.idrc.ca/acacia/outputs/womenicts.html#barriers; accessed February 10, 2002.

Lazowska, Edward D. (1999). *Statement of the Commission on the Advancement of Women and Minorities in Science, Engineering, and Technology Development*. Source: http://www.cra.org/Policy/testimony/lazowska-5.html; accessed February 10, 2002.

Mollison, Andrew (2000). Girls Opting Out of High-tech Jobs. In: The Atlanta Journal-Constitution, April 11, p. A 9.

Odedra-Straub, Mayuri (1995). Women and Information Technology in Sub-Saharan Africa, In: Mitter, Swasti & Rowbotham, Sheila (eds.) *Women encounter technology: Changing Patterns of Employment in the Third World*. Source: http://www.unu.edu/unupress/unupbooks/uu37we/uu37we0u.htm; accessed February 10, 2002.

Past Notable Women of Computing (2002). Kay McNulty Mauchly Antonelli. Source: http://www.cs.yale.edu/homes/tap/past-women-cs.html; accessed February 6, 2002.

Scott, Anne (2001). Grounded Politics: Some Thought on Feminist Process in the Information Age. *Computers and Society*, 31:4, pp. 3-14.

Solinger, Dorothy J. (2001). Globalization and the Paradox of Participation: The Chinese Case. In: *Global Governance: A Review of Multilateralism and International Organizations*, vol.7, no.2, pp. 173-182.

Star, S. Leigh (1991). Power, Technology and the Phenomenology of Conventions: on Being Allergic to Onions. In: Law, J. (ed.). *A Sociology of Monsters: Essays on Power Technology and Domination*. Sociological Review Monograph 38. London: Routledge.

Tsang, Cheryl & Cole, Ida (1999). '*The Independent,*' Microsoft First Generation. New York: John Wiley & Sons.

Vosseberg, Karin & Oechtering, Veronika (2002). *Changing the Male University Culture in Informatics: the Project Informatica Feminale*. Source: http://www.informatica-feminale.de/Papiere/Tromso.html; accessed February 10, 2002.

Yee, Chen Ma (2000). High-Tech Lift for India's Women. In: *Wall Street Journal*, Nov.1, p. B1.

Govind Kelkar

Technological Change and Cultural Ceilings

Abstract
Recent history of technological change in South and South-East Asia has demonstrated that institutions – their structures and procedures – and cultures are not compatible with the enduring traditions of women's domesticity and inferiorized roles. Women are on the move to enhance their capacity for autonomous action in the face of constricting social, cultural sanctions for gender inequalities. While a large number of women continues to work in gendered homes and work sites, balancing work and domestic responsibilities with little help from men, there is an ongoing struggle of these women to challenge the embedded patriarchal relations within the family and in the industry. Conceding that there are socially sanctioned gender inequalities in the market, many women prefer to work outside the home in the attempt to improve their social position and construct a greater scope to enhance their agency (the capacity for autonomous action) rather than to be subject to family-based dependency and coercion. These issues were discussed in the courses taught by the author at *ifu*.

1 Introduction

This chapter attempts to explain how women are affecting and have been affected by the wide-ranging technological advances. The interest in writing this chapter evolved during a three-month experience of lectures, discussions and interactions with women students from Asia, Africa, Europe, and South and North America, at *ifu* (International Women's University, here: *ifu's* Project Area INFORMATION) in Hamburg in 2000. I directed two projects: *Community Development through Information* and *Cultural Modes, Self Expression and Media* and offered two courses: *Gender Research Methods in Science and Technology* and *Indigenous Knowledge and Technology*.

Most discussions during the projects and courses focussed on one of the two major issues: women's role in the new industrial and information technologies; and division of authority between the sexes. We also discussed and debated a seemingly historical fact that universally men have enjoyed authority over women. We reviewed the past fifty years in several cultures in South and South-

East Asia and looked at the change in gender relations from a matrilineal and/or egalitarian system to one where male domination is present as the norm. Cultural traditions of women's exclusion from knowledge and community management delegates authority and prestige to men. Men virtually hold all formal positions of power and decision-making in societies under patrilineal systems. However, in matrilineal systems, women have specially effective power; they have rights and control over ancestral property and knowledge of ritualistic activity, including being the spiritual heads of the community, e.g. *syiem sad* among the Khasi in India and *Bobolizan* among the Rungus in Sabah, Malaysia (for detail see Kelkar, Nathan & Walter, 2002)

In Asia as a whole and particularly in East and Southeast Asia, women have entered the industrial labor force on a larger scale and faster than in any other developing region of the world. This was part of the process of globalization, as export markets provided a scope for developing light industry far beyond what the national, internal markets did. Within the labor-intensive export-oriented industries the employment of young women (the classic 'nimble fingers' case) rose much faster than that of men (Lim, 1985; and Banerjee, 1991). More recently, advances in information technologies have led to changes in the organization of work. There has been a shift of women workers from the status of unpaid family workers to that of employees. This shift represents a change, not within an existing industry, but in terms of the over-proportionate growth of industry, leading to a change in the technological composition of overall economic activity. Did this movement of women as employees into industry or commerce bring benefits to women concerned? Did it weaken the grip of patriarchy, the confines of the cultural ceilings (duties of domesticity and inferiorized social, familial relations)?

Gender is not a form of natural difference but a socially constructed form of power. Women's crushing inequalities of access to knowledge and resources are legitimized by cultures. Gender relations are produced and reproduced to serve certain specific interests of the dominant people – men in this case. Gender relations are complex and constitute the cultural terrain for measuring and feeling in the family and community, including the complicity of the dominated.

Present development discourse emphasizes building women's competence for industry and higher productivity (see also the chapter by Dahms & Faust-Ramos, this volume). The real issue before us is not simply a question of giving Asian women access to technological development but also of how they are enabled to carry forward their responsibility for industry and society. A culture that stresses women's domesticity and inferior social position is unlikely to do very well in relation to problems of production, efficiency, and technological development. And by no means is it likely to be conducive to innovation and technological transformation.

2 Women and Technological Change

In seeking answers to the above questions, it must be pointed out that the new export industries represented the first avenue for the large-scale entry of women into industry. For young women coming from confined rural backgrounds the introduction of modern industry and machinery certainly represented an advance. They learned new technologies and new methods of work organization compared to the craft or agricultural methods or housework they had been used to. After a while they also absorbed the changed and faster rhythms of factory production, even where the basic activity, say, embroidery was no different from that done earlier in the home. Cooperative activity and team skills, based on a division of labor replaced home-based craft-style production.

After the young women from rural areas had been working for a while they were indistinguishable in dress and style from urban women (Tao, 1995: 7). In terms of earnings – though wages were and are very low compared to, say, what is earned in organized large industry – they still represented much more than what could have been earned in the stagnant rural settings from which these women came. The wages of women in Bangladesh's garment sector are at least double what they could have earned in the informal sector or in rural areas (World Bank, 1995: 73). While there was the push of rural stagnation that induced these women to seek employment, it is not as though they were indentured or otherwise bonded laborers. Thus, one must expect that they earned more even in the low-paid garment sector than they could elsewhere.

Along with the above there is the increase in dignity that goes with being a wage-earner, often even the major income provider in the family. In family agriculture, the women's contribution would have been merely subsumed in the general household labor and not even acknowledged, given men are the owners of land in most of Asia. The men also would have greater control over the income from agriculture. But in the condition of women wage-earners they would have a greater prestige in the family and are also likely to have more control over how their income is spent, which is what Amartya Sen's theory of the family as a site of cooperative conflict would predict (Sen, 1990). The World Bank study found that 57 % of women garment workers determined how their own wages are spent and even that their husbands contributed 1.3 to 3.7 hours to household work per day (World Bank, 1995: 73).

The young women also became more proficient in their skills and could take the initiative and promote the development of new technology (Tao, 1995: 10). In the factory studied by Tao, women workers put forward 95 % of the suggestions to improve production. Of course, all this works to the greater profit of capital, but it also demonstrates the greater initiative of women workers after a period of adjustment.

There is no denying that the buyers from the North who buy garments from the South benefit from the low wages of the workers and earn high profits from the sale of these garments. But from the point of view of the women garment workers themselves it represents an advance over their former condition not only in terms of the income status of their families but it also enables them to improve their status and position within the family. Yet it is still sweated women's labor on the basis of which the developing countries have built their competitive positions in world trade.

The development of information technology (IT) in Asia has had a clear impact on women. Overall figures of the number of women in the Indian IT industry are not available owing to the lack of gender disaggregated data in existing literature, including the National Association of Software and Service Companies (NASSCOM) study (NASSCOM 2001a). But it is estimated that women constitute 21 % of the total IT workforce, which is higher than their participation in the national economy as a whole, now at 13 % (NASSCOM 2001b).

What has been the impact of women's entry into the IT sector on existing gender roles and relations? Studies of 'Village Pay Phones' in rural Bangladesh (Richardson, Ramirez & Haq, 2000) and computer aided technologies and teleworking in Malaysia and India (Ng, 1987; Mitter, 2000; Mitter & Sen, 2000; Gothoskar, 2000; Kelkar, Shrestha & Veena, 2002) have observed that household income has increased, and women have more mobility and more say in household matters. But it is also pointed out that women's work has multiplied and the gender-based divisions of labor have been maintained.

There is, however, an undeniable improvement in the social mobility and work participation rate of women in the IT industry. The nature of work (such as flexi-time, teleworking and working from home or from decentralized centers), the tools (such as e-mail and Internet) and the individualization of capacities required by information technology make women more capable to take decisions on their own and construct greater scope to enhance their agency. IT does, therefore, constitute the basis of the redefinition of traditional gender norms and supports a medium of information, understanding and knowledge in which women's interests, opinions and rights are taken into account. Nevertheless, they are restricted by the dominant interests of the market and the state which provides a non-threatening mobilization of women's labor for the benefit of their families and communities.

Gender inequality is embedded in the history and political economy of the Asian region, including India. Yet, women are not silent observers of the male appropriation of traditional and technological knowledge, power and resources. There are women (as evident through women's movement, women's writings, NGOs) who speak publicly against the growing male dominance and control of resources. Others are silent but would speak if power and resource inequality did not create obstacles. There are also women who keep quiet and have no realistic choice other than compliance with the male dominance. This is done as a result of fear of insult and assault on the body. Conceding that there is power and gender inequality in the market, many women prefer to work outside the home, in an attempt to improve their social position, rather than be subject to family-based dependency and coercion.

The two aspects of technological development and cultural ceiling are inter-related. While the former may imply incorporation of women's interests and roles in technological development, the latter tends to emphasize conflicting interactions between gender-specific interests and identity: men may recognize that they can gain from excluding women from certain jobs and knowledge spheres. Women may also share the common attitude that certain jobs and knowledge are more 'appropriate' for them as they are enshrined in traditional culture. Women may continue to accept such gender-specific norms and preferences but if the social cost (in terms of women's constraints in certain forms of work and knowledge) increases, they are likely to be inclined toward a secular, gender-responsive action.

3 The Need for Gender Knowledge in Technology Studies

Technology has its roots in indigenous, non-Western and pre-'industrial revolution' systems. Women have played an important yet unrecognized role in these systems and in the history of technological development. The 'technology question' for women is not whether technology represses or liberates, or whether women have equal access or entry to new technologies, but rather how to restore and carry forward an equality-based participation of women in technology development[1]. Political and economic empowerment, combined with enhanced knowledge, skills and education, are crucial preconditions for the transformation of social and gender relations through development in science and technology.

There has been much interest in the relationship between technology and social change in the past decade. The sociology of technology shows that political choices are embedded in the design and selection of technology. Many argue that patriarchal values and biases are particularly embedded in Western technology and science (Mies & Shiva, 1993; Shiva, 1992). Dramatic changes in technology, the challenge of feminism and the awareness of the vulnerability of the environment have made much of this ideology untenable.

The almost complete exclusion of the gender question from technological studies points to the need to take account of the underlying structure of gender relations (see also Bratteteig, this volume). There is little literature on women

---

1   This appears to be in contrast to the position of Woodbury, this volume.

and technology despite the proliferation of technology studies, and little attention to how technology studies may be shaped by the incorporation of gender interests. Even the sociology of the new technology is largely blind to gender issues (see Nandy, 1988; Banuri & Marglin, 1993). Because technological change is subject to struggles for control by different groups, the outcomes depend on the distribution of power and resources in societies in which women are at a disadvantage. *ifu* illustrates a critical role of providing for women cross-culturally access to knowledge of both gender relations and of technology fields.

In Asia, technologically changing cultures in the midst of rapidly growing technologies demand urgent attention to socially entrenched gender relations. This requires interdisciplinary thinking, targeted research and policy institutions as well as international development planners. Education and training institutions can impact gender-relevant knowledge, carry out research on valuation of women's work and roles, establish mechanisms to assess the implementation and impact of development policies and programs on women and ensure their contributions and extension of benefits. As pointed out in the UN Conference on Environment and Development (UNCED) Agenda 21, Chapter 24, academic institutions can also collaborate with researchers on developing gender-sensitive databases on women's knowledge and experience of the management and conservation of natural resources, the impact of environmental degradation on women, and the structural linkages between gender relations, environment and development (Agenda 21, 1992).

While analyzing the reasons for women's underrepresentation in technology education and employment is critical, a more important question is why there are so few women directing the agenda of these fields. There is further need for gender-knowledgeable professionals in technology studies.

However, there is another issue beyond that of access to education or even authority in science and technology. The equal opportunities strategy does not address the division of knowledge and division of labor by gender. A holistic perspective on technology demands a transformation of gender relations in academia and industry.

4 The AIT Experience

Setting up Gender and Development Studies (1991-1997) at the Asian Institute of Technology (AIT) has been both a challenge and a tough experience. Some of my efforts did not cause problems and sailed smoothly, while others were seen as blatantly 'feminist,' with an advocacy for gender equality, and therefore subversive of cultural norms. The latter caused enduring, tiresome controversies. There were repeated deadlocks leading to fatigue and demoralizing experiences.

There were many occasions in the initial five years when I felt indignant and questioned whether my struggles at AIT were worth the effort. I carried on because of the undying support I received from my friends, a large number of them being feminist (including some men) and at strategic positions in various places within AIT, across the region, and outside the region as well.

There were also others at AIT (both women and men) who in a somewhat pragmatic manner advised me not to be 'confrontational,' 'wait for some change' (of hearts, perhaps) and dress in a *Saree* to look more 'feminine and nice.' Further, advice was that I should conduct research quietly and not insist on teaching or advising students. If there was an opportunity, I should accept the position of co-advisor, along with a male colleague who would be the advisor. My demands for equal and just treatment in the academic system were interpreted as that of a 'non-Asian woman, with a strong undercurrent of feminism.' Several times I was reminded by some senior colleagues (from Asia and male): "our expectations are different from an Asian woman." A couple of years later, one of the male colleagues admitted to me that "the AIT system has been unfair to you."

In 1992, during my negotiations with an AIT professor on the inclusion of gender aspects in technology studies at AIT, I was given a copy of an article that claimed women's low brain weights and deficient brain structures, and that their inferior intellectual capacities were explained on this basis. I questioned his thesis and argued with him on the analogy of caste and gender in India, which carried an interpretation that women shared with 'the low castes' small brains and polluting elements rather than original thinking, an intellectual quality found in upper caste men.

Against my struggle for a degree-awarding program Gender and Development Studies, there were efforts to keep Gender and Development Studies as a non-credit 'gender-sensitization limb' of the graduate studies at AIT. The organizational placement of Gender and Development Studies as a non-ranking discipline becomes the way in which the reality is perceived, so that even the existence of constraints is not recognized. "Of all forms of hidden persuasion the most placable is the one exerted quite simply by the order of things" (Bourdieu & Loic, 1992). The unrecognized nature of these constraints means that steps are not taken to remove them and the constraints are instead accepted as being unchangeable aspects of institutional culture.

5 Gender Knowledge in Technology Makes a Difference

The structural discrimination (the cultural ceiling) against women does not just mean injustice and inequality for half of the world's population, it also "constrains a society's productivity and ultimately slows its rate of economic growth" (World Bank, 1995). Discrimination of and under-investment in women means a missed opportunity for a higher rate of human capital formation, losses in productivity, retardation in technological change, lower well-being of families and society at large. There is extensive data to prove, for example, that women's education functions as a catalyst that increases the efficiency of other investments in health, nutrition, family planning, agriculture, industry and social infrastructure.

In the analysis of the interface between technology and society, there is growing recognition of the specific roles of women in various spheres of production. This has led to the shift from earlier emphasis on 'community' participation to one that recognizes the necessity of 'empowering women' as part of the development process in various fields (Dahms & Faust-Ramos, this volume). Agenda 21 clearly recognizes that 'empowering women' has a role not just for welfare reasons, but for the development process and for the development of technology itself. Among its other recommendations, it asks governments to take steps to "promote the provision of environmentally sound technologies which have been designed, developed and improved in consultations with women [for] accessible and clean water, an efficient fuel supply and adequate sanitation facilities" (1992).

Gender studies have introduced a new set of analytical frameworks to look inside the household in order to understand its resource use pattern. To what extent is the gendered control of household and community resources a factor in the adoption and success of technological interventions? Despite the officially acknowledged feminization of agriculture, are there conceptual differences encountered in recognizing women as farmers and their rights over land?

Women's contributions to agricultural production, for example, is concealed behind their domestic tasks because they are regarded as merely doing 'domestic work.' A large part of women's labor is not even seen as 'labor' but only as 'service' performed by the woman for her family. Enhancing women's agency requires action on several points. Property rights, access to finance including micro-finance, building women's organizations, effective participation in community forums, measures to curb domestic and other violence on women, tackling discrimination against the girl child in matters of nutrition, health care and education – these are aspects of transformation.

The needs of domestic or reproductive labor are the least addressed in technological development. In the market-dominated system, the extent to which reducing the drudgery of domestic labor and its health hazards are dealt with, depends on the extent to which women's work is remunerated. It also requires attention to what are now 'women's needs' in the existing division of labor. For instance, changes in house or kitchen design to promote more gender-equal roles (sharing of domestic labor between women and men) and to make the labor less

hazardous need to be integrated into new architectural practices. But this requires both more women as architects and technologists, and consultation with
women users of these technologies, so that they can participate in their design,
and changes in gender relations, which make these technological changes necessary.

6 Telecommunications and Culture

The combination of IT with telecommunications, particularly satellite communications, has transformed the world of communication. To take an example of
this transformation: during the 'internal emergency' regime in the mid-70s in
India, when there were strict controls on the press, it was through word of mouth
and flyers that opposition to the excesses of the regime was transmitted, which
finally ended in the defeat of the ruling party. On the other hand, in the early
1990s, during the demonstrations against military rule in Bangkok and other
Thai cities, sections of demonstrators often kept in touch with each other by mo-
bile phones and, although Thai TV did not broadcast pictures of the demonstrations, those who had access to satellite dishes could watch them on various foreign TV networks.

Women's groups in various parts of Asia are able to keep in touch with each
other and with groups in other parts of the world through e-mail and other such
communication systems. The resulting networks of such organizations are able
to work in very close coordination with each other in conducting campaigns on
various issues affecting women. Indigenous women's groups, indigenous people's organizations, organizations of those protesting against large dams – all
such groups are now networking with each other in a manner made possible by
the new communications technology (see Harcourt, this volume) including self-
organizing *ifu* alumnae discussing political issues, supplying each other with
job- and conference opportunities, and supporting each other in everyday issues.

Significantly, the new medium does make it possible for the small groups
and people's movements (the women's ecology and other movements) to put
forward their positions more effectively in the various discourses. To give an
example, in the course of the women's anti-liquor movement in the state of
Andhra Pradesh in India, the Women's Feature Service was able to put out news
about this movement and the views of its participants to women's organizations,
civil rights groups and other NGOs around the world. While in the days of the
print media it would have been very difficult for groups of rural women to project their views nationally, let alone globally, now with the electronic media it is
very much possible, and in fact it is difficult to stop such transmission of news
and views. The transformation of telecommunications does not end the power

equations that exist, but it does allow the disadvantaged groups more scope to project themselves than was possible during the era of print media. In this volume, several chapters deal with the potential of electronic media for democratization: Williams discusses the role of the Internet in democratization processes in Fiji, Druke looks at IT in connection with promoting the cause of refugees, while the situation of indigenous women is specifically addressed by Calleja.

Since such use of telecommunications is largely by groups and not individuals, the cost of, say, a personal computer (PC) and related equipment is not such a major factor restricting its spread in Asia. What is a factor restricting women's use of these facilities is the required familiarity with the English language. The localization of programs into various languages is necessary for the use of the new telecommunications systems to become more widespread. This, in turn, depends on the depth of the market for software in a language; thus women's use of computers would benefit from higher incomes that would increase the market for PCs, or for the cheaper internet-based systems that are being developed. But localization of the software in local languages is essential for moving the new telecommunications system beyond its current elite use. Recently, M. S. Swaminathan Research Foundation set up an important innovative program of Village Knowledge Centers in a group of six villages in Pondicherry in India. Two major features of the project are: development of local language, Tamil Software, and gender sensitivity (including rural poor women's health needs) in assessment of information needs of local people.

The discourse on community is very much a non-Western contribution to the discussion on rights and development. But it should not be assumed that these communities are homogenous, possessing no further groups within them (see Dahms & Faust-Ramos, this volume). Women and men form two obvious groups within these communities. They have more or less well-defined and different social roles. Women, for instance, even in matrilineal communities are not the political representatives of the community. Thus, community, while a valid unit of analysis, itself needs redefinition in terms of the roles of women and men. This redefinition comes about through conflict and struggle, which are themselves part of cultural practice.

We should note that cultures are not static, something given for all time. They change and the sources of change may be varied. Many changes originate in ideas gained from other cultures, from inter-cultural discussion and communication, as was evident in many collective discussions of *ifu* students, particularly of the project *Cultural Modes, Self Expression and Media* (see the chapter by Akande, this volume, who was the facilitator for this project). But whether a particular idea originates from an intra-cultural critique or from inter-cultural discussion, the ideas change the existing cultural practice of the group or community concerned. It is this changing cultural practice, resulting from intra-cultural critique and inter-cultural exchange that forms the basis for the recognition of women's rights. Women's rights clearly have become part of a much wider, globalized, cultural network of perspectives. The multiple cultural flows are still asymmetrical. Power is a factor in all communications. While new technologies enable the weaker sections, women and other groups, to put forward their positions in the world flow of culture and human values, they have not yet ended the asymmetry of the flows.

7 Beyond Cultural Ceilings

New visions – and new technologies that enable them to be realized – can only be developed in an atmosphere that encourages non-conformity. Major innovations always start out small and in some individual's thinking. Over time what starts out as an individual's defiance may become a new social norm. In technology, too, innovation starts out in individual thinking or action or in small organizations, which then grow (or are taken over by others). An over-emphasis of conforming to the norm, other than in such general matters as adhering to the principles of justice and goodness, will only stifle initiative.

In the post-colonial world of the fifty years since the end of the Second World War in Asia one broad conclusion can be stated: overall women have advanced in search of more equal gender relations in most of the continent. The challenges to patriarchy are increasing and patriarchy is weakening. The gender-specific position of women is currently in the midst of a whirlwind of critical reflection in development and academic circles. However, all is not well. The texts of technological development are still the texts of the dominant people – the male gender and the Northern/Western region. While the new technologies, particularly the new information technologies, whether in manufacturing, services and communications, have great promise in terms of dissolving old bases of discrimination, such as heavy and light work, etc., the potential of these technologies for decentralized and more humane development, with participatory political structures, has yet to be realized because of continuing patriarchal relations and the domination of accumulation over development goals.

The cultural ceiling exhibits itself very starkly in relation to the role of women. The idea that technology is not for women, that women are not technologically minded, is strongly embedded not only in Asian thinking, but also in that of Europe and America. The many technological innovations that women have historically been responsible for, including the creation of agriculture, are ignored in such thinking. Women's knowledge, based on their labor, is virtually ignored in the creation of new technology. The cultural ceiling that effectively debars women from contributing to creating new technologies needs to be overcome in order to increase the potential of human society.

It is critically important to address culturally sanctioned social resistance (largely male and often with women's complicity) and set up local, regional, national and international organizations and academic institutions which formulate and implement anti-patriarchal programs. In this regard, examples can be drawn from various courses and projects offered on the Hamburg campus at *ifu*. Significantly the International Women's University with its painstaking efforts to draw students and faculty from South, East, North and West made an exemplary beginning in providing women with access to knowledge in new technologies and networking. Furthermore, the students and faculty members never lost sight of the relevance to discuss not only gender relations across cultures and regions, but also asymmetrical flows in information, knowledge and power. These, in turn, provide a step forward toward building an egalitarian feminist collectivity to learn, understand and make use of new technologies. The essential issue for women's empowerment is a transformative change of culturally sanctioned institutional resistance to women's advancement. The rest of it is window dressing.

References

Agenda 21 (1992). *Global Action for Women Towards Sustainable and Equitable Development.* Rio de Janeiro, Brazil. Chapter 24, pp. 21-24.

Banerjee, Nirmala (1991). The More It Changes, The More It Is the Same: Women Workers in Export Oriented Industries. In: Banerjee, Nirmala (ed.). *Indian Women in a Changing Industrial Scenario.* New Delhi: Sage Publications.

Banuri, T. and Marglin, F. A. (1993). *Who Will Save the Forest? Knowledge, Power and Environmental Destruction.* London: Zed Books.

Bourdieu, P. & Loic, J. W. (1992). *An Invitation to Reflexive Sociology.* Cambridge: Polity Press.

Gothoskar, Sujata (2000). Teleworking and Gender. In: *Economic and Political Weekly.* Mumbai, India: Sameeksha Trust Publication, Vol. XXXV, No. 26, June 24-30, pp. 2293-2298.

Kelkar, Govind, Girija Shrestha & Veena N. (2002). IT Industry and Women's Agency: Explorations in Bangalore and Delhi, India. In: *Gender, Technology and Development.* New Delhi: Sage Publications, Volume 6, No. 1.

Kelkar, Govind, Nathan Dev & Walter Pierre (eds). *Patriarchy at Odds: Women in Forest Societies in Asia.* New Delhi: Sage Publications, forthcoming.

Lim, Linda (1985). *Women Workers in Multinational Enterprises in Developing Countries.* Geneva: ILO.

Mies, Maria & Shiva, Vandana (1993). *Ecofeminism, Kali for Women.* New Delhi and London: Zed Books.

Mitter, Swasti (2000). Teleworking and Teletrade in India: Combining Diverse Perspectives and Visions. In: *Economic and Political Weekly.* Mumbai, India: Sameeksha Trust Publication, Vol. XXXV, No. 26, June 24-30, pp. 2241-2252.

Mitter, Swasti & Sen, Asish (2000). Can Calcutta Become Another Bangalore? Looking for Windows of Opportunity in International Telework. In: *Economic and Political Weekly*. Mumbai, India: Sameeksha Trust Publication, Vol. XXXV, No. 26, June 24-30, pp. 2263-2268.

Nandy, A. (ed.) (1988). *Science, Hegemony and Violence: A Requiem for Modernity*. Tokyo: The United Nations University and Oxford University Press.

Ng, Cecilia (ed.) (1987). *Technology and Gender: Women's Work in Asia*. Kuala Lumpur: Women's Studies Unit.

NASSCOM (2000). *IT Industry in India*. NASSCOM, Delhi. Source: http://www.nasscom.org/ it_industry/indic_statistics.asp; accessed on October 24, 2001.

NASSCOM (2001). *First Ever Workshop on IT Enabled Services for Women Entrepreneurs*. Workshop jointly organized by NASSCOM and Government of NCT of Delhi. NASSCOM Press Release, Delhi, February 22, 2001.

Richardson, Don, Ricardo Ramirez & Moinul Haq (2000). *Grameen Telecom's Village Phone Programme: A Multi-media Case Study*. Canada: TeleCommons Development Group. Source: http://www.telecommons.com/villagephone/index.html; accessed on November 5, 2001.

Sen, Amartya (1990). Cooperative Conflict. In: Tinker, Irene (ed.). *Persistent Inequalities: Women and World Development*. New York: Oxford University Press.

Shiva, Vandana (1992). *The Violence of Green Revolution: Ecological Degradation and Political Conflict in Punjab*. London: Zed Books.

Tao Chunfang (1995). *New Technology and Women's Development:* Report of a Fact-finding Inquiry of the Wanbaozhi Motors Dalian Limited Company. Unpublished.

World Bank (1995) *World Development Report 1995: Workers in an Integrating World*. Oxford, Washington: Oxford University Press.

Part 3: Enhancing Communication

Due to the diversity of the women involved and the variety of settings where they met, *ifu* provided an intricate network for possible communication, mirroring in the small the situation in the globalized world. On the personal level, the diversity of cultures, disciplines, professional standings, ages, sexual orientations, and family situations turned each attempt at communication into an adventure, both rewarding and loaded with risks. In the settings for cooperative learning, different discourses and ways of knowing interacted, and many borders were to be crossed – between scientific disciplines, art and science, theorizing and action, diverging notions of feminism, Western and indigenous ways of knowing, various cultures and social groups, and so on. The chapters in this section show how women dealt with the challenge of communicating in the groups, how communication was supported through artistic means and how creative ways of communication such as visualization and performance were taught and used.

Jutta Weber's account of *ifu*'s project *Reconstructing Gender on the Internet* reflects on interdisciplinary and intercultural communication and focusses on the process of productive tinkering in her group. The participants opted for a playful process, accommodating happenings such as the kidnapping and dressing up of Lara Croft and a poster action, assembling a collage of feminist illustrations. Through self-organization (some competent participants offering skill courses to others) they enabled sophisticated use of the internet, and experimented with cyborgs online. In this creative environment each participant could pursue her own theoretical work.

'Spinning at Computers' as described by Antje Eske and Tatjana Beer shows a playful way of using the computer for human exchange. Drawing on the art of conversation developed in European history mainly by women in the salon culture, computer supported conversational games were used to facilitate exchange between women of different cultures. Examples of six games are given, enabling the participants to open up, revealing something about their personality, their dreams and beliefs and becoming sensitive to the others' perspectives.

134

In her paper on imaginative visualizations, Ina Wagner focusses on communication in creative work. Based on field research with architects, she shows different ways how visualizations are used to communicate ideas, discuss alternatives, or memorize important aspects. The use of inspirational resources is embedded in open planning, a flexible way of considering and pursuing options in search for an aesthetically pleasing and effective solution. This way of proceeding can be generalized to facilitate communication in many activities related to design.

Performativity is the core issue addressed by Ursula Biemann and Berta Jottar in discussing the experience of their art workshop at *ifu* that dealt with borders (in particular, the U.S.-Mexican border) as complex constructions, which become real through the myriad of activities and discourses of people crossing or being affected by the border in various ways. Within *ifu*'s cross-cultural context of international participants they focussed on the relationship between language and translation. Besides theoretical lectures and text-based discussions they looked at a wide range of media and a variety of aesthetical strategies, eventually turning the participants into producers of art themselves.

One of the important experiences of *ifu* was the enrichment owed to these artistic and creative ways of communicating. Beyond words that sometimes reinforced separation, common action, performance and visualizations provided a way of developing deeper mutual understandings that on one hand strengthened group coherence and on the other brought considerable enjoyment.

Christiane Floyd

Jutta Weber
With: *Irene Aterido, Iskra Dimitrova, Claudia Draude,
Miriam Engelhardt, Monika Graus, Martina Kenk, Cheris
Kramarae, Nashrú López Rascón, Boryana Peevska, Ulrike
Peter, Birgit Pretzsch, Juliane Schwarz, Young Sook Shin,
Michelle van Looy, Berna Zengin-Arslan (& Lara Croft)*

Cyberfeminism Crossover: Talking about Intercultural and Interdisciplinary Experiences

Abstract
In this chapter I want to look back on the productive tinkering process we experienced in the cyberfeminist project group *Reconstructing Gender on the Internet* at *ifu*. My aim is to work out some of the conditions and contexts which enabled us to bridge intercultural and interdisciplinary differences (besides others) and to make them fruitful for our work and our lives in no more than three months. This kind of intercultural and interdisciplinary work is seen as very important for feminist and other critical theories and projects in the age of technoscience and globalization, but it is still rarely reflected and theorized. Thus, by analyzing this group process, I want to develop some ideas and groundings for interdisciplinary and intercultural work.

1 Fears and Hopes

What will happen when fifteen women from all over the world come together? What if they have never seen each other before? What if they have no common mother tongue, educational and professional background, nor any particular reason for choosing this cyberfeminist project called *Reconstructing Gender on the Internet*? For practical reasons, being the so-called facilitator of this project at *ifu* (International Women's University, here: *ifu*'s Project Area INFORMATION), I never dared to ask myself this question beforehand. I did not want every night to be a sleepless one even before this experiment started.

But now, a year after the start of the project, I have another, quite relaxed attitude when I look back on this tinkering process in which we put together our experiences, expectations and knowledge. In our *ifu* time we did struggle quite hard to mediate our different viewpoints, cultural, and professional backgrounds as well as bridging our language problems, which were due not only to our own limitations but also to the inherent logic of every language, and in this case the English language, which could not always express and mediate our purposes (an experience which I am reliving while writing this chapter). But I am glad that I could participate in this process where we found ways to translate our visions, needs, and experiences so that they became at least partly understood and accepted by the other participants of the project as well as some other participants in the Project Area INFORMATION.

In the following, I will try to reconstruct the abilities we had and the efforts we made to succeed in sharing our different approaches and viewpoints while exploring past, present and future of cyber/feminism, discussing the relations of gender, knowledge and technology and developing our visions of "better livable worlds," as Donna J. Haraway (1994: 60) calls it. And I will attempt to reflect our intercultural and interdisciplinary work as this is seen as very important for feminist and other critical theories and projects in the age of technoscience and globalization (cf. Haraway, 1991; Braidotti, 1994; Weber, 2002).

I cannot reconstruct the group process without generalizing my point of view to some extent, but I hope I can make this visible again and again. Before writing this chapter, I asked the participants of the project group via e-mail to share their reflections and experience in the project group and some of them sent me their comments, so I included some of their ideas here as well.

2 The Group: Reconstructing Gender on the Internet

To give you a rough idea of the multi-layered mixture of the participants of this project, I want to first of all give some basic facts concerning the group:

*   The participants came from nine countries on three continents: Bulgaria, Canada, Germany, Korea, Macedonia, Mexico, Spain, Turkey, and the U.S..
*   The women's age ranged from early twenties to mid-fifties, so there were nearly three generations gathered in our group.
*   Our academic and educational backgrounds as well as our technical skills were also very diverse. The different disciplines we came from were: art, communication sciences, cultural studies, educational science, electric-electronic engineering, gender and women's studies, history, linguistics, literature, philosophy, political science, and sociology.
*   There were several women in the project who had advanced technical skills like, e.g. website design, even without being academic computer scientists.
*   The organizational structure of the project was determined by the Project Area INFORMATION: every project had a project director (for our project, Cheris Kramarae from the U.S.), a project facilitator (myself, from Germany), and the participants.

To give you a more lively picture of our aims and our spirit, and because I cannot even give a rough sketch of every member of the group, I want to reproduce our manifesto here, the statement I wrote together with Nashrú López Rascón for our home page.[1] It is a statement the members of the project group agreed on and which was intended to summarize our goals, politics, intentions, feelings and experiences in the group after having worked together for months.

> We are a very old-fashioned team, because we are
> FEMINIST and we (at least most of us – sorry for subsuming
> others) like to perform ACTIONS. We thought reconstructing
> and bending gender cannot be only an academic activity. Don't
> get us wrong: we love to theorize, to read and learn from
> books, hypertexts and lectures, but we also like to confront
> other people with our own ideas, our critique, our dreams and
> humor. We enjoy these moments very much – maybe we are too
> passionate.
> To reconstruct gender we got the idea the best way is to
> reconstruct our daily lives, our own habits, patterns of thought
> and feelings and relationships. Something we not only do here during
> our project work, but is our passion before, during and after...
> And – what is most important – we are busy
> reconstructing our relation to TECHNOLOGY. One cannot
> exaggerate the meaning of technology in today's societies. We
> are living in a time where industry, science, technology and
> culture are becoming more and more of a hybrid. Some call it the
> age of TECHNOSCIENCE. There is no life without technology – if
> you like it or not.
> But what kind of relation do we want to have concerning
> technology? This can be a question of life and death..We enjoy
> technology (in many cases), but we are aware that it is also an
> instrument to support and reinforce the subordination of women
> and other Others..los otros under the old and well-known
> patriarchal and capitalist patterns.
> We are technologized women, even if those in power try to
> tell us, we are the natural ones, they try to present us in
> communion with their fetish of nature. Technology can be a
> pleasure – whether high or low technology. We are fond of
> biking, of burning CDs, making films and braids, building web
> pages, or EVEN of cooking (uuuuuuuhhhhh!!!!).
> We are sending thousand of e-mails, turning ourselves
> consciously into cyborgs and wonder what to do with all the
> huge amounts of data whirling around us, within us, through us.
> Data 'R' Us. We turned into data, data turned into us.
> Once we got some attention of journalists and photographers,
> when we hijacked Lara Croft changing the data structure of
> Lara (another sexy package of data we made even more sexy):

---

1   See: http://www.vifu.de/gendering; accessed October 20, 2000.

Figure 1: Lara Croft dressed up at *ifu*

– as the press people did with us.
We explored different ways of being a cyborg, coming from
different countries and contexts. There must be more than
these narrow-minded, destructive heroes and warriors in
cyberspace as well as the oversexualized cybergirls (doesn't
matter which size of breast) just waiting for the console
cowboys – these 'cibervaqueros' with their joysticks and
mobile-belts – to get rescued. So have a look on all the different
expressions of cyberworlds we developed. For those who are
'extraños,' strangers, in the cyberworlds, some of us have built
a Beginner's Cyberfeminist Dictionary to give you a cybermap
for navigating through this bizarre, sometimes 'unheimlich,'
uncanny, but also exciting and desirable world.
Enjoy your selves!

I hope this gives you a more colorful picture of the project's spirit and content.
Having already had some experience of the hardships and difficulties of interdisciplinary work, and considering that to most of us, intercultural communication in such a multi-layered way was new, I still wonder how we could succeed
so well in working together, sharing our knowledge, bridging interdisciplinary
as well as intercultural differences.

3 Stepping Across the Border: Talking about Interdisciplinary and Intercultural Communication

The theme of crossing borders is addressed by different authors of this book. While Biemann & Jottar write about borders between countries, Harcourt refers to crossing boundaries of time, place, space and gender at *ifu* discussions. Klein-Franke in her chapter with Floyd writes about moving between 'knowledge houses' in interdisciplinary and intercultural communication. So what are the essentials and issues of interdisciplinary communication?

3.1 Interdisciplinary Communication

Interdisciplinary work seems to be something which is desperately needed today, in the age of globalization and the growing complexity of problems as well as research fields. Nowadays interdisciplinary or transdisciplinary work is seen as a necessary prerequisite for innovative research as well as political work. The German philosopher Jürgen Mittelstraß describes inter-/transdisciplinary research as "research which transgresses disciplinary borders, which defines and solves its questions beyond disiplines" (Mittelstraß, 1998: 44; my translation).

But many feminist theorists stress that inter- or transdisciplinary research is more than this. Critical transdisciplinary work not only bridges the gap between disciplines but also uses innovative procedures to overcome traditional categories and forms of knowledge production, and to develop new ones.[2] Rosi Braidotti speaks of the development of a nomadic epistemological position, which generates new concepts in the transfer between the humanities and (techno-)sciences: "This transdisciplinary propagation of concepts has positive effects in that it allows for multiple interconnections and transmigrations of notions [...] One just needs to think of the fortunes of a notion such as 'complexity' to appreciate the metaphorical resonance gained by some scientific concepts in contemporary culture at large" (Braidotti, 1994: 23).

But despite the fruitful *theoretical* reflections on inter- or transdisciplinary research in general, there is still an astonishing void concerning interdisciplinary *practice* under contemporary academic conditions. (It also seems to me that there is much more work done on the theory and especially on the practice of intercultural than on interdisciplinary communication.) There is a big gap between theoretical reflection and "the culture of practical interdisciplinary work" (Mack, 1998: 1; my translation). For decades now, there has been a theoretical discussion going on in Germany about interdisciplinary practice, which does not even seem to satisfy those involved in it and which has not taken into account

2   Cf. Dölling & Hark, 2000.

contemporary socio-cultural and political conditions of knowledge production. Most interdisciplinary work actually seems to be governed by practical research and educational politics (cf. Mainzer, 1993: 17).

Most of the people from academia report failures in the field of interdisciplinary work, great difficulties in communicating effectively, problems in translating the different worlds of knowledge, experience and methods. This is especially true of interdisciplinary projects that are intended to bridge the gap between science and the humanities. Nevertheless an interdisciplinary (as well as intercultural) outlook is a popular and effective decoration for universities, research projects, graduate programs and the like in their race for funding. But hardly anybody seems to reflect on *how to do* interdisciplinary work. It must be one of those things that everybody does 'naturally' without knowing exactly how it is done...

3.2 Intercultural Communication

It seems to me that there are a lot more training programs, self-help manuals or courses available designed for raising intercultural awareness. Although they had received no preparation concerning the problems of interdisciplinary work (as well as differences between generations, sexual orientation and the like), at least the facilitators of the Project Area INFORMATION as well as those project directors who were already with us, got some excellent lessons in intercultural awareness from our colleagues Zhang Wei (China), Mona Dahms (Denmark), Tamara Rollocks (USA/Germany) as well as Elke Mätschke (Germany).

The organizers had only planned one day for this training. In retrospect, many of us agreed more time was needed for a "moderated discussion of our own experiences in different modes of learning, teaching, researching as well as working styles and settings, and for reflecting and experiencing different cultural and disciplinary contexts" (*ifu* facilitators' training program, hand-out) – as had been promised in the training program. But most of our training was spent on organizational work and finalizing the concepts for the projects. So in the end there was no training in interdisciplinary work, there were no discussions about the topics of the various feminism/s (a discussion that was started by the participants later), of sexual orientation, age, and the like.

Nevertheless, our short training program in intercultural communication, which consisted, among other things, in discussing 'real life situations' in small, intercultural groups gave me some idea of the problems and difficulties ahead of me, but also of the richness which can come out of these intercultural conversations.

3.3 Getting Together

The starting conditions of our project were strikingly similar to those of most interdisciplinary work in academia today: the participants applied to take part in a project on a given topic and were put together. At *ifu* they had at least the opportunity to get a fairly clear idea of the projects when all the project directors and facilitators presented the project outlines in greater detail at the beginning of *ifu*. So the participants could make up their minds whether they wanted to confirm or change their decision for a project.

I guess the reason for most participants to join the project *Reconstructing Gender on the Internet* was their devotion to the subject of either feminism in general (our project was the only one with 'gender' in the title), or feminism and new information technologies, i.e. cyberfeminism in particular. Shin Youngsook from Korea, for example, who worked for the Korean Research Institute for *Chongshindae* (Japanese military sexual slaves in World war II, the so-called 'comfort women'), participated in the project because she is devoted to feminist goals and wanted to learn more about new technologies, about technoscience and globalization, while others wanted to do more research on 'cyborgology,' gender bending, and the like. Nashrú López Rascón from Mexico[3] wrote about her motivations for joining the project: "*Lara Croft? Cyberfeminism? What's that?* was my first thought when I heard about the project *Reconstructing Gender*. Even more, I thought that I did know almost nothing about feminism and less about gender studies. On the other hand, there were many women from Germany and from the 'Western world', and this was another reason to get curious myself about this project. ... I think there was another motivation, but it was from the feeling, the intuition pulled me in this direction, and it doesn't fail, never, then, I followed it..." So in a way, Nashrú was the 'anthropologist' among us, participating in a project with lots of Western women, who nevertheless came from very different cultures and had to do much translation work.

So all the participants of the project were stuck together in their project room, having different ideas and goals concerning the project and only three months' time to get together, to develop concepts and actions, and a very tough study structure, which did not leave much time for the projects.

4 Helpful Strategies and Tools for Getting Along?

Maybe it was the 'hybrid' existence of many of the members of the group which made the crossing of the border between science and the humanities much easier

---

3   Personal communication by e-mail

and which was not documented by educational backgrounds in terms of disciplines, but by the individual technical and other skills of many of the members. Many women were not officially qualified in computer science, engineering, and the like, but they had wide-ranging technical skills concerning, e.g. (advanced) website design, computing in general, video taping and filming etc., which made this interdisciplinary work much easier, and which helped especially to translate our cyberfeminist ideas into action. As Uli Peter, a German member of the group, stressed very clearly in her reflection of the group process, it was to a large extent the fact that we organized our own (advanced) web design course for our group (and some other participants) that improved and strengthened our team work. And the fact that members of the group were teaching and learning together made us 'stick' together and perfectly helped to adjust the learning program to our specific project goals. We did not only improve our team work and spirit very much, but also our technical skills, which we needed to perform our project actions, artwork and results. Last, but not least, the experience of our competence in the group as a whole strengthened our confidence in the project's success.

Our group not only organized and held a web design course for our own needs and implemented it in the official study structure, we also worked on the history of feminist theory, philosophy of science and science studies as well as carrying out and cooperating on public actions as a group (e.g. our famous Hijacking of Lara Croft,[4] as well as a poster action[5], where we shared experiences, work and fun and which made most of us stick together and also helped us to overcome frustration and disappointment. This frustration was only partly grounded in the sometimes exhausting group process as such – transgressing borders and translating experiences – but also in the start-up problems of this newly set up university and thus its often inadequate computer and networking infrastructure and its sometimes inflexible (time) schedules. But having already a common ground as a group, these difficulties sometimes even helped to make the group stick together, as Nashrú López Rascón wrote in her comments on the *ifu* experience: "Even our not enough technical support and time was another challenge to use our imagination and generate 'actions' in order to get our 'action aims': for example to make posters; because we didn't have the resources to build an installation or to edit a video, and jump some restrictions to do it and demonstrate that we are serious and professional people with skills and knowl-

4   Cf. http://www.vifu.de/gendering/lara/gallery.html; accessed August 31, 2000.
5   Posting the critical cyberfeminist posters made by Nashrú and Michelle all over the campus at Hamburg University; see our posters at http://www.vifu.de/gendering/collage/ Elamex-advertising.jpg; accessed February 12, 2001. Also: http://www.vifu.de/gendering/collage/ WomanGods-advertising.jpp; February 12, 2001. http://www.vifu.de/gendering/collage/ nipple-advertisement.jpg; accessed February 12, 2001. http://www.vifu.de/gendering/ collage/posteradvertisement2.jpg; accessed February 12, 2001.

edge to use high technology applying our concepts and creativity at the same time" (Nashrú López Rascón, e-mail communication). But at the same time there were a lot of members in the group who had the technical equipment to balance problems with the weak infrastructure, working with their own laptops, software, using their mobiles and so on.

The *Reconstructing Gender* project women, on the other hand, spread out and worked in four (or five) small groups, which left more room for developing their own ideas and visions and to translate them into political, artistic and narrative projects manifested in web pages. Cheris Kramarae and I had many conversations and discussions about these different projects with the participants, but I think, at the same time, having accompanied this process for weeks, we had confidence in these projects and didn't try to push or force other things on them. Birgit Pretzsch, a participant from Germany, commented in the good-bye statement: "thanks ... for trusting us to work on our own!"

But I guess the fact that many of us lived in the same place far from home also helped us to stick together, always provided that there was a common ground we could build on.

This is not to say that this saved us from every fight or suffering and that we lived in blissful harmony. But in my view most of the time we managed – despite severe technical and administrative obstacles – to develop, embody and enjoy a way to work that comes near to what Donna J. Haraway describes as an important practice of a responsible and situated science:

> Feminism loves another science: the sciences and politics of interpretation, translation, stuttering, and the partly understood. Feminism is about the sciences of the multiple subject with (at least) double vision. Feminism is about a critical vision consequent upon a critical positioning in inhomogeneous gendered social space. Translation is always interpretative, critical, and partial. (Haraway, 1991: 195)

5 Conclusion: Interdisciplinary and Intercultural – but also Interpersonal in the Hybrids' Community

So in the end I can think of several reasons for our successful and enjoyable group process as well as the performance and production of a wonderful project outcome (actions, posters, web pages and so on).

There was this interactive learning process taking place in the group, especially in the self-organized web design course, which helped us to come together and build a common ground for our work of mediation and translation, but also to build friendships and cooperations. But the interdisciplinary situatedness of many women of the *Reconstructing Gender* project, being experts in the humanities as well as with regard to technical skills, was also very helpful for the group process and outcome – as well as supplementing the inadequate infra-structure of *ifu* with their personal equipment, which meant sharing laptops, mo-bile phones, software and the like.

But from my point of view there were some other important factors that helped a lot in bridging the intercultural and interdisciplinary gaps: I am talking of the curiosity, political commitment and motivation (in very different ways), and the devotion to a kind of collaborative playfulness of many members of the group, which made the enjoyable group process possible. Then there was the tinkering with new and different experiences and ideas: most of us were oriented towards an outcome of the project, but we didn't think that it had to be perfect, we wanted to play around, experiment, and have new experiences.

Figure 2: Lara Croft has been kidnapped!

The ability of every single member to cope with the difficult conditions, to have the patience to do the work of mediation and translation made it possible that we did not get lost in a sterile effort to fulfill an unusual but nevertheless academic exercise, but to enjoy and transform our science of "stuttering and the partly understood" (Haraway, see above), and to develop different angles of a critical but nevertheless partial vision which others could share with us.

I hope that this analysis of the manifold reasons for our successful group process may be helpful to others to do successful feminist and other critical work in the future.

Acknowledgements

Cheris Kramarae is a colleague I really enjoyed working with and who joined us for several weeks during the project work, who supported the group so well with her ideas and her humor and made so many things easy-going... Thanks a lot to our course teachers Michelle van Looy and Martina Kenk, as well as Iskra Dimitrova, Birgit Pretzsch and Monika Graus for supporting our project in other socio-technical ways! Many thanks to Nashrú López Rascón and Uli Peter for sending me comments of their experience at *ifu*. I am grateful to Cheris Kramarae and Uli Peter for their constructive criticism and advice on earlier drafts of this chapter and their invaluable support in many different ways. I am also very thankful to Govind Kelkar, Silvie Klein-Franke and Gudrun Parsons for their critical remarks on my chapter.

References

Braidotti, Rosi (1994). *Nomadic Subjects: Embodiment and Sexual Difference in Contemporary Feminist Theory.* New York: Columbia University Press.

Dölling, Irene & Hark, Sabine (2000): She Who Speaks Shadow Speaks Truth: Transdisciplinarity in Women's and Gender Studies. In: *Signs*, vol. 25, no. 4, pp. 1195-1198.

DAAD (ed.) (1999). *Internationale Frauenuniversität (ifu)/International Women's University.* (Prospectus). Cologne: Deutscher Akademischer Austauschdienst.

Haraway, Donna J. (1991). *Simians, Cyborgs and Women. The Reinvention of Nature.* New York: Routledge.

Haraway, Donna J. (1994). A Game of Cat's Cradle: Science Studies, Feminist Theory, Cultural Studies. In: *Configurations:* A Journal of Literature and Science 1, pp. 59-71.

López Rascón, Nashrú & Weber, Jutta (2000). *Introduction given in October 2000.* Source: http://www.vifu.de/gendering/introduction.htm; accessed July 1, 2001.

Mack, Jürgen (1998). *Nachdenken über Interdisziplinarität. Einige kritische Bemerkungen.* Public lecture given on February 18, 1998. Source: http://www.diff.uni-tuebingen.de/institut/struktur/awm./mack.html; accessed January 25, 2001.

Mainzer, Klaus (1993). Erkenntnis- und wissenschaftstheoretische Grundlagen der Inter- und Transdisziplinarität. In: Arber, W. (ed.). *Inter- und Transdisziplinarität. Warum? – Wie?* Bern/Stuttgart/Wien: Haupt.

Mittelstraß, Jürgen (1998). *Die Häuser des Wissens. Wissenschaftstheoretische Studien.* Frankfurt a.M.: Suhrkamp.

Weber, Jutta (2002). *Umkämpfte Bedeutungen: Natur im Zeitalter der Technoscience.* (Contested Meanings: Nature in the Age of Technoscience). Frankfurt a.M./New York: Campus (forthcoming). Source: http://elib.suub.uni-bremen.de/publications/dissertations/E-Diss228_webersec.pdf; accessed January 31, 2002.

Antje Eske & Tatjana Beer

Spinning at Computers

Abstract
'Spinning at Computers' tests in a playful way the use of computer and telecommunication systems for human exchange. It draws on the art of conversation, which has its roots in the century-long history of the Salon culture in Italy and France. As early as in the Renaissance people searched for new forms of connection and connectedness in human communication through conversational games. In those times the exchange was more or less vertical. It connected and mixed different social classes. The following report is based on an art workshops held at *ifu* and describes mainly horizontal exchanges of cultures due to the participation of women from fifteen countries.

1 Introduction

Artistic means can be very helpful in enhancing intercultural communication. This will be illustrated by the example of the weeklong art workshops *Spinning at Computers* at *ifu* (Women's International University, here: *ifu*'s Project Area Information) which was held twice at the Hamburg Academy of Fine Arts in two successive weeks of August 2000. 'Spinning at Computers' implies the art of conversation that is aesthetically formed communication and a playful 'to and fro' between people in a tangible and associative way. The computer is the medium to play conversational games, which are in the spirit of the historical conversational games. While doing this, new computer skills are easily acquired.

The effort and desire to cultivate human exchange is not that new. In art history the art of conversation in antiquity is referred to as 'ars sermonis.' In European history there is the two-hundred-year period of the French 'salon culture' of the 17th and 18th century, which has its roots in the Italian Renaissance, with just that quest for artistic forms of communication. This culture was mainly developed and formed by women. The following report is based on two art workshops held at *ifu* and describes mainly horizontal exchange of cultures, because women from Argentina, Australia, Belarus, Brazil, China, Egypt, Germany, Hungary, India, Ivory Coast, Korea, Mexico, Rumania, Sweden, and Togo participated in the *Spinning* workshops.

We used the software *HyperCard*, which is actually very easy to handle. Owing to its different levels of complexity it is suitable for beginners as well as for advanced users. HyperCard is a multimedia software that enables you to work with sound, color, and short films; it also offers the possibility to express oneself by using links, and it contains graphics and word processing. The conversational interchange happened via conversational games and IRC-chats on the Internet.

Over a period of ten years, Antje Eske developed these games using the historical games of the Salon Culture as a starting point. Together with the students of the 'Spinnen am Computer' seminar regularly held at the Hamburg Academy of Fine Arts, she has tried out and modified the games since 1992.

2 The *Spinning at Computers* Workshops at *ifu*

Where one works together in a stimulating and playful way, one enjoys aesthetical results and beautiful subjective creations and notices steps of development. This approach also tempts what is witty and funny and induces astonishment about the strange results; participants try to be open, to connect to each other and to follow the others' wild jumps of ideas.

2.1 Direct Results of the *Spinning* Workshops

Playing conversational games by changing computers, every woman was visibly connected to every other woman in the room.

It was possible to get an impression of the peculiarities of others by looking at the different interpretations, which were very rich and complicated by reason of intercultural socialization. By doing this we had the possibility to get to know each other better, to look for mutual interests, to learn a constructive way of cutting into a conversation, to use associations of others for our own expression, and to become capable of acting alone and together.

Thus together we could collect 'the dregs of life,' a kind of moral humus, which is the basis of social changes. We discovered a somewhat unusual way to communicate vividly and tangibly. By doing this we connected ourselves with conversational traditions, having playful conversations.

As a special peculiarity of the alternation between writing and drawing, especially to be seen in the examples of 'Les galères,' we have recorded the culturally based artistic possibilities of expression. For example, the first picture exhibits the European Expressionist style, the second one an African style in painting (Sixth Game: Les Galères, Figures 2 and 4).

We learned to strengthen visual expression skills (the importance of visualizing imagination is brought out by Wagner in this volume). We also noticed the differences between the various programmed stacks, which tangibly show the different perspectives of their respective creators. They trained skills of perception and active viewing, and they created new combinations of meaning by reordering only the cards as a response.

At the same time the participants learned advanced computer skills in a playful, women-friendly way. Our common activity also trained 'linking thinking,' a non-linear way of coming to conclusions.

2.2 What About 'Linking Thinking'?

'Linking thinking' has different aspects: the scientific aspect was put by Charles Sanders Peirce as a method of non-deductive reasoning. He called this 'adductive' reasoning a "strategy for effective guessing." He named this fantastic, digressive, easy playing with ideas 'musement.' According to Peirce, it also contains the possibility, in connection with a transformational process, to turn from pure game to scientific research or artistic productivity (cf. Wirth, 1999).

The artistic aspect and the artistically productive method in our case was conversation. Associative spaces could be opened by thinking and 'talking' (this includes also, e.g. drawing or making music, in links), with the possibility of meeting each other there. In these spaces the meetings are more intensive. The philosophers of Romanticism met and produced together in a free and uncompromising exchange of ideas called 'Symphilosophy' or 'Sympoetry.' Friedrich Schlegel went into raptures about an art in which individuals merge, and Friedrich Schleiermacher evolved a theory of sociable behavior: "All should be interaction... Everyone should be ready to associatively play with ideas." [Translation by A. Eske]

'Linking thinking' in the *Spinning* workshops helps to gain the other persons' perspective. It helps, for example, to understand the feelings of women in Mexico City. During the night they spray tags onto the walls of the houses, feeling like queens... (see the fourth game, Hyper Into). By 'jumping the links,' which means following another person's wild jumps of ideas, one gets the unique opportunity to leave the position of an outside observer. Really to see what the person opposite wants to tell effects an opening to others and has the potential of broadening one's mind and changing one's perspective.

Links are a specific way of expression of computers or data nets. They primarily appeal to our emotions. Sometimes a picture-link in a HyperCard stack we conversed with went 'straight to the heart.' Links fix the associative jumps which briefly appear like lightning.

This moving in multidimensional spheres, especially in the *Spinning* workshops, bound the international group together, in spite of different cultures, different histories –individual and social – and different languages with different layers of meaning.

2.3 The Feminist and Female Approach

In the *Spinning* workshops many obvious differences between the women were involved: different countries, different cultures, different religions, different social classes, different scientific disciplines, different knowledge and practice of speaking English. But common to all of us was the experience of being a woman and to live in societies mainly shaped by the power of men.

An overview of a two-hundred-year epoch of the history of European art was presented in the *Spinning* workshops to give an idea, also to women from other continents, of how to deal with the history of women in their own histories.

This part of history is especially interesting because during the Salon Culture of the Renaissance, Baroque and Rococo women had an influence that has shaped the art of conversation up until now.

Because of talking together and switching from words to drawings, every woman got a chance to be heard and seen. While talking with each other about all those metaphors, creative ideas and expressions it was very important to perceive the perspective of the others in relation to one's own perspective and to get to know each other better. Playfully and with the use of the *Steigrohre des Unbewussten* ('elevators of the unconscious'), creativity and multicultural characteristics are supported, and the precious peculiarity of others appears clearly.

The alternation between writing and drawing also filled the gap between mother tongue and working language.

Nowadays it is an often-heard complaint that feminism is very exclusive and restricted to white, Western, Christian, healthy, well-educated, middle-class women. Poor women, women of color[1], women with handicaps, women from the South are not well represented in the feminist movement of the last thirty years. One way to alter this situation is to listen to each other's stories about one's life histories and the oppression one suffers from, and to respect one another's means to cope with one's situation. For this endeavor you need spaces and the willingness to be touched and changed by the other's story. *Spinning at Computers* is one example of an exciting exchange of different views and aesthetic traditions.

---

1   'Women of color' is a term, which is widely used in the U.S. and Europe by women of African, Asian or Oriental descent to describe themselves.

For many women electronic media are a male domain and their own access seems impossible. With the help of conversational games, one's own motivation grows and the access occurs almost unnoticeably. Therefore artistic means can be very helpful tools to enhance intercultural communication.

3 Description of the Conversational Games

An artistic exchange playfully occurred through seven conversational games.

These games were arranged in a certain manner that allows to overcome technical and social barriers step by step.

3.1 First Game: Silent Mail or Chinese Whisper

To become comfortable with the technical and social conditions we started off with a game which is similar to the one played at children's birthday parties. We began with the first card of a HyperCard stack with a word, a little sentence or a picture like the sailing boat – see the first illustration below. We then changed computers and, on a second card transformed, in this case the picture into a word or a short sentence by using associations, e.g. 'seagul/ly.' By example of the pictures in Figure 1: First game Silent Mail or Chinese Whisper, it can be seen how we moved with associative jumps from a sailing boat dancing on the waves, via verbal transcription to a lion, hiding behind a palm tree. Then, changing computers again, on a third card we turned that word into a new picture, and so on. In this way we easily jumped from one to a thousand, cultivating broader possibilities of thinking, which are beyond logic and one-dimensionality.

Figure 1: Pictures of Silent Mail

seagul/ly

lion hiding behind a
palmtree, watching
the total mess in
the garden

Figure 1: Pictures of Silent Mail (continued)

3.2 Second Game: Metaphor – Draw a Metaphor of Yourself

To learn a little more about each other and therefore feel more familiar with the group, each participant tried to find a metaphor, symbol or picture to characterize herself. It is not usual for women to do this, because normally in the past (and today, too) men created those metaphors to describe women, often in an inadequate way. So, besides those entirely male imaginations the question remains which picture we want to draw –and to show – of ourselves? We did it in an obvious and tangible way. Each woman started to draw pictures to characterize herself or took a fitting bit of artwork out of the HyperCard archive.

Figure 2 shows the metaphor proposed by Ekaterina Sedova from Belarus. She studies musicology and imagined herself as a male conductor. She had been a conductor herself and played a bit with the role. This male conductor turns upside down and in spite or because of this he gets applause.

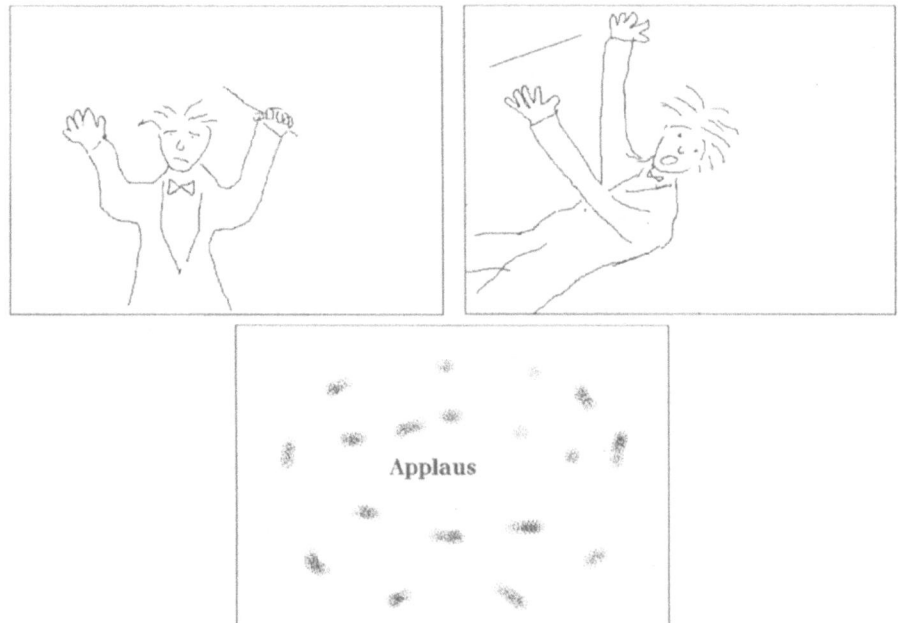

Figure 2: Pictures of Self-describing Metaphor

3.3 Third Game: Jumping Jack or Working with Links

The difference between linear and chaotic story-telling: The pictures in the 'metaphor' stack are linearly connected and so the story is told in an understandable manner. To demonstrate the gap between linear and chaotic thinking, between a one-dimensional and a hyper-dimensional 'view of the world,' we only changed one word in the program. Instead of 'go to next card,' we told the computer to 'go to any card' so that any card of the stack could be chosen and connected with any other card. The sense got lost, but sometimes, by throwing together the unthinkable, a new meaning flashed into our contemplation.

Anke Bornträger from Germany told, as a metaphor, a little story about chickens in which one hen makes friends with another, and nothing can come between them.

In the game of 'Jumping Jack' this story changed into a view of one, two or three happy hens, as pictured in Figure 3.

Figure 3: Pictures of Jumping Jack

3.4 Fourth Game: Hyper Into

Sometimes there is a need to respond directly to a statement from another person. HyperCard lets you do this in that you can connect any part of the surface of one card with any part of another card. You can hyper into a stack. This is a special form of social contact, a kind of an apparent and associative-combined 'to and fro' between people. In this way we were artistically talking about problems, ideas, imaginations, etc.

In the example below you can see a simple way of relating to one another. We used our local area net to hyper into the stacks of others. The pictures on the left show parts of a HyperCard stack from Maria Alejandra Sanchez-Vazquez. She is from Mexico, and she visually told us that at night in Mexico City you can find women on the roofs, spraying tags onto the walls of the houses. Those women feel like conquering the stars and being one with the endless space.

Ronja Perschbacher from Germany answered and encouraged her not only to admire the stars but to 'be a star' herself.

A second answer came from Carina Keskitalo from Sweden. She related to the second idea and showed happy people from all parts of the space, celebrating the night with beautiful fireworks.

Figure 4: Pictures of Hyper Into

3.5 Fifth Game: Modifying Links

In order to be more expressive and simulate the use of hands, modulations of the voice or facial expressions, one can use the visual effects in the HyperCard program. One can connect cards by a button jump, modified by visual effects. This jump connects different cards by fusions, pushing, pulling or squeezing motions in several shades. In that way, everyone is able to find the 'right one' for her own story or a special problem. Djesika Amendah from Togo, for example, chose a squeezing motion. It gradually shrinks the first picture to its center by uncovering a second picture. The sequence in Figure 5 shows, on the one hand, what men can harvest if they open certain doors and, on the other hand, uncovers what women can bring about.

Figure 5: Pictures of Modifying Links

3.6 Sixth Game: Les Galères

At different times in history, conversational games have been played to support the 'to and fro' between people. Those games are a way of presenting themes to a group in an extraordinary way, or to show oneself very witty, to play together, and to acquire new ideas by playful exchange.

Those games were also a bit of a bore, in that they tried to be witty in a strained way to fulfill the high expectations of the circle.

In the 'Spinning' workshops we transformed a conversational game which Madame du Maines played in her salon at the beginning of the 18th century. This salon was called 'Les galères du bel esprit.' Rather than out of a reticule, the participants took a lottery ticket out of a little box. On each of the tickets four end-rhymes were to be found, e.g. beast/at least/gender/tender.

All participants wrote poems with their end-rhymes on the first card of a HyperCard stack. Then, changing computers, we transformed the poem on a second card into a picture or a little film, or maybe a 'jumping jack,' by also using the visual effects. By changing computers again every woman created a new poem on a third card, which was adapted to the picture on the second card, and so on.

Do not be a beast
We are humans
            at least...
Everywhere the same
      North,
            South,
                  West,
                        East,
You are that kind of gender,
it is nice to be
                  Tender ...

two women, when they are in a fight

act very furious, they even might

stick their tongue out, bite and hit !

so listen to me, stay out of that, kid.

Figure 6: Pictures of Les Galères

3.7 Seventh Game 'Haikai-Renga-Chat' – an Artistically Formed Chat

An Internet chat works by typing. People in the same room with several computers and people spread all over the world are able to take part in a chat. Before you enter a chat room you have to choose a nickname, any name you want to, so it is also anonymous. In our case two persons often shared one computer and one alias.

In Japan, there is a very old form of poetry (about 760 B.C.) called 'Tanka,' which developed into an answering poem over the centuries. It was later transformed into a joke chain poem called 'Haikai-Renga,' with beginning and answering verses alternating. The lines of this poetic form have to be either five or seven syllables long. We adopted that form for our chats.

The chat we want to take a closer look at had about ten participants (one of them external). The chat rule was to use the Haikai-Renga form and also to link words that transport a background of meaning, sentimental pictures, and nonsense words. One implicit rule of the chat was to use the English language, as it was the official language of *ifu*.

- The first theme was 'life after death.' Beliefs, fears and hopes about death are closely linked to religious beliefs. To discuss this topic in 'real life' often means to be hurt by others. In this playful and protected way it was easier to open up and share one's beliefs.
- After a while the chatters left the basis of mutual communication and the official language English and created a wonderful international poem.
- After that, they discussed different types of conversational games they could play. They started to create three-word-stories, in the tradition of dada, surrealism and hip-hop poetry.
- At the end of the chat the group returned to their mother tongues for their good-byes.

Our following example of Thursday, August, 17, 2000, is shortened:

> "time: death is mystic but most
>
> ...
>
> dreamer: death is dark and blue
> flower: dead is dead is life
> time: is it so nice or
> unknown: Is God mystic, mystic
> time: stiff and quiet is death
> bettyblue: ashes and moss cover me
> dreamer: of cours but not ...
> newest: Ah, now i know you
> unknown: is bettyblue dead?
> time: you are taking it so serious
> newest: the soul never dies
> unknown: you think soul exists
> bettyblue: it sores and it flies
>
> ...
>
> dreamer: not mystic, it's real
> unknown: What does this mean?
> lila: bei gut wetter
> unknown: This should be english
> time: Hablar aleman no porfavor
> unknown: Nor espagnol
> dreamer: english, english, eng...
> Sasha: Dominate the world, now dominate at *ifu*
>
> ...
>
> lila: please speak your homelanguages
>
> ...
>
> flower: ben cok üzgünüm
> time: Atehere po nisim nga e para
> Sasha: No, star is also actor

aaru: namaskaar
aaru: *ifu* mein aapka swagat hai
bettyblue: chan put pasa Thai duey
lila: das klingt schoen
flower: ana zaalana awi
time: Me preocupa el vacio
unknown: English english en
time: nuk me pelqen ne Anglisht
unknown: Do you know babel tour tour
lila: que es vacio?
bettyblue: English yaag mak mai chop pasa Enlish
aaru: yeh sab kya ho raha hai?
unknown: Another answer please
time: emptyness, filled with nothing
dreamer: we have no communication

...

tatant: commumication, come please

...

time: I ma commung
unknown: Gbe ka gon dom miele han?
bettyblue: If this were really a salon I think we would be thrown out for having too much espirit nes pas?
time: What is going to be at the end

bettyblue: What about telling a story? we all write only 3 words for example i write The girl went ---to the back---of the green ---building where she ,,,,,,,,do you get it?

....

lila: In the harbour
tatant: about my favorite
dreamer: ship is gone
tatant: ship on the
tatant: ocean and now?
flower: waves high beach
tatant: sailor is lost
bettyblue: The captain shouted
tatant: s.o.s.

...

tatant: be careful sailor
lila: the clabauterman
tatant: watch out shark!
flower: magic stick out
bettyblue: and so finally
tatant: clap your hands
lila: all are good
tatant: ask his name
tatant: what a shame

....

*** Signoff: Sasha (o rewoh)
tatant: you wonerful chaters
bettyblue: Goodyed

lila: thats french
tatant: thats the beginning of the end!
*** bettyblue has left channel #*ifu*
lila: adios
time: mirupafshim
flower: iyi günler
flower: maasalama
tatant: lets say Auf Wiedersehn
flower: khoda hafez
flower: allaha ismarladik
tatant: gia sou
tatant: Hej po dej"

4 Conclusion

Aesthetical forms of expression influence all other spheres of life. To discover artistic forms of expression and to carefully play with them is what we were doing during the *Spinning* workshops. We view these games as being valuable in other higher educational situations where one tries to perceive the peculiarity of others, tries to dig out buried possibilities of expression, changes media, e.g. communicates by drawing and typing, tries poetical possibilities or sketches impressions, expresses subjective feelings and regards them as valuable.

References

Alsleben, Kurd & Antje Eske (eds.) (2001): *NetzkunstWörterBuch*. Norderstedt: Books on Demand.
Beer, Tatjana (2001). *ifu, Internationale Frauen Universität*. In: Alsleben & Eske 2001, pp. 232-227.
Eske, Antje (1995). *Spinnen am Computer. Im Hyperraum auf der Suche nach dem Faden-anfang*. Hamburg: material-Verlag, HfbK.
Eske, Antje (1998). *Spinnen am Computerspiele*. Seminararbeit SS 98. Hamburg: edition kuecocokue.
Eske, Antje (2000). *Spinning at Computers. A Link from History to Now*. Seminar at the International Women's University *ifu* 2000. Hamburg: dtp Hfbk.
Eske, Antje & Beer, Tatjana (2000): *International Women's University ifu Spinning at Computers*.
Idensen, Heiko (2001). *Symphilosophie/Sympoesie. Das Romantische Kunstwerk als gemein-schaftlicher Prozess*. In: Alsleben & Eske 2001, pp. 437-440.
Wirth, Uwe (1999). Wen kümmert's, wer spinnt. In: Suter, Beat & Böhler, Michael (eds.) *Hyperfiktion*. Basel, Frankfurt a.M.: Stroemfeld Verlag, pp. 29-38.

Ina Wagner

Imaginative Visualizations:
Enriching Women's Workplace Skills

Abstract
The theme of this chapter is creative work practice and the role of visualizations in express-ing, developing, detailing, communicating, and presenting an evolving piece of work. It is based on extensive fieldwork in an architectural office and on detailed accounts of work practice from early conceptualizations of a design to its implementation. It also makes use of some of the concepts and metaphors that researchers and architects co-developed in the course of their joint investigations for gaining a richer understanding of design practice and for talking about it with others.

The chapter discusses some of the key features of creative work, introducing the notion of 'open planning.' Its focus is on skills such as mobilizing inspirational material and working with it, creating 'persuasive artifacts' and using space for story telling as a way of expressing context and open relationships.

Exploring design practice and the power of visualization is done with a view to enriching women's workplace skills. This was also the objective of a workshop held at *ifu* by the author.

1 Visualizations at Work

A one-day workshop at *ifu* (International Women's University, here: *ifu's* Proj-ect Area INFORMATION) was dedicated to issues of visualization, imagination, and cooperation, with the aim of discussing possibilities of enriching women's work environment. This came at a point when the women were preparing pres-entations of their projects. As it turned out, almost none of the women had expe-rience with visual material, and using such material as part of academic work seemed quite unusual. The idea was to use project material, provided by the participants, for enlarging the women's repertoire of expressing and sharing their work with others.

Looking at issues of visualizations was an open experiment, which drew from the experiences of working with architects. The idea was to offer these ex-periences to the women at *ifu* as a resource for their own work and to explore how they would use different visualization techniques for expressing themselves and for communicating their project work.

The first task was to look at visual material as sources of inspiration – where do you find such material, what does it tell you, and how can you use it in support of an idea, concept, project? The women assembled collages of images and text on large sheets of paper that explained the core idea of their project.

The women were invited to play with the *Wunderkammer* (Figure 1), a visual environment in which multimedia inspirational materials – scanned images, sound, video, rendered 3D objects – can be placed, stored, encountered, found, displayed, and integrated with the flow of the work (Kompast et al, 2000). This 3D Wunderkammer is a result of fieldwork in an architectural office in close cooperation with the architects. It was inspired by the cabinets of curiosities of the 17th and 18th century, such as the Wunderkammer of Rudolf II in Prague. The need for a modern cabinet of curiosity was confirmed by observations of the ways in which architects collect, archive, and search for inspirational material, and how they use it for developing, expressing, communicating, and presenting their work. The concept of Wunderkammer builds on the metaphors of travel and of 'the world as exhibition' as stimulating ways of encountering primarily visual materials. The 3D world with its diversity of places, atmospheres, and landmark objects provides a rich and significant context for placing visual material, with the third dimension dramatically increasing the space for storing, viewing, presenting, and interacting with objects. The architects used it as a visual archive, as a source of inspiration, and as an exhibition and presentation space. The Wunderkammer invites and enables users to experiment with context, scenography, and arrangements.

Figure 1: Placing and discovering inspirational objects in a 3D space

A next step was to explore how assemblies of (visual) material can be used in support of, on the one hand, presenting an idea and, on the other hand, of preserving the memory and history of a project. The women experimented with different orders of material – folders/categories, narrative, layers, post-its, etc. These exercises were based on fieldwork showing that architects often work with assemblies of artifacts. They may arrange these artifacts within spatial vicinity, layering, juxtaposing them, without giving a precise definition of their relationship. This may ease people's conversations and their joint effort to arrive at a solution for complex problems that cannot easily be defined.

This was only the beginning of a learning process. At the background of this work was the aim to learn from designers' work practices, the assumption that looking at how they mobilize inspirational resources, keep a project open to a dialogue with other people and disciplines, and at the role of visual material in this process may help women to extend their own workplace skills.

2 Aesthetic Design Work

Good design implies the ability to take a 'different view' of the myriads of (technical) parameters that have to be taken into account and bring diverse and sometimes contradictory themes and interpretations to work together. The dynamic interplay of 'facts' with images, metaphors, and analogies supports this. An important aspect of this process is to gradually expand and enrich the solution space by mobilizing people and ideas about materials, technical detail, etc., before arriving at particular solutions and fixing them.

This process of mobilizing and interpreting involves numerous multimedia materials, many of them with graphical and visual features. Design work proceeds through producing, processing, sharing, interpreting, and modifying sketches, plans, construction drawings, scale models, samples of materials, images, and 3D visualizations, as well as more mundane planning documents such as Word and spreadsheet documents, e-mail messages, faxes, etc. While some of this material is precise and detailed, much of it is conceptual, metaphorical, and in formation.

Architectural design practice is rich and extremely varied. Each office has developed its own working methods and approaches to solving the numerous problems that pose themselves on the way from a design idea to an aesthetically satisfying, affordable and usable building. While trying to capture this variety, we have also been able to identify some generic features of design work which seem to be relevant for creative work practice in other areas and disciplines (Wagner, 1999).[1]

One of these features is the conceptual nature of design work. Architects develop a design from a variety of resources – the specific project requirements, contextual, sometimes historical information about a site or area, previous proj-

---

1   The examples and materials discussed in this chapter are based on fieldwork in the architectural office of Rüdiger Lainer and represent some of its current project work, in particular *Pleasure Dome*, an entertainment center in the *Gasometer* area of Vienna, and *Eurocity*, a Cinema Center in Salzburg.

ect work, technical solutions, regulations, etc. Many of them use inspirational materials and associations – images, metaphors, and analogies – for synthesis and analysis, concept formation, and formulation (see, e.g. Lawson, 1980). The art of designing consists in gradually assembling these resources into a whole while keeping their connections fluent.

In their work, architects frequently use images for expressing particular qualities. This installation by Lois Weinberger (Figure 2), who works with the principle of 'de-naturation,' leaving cracks in asphalt for wedges and plants, illustrates the architect's notion of 'artificial nature.' In this sketch (Figure 3), which was produced for an urban planning project, the architect explains his idea of constructing an area of high density by 'diving into and cutting out.'[2]

Figure 2:	Figure 3:	Figure 4:
Visualizing 'concepts in formation'	Fuzzy concepts	The column – reinterpreting constraints

A related feature of creative work is the ability to handle constraints in innovative ways. The limitations defined by technology, time, knowledge, economic resources are many, and they are often overwhelming. Good design succeeds in turning a constraint into an opportunity for doing things differently, as in this small example from an architectural project (*Eurocity*), where for structural reasons two columns had to be added which the architect saw as interfering with the monolithic and floating character of the building. With one of the movie theatres having to be shifted outward, there was suddenly a new, never thought

---

2   Unreferenced quotations are from our own fieldwork notes.

of place for the support structure. Its wedge-shape reflects and strengthens the design concept in a dramatic way (Figure 4).

When thinking of creative work, the focus is often on the artist, her/his intuition and creative gift. However, much of design work is intensely cooperative, involving numerous people, viewing each other's work, explaining, sketching, discussing design details, assessing the progress of work, confirming responsibilities, distributing work, etc. Throughout the planning process, architects need to interact with a great diversity of external actors – the client, technical consultants, local authorities, producers, etc. – consulting, co-developing, negotiating. At the heart of design work, therefore, is the need to share materials, and to mobilize support.

3 The Open Planning Metaphor

These characteristics of creative design – its conceptual, complex and highly cooperative nature – require work to be organized in an open, informal and fluent way. We use 'open planning' to express the idea that architects/designers should be supported to work, and also present their work, in an open space of possibilities rather than a set of (pre-)defined solutions. There are many good reasons for maintaining openness: complexity, which implies the impossibility of defining and fixing details in a step-by-step process, the desire to expand the solution space and to see things differently, the necessity to involve and mobilize the competence and cooperation of many others. As women are often silenced when giving their opinion and creative ideas, open planning can also be seen as a strategy of maintaining a space for interventions throughout a project. Openness implies that decisions about possible design trajectories are not made too quickly, and requires that the different actors present their work in a form that is open to change. It puts emphasis on the dynamics of opening and expanding, fixing and constraining, re-opening, etc. (Tellioglu et al, 1998).

Some of the building blocks of this methodology may be translated into other areas of creative work, in particular the necessity of:

- *Mobilizing a wide range of inspirational resources* – objects (metaphors, images, analogies, samples, music, etc.) that have the quality of stimulating associations and expanding the solution space for a design, including techniques such as 'working with contradictions,' and 'defining themes.'
- *Rich and open forms of presenting and communicating a design* – techniques for communicating qualities in ways that narrate and evoke, rather than prescribe, imaginations, and thus invite others into a dialogue.

- *Meandering processes of decision-making* – this asks for a conceptual shift from working with fixed elements or solutions to working with 'placeholders,' and to look at specifications as partial and preliminary.

3.1 Inspirational Objects – Rich Descriptions

Inspirational resources – images, music, materials, and other objects – are ubiquitous. Architects evoke, collect, and use them to capture and express an evolving concept, to emphasize particular features of a site or a material, to bring seemingly contradictory themes together. One of their achievements is that they support what we described as the dynamic interplay of images, metaphors, analogies and 'facts.'

The 'big wall,' impregnated with color and light
A shimmering surface, bright and transparent, as seen from a distance, its structure revealing itself when approaching
The façade as screen, colorful patchwork (Richard Serra, Chartres)

Juxtaposing nature with art
The interplay of 'harsh nature' (Mario Merz) with the luminous wall
The façade as cutting edge between rough concrete and color

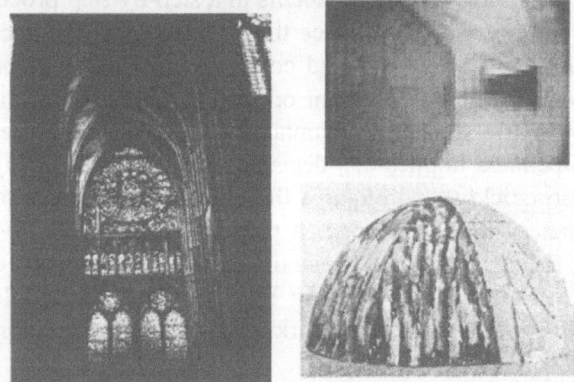

Figure 5: Working with metaphors, images, and associations

This collage (Figure 5) of 3D visualization, text and association images represents some of the central features of the design concept for *Pleasure Dome*. While the 3D image visualizes the idea of a 'big wall, impregnated with color and light,' the association objects (some of which are shown in Figure 4) in this project help to grasp some of the essential qualities of the design. Their use is interwoven with talk and embodied action: sketching, arranging materials on a table, pointing, etc. Gestures, talk, and inspirational objects formulate or translate (Goodwin, 2000) the concept in formation of the building's façade as a cutting edge between the rough quality of concrete and the lucidity and colorfulness of the glass skin.

At a later stage, a scale model is constructed, visualizing the 'stones that dip into water,' the volumes of the movie theaters, which can be lighted from inside (Figure 8). It is used to convince the client of the architects' choice of vivid colors. This process of imagining and expressing reaches far into the implementation phase of a project, cf. the pictures from the construction site shown in Figure 6, enlarged prints of which turn a small meeting room in the architectural office into an inspirational environment. They act as reminders of some of the crucial design principles.

Figure 6: Images from the construction site as inspirational imaginations

Images, objects, and metaphors provide a rich language for forming and communicating ideas. Their sources are manifold. Architects and designers work with inspirations from many different aesthetic and scientific discourses – from the fine arts and the theater to biology and mathematics. Many of the images that are evoked or produced, hung on the walls, shown to different audiences, do not bear any resemblance to what will eventually be designed and built. They rather touch upon specific qualities which can only be described in a visual or poetic language or provide (idealized) versions of certain themes within the design concept.

3.2 Meandering Processes of Decision-making

A second feature of openness is captured by the notion of 'meandering.' Design work rarely proceeds in a linear, step-by-step mode; it artfully oscillates between pre-scribing and de-scribing, fixing and opening. Concretizing a design requires to evoke the main concept, to think it through, and to gradually explore the feasibility of various solutions on different levels of detail. A crucial aspect of this is to be able to work with 'fuzzy concepts' (such as 'diving in and cutting out,' Figure 3), and to maintain things at different stages of incompletion.

This oscillating between details and the whole, between precision and fuzziness, asks for a conceptual shift from working with fixed elements or solutions to working with placeholders, and to look on specifications as partial and preliminary. A placeholder stands for something which might be there, but is still in formation. It underpins the passage from possibility to actuality which is the work of design. It may be represented by a product, image, assembly of everyday objects, example from a previous project. It may only be defined on a conceptual and metaphorical level. An example of this is 'Piranesi's staircase' (Figure 7) – an image and metaphor which the architect used for representing his notion of stairs which superimpose an existing structure in an old building, weaving a new pattern.

Figure 7: Working with placeholders – Piranesi's staircase

Working with placeholders is a method for representing relatively complex systems before they have taken shape. Placeholders facilitate communicating about something which has not been specified in detail. They enable people to focus on the concept rather than on a particular material, product or constructive solution.

4 The Power of Visualizations

Visual and graphic material plays a major role in conceptualizing, mediating, and communicating an evolving design concept. One of its most important advantages is its ability to create persuasion and to invite others into a dialogue

(Latour, 1986). In the design disciplines work and presentation are closely interwoven.

The examples taken from various architectural projects support this view. Many of them are not primarily created for presentational purposes. They are produced as an intricate part of the process of forming an idea, approach, and method. They help in taking a step forward in the common understanding of a design. They support its development, expression, and being shared with others. If visibly displayed in the architectural office, they are frequently looked at and referred to as part of ongoing work. This feature of visual representations – their artistic arrangement in support of an idea – is captured by the notion of persuasive artifacts.

A related achievement of visualizations is that they are 'network-organizing devices,' individual and interactive thinking tools, organizers of interdisciplinary communication (Henderson, 1995). As has been described elsewhere, sketching and explaining ideas are tightly interwoven activities (Wagner, 2000).

Figure 8: Visual-verbal relationships

We see that visualizations are often created and used as part of talk. Many of them contain text as well as visual elements. These visual-verbal relationships (Figure 8) are crucial to many design disciplines. As Mitchell argues: "...all arts are 'composite' art (both text and image); all media are mixed media, combining different codes, discursive connections, channels, sensory and cognitive modes" (Mitchell, 1994: 95). The growing, metamorphosing idea of 'stones dripping into water' is represented in the material that is collected and produced, including the talk around it.

5 Spatial Assemblies

While some of the visual material stands for itself, eventually assuming a key role, others melt into assemblies of materials representing a particular task. In fact, much of the individual *and* cooperative work is done by creating assemblies of materials. People configure materials for a particular task, and reconfigure for the next task.

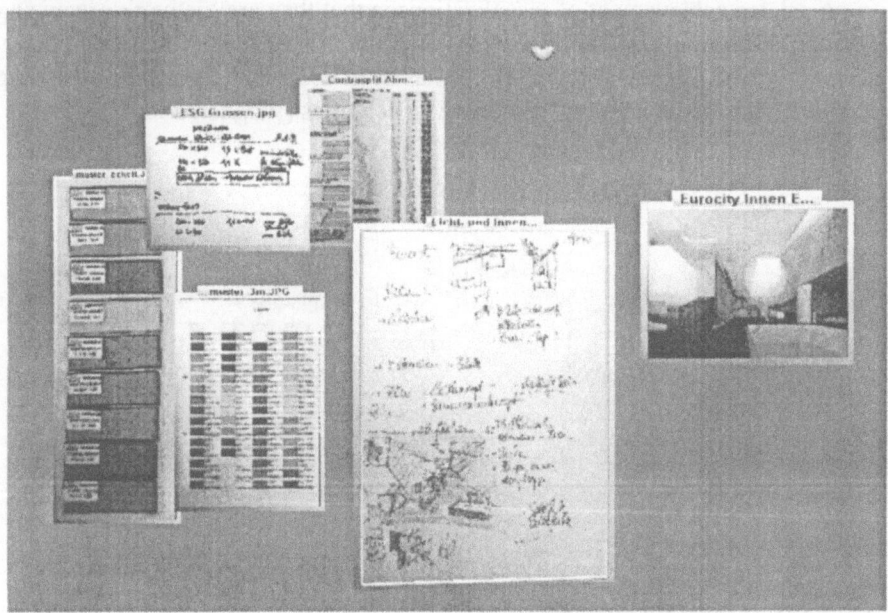

Figure 9: Configuring materials for a particular task

We have analyzed in depth how people arrange materials in their immediate physical environment. Figure 9 shows some of the materials that were assembled in support of a specific task – the design of the projection cabins for *Eurocity*. Light plays a major role in the design concept, and the projection cabins were conceived as transparent light boxes. Designing the projection cabins involved selecting glass and devising a way of mounting it onto the cabins that reinforces the lighting effect.

The architect in charge of this task has assembled all the relevant material in her workspace. In the foreground are a sketch of the lighting concept and a 3D visualization of the interior with the glowing projection cabins. While searching for materials, she has looked into reference material from another project – images of glass, foils and membranes, together with some technical information.

When configuring such materials in their workspace, people use particular techniques (Figure 10) such as foregrounding – arranging materials with reference to the embodied experience of space. Materials that are under direct consideration occupy the foreground – both literally and metaphorically – but they can easily be turned into a background. Particular orderings of materials do not just reflect individual strategies of using space but shared visual conventions. People pile materials that belong together but are not needed at the moment in stacks.

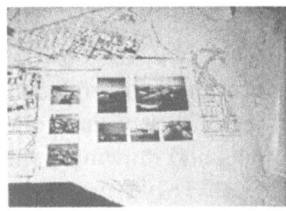  

Figure 10: Orders of materials

Other, more subtle assemblies reveal that there are quite intricate links between documents and objects, such as a post-it note on a particular drawing to remind oneself or others of things to check or to complete. Another frequently observed assembly involves the use of tracing paper, where a blank sheet of tracing paper is placed over a plan, and 'anchored' by entering some positional markers. The tracing paper is then used, for example, to experiment with design ideas. Such an assembly creates a precise relationship between a design sketch and (one or several) other documents.

Assemblies allow an arrangement of artifacts within spatial vicinity, layering, juxtaposing them, without giving a precise definition of their relationships. They represent 'context' – the biography or trajectory of a particular design detail (such as the projection cabins or the search for glass), relationships between parameters and/or to people. They may provide a good overview, including pointers to things that should be kept present.

An important feature of such assemblies of material around a design problem is their narrative character. The material that finally gets chosen is not just a product, but a whole story of searching and testing, which may be used by others who find themselves confronted with a similar problem. The narrative form allows people to go back to earlier solutions, re-assess the constraints, and eventually take another path. It may also help preserve some of the complex reasoning around particular solutions. Such arrangements are not just meaningful for one's own task, but they are reminiscent of the work of others. In addition, they play a major role in preserving the memory of past work.

6 Enriching Women's Workplace Skills

In her analysis of visual cultures in design engineering, Kathryn Henderson stresses the meta-indexical quality of visual materials, their extreme flexibility, their ability to reach and elicit tacit knowledge. She has analyzed the particular ways in which "visual representations facilitate the joining of not only multiple meanings, but multiple forms and formats of coded and uncoded, verbal, visual, mathematical, and tacit knowledge" (Henderson, 1999: 199). We saw how architects/designers capture, express, and detail design ideas through producing and evoking different kinds of visual material. At the heart of their visual communication are sketches, which gradually evolve into plans and drawings, and are sometimes combined with other kinds of visual material. They have developed this art over long years of practice.

Little is known about the gendered aspects of creating visualizations. Working with the women at *ifu* encouraged to think that they may benefit from developing the art of visualizing – sketching, creating collages of images and text – when working at a common project and having to mobilize the understanding and cooperation of others. The women at *ifu* made good use of the expressive qualities of images for talking about themselves and their project. A part of this is the ability to mobilize inspirational resources and to work with them. Inspirational material is ubiquitous. The point is to become aware of it as a potential resource and how to artfully integrate it into one's work. This includes the ability to select and read (primarily) visual material and to use its power of expressing and capturing ideas and concepts. Analysis of designers' representational practices may help develop these skills.

A related skill is the use of both image and text in one's work, and their blending into 'persuasive artifacts' – artifacts that present work in an open way, inviting others in, stimulating their curiosity and imagination, and help combine the analytical with the art of story telling. In most areas of work narrative is restricted to the textual form, which is, however, limited in its linearity. The *bande dessinée* or cartoon enriches this technique using image-text. Including visual material but, in addition, making use of space, further expands the possibilities of expressing relationships in an informal and open way, e.g. of evoking a story (see also the chapter by Eske & Beer in this volume).

We have looked at how designers make use of space for creating meaningful assemblies of materials. Techniques such as foregrounding, layers of transparent paper or post-it notes on drawings and plans reveal intricate and implicit links between documents or objects. One of the lessons to be learned from analyzing these techniques is how to artfully arrange materials in a meaningful way for different purposes. This purpose may be presentational – to create exhibitions of relevant materials for a particular audience. The purpose may be to preserve the memory of past work, to maintain its accessibility and re-usability in a new and different project. Spatial arrangements offer interesting and new ways of building and preserving collections of materials in context.

At *ifu*, creative visualizations were used in some of the projects (for example in the *Health Care Information* project described by El Tobgui & Gregory in this volume) and in the course on *Knowledge Co-construction* (see Floyd, this volume). To make these skills of creative designers accessible to women in other walks of life needs careful nurturing so that they grow into taken-for-granted aspects of their work.

References

Büscher, Monika; Kompast, Martin; Lainer, Rüdiger & Wagner, Ina (1999). The Architect's Wunderkammer: Aesthetic Pleasure & Engagement in Electronic Spaces. In: *Digital Creativity* 10/1, pp. 1-17.

Büscher, Monika; Mogensen, Preben; Shapiro, Dan & Wagner, Ina (1999). The Manufaktur. Supporting Work Practice in (Landscape) Architecture. In: Bødker, S.; Kyng, M.; & Schmidt, K. (eds.). *Proceedings of the Sixth European Conference on Computer Supported Cooperative Work.* Copenhagen: Kluwer Academic Publishers, pp. 21-40.

Goodwin, Charles (2000). Action and Embodiment Within Situated Human Interaction. *Journal of Pragmatics* 32, pp. 1489-1522.

Henderson, Kathryn (1995). The Visual Culture of Engineers. In: Star, S. Leigh (ed.). *The Cultures of Computing.* Oxford: Blackwell, pp. 97-218.

Henderson, Kathryn (1999). *On Line and On paper. Visual Representations, Visual Culture, and Computer Graphics in Design Engineering.* Cambridge MA: MIT Press.

Kompast, Martin; Lainer, Rüdiger & Wagner, Ina (2000). Multiple Voices in the Graphic Design of a Visual Information System. In: Cherkasky,T.; Greenbaum, J.; Mambrey, P. & Pors, J. Kaaber (eds.). *Proceedings of PDC '2000 Participatory Design Conference. Designing Digital Environments.* New York, Nov 28 – Dec 1, 2000. Palo Alto: CPSR, pp. 202-211.

Latour, Bruno (1986). Visualization and Cognition: Thinking with Eyes and Hands. In: *Knowledge and Society: Studies in the Sociology of Culture Past and Present,* Vol. 6 Greenwhich, CT: Jai Press, pp. 1-40.

Lawson, B. (1980). *How Designers Think.* Chatham, Kent: W&J Mackay Ltd.

Mitchell, William. J. T. (1994). *Picture Theory. Essays on Verbal and Visual Representation.* Chicago: The University of Chicago Press.

Tellioglu, Hilda; Wagner, Ina & Lainer, Rüdiger (1998). Open Design Methodologies. Exploring Architectural Practice for Systems Design. In: Chatfield, R.H; Kuhn, S.; & Muller, M. (eds.). *Proceedings of PDC '98 Participatory Design Conference,* Seattle, Nov 12-14, 1998. Palo Alto: CPSR, pp. 19-28.

Wagner, Ina (2000). Persuasive Artifacts in Architectural Design and Planning. In: Scrivener, S.A.; Ball, L.J. & Woodcock, A. (eds.). *CoDesigning 2000*. London, Heidelberg, New York: Springer, pp. 379-390.

Wagner, Ina (ed.). (1999). *Desarte. The Computer-Supported Design of Artifacts and Spaces in Architecture and Landscape Architecture*. Vienna: Institute of Technology Assessment & Design, Vienna University of Technology.

Ursula Biemann & Berta Jottar

Performing Borders:
Gender and Technology in Diasporic Culture

Abstract

Focussing on the U.S.-Mexican border from a multi-disciplinary perspective, this is a reflection about the role of female migrants, gender and sexuality in this border's constitutive moments of post-Fordism from a multi-disciplinary perspective. What is the role of labor in these new diasporic subjectivities? What is the relationship between visual culture and technology in the practice and representation of migration? The dialogue between the authors in the second part of this chapter is also about the paradoxes of speaking in translation within and without borders. Like the art workshop held by the authors at *ifu*, the text is about the collapse of the theoretical with the practical, and the intersections of – rather than borders between – art, theory, and activism.

1 Introduction

Strongly embedded in the Project Area INFORMATION of the International Women's University (*ifu*), our art workshop set out to enable participants to use new media and technologies while at the same time offering alternative visions and strategies for dealing with some of the problematic issues created by this very technology.

The challenge we were facing was twofold. We decided to tackle the core of the problem that emerges when artistic and scientific practices are brought together in an institutional context: the maintenance of the binary categories that are fundamental to Western conceptual frameworks. Our plan was to challenge the idea that clear boundaries could be drawn between categories such as *public/ private, global/local, body/technology, masculinity/femininity* and to acknowledge, by the same token, the existence of a different kind of space.

Our workshop was to open a space in which we could elaborate on the relations between these categories and seek to understand how the boundaries are being performed. We used the concept of *performativity*, born at the intersection of disciplines such as anthropology, theater studies, linguistics, and queer theory, as a liminal space in which discursive mechanisms constitute themselves as the real and material via the regulatory practices of naturalization and normalization. For instance, the space in which gender becomes real, or females become feminine as a 'natural process,' is not when they are born, but when (as Valerie Hartouni has stated in her seminars) a female baby is first dressed in pink rather than blue.

It is the possibility of material consequences that is the constitutive moment of the performative space at the intersection between discourse, practice and the real[1]. One of the reasons for the usefulness of understanding the dynamics of performativity is that it is deconstructive, as it makes evident the relationship between the 'real' and the discursive. However, the deconstructive nature of performativity does not necessarily presuppose a conscious ideological position. For instance, the performativity of gender does not presuppose a progressive behavior since we do not perform gender. Rather, gender is ascribed to us via normalization and naturalization.

Indeed, the case of transvestites and their performance of gender is meaningful since it is their mastering of gender that deconstructs gender realness and biologisms. It is the performativity of passing as a biological, therefore 'real,' woman, rather than the mastering of gender, that makes evident the ideological contradictions between constructivist and essentialist positions about gender, (gender-) passing and transvestites.

Thus, the notion of performativity is crucial in exposing how dichotomies and boundaries are not only central to Western ways of looking at the world but are also expressed materially in the way the world is organized. This insight also recognizes that scientific research practice always implies a constitutive moment as well. We consider these questions to be the subject of cultural investigations and art interventions and made them our prime concern of the workshop.

To enable the participants to grasp these ideas theoretically as well as to position themselves in relation to the major factors which frame the situation of women in the information industry, our border workshop drew on a range of discourses, philosophical, cultural, and economic. We incorporated contemporary ideas from cyberfeminism, critical geography, cultural studies, and performance theory to do a gendered reading of technology both with regard to our proper application of communication technology and particular geographic spaces like borders, where questions of gender and technology are articulated in specific ways. The understanding of these connections was a main objective of the workshop.

---

1   In one of her seminars on gender, Peggy Phelan discussed Austin's example of the power of words in their function as speech acts. For instance, the utterance 'I promise' is an example of the constitutive moment which is in itself performative, i.e. the utterance performs the act (whether the promise is kept or not) because it is the legal and moral consequences that give the utterance great transcendence.

Borders are complex constructions in both a discursive and material sense and new technologies play a major part in facilitating, transgressing and controlling them. National borders also function as powerful metaphors for difference while reflecting and materializing measures of marginalization. The U.S.-Mexican border is a particularly interesting case for our investigation, because it embodies and localizes the basis on which the Information Society is built. On the South side of this border, U.S. corporations assemble their electronic equipment for the communication industry. In this particular site, two major factors of postmodernism converge: post-Fordist production, which draws predominantly on a female assembly labor force, and the migration of women into urban and industrial areas, which is often accompanied by the formation of diasporic identities. We entered the discussion of how bodies, gender and femininity are being produced by the hi-tech industry on the border by looking at two major border regions: Tijuana/San Diego and Ciudad Juarez/El Paso.

The art workshop at *ifu* focussed on the border zone as a discursive, representational space as well as a material space in which border women, who mark the margins of the New World, are affected in their real existences. To give an impression of the visual materials we used, see Figures 1 and 2, both showing scenes at the U.S.-Mexican border.

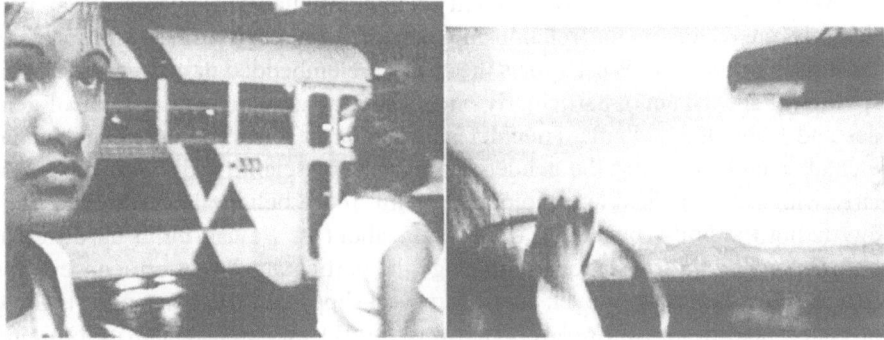

Figure 1: 'Bus Portrait'   Figure 2: 'Desert Ride'

2 Dialogue on Issues Raised in the *Performing Borders* Art Workshop

Question: Berta, as an art project within a scientific program, we continuously discussed the conditions under which our work was elaborated and received in the context of *ifu*. How did you perceive this particular situation and where do you locate our strategies and what was your focus?

Berta: ifu, at large, is a context of communication and negotiation, a multi-lingual place of dialogue. Nevertheless, the dialogue between artists and scientists within *ifu*'s scientific institution was constantly in jeopardy because of the structural deficiencies that the belief in this very split between the arts and sciences entails (for example, a separate committee outside the project areas had been set up to prepare the arts' program).[2] This belief was constantly reconstituted on both sides: the artists not seeing the arts of science, and the scientists not seeing their practice as a representational realm.

Presumptions about the instrumental use of art became more evident in terms of institutional priorities: which fields occupy the core of the program, whose voice has more volume than others, and how much time can be dedicated to art versus 'the scientific core' of the program?

Within the limits of this bipolar context, our strategy then was to depart from the very theories about borders. By locating physical and metaphorical borders, we attempted to deconstruct them from within. We were interested in breaking through these assumed splits not only internalized within *ifu*'s structure, but by participants as well. How, then, could we deconstruct the belief in the discursive split between scientific knowledge versus the production of art and culture?

Within *ifu*'s cross-cultural context of international participants, I was particularly interested in the relationship between language and translation, and how discourses of the West versus the 'rest,' are embedded in our articulation of speech (or speech acts), particularly once we speak and translate notions of gender and technology.[3] Paula Treichler and Donna J. Haraway have been fundamental in understanding the gendered semiotics of scientific discourse, particularly within the medical and biological realm. If we believe Haraway that biology is not the body, but rather a discourse about it, we can build up different lexica which – via translation – challenge the participants' Western conceptions at a rigorous theoretical level. In our art workshop, the Western understanding of gender had to be exposed yet. Haraway (1991) was a basic start to bringing back the split between the cultural/constructivist understanding of gender ('gender is a cultural construction') versus the essentialist/scientific naturalization of sex ('the biology of females predisposes their feminine affinity to motherhood'). Some participants were bored by examples as simple as the above to show how

---

2   Andrew Ross has historically situated the various ideological tendencies embedded in the discursive split between science and the humanities; he has demonstrated how these splits also imply a contractual relationship between their respective representatives. Even though the meaning of this contract has not been a fixed one historically, the rationale of 'not my department' has benefited the 'managerial elites' within both fields (Ross, 1999: 293). Ross closes his essay by asking: "How can science qualify *us* to sustain a critical view of society?"

3   See also the chapter by Akande in this volume.

femininity and sexuality are not the same. On the other hand, and within the context of *ifu*, how can we translate this predominant understanding of sex, and even the established deconstruction of it, when a large number of females in the world believe and own their own essentialisms not only through their own cultural institutions, but via colonization and cultural imperialism? How can we talk about gender and sexuality when there is not even a translation for this very split?

One of the points of talking about (U.S.) transgender and transsexual cultural practices such as gender-passing (in Afro-Latin communities) was to arrive at questions such as: How does technology become the same structure that permeates as well as deconstructs the realness of nature, biology and even race? We juxtaposed various theoretically evident (and not so evident) texts. For instance, by opening the layers of Jenny Livingston's documentary *Paris is Burning*, juxtaposed with Sikay Tang's *In Search for an Allison*, we could unpack cultural practices from a performance studies' point of view.[4] We analyzed the documentary form of realness, in the context of Livingston's paradoxical topic, the realness of gender performance. Why is the realness of gender performance paradoxical? What do scientific discourse and the humanities tell us about realness? How does realness translate across the multicultural, multiracial body of *ifu*? And what is the role of performativity, a space of improvisation between representation, identification and cultural scripts, in the construction and performance of gender? What is the role of translation in the representation of racialized bodies? Hopefully during our workshop, it became evident that biology is not enough, technology fails, and the impermeability and fixedness of borders are desires with real consequences.

Question: Ursula, as a practitioner in between art and activism, theory and practice, always being on the border, how does your border *positionality* enable you to produce alternative pedagogical spaces by creating strategies that look beyond the instrumentalist use of art? From your experience, could you expand on the possibilities of art within theoretical and pedagogical paradigms or practices?

Ursula: I don't know how alternative these spaces are, but it has always seemed highly problematic to me to segregate theory and practice. At most art schools today, students are left alone with bringing their artistic projects into relation with the complex ideas taught in the theory seminars and they are completely overwhelmed by it. If the teachers aren't able to bring the two together, how can

---

4   This is an interdisciplinary approach that borrows from anthropology's understandings of the relationships between cultural scripts and liminality (Richard Schechner), linguistic analysis of the discursive imperative of speech acts (Austin, 1975) and queer studies that coin gender, race, culture and resistance such as Judith Butler, Barbara Browning, Peggy Phelan, Gloria Anzaldua, José Muñoz, etc.

we expect students to perform this difficult task? A workshop, be it announced as a theory or studio course, will always be an opportunity for me to open a space in between and make it productive in a collective way. This was also a major concern for the *ifu* workshop. Besides the theoretical lectures and text-based discussions, we wanted to look at a wide range of media and art projects elaborating the same questions but using a variety of aesthetic strategies. In the second week, we took it a step further and made the participants into producers themselves. We constantly switched between a discursive, representational space and the material space of producers who no longer mediate ideas from a distance but progressively embody the issues by placing themselves in the picture. In this manner, we not only look at the way in which theory can be useful in analyzing cultural productions, but the other way around, how theory can be a visual practice and how this visual practice informs theory. It's performative!

The other point you are addressing is that there is no clear inside or outside the arts anymore. The art space is above all a space in which symbolic productions and their meanings are negotiated. In this capacity, art has expanded its interests to include the rather fuzzy entity of visual culture, which encompasses many media and processes of visualization, also used by sciences and popular culture etc. (see Wagner, this volume). As soon as we enter these contemporary cultural arenas through our art production, we set one foot outside the arts and start operating in a variety of fields in which meaning is produced today. I would find it very limiting to operate merely within the strict confines of the art institution. My videos enter labor union conferences, cyberfeminist cafés, modern art museums and activist networks alike and this is one of the merits of working in between all these categories.

Question: Berta, through your own art practice and extensive research in performance studies, you brought in the notion of performativity, which has been fundamental in rethinking gender in the 1990s. I was very interested in how you apply this concept to the way borders in general, and the U.S.-Mexican border in particular, are being constituted on a daily basis by people crossing it. In the workshop, you extended the border crossing activities into the cultural arena. What place does border art have in all this?

Berta: My approach to the border is that there is nothing natural about it, but that it is a place constituted physically and discursively through its daily crossings. In other words, the border is performative because it materializes through its practices, such as surveillance and control; but once you cross it, it becomes real. When I moved to Tijuana from Mexico City, and in spite of the large migrant but static population working in Tijuana's *maquiladora* [5] industry, I became interested in the crossing back and forth of bodies, mine being one of them. I noticed that the representations of the crossing migrants were highly gendered. For instance, male workers crossing north were constantly feminized by U.S. state and media narratives, which portray them as passive bodies: reproductive in numbers but not productive in the economic sense of growth and profit. However, these overly narrated bodies were, and still are, vital to California's large agricultural and floricultural industry. Even more interesting is the way in which the female migrants disappear in these border crossings. If males are feminized, females are entirely eradicated from the narratives of the illegal alien invasion. These invisible bodies, however, support U.S. middle class women, who can work in the public domain thanks to the informal slavery of domestic workers whose life is reduced to seven days a week live-in cleaning, cooking and baby-sitting, all for the price of two hundred dollars a month. On both sides of the border the possibilities of crossing are central to everyday life and power relations and thus to the region's culture of resistance against border inequalities.

Tijuana is a cosmopolitan and eclectic city, the backyard of U.S. junk and the front yard of San Diego cultural life. It is no coincidence that there is a large number of local artists who are part of the motion and effervescence of border crossings. During the mid-1980s and early 1990s the regional way of producing site-specific art eventually became known as border art.

I was lucky to live in the region at this intersectional moment, when the first generation of Tijuana artists such as Felipe Almada, Federico, Carmela Castrejon, Angelica Robles, Hugo Torres, Gerardo Navarro, and Rosina and Gilberto Conde, and those in the diaspora like me, Maria Eraña, Marco Vinicio, Guillermo Gomez Peña, were collaborating on public installations and performances with Chicana/Chicano and Anglo artists from the other side. This culture of resistance functioned (through the production of art) in public spaces such as plazas and markets, or site-specific places such as the fence and the Garita Internacional (the gate of the U.S. Immigration and Naturalization Services, INS). These happenings contested mass media representations of the border as a war zone, and of its crossers as passive receivers of U.S. benefits, creating a counter-public sphere. Artists used the border fence as a prop and the border as a space of deconstruction, a site of anti-colonialism. We crossed back and forth with 'goods' and art supplies. Recycling, already a fundamental element of Tijuana's life, was a basic strategy of local art practices. The performances and installations were made of re-used materials, cardboard, xeroxes, brown paper bags,

---

5   *Maquiladoras* are outsourced low wage assembly plants located in the tax-free zone predominantly along the U.S.-Mexican border, producing hi-tech equipment for the advanced countries.

used clothes. But owing to Tijuana's softer legislation on the use of public space, these street installations and happenings occurred mainly on the South side of the border. It was always clear that the final destination of the projects/objects was a binational trash can. The artistic attitude behind these actions was interventionist and situationist.[6]

The reason for bringing to our workshop these crossing bodies in relationship to Tijuana's cultural life was to understand how the realities of border violence, including the physical and discursive disappearance of migrants, occurred in a context of cultural resistance manifested beyond the Mexican state and gallery scene from both sides of the border. It was fundamental to point out that the border is a cultural phenomenon constituted not only through its daily crossings but the resistance against the uneven power relationships that these entail. The questions that we raised were: How do we document the undocumented? How do we represent the subaltern, the unrepresentable? How do we record disappearance?

Question: Ursula, from a feminist perspective, what were your priorities in the course?

Ursula: I can think of a number of different facets in a feminist perspective, all of which were brought into the art workshop, at one point or another. One aspect of a feminist view would consist in the focus on women's lives, foregrounding their roles as key actors in migration movements, cross-border circuits and in the global economy. Women are the producers of the hardware that enables cyberspace. In these repetitive processes, the female body is tightly linked to technology on the workbench. On the U.S.-Mexican border, women make up the large majority of the migrated population in the border towns, they have moved from a reproductive to a productive role in society, created new living spaces, enjoy their own entertainment culture and by doing so, they have changed social structures and gender relations. But as you illustrated with your powerful example of the crossing bodies, these facts and stories are often effaced, underrepresented, streamlined or marginalized in favor of majority driven discourses which portray the border and border crossings as a site of male ac-

---

6   Paradoxically, in the early 1990s, as the border stopped being represented as a war zone and became fashionable in the U.S. owing to the Hispanic boom, the multi-culturalism movement, the consolidation of the Free Trade Agreement, and Mexico's shift to an integrationist 'good neighbor' discourse, the happenings south of the border also vanished into institutionalized contexts designed for Border Art on both sides of the border. The most obvious example of this binational phenomenon was INSITE 94, the first binational exhibition of installation and site-specific art with the participation of 100 local and international artists. The event was sponsored by 38 non-profit institutions from San Diego and Tijuana and has become a biennial show.

tivities and masculine control mechanisms. The feminist strategy would consist in filling in missing information and expanding the narrow space in which we speak of the feminine.

Another aspect of a feminist approach examines power relations in their gendered dimensions. How is gender produced and inscribed in the built reality of urban environments and work settings, in economic structures, social regulations, media representations and other public discourses? On a deeper level, we ask in what ways the languages which articulate these discourses are already gendered. Our strategy would be to look at knowledge not as a means to create difference and boundaries by reinforcing binary categories, but in a relational view of social and material spaces, understanding how one type of knowledge conditions another. A feminist methodology would necessarily have to acknowledge one's own positionality to contradict a positivist and masculine assumption about the objectivity of the author/researcher. These assumptions have been challenged by postmodern authors (male and female) for many years now, but in practice we encounter residual encrustations in every institutional corner. Our team teaching in the workshop opened a dialogical space between two positions which were already defined by a difference in cultural backgrounds and disciplinary fields. In this manner, knowledge is less easily perceived as absolute and monolithic but open to reinterpretation.

One of the major benefits provided by a feminist perspective is a situated, gendered understanding of globalization. Technology and gender are entangled in a number of ways: on the level of production since the hi-tech hardware is assembled by women in the South for the advanced world; on the level of consumption through the use of e-mail and the Internet, where women gain access to the global community but are also commercialized and capitalized as the booming bride market exemplifies; and through the ways new media and technologies are implemented to produce new forms of representation of women and their life worlds. Feminist criticism needs to address all these different points of intersection between gender and technology in the global context. A cyberfeminist practice engages furthermore in the generation of new and exciting figurations of the female body in the virtual and the representational realm and to map out new spaces where women appear as agents.

Question: Ursula, on what level do you think artistic practice is contributing to change?

Ursula: The question whether and how we can improve situations is a complicated one for people who are involved in the symbolic production of images. Even if videos as a medium promise to be of great use for activist work, I don't see their primary potential so much in effecting direct social change. I wouldn't reduce it to a mere contribution to an ongoing discourse either, but see its potential in mediating between the two, as active intervention on a symbolic level of cultural production. The image of Woman is, after all, a matter of cultural imagery and in terms of the feminine, the cultural imagery is extremely limited. There is a need to displace and expand the boundaries that limit our imagination and to re-signify the feminine within sexual difference by visualizing the ongoing negotiation between the sexes in all the different areas of social and cultural interaction. The process of re-signification takes place in between the images and our lives, in between the limitations of representation and the existential or political struggle of women. It is never merely a matter of replacing negative images with better ones, social change doesn't depend merely on more accurate information. It is the viewing structures and image regimes, as Kaja Silverman (1997) writes, that need to be transformed. In that sense, the terrain of symbolic production is a performative one: it simultaneously constitutes the situation it tries to describe and that's where the main effectiveness of a visual intervention lies.

To return to the workshop, this dynamic became very evident in the participants' verbal activities and visual productions. In generating a visual language for their intellectual concerns, many of the participants realized that images ultimately embody, even materialize, the borders caused by the rationale of difference and the unresolved dilemmas it entails. Working through these limitations in the video narratives and visual representations of their short videos was an active and effective part in the process of dissolving the mental boundaries that they encounter in their professional and personal lives.

Videography

Biemann, Ursula (1999). *Performing the Border*. Ciudad Juarez.
Jottar, Berta (1992). *Border Swings*.
Lerner, Jesse (1994). *Natives*. San Diego.
Livingston, Jenny (1991). *Paris is Burning*. Paris.
Tang, Sikay (1993). *In Search for an Allison*. New York/Hong Kong.

References

Austin, J.L. (1975). *How to Do Things With Words*. 2nd ed. Cambridge, MA: Harvard University Press.
Biemann, Ursula (2000). Performing the Border: on Gender, Transnational Bodies and Technologies. In: Biemann, Ursula. *Been There and Back to Nowhere: Gender in Transnational Spaces*. Berlin: b_books, p. 133.

Brah, Avtar (1996). Diaspora, Border and Transnational Identities. In: *Cartographies of Diaspora: Contested Identities*. London & New York: Routledge, pp. 178-210.

Braidotti, Rosi (1994). Refiguring the Subject. In: *Nomadic Subjects: Embodyment and Sexual Difference in Contemporary Feminist Theory*. New York: Colombia University Press, pp. 95-111.

Butler, Judith (1990). Performative Acts and Gender Constitution: An Essay in Phenomenology and Feminist Theory. In: Case, Sue Ellen (ed.). *Performing Feminisms*. Baltimore: Johns Hopkins University Press, pp. 270-282.

Haraway, Donna J. (1991). A Cyborg Manifesto. In: Haraway, Donna J.. *Simians, Cyborgs, and Women: The Reinvention of Nature*. New York & London: Routledge.

Jones, Amelia (1998). Dispersed Subjects and the Demise of the 'Individual'. In: *Body Art Performing the Subject*. Minneapolis: University of Minneapolis, London, pp. 197-240.

Jottar, Berta (2000). Movimientos discursivos del cuerpo: Reflexiones sobre performance y Light Up The Border. In: Borras Castanyer, Laura (ed.). *Escenografias del cuerpo*. Madrid: Fundacion Autor, pp. 36-57.

Laurie, Nina; Smith, Fiona; Bowlby, Sophie et al (1997). In and Out of Bounds and Resisting Boundaries: Feminist Geographies of Space and Place. In: Women and Geography Study Group (eds.). *Feminist Geographies*. London: Addison Wesley Longman, pp. 112-145.

Penley, Constance (1998). *The Visible Woman: Imaging Technologies, Gender, and Science*. New York: New York University Press.

Penley, Constance & Ross, Andrew (1991). Interview With Donna J. Haraway. In: *Technoculture, Cultural Politics*. Minneapolis & Oxford: University of Minnesota Press, vol. 3, pp. 1-20.

Phelan, Peggy (1993). *Unmarked: The Politics Of Performance*. New York: Routledge, Chapman & Hall.

Ross, Andrew (1999). The Challenge Of Science. In: During, Simon (ed.). *The Cultural Studies Reader*. London & New York: Routledge, 2nd ed., pp. 292-304.

Schechner, Richard (1985). *Between Theater and Anthropology*. Philadelphia: University of Pennsylvania Press.

Silverman, Kaja (1997). Dem Blickregime begegnen. In: Kravagna, Christian (ed.). *Privileg Blick, Kritik der visuellen Kultur*. Berlin: Edition ID-Archiv.

Treichler, P. A.; Cartwright, L. & Penley, C. (1998*). The Visible Woman: Imaging Technologies, Gender, and Science*. New York: New York University Press.

Part 4:
Supporting Cooperative, Interactive Learning

The information age comes with the need for life long learning to take advantage of changing options, to enable autonomous use of information and to make available information resources for individual and community concerns. This requires new forms of learning – implying a shift from a teaching paradigm, where a teacher imparts existing knowledge to students, to a paradigm of cooperative learning – and media competence in information technologies as the prerequisite for actively engaging in interactive learning. In knowledge projects situated cooperative learning processes using printed and online information resources unfold through self-organization, and the teacher assumes the role of a moderator. In online education, learning is based essentially on interaction with electronically available material, and the teacher, if there is any, monitors the learning progress from a distance. The chapters in this part of the book deal with several aspects of this complex educational challenge on a local as well as on a worldwide scale.

Five participants of *ifu*'s project *Future of Education*, Lisa Link, Therona Moodley, Heike Pienkoss, Sara Sanchez Mera, and Birgit Thies deconstruct the experience of their project group and thus give an account of a knowledge project from within. Key issues are the difficulties of establishing cross-cultural communication, the challenges of self-organized group work, the value of moderation, and finally the cooperation on common results. To communicate the insights gained in this process the participants staged a theater play showing their struggles and their eventual success.

Drawing primarily on experiences gained in organizing and teaching at *ifu*, Christiane Floyd presents a constructivist understanding of knowledge projects as cooperative settings for self-organized group learning, and discusses how knowledge projects can be guided by the teachers, framed by the organizers, and supported by information technologies so as to facilitate the unfolding processes. In social settings shaped by constraints, clashes of interest and hierarchies, the utopian vision embodied in knowledge co-construction can only be realized to a limited extent.

Ingrid Wetzel, *ifu*'s Internet Training Advisor, focusses on teaching computer usage skills as a basic prerequisite for media competence (this was a major interest of many *ifu*-participants). Computer Usage skills are acquired by doing, updating and dealing with uncertain, incomplete and scattered information. In a woman-friendly learning culture background, basic and meta-knowledge have to be provided, and concrete experience at the computer needs to be reflected in group settings to develop a shared understanding of the challenges and difficulties involved.

Cheris Kramarae & Zhang Wei assess the potential of online education for women at a global level. They see globalization as affecting the whole world but benefiting only a few countries, driven as it is by the interests of capital and worldwide corporations. Online education might reach women who are tied to their homes, but it is expensive. Also teaching materials often provide a monocultural Western view with no local embedding. To remedy the situation, experts from different cultures and in particular women should be involved in curricular design.

The overall situation of women and education is aptly visualized in the *Future of Education* website. There is a wall to show the obstacles, with individual bricks named 'access', 'discrimination', 'gender roles', and so on. But there is also a ladder that allows women to take steps for overcoming the barrier. The work at *ifu* and the website itself will hopefully contribute to providing a ladder!

Christiane Floyd

Lisa Link, Therona Moodley, Heike Pienkoss, Sara Sanchez
Mera, Birgit Thies
With: Joyce Agalo, Francoise Amye Menyengue, Uppuluri
Ananta Laxmi, Ilona Blinova, Mamota Das, Bokang Gwebu,
Vibha Joshi, Cheris Kramarae, Sabine Prechter, Farzaneh
Raji, Viktoria Sukovataya, Zhang Wei

A Culture of Cooperation:
Making the Journey the Destination

"We must recognize that underneath the superficial classifications of sex and race the same potentialities exist." *(Margaret Mead)*

Abstract
This chapter subjectively examines the experience of five members of the *Future of Education* project group at the International Women's University (*ifu*). Their voices reflect the multi-cultural, multi-disciplinary, and multi-generational composition of the group. It is an examination of the processes which took place in summer 2000 and describes how the group's journey towards a tangible project outcome became an important factor in the creation of an ongoing culture of cooperation.

1 Introduction

This chapter is an attempt to deconstruct the very particular group experience of the *Future of Education* project group in the Project Area INFORMATION at *ifu* in Hamburg. By adopting a subjective approach to what is often perceived from outside as a radical feminist notion – an international university for women – we are acknowledging the continuing experimental nature of our group process. Almost a year after our period of residency, our group is still evolving and dealing with the challenges of sustaining collaborative ventures via the new digital media. To position ourselves within a static theoretical framework is to negate the 'white-water' metaphor which characterizes collaborations of this composition and nature.

If the authors are to define a guiding ethos of this chapter, it would be couched in the Zen belief that 'the journey is the destination.' While 'living *ifu*' – the three-month residency as members of the *Future of Education* project group (see also Kelkar et al in this volume) – the significance of the actual *process* as opposed to merely the 'end-product,' began to manifest itself. This chapter strives to make explicit and deconstruct this particular group process by reflecting on both the adverse and favorable elements of this collaboration.

Following this, we would like to situate our discussion within the subjective realm. This chapter is, essentially, a compilation of personal and subjective thoughts by members of the *Future of Education* project group. We do not intend to offer a scientific, theoretical and statistically proven synopsis of the possibilities and pitfalls of multi-cultural, multi-generational and multi-disciplinary cooperation. This approach, we feel, also bears testimony to our ongoing experimentation with long-distance collaboration via the new digital media.

This chapter is structured in the following manner: Section 2 (The Setting); Section 3 (Puzzling the Pieces: the Group Process); Section 4 (The Pieces Fit: Results) and Section 5 (Conclusion).

Symptomatic of the nature of our interaction, it is an interesting fact that despite this chapter being the collaboration of five women, oral communication was significantly absent during its preparation. Owing to geographical constraints – we represent three continents – e-mail communication was paramount, with evolving versions of the text being stored in a community system created on the Internet (see CommSy, 2001). You will encounter different writing styles and even different 'Englishes,' a fact which reflects the diversity of the group.

2 The Setting

> We were wedded together on the basis of mutual work and goals.
> *Judy Chicago*

The International Women's University (*ifu*) and its Project Area INFORMATION, residing at the University of Hamburg from July 15 to October 15, 2000 (cf. Virtual *ifu* 2000), gave us the unique opportunity to share lives, ideas and emotions with over a hundred women from all over the world.

Fifteen of these women, representing thirteen nationalities, were assigned to the project group *Future of Education* on the basis of their own choice and interest. This interdisciplinary team initially thought to examine developments and trends in higher education, focusing on their effect on women throughout the world, and to come up with some kind of final representative result (for the initial outline of the group compare *vifu* INFORMATION 2000). The 'director' and 'facilitator' of the group were, respectively, Cheris Kramarae, Professor at the Center for the Study of Women in Society, University of Oregon, USA, and

Zhang Wei, lecturer in the Department of English at Peking University, China (see Kramarae & Zhang, this volume).[1]

Figure 1: Photo of the group

3 Puzzling the Pieces: the Group Process

3.1 The Beginning

It would be fair to say that the first few group sessions were characterized by a state of pressure: the pressure to perform, both as individuals and as representatives of our institutions and countries, as well as the pressure as female researchers and scientists to produce a quality 'product' that would be scrutinized by the various donors, sponsors and the academic community at large. The urgent questions were: How do we define a topic? How do we address our various needs and institutional agendas? How do we balance personal expectations within the group dynamic?

With the benefit of hindsight, it is clear that the group dynamic was initially flawed by its dependence upon traditional, conservative methods of interaction often favored by the tertiary education institutions from which we came. After all, we were a group whose members were tenuously linked by their work in the field of education. Even within this common domain, it soon became apparent that our particular interests were as divergent as our expectations. As participants we did not all enjoy the same liberties regarding choice of end product –

---

1   For further information on the participants, please refer to the group's website – *see Future of Education 2000*.

some participants were pressurized by institutional expectations, which were often conservative and traditional and in direct opposition to the radical assumptions of *ifu*.

Driven by this performance and deliverance anxiety, members reverted to the seminar format, trusting that this mode of interaction would be both an introduction and a 'way in.' We compiled reading lists and delivered presentations following a makeshift round table format. It was not long before the frustrations induced by this method became obvious. This process also highlighted a peculiar phenomenon – excessive politeness and diffidence, which ironically had the effect of hampering the group dynamic rather than fostering it. The accepted ethos of political and cultural sensitivity, especially heightened in those early days, while a cogent element of such a diverse group, often resulted in a blurring of the distinction between individual personalities and cultural stereotypes. Thus, members metaphorically tip-toed around discussions, in an ever widening circle of frustration and anxiety.

Having, at this initial juncture, no group-sanctioned forum for disagreement, some members retreated into silence, a few absented themselves without explanation and others engaged in an over-enthusiastic attempt to find solutions.

The experimental nature of *ifu*, while fostering creativity and innovation, also meant that there was a profound redefinition of roles and expectations. Concomitant with our assumption of the role of learners, there was an expectation of guidance (not to be mistaken for dictation) from the appointed director and facilitator, especially since they were selected on the basis of their expertise and research in the particular field. In the initial stages, considerable confusion arose when the director and facilitator performed as 'ordinary' members of the group by participating rather than directing or guiding.

The role of gender in the group dynamic cannot be fully analyzed as we lack a comparable experience in a mixed-sex group setting. Nevertheless, certain observations made during this phase can assumedly be ascribed to gender. Despite an increasing level of frustration during this phase – it seemed as if no progress was being made – there was a notable reluctance of any one person to assume the leadership position. Even the more assertive and vigorous members of the group refrained from taking on this role. It can only be speculated whether this behavior is attributable to various motives (e.g. a fear of appearing authoritarian) or values (importance of group consensus). This phenomenon nevertheless illustrates that the manifestation of rivalry and power-play for leadership, common in mixed-sex and all-male groups, was not observed in the group process.

It should be clear that while the group dynamic was indicative of an internal struggle for an identity and focus, a profusion of ideas were, nonetheless, being generated. Relying upon tested methods of cooperative work, such as brainstorming, the group churned out various topics in the search for a relevant project theme – the search for a symbol (3.2) is a vivid example of this. And it remains to be said that despite the obvious frustrations, most group members re-mained passionate about the project area.

3.2 In Search of a Symbol

Following two weeks of intensive, regularly scheduled meetings, without any tangible outcome or satisfactory direction for further group-work, the possibility of developing a symbol was earnestly discussed. The symbol, intended to be a visual metaphor for our project group's central focus on women's education, was to transcend cultural differences and interpretations. This symbol-search aptly captured the group's desire to concretely represent, to both ourselves and others, a common agreement about our goal and expected outcomes.

The search for a 'guiding' symbol led to numerous creative suggestions, which were first collated and then presented and explained by their 'advocates.' The following description gives an overview of the proposed symbols:

- *The quilt*: A symbol for the joint group work: everyone brings in her different ideas, ways and patterns of 'quilting,' which will be connected with the others' contributions. At the end of the work process there will be a coherent whole which is both useful and beautiful.
- *The garden*: A visual image providing a 'wholesome view on education' with all the different categories and types of plants symbolizing different educational 'levels.' Wise gardeners (educators) are needed to sustain this garden as a good place to be, a place where seeds are sown, plants nurtured to grow and mature.
- *The city*: A city in the form of a web page standing for a multi-cultural community, each nation living in its own house. Parts of the houses are in disrepair, thus symbolizing the specific national problems (regarding not only education but also culture, economics, politics and social affairs). One 'model house' with an ideal shape represents solutions for the shortcomings of the other homes.
- *The tree*: Equally imagined as an image on a website. The tree provides a global view on higher education, which is not static but growing. The branches symbolize the different continents, the boughs respective countries with flowers, leaves and fruits showing intra-country differences in educational affairs and strategies.
- *The dictionary*: A feminist dictionary for the 'future of education' in a flexible and workable form – more of a process than a ready result. By collecting and connecting relevant words we could find out cultural differences as well as commonalties regarding education – acting in the tradition of feminist research, which has often stressed the importance of language.

- *The city-map*: Education symbolized via a transportation route map in a city. To get to a certain point one may have to change the mode of transport, speed or direction. The map would be graphically conceived so as to provide the user with the most appropriate method to achieve an educational goal.
- *The recipe book*: Giving 'recipes' for education as pieces of constructive and flexible 'how to'-advice for solving educational shortcomings. The book would contain 'recipes' stemming from very different (cultural) experiences, allowing the 'cook' to adapt the ideas to the local situation.

The remarkable profusion of seemingly 'common' symbols proposed by the group members very clearly showed how different the concepts and 'worlds of ideas' were. The images were meant to convey numerous aspects – and naturally no single one could incorporate all of these:

- to show a global view on education and connected fields;
- to connect the global and the local and bring together different individual cultures in one 'unifying' image;
- to critically identify (educational) weaknesses and provide constructive suggestions to find remedies;
- to ensure openness and flexibility and show the evolving nature of the subject.

The symbols had one aspect in common: they all provided for *diversity* on different levels, bringing differences together into a common whole. This was the crux of the matter for the group at this particular stage – how to creatively and successfully utilize the diverse strengths, attitudes, cultural and social beliefs of fifteen women to a common end?

Initially the search for a guiding symbol was a failure – we did not succeed in finding an image equally relevant for the whole group. The demands on the symbol were simply too high and furthermore opinions about its focus differed – it had to be generally understandable, preferably 'culturally neutral,' adaptable and flexible, appealing and relevant, feasible for future work. Even a culturally homogeneous group would have found such a multi-functional image difficult to conceive.

With hindsight, the 'fruitless discussions' were not as unproductive as initially experienced. They had the unexpected effect of highlighting the features significant to the members within the project: the harmonious view, a hands-on approach, a socio-political perspective. They also defined our different perspectives and reinforced a strong desire to develop a project sanctioned by all its members.

3.3 Moderated Discussions

Stuck in an increasingly frustrating search for a topic and working structure, relief appeared in the form of a professional discussion moderator. Being an outsider to *ifu*, she approached both the group and the content from a neutral stance. After two moderated sessions, initial group skepticism about the value of moderation ceased. Moderation may be credited with a significant shift in the group dynamic.[2] The moderation company's philosophy (see Metaplan, 2001) promised to deliver what the group was striving to achieve:

> We facilitate processes that generate shared understanding, ... (We) develop possibilities for action and encourage venturing into new territory. ... We 'translate' between different constructions of thought and build bridges of understanding.

In the multi-generational, multi-cultural and multi-disciplinary academic milieu of *ifu*, this moderation method proved to be a non-threatening form of communication allowing for 'safe' expression of discontent and approval. More significantly, it was a way forward, through the diverse ideas, opinions and emotions.

The general baselines of this moderation technique may be summarized as follows. Before the start of a moderated discussion relatively strict *rules* are put up:

- there are only 30 seconds of speaking time;
- the contributions to the discussion are written up on rectangular cards – only one argument per card of more than one word but less than three lines;
- objections are marked right away in the form of red flashes on the respective cards, the comments are subsequently written on oval cards and posted nearby.

The purpose of these discussion rules is to guarantee an 'efficient and effective discourse.' Everyone is given the opportunity to speak, and argumentation chains and relations are made visible as the discussion proceeds by writing down every argument on a single card and pinning it to a large pin board. By doing this, all comments are condensed and clarified by the moderator, who paraphrases the argument and gives the author the possibility to fix misunderstandings. There may be different colors to differentiate between argument categories if necessary.

The *flashmark* facilitates the expression of doubts and contradictions in a structured and – in connection with the paraphrase technique – objective rather than emotional way. The idea of visualizing the whole bundle of ideas and ob-

---

2   We would like to take this occasion to thank Bérengère Gonin from Metaplan GmbH, Hamburg, once more for her voluntary commitment and her interest in the demanding multi-cultural setting of the group.

jections on one sheet of paper is to encourage the acceptance of divergent ideas. On the other hand, similar arguments and topics can be easily spotted and grouped together, to stress the agreement already existing in the group.

When different relevant topics have been identified it is often necessary to rate their importance for the group – especially if restrictions of time or money have to be considered. In the moderation method this is done in a democratic procedure – every group member distributes a fixed amount of 'votes' symbolized by sticking points onto the topics. Here the allocation of several votes permits a more detailed picture of the group preferences than a single vote could give. In addition, there are less 'left over' ideas and it is clear that their rejection does not apply to their authors but is instead based on the overall picture of circumstances and ideas present. Another aspect worth mentioning is that the personal posting of votes is in itself an expressive process resulting in a more convincing and enduring picture of the group's opinion than a vote by show of hands could ever give.

All in all the moderation method provides both flexibility ('movable' ideas on the pin board, openness to extensions) and structure (written arguments and contradictions, grouping and valuation of topics) to cope with the initial 'fluidity' and diversity of ideas and thoughts. The mere 'collection' of arguments related to each question is structured and evaluated step by step, and finally shaped into a firm notion acceptable to all parties.

How did this moderation method help our group? We began with a reflection of the current deficits in women's contemporary education, differentiating between problems of developed and developing countries and worldwide problems. We then prioritized the topics we found and formed working groups to tackle the five issues which we deemed the most important: problems connected with women's learning styles, discrimination, access, language, and gender roles. After this crucial first step we still had to define the subtopics and working modes within the subgroups as well as a way to convey our results. In the second moderated session, the group was able to work in independent subgroups, using the new visualization methods.

It became apparent that the cardinal benefit of the moderated sessions was a revitalization of team spirit and the ability to critically engage with each other in a constructive and relaxed atmosphere. The (humorously utilized) notion of the *flashmark* continued to function as a group-sanctioned forum for disagreement.

4 The Pieces Fit: Results

> It is better to travel hopefully than to arrive.
> *Robert Louis Stevenson*

4.1 The Theater Play

An important moment for the *Future of Education* group occurred when project groups were required at mid-term to deliver a presentation on their intermediate results and their visions. By adopting a theatrical play as our mode of presentation, we showed that the process itself was as significant as the end result of developing a resource space on the web (see 4.3). Our struggle, for indeed that was what it was, to define a project and situate ourselves within it, offered as much insight into women's education as our final product did.

Against this background, we developed the rather unorthodox idea of staging a play instead of giving a formal presentation of findings, which at that stage, would have been a rudimentary factual framework only. Our decision to utilize drama as a medium was a significant, unanimous group decision. It also provided us as a group with the license to explore and integrate alternative, creative methods of communication and interaction within the academic environment.

The play[3] started with a verbal metaphor of our different origins: one project member after the other rose up from their seats in the auditorium saying "I am the future of education" in their respective native languages.

After this the play took the form of a pantomime relying purely on non-verbal communication. Basic body language, gestures, and facial expressions were used as the common ground of all human beings in a multi-cultural setting. Upon gathering at the front of the auditorium, the project group members shook hands as the Western form of first formal contact between strangers, which represents the will to cooperate as well as initial distance. Then we displayed how we overcame our superficial differences, individual interests, and in some cases personal shyness with the aid of the moderation technique. In the final scene the group members stood in a line facing the audience and holding hands. To express the bonds which had developed by then, all group members spoke in unison saying "We are the future of education" in English.

Judging by the audience's reaction we struck a chord in them. Apparently, by exhibiting our initial confusion and vulnerability, as well as openly admitting our struggle and aggression, we had reflected a process all the groups could relate to. Yet, it was this combination of process and result which was unique.

---

3   A video of the performance is available. Please contact Heike Pienkoss (pienkoss@gmx.net).

4.2 Ambitious Plans: the Conference Application

Another distinct manifestation of our new group identity was our application to hold a discussion workshop at the International Conference on Open Learning and Distance Education, to be held in Düsseldorf (Germany) the following year (see ICDE World conference 2000 for the related website). The main objective of the conference, organized by the International Council for Open and Distance Education (ICDE, see ICDE 2000), was to analyze the development of learning and to explore how open learning and distance education, virtual training and 'e-learning' would locate themselves in the technologically evolving learning environments of the future.

Despite the incomplete status of the final project, uncertainties surrounding funding and which group members would be able to attend, as well as an imminent closing date for application, members were sufficiently encouraged by the positive and creative group spirit to submit a proposal. A successful application would be a validation of our work in the field of women's education as well as an opportunity to extend the life of the project group beyond the *ifu* residency period.

The application was successful and our proposed discussion workshop on 'The Future of Women's Global Education' was scheduled as an extension event at the conference. Subsequently, five members (the authors of this chapter) participated in the conference, where aspects of the moderation system were utilized to structure and initiate discussion in our workshop. The workshop was positively received and the level of active participation by those attending – of both sexes – confirmed the relevance of and a renewed interest in the issue of women's education.

Of the five topics proposed by the moderators, the participants chose the following three statements for critical scrutiny:

- "The Internet will make education available to women throughout the world."
- "Online education will reduce gender bias."
- "Women's education is a largely untapped market."

As with our *ifu* experience, the participants especially valued and praised the methodology utilized to conduct the workshop. Again, the moderation technique provided for a lively discussion among all attendants (for an outline of the contributions and the final conclusions see Link, 2001).

4.3 The 'Resource Space' on the Internet

With women representing more than half of the world's population we believe that women's education will be one of the biggest issues in the development of the global economy and in the revolution of communication and information technology (see Moodley, Pienkoss & Prechter, 2001). Therefore, one of our aims was to raise awareness of the barriers that confront women globally in their quest for higher education.

Given the limited time span within which the project group had to effectively produce a final outcome, we decided to install a website. Other reasons which motivated this option: at the present time, it is the most flexible platform for and means of publication since it may be enlarged and updated continuously even after the phase of face-to-face contact has ended. With the subject 'The Future of Education' being of extraordinary scope it has been impossible to cover and work extensively on every aspect. Therefore we developed an online presentation which serves as a 'resource space' aiming at giving an overview and inviting other researchers and practitioners to participate and comment.

Concomitant with our attempt to find a visual expression for our area of research which is both easily understood and as culturally neutral as possible we created an image of a wall for the first page of the website. Each brick represents an impediment that women encounter in their quest for higher education. A ladder symbolizes the steps that have to be taken in order to overcome the barriers. We hope that our website will, in part, help to serve as a ladder, highlighting some of the major issues in women's higher education and providing relevant resources to anyone interested in this field.[4]

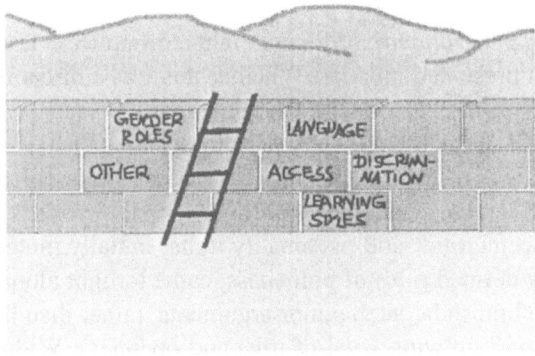

Fig. 2: Picture of the wall

---

4   See *Future of Education 2000* for the web address of the site, a more detailed description is also given in Moodley, Pienkoss & Prechter, 2001.

Due to time restrictions and for feasibility reasons the project group had split into five subgroups working on those subjects identified and voted 'most important' or 'most interesting' in the moderated discussions. Within the subgroups the workload was again divided between the members so that each individual member contributed to our common goal according to her own preference. Two members of the project group volunteered to design, program and install the web pages while the other members mainly delivered content. Against the background of time constraints and with participants returning to the demands and obligations of regular life, the commitment towards the maintenance of the site has proved somewhat problematic. Furthermore, despite the new technologies fostering long-distance interaction, it is a meager substitute for the bond of physical proximity. A more salient point is the fact that the Internet is not equally accessible to all participants. Although we have had to readjust our over-ambitious targets in terms of update frequency, the website still serves as a source of inspiration and as a basis for further research.

5 Conclusion

The continuing, if not intensified interaction of certain members of the group on various projects bears testimony to the successful dynamic in existence at the end of the three-month residency at the University of Hamburg. Aware of the vagaries of distance communication and the demands of work and 'real' life, the group nonetheless remains committed to developing research begun under the auspices of *ifu*. If we were to critically examine our process, the following would be considered key areas in the development of a healthy cooperative dynamic.

Cultural and generational differences in the group were less significant than might have been presumed initially. Whether this was a direct result of personal interaction between individuals and each member's personal contribution or of the shared interest in the topic is very hard to decide. Whatever the reason, it is insignificant in light of the end results. It certainly helped that most members were highly proficient in academic English.

Individual peculiarities and personality traits, initially muted by an acquiescence to socially defined rules of politeness, came to light along with a growing familiarity. With hindsight, such minor arguments, rather than being destructive, were indicative of a growing level of trust and openness. Within the context of our project group, these verbal indicators of particular personality types actually fostered communication rather than hindered it. Our adoption of the moderation method (see 3.3) with its highly structured management of dissenting opinions was critical in the formulation of our eventual research topic and in the devel-

opment of a relaxed, healthy and cooperative environment. Considering the severe pressure the time constraints exerted on the group dynamic, the implementation of the moderation method extracted our debates from the realm of the personal and cultural and firmly situated them within non-emotional academic discourse.

A major impediment to the group process was, undoubtedly, the *time factor*.
As explained in the introduction, members began group interaction as absolute
strangers and continued in this vein for a considerable period. The various pressures detailed earlier, worked against the development of an atmosphere which
would have engendered progress – academic progress as well as the development of an informal network. It should be mentioned that despite the radical
nature of *ifu*, the restricted time period coerced groups into relying on rather traditional forms of co-operative interaction.

The ideal solution would of course be an extension of the residency period.
Since this was not possible, a formal implementation of a moderation method or
similar scaffolded management methods of discussions and decision-making
processes would stimulate this environment and function as a springboard to a
more significant group interaction. The differences evident in the 'pre-' and
'post-moderation' images of our group speak to its significant role in both our
academic and social interactions. Ironically, it was only after the identification
of our project theme and its sub-sections that members displayed any interest in
developing a *social dimension* to the group. Prior to this we would adhere
strictly to the stipulated group time within the university work environment. This
social interaction, however, had the not entirely unexpected effect of enhancing
our project interaction. Jokes and jests on issues considered sensitive in the
work environment became permissible in the informal setting. This had the effect of making it possible for us to deal with and to ease the tensions accumu-
lated around these topics.

Again, the fluid definition of the *role of the project director and the facilitator* within the group process and their often perceived ineffectiveness may be
attributed to the time factor. Had we had more time, the director, the facilitator
and the group would have been able to re-formulate duties and expectations.
Within the implemented work schedule, however, groups initially, in the absence of any structure or perceived goal, adopted a rather traditional view of the
function of the directors and facilitators. By the end of the three months the
group was effectively responsible for all aspects of the process as well as being
self-motivated and functioning. Obviously this was an intended aim of the project work – one that might have benefited from more structural and methodologi-
cal guidance at the very beginning (see the chapter by Floyd in this volume for a
general discussion of this problem).

All in all, our experience shows that especially in such a highly experimental setting as *ifu* one has to allow for enough time and space for people to build

up mutual trust, to open up and to find a 'common tongue' beyond their multi-cultural versions of English. Although these internal, social cohesion developments are generally not appreciated in academic discourse – probably because they are not scientifically measurable – an understanding of the process enhances future collaborative work. If a focus is put on these processes and on the ways in which they may be supported, one may gain knowledge which is far beyond any academic agenda.

References

CommSy (2001). *Community System Server*. Source: http://commsy.uni.de/; accessed June 21, 2001.
Future of Education (2000). *Future of Women's Higher Education*. Source: http://www.ifu.uni-hamburg.de/webspace/education; accessed March 2002.
ICDE (2000). *International Council for Open and Distance Education*. Source: http://www.icde.org/; accessed August 2000.
Link, Lisa (2001). *Summary of the Contributions and Conclusions of the Workshop at the ICDE-Conference 2001*. Unpublished.
Metaplan (2001). Source: http://www.metaplan.com/; accessed July 17, 2001.
Moodley, Therona; Pienkoss, Heike & Prechter, Sabine (2001). Strategies for Web-Based Women's Education. In: *Education and Science*, no. 2, pp. 29-32. Source: http://www.inter-nationes.de/d/pub/bw/e/bw.html; accessed September 2001.
Vifu INFORMATION (2000). Source: http://www.vifu.de/areas/information/projects.html#three; accessed March 2002.
Virtual *ifu* (2000). Source: http://www.vifu.de/; accessed March 2002.
World Conference (2000). *Proceedings of the ICDE World Conference 2001 in Düsseldorf, Germany*. Source: http://www.fernuni-hagen.de/ICDE/D-2001/; accessed August 2000.

Christiane Floyd

Towards Knowledge Co-construction

Abstract
This chapter focusses on cooperative processes of building knowledge in contexts such as learning, decision-making or design. Starting from individual perspectives, knowledge co-construction involves unique, creative ways of appropriating and interpreting existing knowledge, and integrating different views into common results. Knowledge projects unfold through self-organization, where each actively engaging participant at once contributes to and intervenes in the process. Thus, group work and organization, management and team leadership, as well as the roles of teachers and learners, appear in a new light. Drawing on experiences gained in organizing, teaching, and providing technical support for *ifu*, the discussion is centered on how knowledge projects can be guided, framed and supported.

1 Introduction

The term 'knowledge co-construction' originating from recent debates in applied epistemology is used here in a broad sense to evoke a re-thinking of knowledge in comparison to established views of the rationalist tradition embedded in Western philosophy of science. *Knowledge* is seen as situated – shaped by individual standpoints and collective thinking styles, embedded in activity and fitted to needs and interests. Knowledge *Construction* denotes a shift of emphasis from a static view, in which knowledge can be 'had' – acquired, possessed, or passed on – to processes of building insights unfolding in time in unique, creative ways. *Co-*construction suggests that these are not processes carried out by individuals alone, but through interaction with others in communities or groups.

In what follows, I shall use the term 'knowledge project' as a common label for goal-oriented group work involving knowledge co-construction in different contexts. These include cooperative forms of learning and practice, the organization of scientific events and study programs, participatory approaches to community development, or design and use of technical artifacts. In all these contexts, knowledge projects can contribute significantly to democratic ways of proceeding and to the empowerment of individuals or groups. This, however, requires

1. for the participants: engaging in knowledge projects through bringing in one's own perspective and allowing it to be exchanged with others;
2. for the teachers or project leaders: guiding knowledge projects so as to facilitate insight building processes involving all participants; and
3. for the organizers: framing and supporting knowledge projects so as to enable autonomy and self-organization.

In particular, knowledge projects may provide a women-friendly learning environment based on cooperation and networking, accommodating different ways of knowing, and allowing for a combination of action and theorizing in flexible ways. In the present discussion, my aim is to promote a deeper understanding of knowledge projects, to propose ways of guiding and framing them, and to bring out options for their technological support.

In doing so, I will draw mainly on my experience at *ifu* (International Women's University). In *ifu*'s study program at the University of Hamburg I was engaged in several, interleaved roles: as the local dean of the Project Area INFORMATION, as the head of the Hamburg local team, and as a subcontractor for the virtual *ifu*. This meant that I was involved with and co-responsible for the curriculum, the organization of the study program and the technical infrastructure. Thus, I participated in *ifu*-activities at different levels and was able to perceive them as interconnected. In this chapter I will address the following levels:

• A one-day course on knowledge co-construction; my only opportunity of working directly with the students.
• The curricular projects, unfolding in twelve parallel groups throughout the study program.
• The joint effort of discussing and monitoring the ongoing curricular projects amongst the faculty and staff.
• The technical support for the curricular projects using the community system CommSy.

Apart from the course which I (like the other teachers at *ifu*) held on my own, all levels of the study program were prepared and conducted cooperatively.

Designing the curriculum in itself was a knowledge project, carried out by Silvie Klein-Franke and myself (and to some extent by Dorit Heinsohn) of the Hamburg local team with the curricular working group of our project area.[1] The other members of this group were Tone Bratteteig, Edla Maria Faust-Ramos, Govind

---

1   See the chapter by Floyd and Klein-Franke in this volume.

Kelkar, Cheris Kramarae, Irma Avila Pietrasanta, Heidi Schelhowe, Esther Williams and Marsha Woodbury. We each brought in our own experience from research, teaching, curricular design and the organization of scientific events.

None of us had ever been involved in an effort similar to *ifu* before. The unique character of this study program (as interpreted by us) challenged us to invent a mixture between a summer school and a graduate course for an unknown and heterogeneous audience. We had little time and very limited resources to do that. Like any other group, we had difficulties finding a common ground. To some extent we shared visions of how we hoped things would develop. To realize these visions, we proposed specific ways of proceeding. Although we had to cope with different teaching styles, expectations and constraints, as well as with continuing uncertainties regarding faculty members, participants, and resources, we produced results that provided the frame for the unfolding *ifu* in Hamburg.

We concentrated on the curricular projects, which we saw as the key element of the study program, though what we meant by 'project' varied according to our culture, discipline, and personal experience. During *ifu*, our roles would be different. The Hamburg local team would be engaged in enabling work, creating the conditions and providing the resources for the various learning activities. Heidi would concentrate on virtual *ifu*. All others would build up and direct curricular projects. We conceived these projects as interdisciplinary and intercultural forms of cooperation with a high degree of autonomy. We did not, however, fully foresee the difficulties involved in moderating and coordinating the ongoing project works.

The technical support for the project area was discussed in a separate group. The so-called virtual *ifu* (*vifu*), operating under Heidi's guidance from Berlin, provided an educational website for the whole *ifu*. The Hamburg part of *vifu*, with Wolf-Gideon Bleek as the central figure, was responsible for the technical infrastructure connecting the individual workplaces with the *vifu* server. It also provided computer support for the ongoing group work in the projects, relying on the web-based community system CommSy. Due to time and other constraints there was no systematic interaction between the infrastructure and the curricular working groups and no clear understanding beforehand of what the needs for technical support would be.

While we tried to prepare the study program as a coherent whole, I only learned during the *ifu* experience itself to consider it an overall knowledge project, which might have benefited from being recognized and framed as such. In retrospect, some measures taken seem appropriate, while others appear to have hindered the actual learning processes amongst the participants. In some cases the need for appropriate measures had not been anticipated and we were left to improvisation. Learning from these experiences may be helpful to others engaged in promoting cooperative forms of learning.

2 A Flower Bouquet of Knowledges

To illustrate the potential of knowledge co-construction, I would like to start
with an example from a teaching experience at *ifu*. My one-day course *Building
Insights Together – Knowledge Co-Construction* attracted 19 participants from
Albania, Bosnia-Hercegovina, Argentina, Australia, Brazil, Chad, Egypt, Germany, Kenya, Mexico, Nigeria, Romania, South Korea, Sri Lanka, Sudan, and
Tanzania with various disciplinary backgrounds. In planning the day, I wondered how I could engage this mixed group in a discussion on my topic. Just
going into applied epistemology seemed very dry. Fortunately, I could draw on
the inspiration from two recent *ifu*-lectures. Govind Kelkar had reminded us
how, in an international context, we should be talking in the plural about
'knowledges', and Ina Wagner had just delivered her talk on creative visualization (see Kelkar and Wagner, both in this volume).

This gave me the idea to start the course with a group activity which provided an example for knowledge co-construction by working together on the
concept of 'knowledge' itself. I introduced this with three transparencies shown
in Figure 1.

From the "Tree of Knowledge" – Part of Judeo-Christian and Islamic Tradition – Title of a highly relevant book by H. Maturana and F. Varela *to a "Flower Bouquet of Knowledges"* – How do we view knowledge (as individuals, in our culture)? – How does this relate to established philosophical views? – What would be a rich notion of knowledge?
"Knowledge" is a constructed concept Originating from a history of usage going way back to Indo-Germanic roots – Drawing (at least) from Greek, Latin, Germanic, and Celtic sources – Located in a field of semantic connotations in the English language – Shaped by centuries of English-based philosophical discussion
Making your Knowledge Flower – What is the word for knowledge in your language? Write it down in your script, and if needed, in ours as well! – What are related words in your language? Re-translate some (3-5) into English and write them down! – What concepts are related to knowledge in your culture? Name some important connections or contrasts! – Visualize your conceptual structure by using the words as petals, arranged in a flower shaped any way you like.

Figure 1: Guidance for Group Activity on '*Knowledge* Co-construction:
Building the Concept of Knowledge Together'

To start the process, I gave an example drawing on my own language, German.
Translating 'knowledge' into 'Wissen', I pointed out that the associated field of
connotations is different from its English counterpart. On the language level,

related words include 'Weisheit' (wisdom), 'Bewusstsein' (consciousness), 'Gewissen' (conscience) and 'Wissenschaft' (a collective term for the humanities and sciences). Important concepts connected with 'Wissen' are 'Können' (the former denoting 'knowing that', the latter 'knowing how'), and 'Glauben' (belief, often contrasted with knowledge).

After that, I equipped the students with basic materials such as colored cards, scissors, scotch tape and marking pens, and set them to work. Some stayed on their own, others joined with partners speaking their language. After one hour's creativity fourteen magnificent flowers were presented, showing a rich diversity of culturally shaped views of knowledge. The comments given to explain the individual flowers showed fundamental differences in approach.

For presentation in this chapter I have chosen a subset of flowers that in my eyes exemplifies specific ways how conceptions of knowledge differ[2], namely: How is knowledge seen as related to human beings? And how is knowledge connected with religion? Since the participants are no longer available for discussion, the interpretation given here is mine – based on the shapes of the flowers as well as on the inscriptions of the petals – and undoubtedly reveals my own background as a Catholic Austrian, having lived in the U.S. and in Germany. I hope that the account given is sufficiently accurate to be acceptable to the authors.

The Australian Knowledge Flower (Figure 2) renders the view of knowledge familiar in the English language.

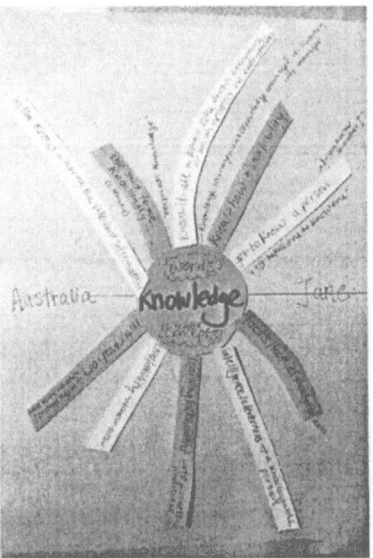

Figure 2: Australian Knowledge Flower by Jane Gibian

---

2   The figures are based on slides of the originals made by Tatjana Beer.

It shows different shades of meaning: 'to know' can refer to having information or factual knowledge, to possessing a skill, or to being acquainted with a person[3]. Through learning, you can come to possess knowledge and thus be 'a knowledgeable person'. 'Being in the know' shows how knowledge becomes operational. So, knowledge is something that individuals can acquire and have, that can be passed on, and that enables you to act.

By contrast, the Kiswahili Knowledge Flower (Figure 3) shows knowledge linked with human faculties. Around the inscription 'knowledgeable' in the center, we find petals labeled 'experience', 'awareness', and 'understanding'. 'Intelligence' and 'wisdom' are so closely related that they appear together on one petal. In commenting, two different notions of wisdom were distinguished: one that anyone can aspire to, and another that can only be acquired through age. In this conception, there is no way to separate knowledge from the human individual and no sharp boundary between knowing and other forms of human experience (similar ideas were visualized in knowledge flowers based on other black African languages).

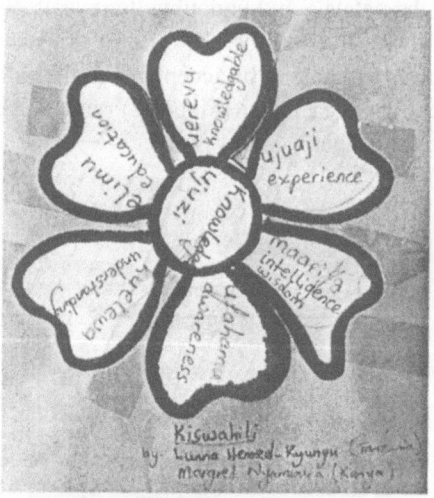

Figure 3: Kiswahili Knowledge Flower by Lunna Hemed-Kyungu (Tanzania) and Margaret Ndung'u (Kenya)

The Brazilian Knowledge Flower (Figure 4), embedded in the Catholic tradition, displays a double flower with two options available to the human individual. Knowledge and belief grow on one stem, but are separate. In the petals of the main blossom both knowledge and wisdom can be found. Branching off at the side, we find the believer and the act of believing. Duality, contrasting, for ex-

---

3   In German there are three words 'wissen', 'können' and 'kennen' to convey these different shades of meaning.

ample, science and religion, or facts and values, is constitutive for the conception of knowledge displayed here. These dichotomies, originating in the European history of thought, have, through colonialism, been influential in other parts of the world as well.

Figure 4: Brazilian Knowledge Flower by Maria Luiza de Mello e Souza

A quite different arrangement, suggested by the Muslim tradition, is visualized in the Arabic Knowledge Flower (Figure 5).

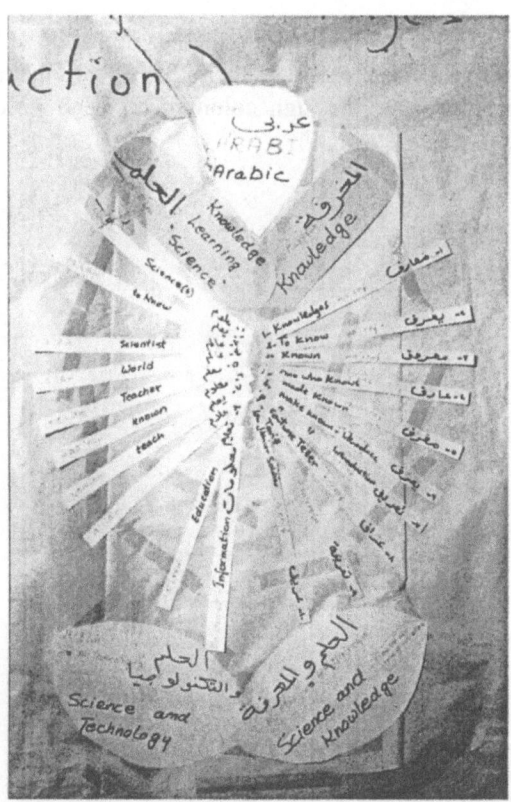

Figure 5: Arabic Knowledge Flower by Mona El Tobgui (Egypt) and Hanan Satti (Sudan)

Here, the concept of knowledge appears to be twofold: in a narrower sense it pertains to knowledge in connection with science and technology, this appears as linked with a broader notion of knowledge that includes religious ways of knowing. Both have a wealth of connotations relating to activities of learning and to people working with knowledge, for example, associated with the narrower concept we find the teacher and the scientist, and in the broader context also the fortune teller and even a junior rank in the army. Knowledge in the broad sense definitely goes beyond the individual, as it is said to come 'from the solid base of societies'.

The Sri Lankan Knowledge Flower, in the Buddhist tradition (Figure 6), views 'knowledge' in the sense of cognition, and displays it as conditioned by influence factors. The most important ones, shown above, are education, the local Sinhala culture, and Buddhism. To explain the intricate combination of influence factors, three more religions (Christianity, Islam and Hinduism) are brought into play, as well as history, foreign relations and the modern media. Note that there is no mention of individuals here, no dualism of knowing and believing, no separation of knowledge and wisdom, and no suggestion of any relation of knowing to action.

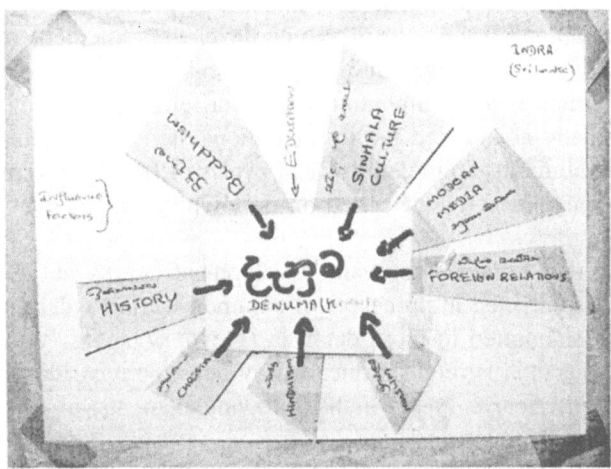

Figure 6: Sri Lankan Knowledge Flower by Indra Ranasinghe

The diversity of the fourteen flowers was greatly admired in the group. Regrettably, we had to restrict ourselves to being fascinated by and trying to appreciate the individual conceptions. Attempting to understand and relate the differences, or even building a rich notion of knowledge taking them into account, would be an immensely difficult undertaking, way beyond what our group could hope to achieve or I was able to facilitate. And it would take time.

3 Engaging in Knowledge Co-Construction

Engaging in knowledge co-construction is more than just participating in knowledge projects, it means doing so with an awareness of the processes involved. As we found out at *ifu*, there are different avenues for becoming sensitized to knowledge co-construction. Amongst them are adult education, participatory design and development, and feminist discussions on standpoint-related knowledge.

My understanding originates from design in the area of software development. The work within the development team and the cooperation between developers and users can both be seen as knowledge projects. In traditional software engineering, knowledge building is understood in strictly rationalistic terms as proceeding through abstraction and formalization. But in supervising students I found that any two groups – even when confronted with the same problem and supposedly following the same method – proceed differently, each participant bringing in his or her perspective. They elaborate their own problem view, interpret the method in their own way and work towards what they consider an appropriate solution. Thus, 'problem setting' and 'problem solving' are intertwined in unique creative ways. When developers interact with users, even more perspectives are brought into play, relating to a variety of interests and fields of experience, and communicated in different professional languages. Thus, I eventually abandoned the linear notions associated with the top-down method in my home discipline, in favor of cycles of (re-)design, (re-)implementation and (re-)use of software, based on prototyping and evaluating partial results.

In the present context, software development serves as an example for working groups engaged in processes of common learning, decision-making or designing. As elaborated in more detail in (Floyd 1992), my understanding of knowledge projects is strongly influenced by constructivist ideas (in particular by Heinz von Foerster) and rests on the following elements:

- Knowledge projects are constituted by the participants, unfold through self-organization, and cannot be pre-determined.
- Project groups set (and revise) their own goals, the goals imposed from outside are reinterpreted and turned into own goals by the group.
- Knowledge projects build their own common ground in terms of how they set up and maintain an agenda, negotiate priorities, distribute work, make decisions and handle conflicts.
- Knowledge building rests on the appropriation of existing knowledge – facts and interpretations, theories, methods, and so on – from different areas and the configuration of these elements in a relevant way.
- Knowledge building is enabled through diversity and options for choice and consists in networks of distinction- and decision-making.
- Knowledge co-construction proceeds through shared activities resulting in artifacts that are evaluated, and through communication providing feedback.
- A knowledge project succeeds if the group produces common results that it deems fitting to the established goals and articulated concerns.

In literature, cooperative processes of learning are dealt with in the light of hermeneutic, pragmatic, culturalist, and constructivist schools of thought, all challenging the claims of science to objective knowledge. Depending on the author, these theories are considered to be (partially) contradicting or complementing one another. As may have become evident in the introduction, I am committed to the latter approach.

The views proposed here relate directly to the ideas on learning processes based on Maturana's notion of autopoiesis and Freire's notion of autonomy, as introduced by Dahms & Faust-Ramos in this volume. There is also a strong connection to the ideas of Bratteteig and Wagner in this volume, both emphasizing (in different ways) how design proceeds through creative work with materials and artifacts.

4 Guiding Knowledge Projects

When I became aware of knowledge co-construction, I was teaching and guiding knowledge projects in a university setting. Thus, I devised principles for group work along the lines described above, originally intended for software development, but more generally applicable (Floyd 1996). The most important arena for knowledge co-construction at *ifu* were the twelve curricular projects conducted in parallel over a period of three months and involving groups from five to fifteen participants. Thus, I introduced these principles through a lecture and a brief handout (consisting essentially of the recommendations given below) for the curricular projects where they were to be applied in an interdisciplinary and intercultural setting. In Figure 7, the general principles appear on the left side. On the right side, they are made concrete through specific suggestions addressed to those who would guide the *ifu* curricular projects.

These principles are called 'gestalt-oriented' because the idea is to promote the emergence of a shared understanding in groups. The German word 'gestalt', which has found its way into English usage, suggests a *whole* formed through perception from a collection of disparate elements. Since 'gestalten' is also the German word for designing, the term further suggests that the emerging whole is formed so as to be fitting to an intended purpose and at the same time be aesthetically pleasing. Depending on the context of the knowledge project, the emerging 'Gestalt' can be a vision, a plan for action or some kind of product – material or formal – as the result of knowledge co-construction.

As explained in my chapter with Klein-Franke, this volume, the curricular working group had decided that each project should be guided by one of its members as project *director* in cooperation with a project *facilitator* who would only join us shortly before *ifu* started. Therefore, the director was responsible for preparing the contents, goals and methods for the projects, while the facilitator was in charge of moderating the process. Furthermore, the idea was that each participant should be encouraged to bring in her ideas, concerns and case studies.

Establish and renew a common ground	– State objectives, make goals concrete – Bring out interests, expectations and responsibilities – Clarify modalities for co-operation – Insure quality management – Make the project plan concrete – Come back to these points regularly
Include and interrelate all participants	– Bring each participant into the group – Keep each participant in an active position – Empower interaction-weak participants – Form subgroups to strengthen networking
Articulate and exchange perspectives	– Be aware of dominating and implicit perspectives – Encourage the voicing of authentic perspectives – Strive to identify common points and differences
Bring out and accommodate diversity	– Do not impose, but propose your own plans, views and structures – Allow for alternative proposals – Acknowledge and deal with differences – Aim for a common understanding accommodating differences
Develop and reflect on a project language	– Bring out differences in concept-use – Deconstruct and reconstruct key concepts for the project – Be sensitive to emerging project-language – Keep track of project history in terms of language development
Adopt and exchange project roles	– Clarify the pre-established roles of director and facilitator – Assign and rotate special tasks (facilitating a session, keeping time, writing a protocol, evaluating results) – Make each participant a valuable specialist with a responsibility to the group
Support and co-ordinate incremental work	– Define small work steps and intermediate results – Set up quality criteria – Form subgroups for evaluating results – Find out how feedback is acceptable in different cultures – Give and take constructive criticism
Create and keep alive a milieu of trust	– Reflect on your own role (as director or facilitator) – Respect each participant – Negotiate responsibilities – Counteract destructive group mechanisms – Keep decisions transparent – Motivate and justify necessary changes – Do not take anything for granted

Figure 7: *Gestalt-oriented Principles of Group Work* as Presented to the Directors and Facilitators of Curricular Projects at *ifu*

Due to various circumstances and constraints – such as: some pairs of directors and facilitators had known each other before *ifu*, while others first met there; between some there was a distinct difference in seniority, while others were more or less equal; some directors stayed on site throughout the study program, while in other projects the facilitators worked largely on their own – the actual cooperation of project directors and facilitators took very different forms in the individual projects.

In my role as an organizer, I was not directly involved with any project and so I am unaware to what extent the directors and facilitators explicitly drew on the Gestalt-oriented principles in planning and reflecting their work. Rather, these principles sum up ways of proceeding that have been developed by many people involved in teaching and projects in different parts of the world. In this book, five project accounts (by El Tobgui & Gregory; Weber; Link et al; Kerr & Mätschke; Keskitalo & Limpangog) illustrate the struggles and the drama involved in moderating the group processes and show how different techniques were successfully used to promote communication. Also, my co-editor Lilac (Cirila P. Limpangog) gives an account of the open process in the project *Visions of Citizenship*, directed by Esther Williams, where she was the facilitator (Kelkar et al, this volume).

It is easy to see the relation of her account to several of the Gestalt-oriented principles: it is an excellent example of 'proposing' but not 'imposing' contents, methods and plans; a common ground is established by first discussing how to work with the participants; each participant is given the opportunity to voice her perspective (by using meta-cards); own goals are set by the group by re-interpreting what has been proposed in keeping with individual and shared perspectives.

The group processes were by no means always smooth – depending on the individual project it took between two and five weeks for the groups to establish their goals, find their concrete topic and plan their work. In some cases this brought about a good deal of uncertainty, frustration, and conflict that the pair of director and facilitator needed to handle.

I still think the double guidance of projects by director and facilitator was a good idea in principle. However, we grossly underestimated the difficulty of moderating the group processes, and we left the directors and facilitators more or less alone with them. The directors had volunteered for the projects because they related to their research interests. The facilitators were selected on the basis of relevant scientific qualifications so as to form international and interdisciplinary teams, but we had not paid much attention to whether they had experience with moderation. Guiding the project works was not only difficult for them because it involved communication both between disciplines and cultures. Moreover, the facilitators were in many cases on the same level of seniority as the participants themselves which made their role in the group problematic.

In retrospect, it seems clear that we should have provided for a moderation training at the beginning of *ifu* and for a supervision of the ongoing work by professional moderators having experience with interdisciplinary and international groups. This brings us to the more general question of how knowledge projects should be organized to promote knowledge co-construction in a felicitous way.

5 Framing Knowledge Projects

'Framing' will be understood here as the collection of all measures taken to create conditions for, organize and monitor knowledge projects. This means an interplay between project 'outsiders' who in one way or the other are responsible
for conducting the projects and 'insiders' comprising both the project leaders
and the other participants. Clearly, there is a hierarchy here, giving rise to questions such as how much autonomy is granted, how much control is attempted
and what efforts are made to influence the results.

In the case of framing the curricular projects the 'outsiders' involved were
the members of the Hamburg local team, including myself, not acting entirely on
our own accord but within the general framework of *ifu* that only gave us partial
autonomy for the Project Area INFORMATION. Some conditions we simply
passed on. For example, the fact that credit points were assigned for project
work brought about the need for keeping track of attendance, and the fact that
there would be a presentation at the end contributed significantly to the pressure
felt by the groups to produce results. While for the participants those constraints
may have been some of the most noticeable ones, the emphasis here will be on
the measures we took by choice in order to reflect on their merits.

The project directors had the double character of outsiders and insiders. As
members of the curricular working group they had taken many of the basic decisions for framing the projects together with us before *ifu* started, but then they
lived through the experience of the projects themselves. To some extent the
project facilitators can also be considered as both insiders and outsiders, as they
were involved in those framing decisions that were taken right before *ifu* started.

There was no systematic way of including the participants in the framing effort. Regrettably, *ifu* had not provided for a democratic forum of student representation. In our project area, there were occasional attempts at bringing in participants' initiatives, some of which we were able to accommodate, but mostly
the students' viewpoints reached the organizers either through personal conversations or through the directors and facilitators telling about their projects.

The most important measures for framing the projects were:

- *Organizational Model*: establishing the roles of project directors and facilitators; this was helpful but brought about the difficulties of how to cooperate
  which have already been described.
- *Project Definition*: ensuring that a project outline would be available ahead
  of time giving the problem, the methods, the expected results and so on.
  This made it possible for students to make a project choice before *ifu* (required in some cases to get a leave) and provided the basis for the project
  works.

- *Project Selection*: organizing a 'project bazaar' in the first week, enabling students to make an informed choice. This was a measure chosen in the last moment and certainly helpful, but since it had not been planned ahead of time, it caused a lot of extra work and made the first week very crowded.
- *Project Input*: planning courses, art workshops and lectures with a view to providing theories, methods and skills to the projects. This was a good idea in principle, but fraught with problems in practice due to difficulties in scheduling time, finding the appropriate level for the heterogeneous group of participants and keeping the work load at a reasonable level.
- *Work Reports*: requiring the groups to give a weekly summary of their on-going work. This requirement of the organizers was first considered a measure of unwanted control by the facilitators. It had to be implemented with great tact so as not to interfere with the privacy of the project groups, but eventually allowed to keep track of the ongoing work in a way that was satisfactory to both project insiders and outsiders.
- *Project Consultation*: inviting lecturers, expert *ifu* participants and guests to visit the projects. This arrangement worked very much on an individual basis and affected project groups in different ways. Some made their own contacts, others profited from guest lecturers.
- *Time Frame*: structuring project time in two stages (of about four weeks each) divided by a reflection point and a break. This subdivision was suggested by the 'excursion week' placed in the middle of the *ifu*-period; it was used successfully to encourage a shift from defining the project topics to working towards results.
- *Pairing Project Groups*: ensuring a mutual evaluation by a partner group engaged in related work. The requirement to give a presentation to another group at the end of the first project stage turned out to be very helpful to the groups for focussing their discussions, enriching their ideas of how to proceed, and understanding better their communication problems by comparing themselves to their partner groups.
- *Reflection on Project Work*: providing for a reflection at mid-time both in the project groups and in the home groups. In the project groups, the reflection was focussed on the ongoing work and greatly stimulated through the feedback from the partner groups. In the home groups, the participants had the opportunity to discuss their general experience at *ifu*, including problems they might have with their project group, to enable them to make the best possible use of their time at *ifu*.
- *Informal Project Presentations*: using plenary discussion times for allowing each group to present their ideas and partial results.
- *Strategy Group*: forming a team of international experts to discuss continuation of the project after *ifu*. The strategy team involved resident faculty members as well as guest-lecturers. Due to time constraints, visits to the in-

dividual projects, as originally planned, had to be dropped. The plenary discussion focussed mainly on networking possibilities.

To monitor the resulting complex processes in a way that was feasible for all projects, there were regular meetings of the directors, the facilitators and the Hamburg local team during the three months of *ifu*. The cooperation in this group was very difficult and loaded with conflicts that we were not able to overcome. In retrospect, I believe that this partly due to the fact that the cooperation amongst the faculty during *ifu* had not been thought of as a knowledge project in advance and, thus, not carefully been prepared according to the same principles as the curricular projects themselves (I became aware of this through a critical comment by one of the facilitators).

If I were to conduct a similar effort again, I would attempt to promote knowledge co-construction *about* knowledge co-construction amongst the faculty as a central part of our cooperation. It would be helpful to invite a moderator from outside to facilitate a group process between the organizers and the faculty to allow everyone to bring in their own perspectives on how projects should be framed, and so on. We would have to find a common ground in terms of how we would cooperate, how we would set priorities, how we would make decisions.

The main requirement for that would be to allow for a lot more time than we had available, so as to initiate a group process (about group processes). This would introduce more openness into the overall process and perhaps make the results less predictable, but it might enable a very rich learning experience for everyone involved.

6 Supporting Knowledge Projects

In this section, I would like to discuss the potential of software support for knowledge co-construction in a way that relates concretely to the requirements of working together in knowledge projects. At *ifu*, this was a research issue for the software engineering group headed by me, in cooperation with virtual *ifu*. The *vifu* project *Knowledge Co-Construction* aimed at supporting the ongoing work in the twelve curricular projects through the web-based community system CommSy (http//:www.commsy.de), developed at the University of Hamburg.

CommSy supports the communication and the coordination of work in groups. It provides the possibility for participants to introduce themselves, for sub-groups to be formed, for agendas to be kept, for news to be exchanged, for discussion forums to be set up, and so on. Thus, the focus is on internal project communication. It also allows to embed shared materials and to work together towards common results. Since CommSy does not require any special technical resources (just the browser), so it could be used not only during *ifu* but also afterwards to support project groups in finishing their work.

Introducing CommSy at *ifu* was made difficult due to recurring problems with the infrastructure that caused a lot of frustration at the beginning, but most project groups adopted CommSy at the end of the first project-stage. Through this experience, we learned to distinguish different needs of projects for software support, some of which were well covered by CommSy as it was, others could be introduced in CommSy during *ifu*, and yet others pointed to difficulties in providing a learning environment that was, at the same time, easy to use and simple to install, and comprehensive in the features offered.

Knowledge projects require support for different aspects of their practice:

- *Internal Communication*: introducing participants and their perspectives, making networking easy, coordinating work in a reliable way. The idea is to provide a private space where the unfolding history of the project is made available as a resource to the participants. This is well supported with the CommSy features explained above.
- *External Communication*: allowing for the presentation of (partial) results, announcing public events and exchanging news with others. This was not provided by CommSy, but only by the general *vifu*-server, so the audience addressed by external publication was quite general and could not be restricted to specific target groups.
- *Embedding Materials and Sources*: this is required for enabling a group to assemble their own 'knowledge base'. The CommSy features in this area were enhanced on the basis of the experience at *ifu*.
- *Working Together on Common Results*: these may be, for example, papers or websites. The difficulty here is the interaction of a system like CommSy with other tools such as text processing. This was not possible by staying in the uniform CommSy environment but required changing to other platforms.

In spite of various shortcomings, the results of using CommSy were encouraging. The experience has shown, however, that not only the technical features of a software support system matter but also the way it is introduced into the group process. While, in principle, the organizers were already aware of this before *ifu*, persistent technical troubles and the general scarcity of time and resources made a felicitous introduction difficult in practice. It was fortunate that due to an unforeseen change in work assignments, one of the facilitators became available as the person responsible for introducing the system into group work. The experience of using CommSy at *ifu* has been reported by Bleek et al (2000), some of it can also be found in the project reports already referred to in section 2, and in Kelkar et al, this volume.

7 The Paradoxes of Knowledge Co-construction

To some extent, the idea of knowledge co-construction embodies utopian visions of equality in social settings shaped by power structures. It suggests a playful creative environment in a time of pressure and goal orientation, and seems to require unlimited resources. In the real world, the conditions are very different, and the possibilities of flying high are limited through many constraints. This was experienced very clearly at *ifu*. These were the most important fields of tension we came across.

- *Hierarchy vs. Networking*: Knowledge co-construction unfolds through the self-organization of participants having equal rights, and yet it is embedded in hierarchical structures, both within the project and in relation to the outside. At *ifu*, it was painful to see how the clash between the hierarchy: student / project facilitator / project director / local dean of the Project Area / *ifu*-president interfered with the hopes for free communication. This structural property could not be circumvented by the people involved. Since hierarchy can not be avoided altogether, the levels of hierarchy should be decreased, the roles should be better clarified, and democratic procedures for negotiating between the different groups should be established. Also the hierarchy student / teacher becomes problematic in a setting where the so-called students are themselves experienced scientists and professionals.
- *Pre-Planning vs. Self-Organization*: Study programs need to be planned ahead of time. Programs need to be prepared, lecturers invited, contents made available. But knowledge co-construction evolves in an unpredictable manner through the interaction of the group, and is stifled by too many scheduled activities. We had designed a fixed time table, which turned out to be too crowded and were left to improvisation trying to accommodate students' initiatives. An alternative might have been to leave more space in our time table, not empty, but devoted to activities like 'self-study' or 'self-organized group work' that could then be filled in as required during the study program.
- *Cultural Dominance vs. Meeting on Common Ground*: In knowledge projects, participants need to find their common ground. Whose ground? At *ifu*, for example, in spite of all our efforts at providing an internationally relevant curriculum, it was nevertheless experienced as Euro-centric by participants from overseas. Although the Germans were only a relative majority and could not even use their own language in the study program, they were the only ones familiar with the surrounding culture to which the others had to adapt. The way communities are formed, conflicts are handled, decisions

are reached varies in different cultures. It would be naive to expect that we can overcome these difficulties by curricular measures.

While it seems very important to me to acknowledge these limitations, they will certainly not discourage me from continuing to work towards enabling knowledge co-construction wherever I can. The most important lesson I have learned from *ifu* is to value the enrichment from unique personal encounters fundamental to knowledge projects. Perhaps we should learn to think of knowledge co-construction as celebrating a community – not blinding ourselves to the disappointments, conflicts and power struggles that will inevitably arise, but nevertheless aiming for accepting each other's perspectives with mutual respect. Thus, while we may not be able to remove structural obstacles and our foresight will remain limited, our ability to engage in knowledge co-construction will grow.

Acknowledgements

I would like to express my sincere thanks to all those who contributed to and cooperated with me at *ifu*. In particular, I gratefully acknowledge the extraordinary commitment of Tina Bach, Wolf-Gideon Bleek, Dorit Heinsohn and Silvie Klein-Franke, and of all other members and helpers of the Hamburg local team. I owe many thanks to our international dean Cheris Kramarae for allowing us to benefit from her wisdom at critical times, to all members of the curricular working group, mentioned by name in the introduction, for shaping *ifu* together with us, and to all guest lecturers and artists for bringing in their valuable ideas. I also greatly appreciate the contributions of the facilitators Dorcas Mofoluwake Akande, Aleida Calleja, Mona Dahms, Yvonne Dittrich, Judith Gregory, Cirila Lilac Limpangog, Monika Pater, Jutta Weber, Heike Winschiers and Zhang Wei, who met the tremendous challenge of moderating one or two project groups, as well as of Tatjana Beer and Katja Fischer who facilitated the art-workshops.

Last, not least, I would like to thank Anke Bornträger, Maria Luiza De Mello e Souza, Delphine Djiraibe, Mona El Tobgui, Stephania Evboikuokha, Inge Gavat, Jane Gibian, Lunna Hemed-Kyungu, Martina Kenk, Jeong Soon Kim, Kerima Kostka, Margaret Ndung'u, Birgit Pretzsch, Indra Ranasinghe, Sara Sanchez Mera, Maria Alejandra Sanchez-Vazquez, Hanan Satti, Mirela Skenderi, Dumanic Suhreta-Shura for their participation in the course on *Knowledge Co-construction*, which provided me with deep insights into the diverse ways of knowing, as conceived in different parts of the world.

References

Bleek, Wolf-Gideon; Dittrich, Yvonne & Jeenicke, Martti (2000). *Classifications as Tools.* Workshop Paper, CSCW 2000, Philadelphia, USA.

Floyd, Christiane (1992). Software Development as Reality Construction. In: Floyd, Christiane; Züllighoven, Heinz; Budde, Reinhard; Keil-Slawik, Reinhard (eds.). *Software Development and Reality Construction.* Berlin, Heidelberg etc.: Springer, pp. 86-100.

Floyd, Christiane (1996). Choices about Choices. In: *Systems Research*, vol. 13 (3), pp. 261-70.

Ingrid Wetzel

Teaching Computer Skills: A Gendered Approach

Abstract

Participating in the Internet age requires skills in computer usage. Accordingly, a high importance has to be assigned to pedagogical efforts in computer-related education. However, acquiring computer skills seems to deviate from traditional forms of learning. Knowledge in this area is aging rapidly and necessarily deals with uncertainty. Required new information is not available in books, but acquired by trial-and-error at the computer, by gathering scattered pieces of information from magazines or the net itself, and by communication in interested (virtual or not) communities. These factors point to the need of alternative teaching and learning principles. This is particularly important for women, who tend not to be attracted by experimental modes of proceeding at the technical level. Thus, suitable forms of learning, based on careful consideration of gender-related differences, need to be integrated into what amounts to a women's learning culture. It should provide a setting where an experience at the computer is intentionally interwoven with reflection about the experience. It should nurture communication by those whose personal interests may not be drawn to these kinds of skills. It needs to address subjects at the meta-level, such as methods for acquiring new skills or how to find the information needed. And it needs to train basic, rarely taught skills. Based primarily on the author's experience at *ifu*, concrete examples about how to translate these requirements into action are given.

1 Introduction

In this chapter, I will reflect on my experiences in teaching advanced computer skills to women in the light of feminist theories. In doing so, I will primarily draw on my experiences at *ifu* (International Women's University, here: *ifu*'s Project Area INFORMATION), where I helped design the Internet training at basic and advanced levels offered to all participants and taught a weeklong course on *Overcoming Barriers to Mastering Technology*. This work, in turn, was based on a long standing interest in pedagogical questions in the area of computing and on previous teaching experience, for example in the course *admina*, designed by me to help women students in informatics acquire skills in (computer) system administration. As I live in Germany, the reflection depicts the situation in this country in particular.

In the last years, the explosive growth in Internet usage, advancing web-technologies and new digital media have accelerated profound societal changes leading from the industrial to the information society. Future transformations are forecasted to be even more radical than in the past. Educational systems are challenged to respond to these developments as quickly as possible. Accordingly, there are projects, research and educational debates in different countries that demand large-scale education initiatives (see Westram, 2000; Balka & Smith, 2000; Hapnes & Rasmussen, 2000; Schründer-Lenzen, 1995). Most authors agree that schools and universities have the responsibility to prepare young people for the rapidly changing realities (at least in industrialized countries). Although some argue that it was never the school's task to prepare for occupational competence but to give a solid foundation in the sense of a broad general education,[1] there now seems to be agreement to respond to an environment that is more and more influenced by new media and affects children's habits and learning behavior from a very early age on. Increased ability in perception and quickness in handling with regard to smart devices, possible stimulus overflow and a tendency for young people to outdistance older ones in their abilities to deal with technology need consideration as well as the potentials new media offer for education in general.

Thus, there is a growing conviction that unless the profound changes, which so deeply affect public and private life, are quickly mirrored in new educational goals and pedagogical concepts and realities, the future prospects and ability of whole societies as well as individuals to compete will be jeopardized. Significantly varying prognoses are made for different countries. Westram (2000: 57) refers to estimations for Germany from 1996 stating that by the year 2000 only a third of all employees would be able to do their jobs without computer skills. Leaving the educational issues to be dealt with to private efforts will likely favor those people whose ability, interest, background, potentials and economic interests draw them towards the new computer culture. Authors warn us of a digital divide (Spender, 1995), a two-class society, or an increased 'knowledge gap' intensified by the new media (Westram, 2000: 48).

As research shows, the diversification in what is called computer literacy or media competence starts at early age. Especially significant and widely observed are differences between male and female students, observations I am concerned with in this chapter. Furthermore, with a special focus on the technical aspects of media competence as taken here, we are dealing with exactly that aspect of education and career choice which has constantly been avoided by a majority of women over the past decades and in almost all countries.

---

1   See, for example Chegwidden (2000) or Schründer-Lenzen (1998).

In keeping with the broad agreement on media competence as a basic pedagogical goal and as a central task and challenge for the educational system on all
levels (Forum Info 2000, 1996, cited in Westram, 2000: 44), I want to draw attention to new didactical concepts for conveying technical skills in computer usage. And I claim that these concepts need to play an important role in any critical plans for pedagogical changes.

In what follows, I will argue that skills in computer usage are an important
aspect of the required overall media competence and analyze factors that make it
difficult for women to achieve these skills and to participate in computing education in general. Then I will propose possible contents and educational objectives, taking into account the special character of the skills and knowledge to be
taught, and relating these characteristics to reported preferences and attitudes of
women. On this basis, I will develop didactical concepts for a women's learning
culture which, I believe, is better suited to both the specific skills and knowledge
required and women's preferences.

By way of illustration, the course on *Overcoming Barriers to Mastering
Technology*, held in the cross-cultural setting of *ifu*, will be presented.

2 Skills in Computer Usage as an Important Part of Media Competence

Definitions of media competence are manifold as they are based on the somewhat vague term *multi-media*. Multi-media comprises the integrative and interactive usage of different media, and the computer-based provision and management of various information provided by different media, or it is used as a generic term for new products or services from the computer, telecommunication
or media fields. Hence, the term comprises information and communication
technologies which emphasize the more technical aspects.

As discussed in Germany, media competence or media pedagogy (Westram,
2000: 41 and Forum Info 2000, 1996) involves the ability to

- achieve knowledge about and access to different media (hardware and software) paired with the ability to use them and to constantly update these
  skills;
- select and evaluate media-conveyed information by relating it to its social
  and economic conditions of production;
- actively, self-confidently and responsibly participate in the media-dominated
  society, including shaping and designing one's own contributions.

Considering these goals, the Internet seems to play a central role in media education with its various opportunities to be integrated into classes and curricula.

However, the fact that the Internet needs a computer as a prerequisite raises questions. Westram (2000) reports on a perceptible shift of emphasis in the definition of media competence over the past years towards active participation in using computers, software and communication technology. She raises the question of how the new medium Internet will be related to computer science – whether the technical device computer will dominate the medium Internet, and whether this may lead to a repeated formation of conditions known from computer science, such as the dominance of male students and developers in this field (see Woodbury, this volume). Although some of the developments seem very promising in that there is an increase in women's access and usage of the Internet reported, differences in the kind of information accessed and the kind of activities the Internet is used for remain significant.

Some authors warn that we must not underestimate the technical complexity related both to learning how to work with the Internet and also to providing the needed infrastructure. They point out that educationalists faced with technical media often reject suggestions for change or react in a helpless manner (Westram, 2000). Glotz puts it this way: "The resistance of the pedagogical province to the usage of modern media is strong and has deep roots" (quoted in Westram, p. 55, my translation). One result is that many children and young people acquire computer competence on their own, a situation that is partially responsible for the increased 'digital divide' mentioned above.[2]

Thus, if we consider skills in computer usage an important part of media competence, new didactic concepts are required in order to avoid a repetition of imbalance in educational and occupational opportunities for women and men. These concepts include consideration of the reasons why in the past work with computers has been avoided by certain groups of people, especially women.

3 Women and Computer Usage

Although the social and economical demand for media/computer competence is great, women are still highly underrepresented regarding the development as well as the usage of computer artifacts or Internet applications. There are many reasons for this phenomenon, and investigations show a diversity of different

---

2   "Many girls are not receiving the same kinds of opportunities to become technologically
     skilled as boys are. ... Boys develop alliances with computers largely due to their exten-
     sive out-of-school computer experiences. ... These factors relating to amount of experi-
     ence with computers have a significant effect on students' attitudes and perceptions"
     (Ching et al, 1998 quoted in Westram, 2000: 34).

viewpoints. While gender differences seem to apply in different ways to Internet usage on the one hand and higher education for information technology (IT) professionals on the other hand, significant gender variance is reported in both areas and may have similar roots.

Some recent figures illustrate the divide. For example, in Germany the number of women computer science students has even decreased over the years, from 20% in 1983 to about 10% in 1997. Between 1991 and 1994 the percentage was only about 6% (Schinzel, 1997).[3] Significant differences in computer or Internet usage and educational efforts exist among countries, although the reasons are still not too well investigated.[4] Here, Europe seems to be less gender-balanced than, for example, the U.S. (Suriya & Panteli, 2000). Too few researchers seem to address the situation in third world countries where potentials in gaining education or participation in virtual communities could especially contribute to women's quality of life.

On the basis of the research results available and my own experience as a software engineer in research, business, and university education, I want to group possible reasons for this gender bias into six major areas. The first three address gender differences in general orientation, self-concept, and self-confidence, while the other three aspects refer to the social, gendered world of IT: the general environment, artifacts and their usage, and education.

3.1 Gender Differences in Orientation

Research suggests that many women have a general *multi-perspectivity* including a broad distribution of intellectual interests among different fields (Schründer-Lenzen, 1995). This relates to research results showing that women in technical fields often pass up sense-making relations while moving towards the use-context (Schade, 1998), which in turn matches with higher participation of women in application-oriented fields of informatics. This in turn relates to investigations made by Erb (1996), who points out that the traditional (mainstream) computer science still disregards these user-oriented and interdisciplinary topics.

---

3   I suggest that the decrease could also be related to a change in programming technology, from a focus on (abstract) programming concepts to an emphasis on (technically) complex programming environments.

4   Westram (2000: 62) gives the following examples: whereas investments in new technologies at schools until 2005 are to be around 21 Billion Deutsch Marks in Japan, Germany invested only 160 Million Deutsch Marks in the last years. In Europe, Scandinavian countries show a high support of school initiatives, see, e.g Hapnes & Rasmussen, 2000 and Finnish Ministry, 2001.

Often women do not focus on the technology itself but on using it within a general interest in relationships (Durndell & Thomason, 1997). This is confirmed by recent findings of Peiris et al (2000), who state that out of all areas of computing, the Internet, as a communication tool, has been singled out as the most 'women-friendly' and that women are changing the way the Internet works in that they are more task-oriented and frequently use its networking facilities to contact friends. This is perceivable in characteristic online styles, emphasizing expressions of appreciation and community building, in order to make participants feel accepted and welcome, while men often use putdowns, strong assertions, lengthy postings, self-promotion and sarcasm.

The task orientation of women is further related to more pragmatic ways of using computers. Instead of playing games and downloading or installing software, many women prefer using e-mail and the Internet as a source of information in concrete professional contexts (Turkle, 1995). However, women's lack of passionate attitudes towards hardware and software themselves is seen as a possible source of their lack of experience with computers (Symonds, 2000).

3.2 Gender Differences in Self-Concept

Personal interest and ability are viewed as the most important factors influencing career choices for men and women (Chan et al, 2000). As career choices are suggested to be linked to the interests of children aged 11 through 14, the influence of peer groups is strong. While peer group pressure is seen to draw girls away from computers, the opposite applies to boys (Symonds, 2000). Computer competence is seen as a stabilizing factor for masculinity (Schründer-Lenzen, 1995), whereas interest (not competence) in computers may be regarded as unfeminine.

In more detail, women's relationship culture is based on an interaction process that is sensitive and experiential. Since computers, being technical objects with immaterial action, lack the emotional element that constitute women's sensitivity to something or someone else, computers have critical limitations in satisfying women's 'relationing.' In contrast to this, computers as 'inferior' objects may provide additional practice of dominant behavior (Dorer, 1997), which may help explain male interest as a permanent phenomenon beyond profession-related applications (Schründer-Lenzen, 1995: 133). This may lead to the kind of technical competence that "has come to constitute an integral part of masculine gender identity" (Grint & Gill in Tuuva, 2000).

3.3 Gender Differences in Self-Confidence

In several investigations a gender difference in self-confidence towards the use of computer technology is reported (Symonds, 2000; Schründer-Lenzen, 1995; Durndess & Thomason, 1997). Even if similar efficiency is achieved, women tend to feel less confident about their abilities than comparable male participants, as reported by McDonald & Spencer (2000), who examined gender differences in navigational efficiency, navigational strategy, and user confidence in web navigation. Differences in self-representation are also related to differences in self-confidence and self-esteem (Schründer-Lenzen, 1995: 137). Again, 'computer language' serves the purpose of obtaining attention and allows for masculine identification and evidence of belonging to a male subculture.

3.4 Male-Dominated Environment

Owing to the low percentage of female computing graduates and even fewer women working in this domain, only a small proportion of software designers are women. Miliszewska & Horwood (2000: 51) speak of a "macho-image" presenting an obvious problem in attracting women to computer science in tertiary education. According to Dole Spender (1995) boys and men have access to more computers, spend more or their time with them, and are the dominating presence in cyberspace.

As with technology in general, computer technology in particular is seen as being rooted in values that are considered masculine, such as objectivity, progress, rationality and competition (Tuuva, 2000), which again can be traced to the intertwining of technology and masculinity or to technology being understood as an integral part of masculine gender identity.

A by-product of this bias is that women pursuing an IT career usually find themselves working in male environments (see the chapters by Bratteteig and by Woodbury in this volume). "That some women feel uncomfortable in mostly male environments is not primarily a result of men trying to make them feel unwelcome but of dynamics resulting directly from the male majority and societal sex-based differences in behavior. While perhaps it is comforting to know that no conspiracy exists against women computer scientists, it also means that the problem is harder to fight" (Spertus, 1991: 87).

Kuosa (2000) observes gender-neutral ways of talking among computing professionals and gender issues being efficiently hidden in working organizations or not perceived to matter in everyday working practices. She then asks: "Why is it so important to study gender when professionals do not give it any importance? Bjorkman et al give an answer: 'By creating a community of genderless 'computing people', where the function of gender and power is hidden, and indeed regarded as irrelevant, women are effectively excluded'. This means that women are allowed to enter the profession as long as they behave like men..." (Kuosa, 2000: 122).

However, actual cases of gender discrimination and perceived preferences for male IT professionals are also reported as excluding factors for women (Symonds, 2000). Further factors are seen in the lack of role models and the rapid development in IT, the latter of which seems to intensify general difficulties for many women involving the balancing of career and family responsibilities.

3.5 Computer Artifacts and Dealing with Them

Male domination in the IT sector has its effects on computer artifacts. As most software developers are male, even when user-centered approaches are undertaken, applications are usually developed from a male perspective resulting in interfaces that the developers themselves like (Peiris et al, 2000; Dorer, 1997). In order to be inventive they often set involvement of users aside, and design for masculine, young, and technologically highly competent users (Rommes, 2000). According to Peiris et al (2000: 35) "this leads to software which requires the user to 'play' in order to determine functionality, and systems with difficult to understand commands, icons and menu names. This enforces the view that computers are male things. Few girls wish to study such a subject, and so the cycle continues".

This "cycle of imbalance" (Peiris et al, 2000) may also explain the often stated observation that new technology is learned through trial and error. "This is considered the normal practice everywhere in computing culture, for example, in computing professionals' education" (Ylijoki, 1998: 170-175). Many professionals recommend it for learning to use the Internet. If this attitude seems to be a requirement in learning to deal with computer artifacts, careful consideration has to be given to the different learning behavior of women students observed by many authors. Dorer (1997, (translated) in Westram, 2000: 39) remarks: "Men are dealing with this technology in a considerably more intensive playing manner than women." And Augstein states (translated): "Whereas men are more likely to 'hammer away at the keyboard' in a spontaneous and playful manner, women prefer to mentally anticipate their doing and to understand the meaning of their activity. Thereby their learning rhythm is different from that of men" (1996: 13). Augstein concludes that this may explain why women often feel left behind in mixed-gender courses.

3.6 Education

Statistics showing that the gender bias in choosing an IT education at the tertiary level still remains or increases lead to a discussion of coeducation at schools. The fact is that with coeducation girls demonstrate stronger gender-conforming tendencies in their choice of main subjects and in the development of interest profiles, and also the grading exhibits gender-conformity (Schründer-Lenzen, 1995). The subject of single gender education is very controversial (although a significantly higher percentage of women computer scientists come from former girls' schools). Critics discuss the advantages and disadvantages of suspending coeducation in natural and computer science with caution since consequences may have broad implications. For details see Schründer-Lenzen (1995: 38-43).

Another recently posed question rapidly gaining importance is to what extent computer-mediated and distance learning and the use of the Internet affects the learning situation of girls and women (Leong & Al-Hawamdeh, 1999). Here, Chegwidden (2000) offers a valuable statement: "Interesting pedagogy with computer applications is possible, but only if teachers and students do not have to think about the computer very much."

4 Towards a Women's Learning Culture around Computer Skills

I consider it a priority to shape new educational programs in order to invite and qualify young people in computer skills (as an important part of their overall media competence) – especially those with less interest and experience in technology, whether these are women or men, from whatever social status, and from whatever ethnic or national backgrounds.[5] However, as pointed out above, there are good reasons to focus especially on supporting women students.

4.1 Characteristics of Skills in Computer Usage

To find appropriate ways of teaching, we have to determine the content of knowledge and skills we want to convey and to reflect on the special character of this knowledge and skills.

---

5   Apart from this goal another major professional and personal interest lies in shaping new methods for information systems development emphasizing the intertwining of social and technical aspects, (possibly attracting 'people-oriented' students to the design of computer artifacts and) hopefully leading to (more) adequate organizational solutions, see Krabbel, Wetzel & Ratuski 1996, Wetzel & Klischewski 2002.

Possible topics regarding the technical aspect of media competence are broad in range and will, therefore, be grouped in three areas (although the separation between these categories is not clear-cut): *basic skills, background knowledge and meta-knowledge*. Basic skills address the concrete aspects of using software tools and the Internet or comprise the concrete steps in selecting and running computers, periphery and smart devices. Background knowledge provides context knowledge for basic skills and error handling and prepares for dealing with complexity, whereas meta-knowledge addresses strategies and structures to support constant learning based on reflection and awareness of gender-related differences.

These given areas exhibit the following characteristics:

- *Doing.* First of all, computer usage-related knowledge is highly experience-based; these skills can only be acquired by doing. This 'doing' usually takes place in a trial-and-error manner. To succeed with this attitude means investing time, and in order to memorize the many steps necessary (including back-tracking) it requires a lot of repetition – or in case of failure, a lot of patience and motivation.

- *Updating.* Given the pace of innovation, it is not surprising that knowledge and skills rapidly become out-dated. Even though former basic knowledge often relates to upcoming technology, users need time to discover the changes or often to learn completely new ways of proceeding with the rapidly developing technology.

- *Dealing with uncertain, incomplete and scattered information.* Knowledge is often incomplete and uncertain since only a slice of the whole picture is available. It is offered in scattered details, i.e. teaching material for brand-new technology is often not available in textbooks (they will be published one or two years later when the technology is known and widely applied), where it is usually presented in a structured way and from a certain abstract point of view. Instead, information has to be gathered from computer magazines and technical journals or from news groups. Furthermore, information is linked to economic contexts or other interests, for example one needs to know which company offers which kind of tools, whether a firm may prevail or succeed, how to receive test versions, how to distinguish reliable information from mere advertisement etc. Thus, the learning situation seems to lack a 'protected' ground of manageable size.

4.2 Computer Usage Skills and Preferences of Women

It is very interesting to relate these specifics to women's preferences as we do in the following.

- *Doing*. As pointed out above, women seem to prefer to understand action before doing it. This clashes badly with the necessary trial and error approach or game-playing attitude. Furthermore, in relation to the already low self-confidence, understanding before doing can be seen as a strategy to avoid mistakes. In contrast, making mistakes is central to the trial and error approach. Additionally, self-confidence may allow male users to recognize badly styled user-interfaces or networking environments as potential sources of failures, leading to a 'healthy' assessment of and a distance to 'human-made' systems, whereas a lack of understanding the system may mislead insecure users. This means that women more often and in more cases seek the causes of breakdowns in their own (imagined) mistakes rather than in badly designed systems. Furthermore, the required trial-and-error attitude does not agree with the usual task-orientation of women, which is application-oriented, whereas the 'doing' requires interest in the computer as an end in itself (Durndell & Thomason, 1997: 8). Also, due to the time computer work requires, it stands against a clear separation of leisure and working time, which women seem to make.
- *Updating*. Similarly, the rapid outdating of skills and knowledge requires a constant interest and much time in order to keep up with changes or innovations. For a single person the ever-increasing variety of software, systems, devices etc. can be overwhelming; intense identification, exchange and competition in a clearly technically focused peer-group is required. This again clashes with the application-orientation and the much broader interests reported for women and in some cases even causes fear regarding a successful re-entry into professional life after maternal leave.
- *Dealing with uncertain, incomplete and scattered information* throughout computer usage collides with the reported general lack of self-confidence of many women. The never-ending intertwining of different factors may cause a feeling of helplessness in contrast to the wish to master a clearly delimited subject. Scattered details clash once more with a preferredly structured and abstract way of understanding and an interest in concrete achievements. The 'places' where information is offered (and the kind of information itself) seem to be highly male-oriented. Computer magazines, computer shops, news groups, and markets are still male environments sometimes exhibiting a 'macho-image' in keeping with well documented male-oriented styles in communication.

4.3 Concepts for a Women's Learning Culture

Considering the mismatch between characteristic skills in computer usage and preferences of women, the reports of low female participation should come as no surprise. However, new statistics show that women realize the possible options of the Internet and computer usage to mediate their own contents, participate in social life and at their work places and are catching up in this area (see Fittkau & Maaß, 2001, for details). From experiences at *ifu* and other university courses I can only underline this emerging interest of women in at least Internet-related technical skills. These students are explicitly asking for different didactical concepts. Hence, more adequate ways of teaching, especially for women, need to be found in the future.

Westram (2000) argues for new didactic concepts that consider gender specific differences, try to meet women's interests half way, provide female role models and motivate and enable self-learning by initiating cooperation and initiative. However, Balka (Balka & Smith, 2000: 3) reports a "near absence" of alternative approaches to computer science education. Following Westram and on the basis of several courses I have held, I would add that new didactic concepts have to correspond with the special character of the skills that are to be conveyed. Moreover, concepts should take advantage of the strengths of female attitudes, such as communication, searching for mutual help, openness to share, teamwork and reflection.

Hence, the women's learning culture proposed here is to comprise all the factors necessary to achieve a learning process toward chosen goals, i.e. the definition of objectives and goals combined with appropriate didactical forms, a learning environment which nurtures interest and communication, and the preparation of teachers and lecturers.

In order to support women according to gender-specific differences in acquiring skills in computer usage and to initiate reflection about these differences, the proposed courses are given for women only. They are prepared and held by a team of women (usually one lecturer together with advanced students). The chosen topics should include aspects in computer usage that are new or absent from usual curricula. The didactical concepts combine:

- Structured input of background, basic and meta-knowledge;
- Doing by performing concrete tasks at the computer usually new to the audience (through the provision of scripts to follow lessons or to answer questions);
- Reflection by communicating about performing of the tasks and the overall attitude in accumulating computer-related knowledge.

Thus, the women's learning culture becomes manifest both in the setting of the courses and the chosen content. The atmosphere of mutual action, reflection and communication helps students to enjoy technical subjects and allows for waking their interest in them. It enables the sharing of reflection, frustration, fears or anguish at a level of depth and honesty which can be seen as a strength of women. It opens a terrain women are often feeling comfortable with or which they are searching for (see also the discussion on the potential of knowledge projects by Floyd in this volume). Moreover, being centered around new contents or subjects missing from usual curricula and women-oriented examples, the courses seem to be very attractive to women. As a result, the courses held so far all closed with the wish for more permanent courses.[6] Permanent courses with a constant obligation to attend as well as the occupation in a settled environment would help to give these subjects the right place among other activities whereas otherwise, too often, they risk becoming less important in the complexity of other demands.

5 The Course 'Overcoming Barriers to Mastering Technology' at *ifu*

Giving an example of the women's learning culture, I will briefly describe a course held at *ifu*. The course *Overcoming Barriers to Mastering Technology* was embedded in a series of courses devoted to technical subjects. The idea was to support the project work of *ifu* by continually providing basic and advanced technical training and to offer some additional courses for students with further interests. Owing to the very tight schedule during *ifu*, the course was held as a block on (only) four consecutive days. Over twenty *ifu* participants attended. They came from countries around the globe and different research areas. The instruction team consisted of five women students of computer science and a woman university lecturer in software engineering.

Four topics were chosen, each of which addressed basic skills in computer and Internet usage. Each day was devoted to one topic: mastering a new tool, the structure of Internet pages, Internet transactions, download from the Web.

Each topic was approached following the same pattern:

1. Introduction to the subject;
2. work at the computer;

---

6   A real achievement was one course that brought forth an ongoing initiative of women students at the Computer Science Department in Hamburg University, called *admina*, with self-organized tutorials over the past six years.

3. group discussions; and
4. group presentations and summary in the plenum.

As an example, the first topic is presented in a bit more detail.

The introduction centered around different attitudes to tool usage: a general task-orientation and an approach of 'tool awareness.' While task orientation may result in impatience and anger if a tool does not support the task as smoothly as expected, tool awareness pursues tool 'understanding' (i.e. knowing about patterns and specifics of software tools, the comparison between the purpose of tools and one's own expectations, and the 'philosophy' of tools) and the necessary translation of the task at hand to the functionality offered.

Ten software tools were available during work at the computer, and each participant was asked to choose a tool with which she was not yet too familiar. The goal was to master a new tool by 'playing around' (given some guidance in the form of exploration tasks for those who wanted it while the team helped by answering individual questions).

The following group discussion and plenary presentation centered around discovering menu patterns across tools and reflection about (unfamiliar) ways to proceed.

Concerning the reflection about women-oriented aspects, it was totally amazing for me to recognize similar patterns in attitudes of women across the different cultures. For example, nearly all of the participants recognized themselves instantly as usually pursuing a task-orientation, a fact which was eye-opening for them (even after years of computer usage). The exploration of tools with 'tool awareness' and the surprise about how much could be achieved in a short time was new and helpful to many. Similarly, they welcomed the structured input for assessing websites; hesitation in performing order transactions or downloading seemed to be a wide-spread phenomenon. And the connection to respective background knowledge was considered very helpful.

Finally, a very brief evaluation of the course shows the following: As participants suggested, the course could certainly have been longer, especially the segment scheduled for work at the computer. Much content was covered in a very short time. Nevertheless, most participants were very committed and very grateful. The intertwining of input, doing and reflection created an atmosphere of excitement. All topics were of high interest. With more time, even more student initiative in preparing input and examples would have been highly welcomed from both sides – participants and instructors.

Hence, most of the participants would have liked to have such a course to accompany the whole *ifu* experience. More advanced subjects such as building active web pages were requested (and a further course was held). The atmosphere of interest, communication and exchange in addressing these technical objectives in computer usage was highly stimulating. Overall, the course experience was profoundly encouraging for us to pursue a combination of training for skills and reflection about women attitudes as a basis for a promising 'women's learning culture.'

Conclusion

In view of a growing impact of media, computers, the Internet and smart devices in social and professional life, women with their multi-perspectivity, relationship-oriented interest and emphasis on practical achievements have to devise their point of view, shape their contributions and find places of influence. Accordingly, the overall educational goal of a women's learning culture for acquiring computer skills is twofold. While conveying computer skills and lifting the background knowledge the aim is also to pave the ground for a fuller understanding of the situation of women in technical areas. This should help each woman to find her own individual position and choices and be more conscious about which ones to take. No one should be pushed towards technology. For those, who are attracted to further advances in computer usage, this approach opens options to proceed. But for those whose orientation is still mainly toward people and who have a broad rather than a specialized perspective, computer skills and knowledge may yet nurture self-esteem. This contributes to achieving more self-confidence, on the basis of which women will hopefully raise their voices and influence situations in which their broader application-oriented view is very much needed.

Acknowledgements

I owe many thanks to Christiane Floyd, local Dean of *ifu*'s Project Area INFORMATION, who encouraged me to participate in *ifu* and later initiated my writing and reflection about my experience and concepts, which again caused me to reflect on my own way through computer science as a woman. Thanks to the editors for thoughtful suggestions encouraging feedback, and to Gudrun Parsons for the final editing of this chapter.

   I would further like to thank Anja Hennemuth, Antje Großmann, Dorina Gumm, Ulrike Najmi, and Jutta Schenk, who helped me to prepare and conduct the *ifu* courses with great commitment, and to my friend and former colleague Anita Krabbel, with whom I share reflections on women's approaches to software developing projects and who thought up the name *admina* for the first women-only course I held.

Also thanks to the male colleagues in the department who took time to discuss their attitudes, to help prepare 'stable' environments for the courses, and to share insights, practical knowledge and many details with me, especially Wolf-Gideon Bleek, Michael König, Andreas Rudloff, Reinhard Zierke and Uwe Zimmer.

And last not least, thanks to the participants in the *ifu* course: Diana Andone, Irene Aterido, Lynda Awasum, Zubeeda Banu Quraishy, Mildred Kiconco Barya, Yolisa Faith Bomela, Evelyn Fogwe née Chibaka, Inge Gavat, Bokang Gwebu, Emebet Hassen, Ila Joshi, Roxanne Kavarana, Kerima Kostka, Faith Nebo Legoabe, Pretty Lilly Majola, Boryana Peevska, Farzaneh Raji, Sara Sanchez Mera, Hanan Satti, Veronika Schulze, Juliane Schwarz, Dumanic Suhreta-Shura and Ciler Tüzüner, to whom I owe one of the most rewarding teaching experiences in my career.

References

Augstein, Rudolf (ed.) (1996): *Online – Offline. Hauptergebnisse Nutzertopologie*. Hamburg: Spiegel-Verlag.

Balka, Ellen & Smith, Richard (eds.) (2000). *Women, Work and Computerization – Charting a Course to the Future*. Proceedings of the IFIP TC9 WG9. 17th Int. Conference on Women, Work and Computerization. Boston, MA: Kluwer Academic Publishers.

Chan, Vania; Stafford, Katie; Klawe, Maria; Chen, Grace (2000). *Gender Differences in Vancouver Secondary Students*. In: Balka & Smith 2000, pp. 58-69.

Chegwidden, Paula (2000). *Feminist Pedagogy and the Lap Top Computer*. In: Balka & Smith 2000, pp. 292-299.

Dorer, Johanna (1997). Gendered Net: Ein Forschungsüberblick über den geschlechtsspezifischen Umgang mit neuen Kommunikationstechnologien. *Rundfunk und Fernsehen* 45 (1), pp. 19-29.

Durndell, A. & Thomson, K. (1997). *Gender and Computing: A Decade of Change?* Computers Education, vol. 28, no. 1, pp. 1-9.

Erb, Ulrike (1996). *Frauenperspektiven auf die Informatik: Informatikerinnen im Spannungsfeld zwischen Distanz und Nähe zur Technik*. Münster: Westfälisches Dampfboot.

Finnish Ministry of Education (2001). Source: http://www.minedu.fi/; accessed September 2001.

Fittkau & Maaß GmbH (eds.) (2001). *W3B-Profile – WWW-Benutzer Analyse, April/Mai 2001*. Source: http:// www.fittkaumaass.de; accessed September 2001.

Forum Info 2000 (eds.) (1996). *info 2000. Deutschlands Weg in die Informationsgesellschaft*. Berlin: Bundesministerium für Wirtschaft.

Hapnes, Tove & Rasmussen, Bente (2000). *New Technology Increasing Old Inequality*. In: Balka & Smith 2000, pp. 241-249.

Krabbel, Anita; Wetzel, Ingrid; Ratuski, Sabine (1996). Participation of Heterogeneous User Groups: Providing an Integrated Hospital Information System, In: Jeanette Blomberg; Finn Kensing; Elizabeth Dykstra-Erickson (eds.) *Proceedings of the Participatory Design Conference* (PDC96). Cambridge: MA, pp. 241-250.

Kuosa, Tarja (2000). *Masculine World Disguised as Gender Neutral.* In: Balka & Smith 2000, pp. 119-126.

Leong, Siew Chee & Al-Hawamdeh, Suliman (1999). Gender and Learning Attitudes in Using Web-based Science Lessons. In: *Information Research* 5 (1). Source: http://informationr.net/ir/5-1/paper66.html; accessed March 18, 2002.

McDonald, Sharon & Spencer, Linda (2000). *Gender Differences in Web Navigation.* In: Balka & Smith 2000, pp. 174-181.

Miliszewska, Iwona & Horwood, John (2000). *Women in Computer Science.* In: Balka & Smith 2000, pp. 50-57.

Peiris, D. Ramanee; Gregor, Peter & Indigo, V. (2000). *Women and Computing.* In: Balka & Smith 2000, pp. 34-41.

Rommes, Els (2000). *Gendered User-Representations.* In: Balka & Smith (2000), pp. 137-145.

Schade, Gabriele (1998). Geschlechtsspezifische Medienkompetenz. Ein Erfahrungsbericht der TU Ilmenau. In: Winker, G. & Oechtering, V. (eds.). *Computernetze – Frauenplätze. Frauen in der Informationsgesellschaft.* Opladen: Leske + Budrich, pp. 157-166.

Schinzel, Britta (1997). Why is Female Participation Decreasing in German Informatics? In: Grundy, F. & Oechtering, V. (eds). *Proceedings of the 6th International IFIP-Conference on Women, Work and Computerization.* Berlin, Heidelberg: Springer Lecture Notes in Computer Science, pp. 365-378.

Schründer-Lenzen, Agi (1995). *Weibliches Selbstkonzept und Computerkultur.* Weinheim: Deutscher Studien Verlag.

Spender, Dole (1995). *Nattering on the Net – Women, Power and Cyberspace.* Melbourne: Spinifex.

Spertus, Ellen (1991). *Why Are There So Few Female Computer Scientists?* Boston, MA: MIT Artificial Intelligence Laboratory Technical Report 1315.

Suriya, M. & Panteli, Androniki (2000). *The Globalization Of Gender In IT.* In: Balka & Smith (2000), pp. 42-49.

Symonds, Judith (2000). *Why I.T. Doesn't Appeal to Young Women.* In: Balka & Smith (2000), pp. 70-77.

Turkle, Sherry (1995). *Life on the Screen: Identity in the Age of the Internet.* New York: Simon & Schuster.

Tuuva, Sari (2000). *Local Interpretations of Information Technology.* In: Balka & Smith (2000), pp. 208-216.

Westram, Hiltrud (2000). *Internet in der Schule – Ein Medium für alle!* Opladen: Leske + Budrich.

Wetzel, Ingrid; Klischewski, Ralf (2002). Serviceflow beyond Workflow? Concepts and Architectures for Supporting Inter-Organizational Service Processes. To appear in: *Proceedings of the CAiSE '02* (Fourteenth International Conference on Advanced Information Systems Engineering), Toronto, May 2002.

Cheris Kramarae & Zhang Wei

At Home in Education: Making Online Education Work for Global Women

Abstract

Online education has been touted by many educational and governmental leaders as ideal especially for 'home bound' women or women with heavy family and employment responsibilities. This essay looks first at the interests of people involved in decision-making regarding online higher education; second, at the varying ideas about the educational needs and capabilities of women; and third at the usually too limited concepts of 'access' and 'digital divide,' which don't consider women's situations or power relationships within the family. We also suggest some critical questions to help redesign women's online education. What are now usually considered as individual women's educational issues need to be recognized as global social issues involving the development and potential of all societies. These were discussed in the *Future of Education* project guided by the authors at *ifu*.

1 Introduction

The term 'online global education' sounds so good, suggesting qualities of teaching and learning that are inclusive, organic, holistic, connected. The term calls to mind those advertisements that utilize illustrations of students with different skin tones and costumes, sitting with computers that have connecting cables attached to various parts of the globe. We may come from different cultures and parts of the world, but, the ads seem to suggest, we can all study together electronically.

The possibilities for intercultural collaborations in higher education have increased dramatically, of course, with the spread of the Internet into many parts of the world. Online higher education is increasingly seen as at least a partial answer to the problems of women in many parts of the world who have primary responsibility of home and childcare (and often other work responsibilities), do not have funding for babysitters and expensive courses, and cannot attend campus classes. However, we argue for considering what is happening as not only a technical revolution but as primarily a social and political revolution that has

different impact on women and men around the world. For this reason, this
theme was proposed as a curricular project for *ifu* (International Women's University, here: *ifu*'s Project Area INFORMATION). Our analysis grows out of our
work with the women in the *Future of Education* project (see the chapter of
Link et al in this volume).

2 How Is Globalization Spinning the World?

As other critics have noted, globalization is neither accidental nor inevitable. It
is happening, in good part, because many people and institutions are interested
in moving people, materials, institutions, plants, and information around the
world, often for the primary purpose of making money. Much of the information
is coming from 'First World' countries via cable TV and the Internet, and going
to 'Third World' countries. Much of it is organized with a strong linguistic imperialism, since English is the dominant language of much of the information on
the Web as well as the major language of 'information' programming of the new
media technologies. According to the latest Internet statistics by language, Internet users using English language make up almost half of the online language
population today (Figure 1).

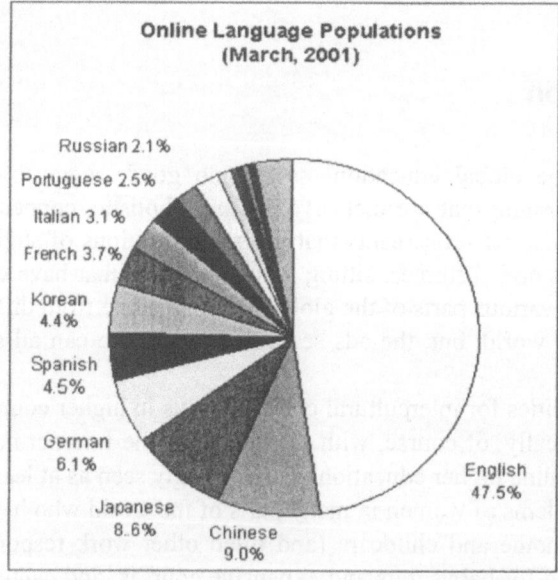

Figure 1: Chart of Online Language Populations,
from *Global Internet Statistics* (Global Reach, 2001).

Some of the 'experts' who are most interested in the use of global digital knowledge and education are venture capitalists interested primarily in good returns on investments, and educators interested primarily in increasing people's access to education. According to International Data Corp (2001), worldwide revenues in the corporate e-learning market will surpass $ 23 billion by 2004 from less than $ 2 billion at the end of 1999. The unprecedented influence from the corporate world has brought in ethics, values and goals that are often counter to what educators hold for good education. Consider Microsoft's goal in its cooperation with British schools, as a newspaper reporter summarized in this adapted slogan: "Give me a child of seven and I will give you a Microsoft user for life" (cited in Faigley, 1999: 131). The interests between these venture capitalists and the educators advocating online higher education for women are not only often in conflict, but are also often based on very incomplete information about women's lives, and educational needs.

3 Where Are Women Online?

The specific figures will change over the years, but the trends are well worth noting. At the end of 2000, an estimated 377 million people, half of them in the U.S., had access to the Internet (U.S. Department of Education, web-based Education 2000). The World map of Internet users suggests a high density of online population in North America, Europe and some developed areas in Asia (Figure 2). For an account of the situation in Fiji, see Williams, this volume.

While the number of female Internet users appears to be catching up with male users in some places, male users are still dominant on the Web outside the U.S. (Nielsen//NetRatings, 2001). In developing countries such as the People's Republic of China, female Internet users were only 30.44 % of the total Internet users at the end of 2000 (CNNIC, 2001). Even in the U.S. where the gender gap seems diminishing in Internet access, the gap between females from different ethnic groups still remains; female Internet users are more likely to be 'well-educated' whites with above-average family incomes (United States General Accounting Office, 2001).

For those who have access to the Internet, most of the current online education programs at the tertiary level are provided by traditional universities and single-mode Distance Universities (such as the Open University in UK, Fernuniversität Hagen in Germany, the Open University of Hong Kong, Anadolu University in Turkey, the Central Radio and TV University in China, and the Indira Gandhi Open University of India) that are transforming into the third-generation Distance Universities.

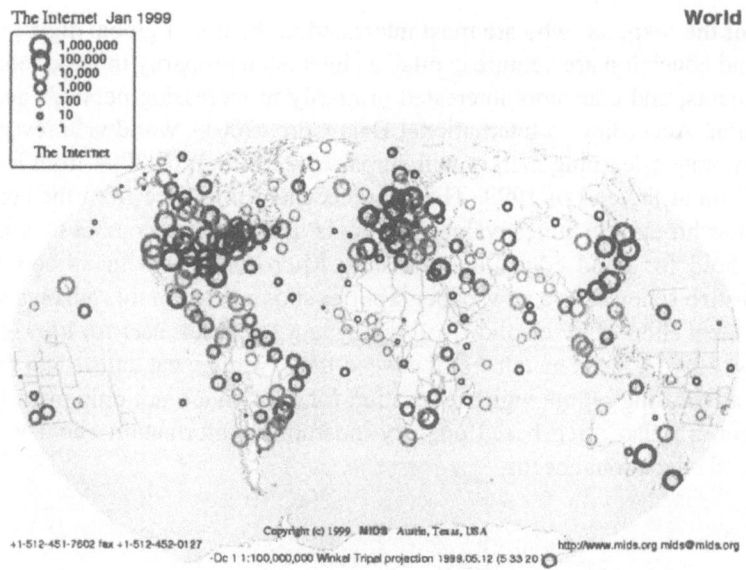

Figure 2: World Map of Internet Users (An Atlas of Cyberspace, 2001).

With most of the current online programs offered by traditional institutions of learning, they are largely benefiting the very people, who can, in the first place, afford the tuition costs and at the same time have access to the Internet. A national survey in U.S. universities indicates that three quarters of universities offering online learning courses charge the same tuition fees as for the on-campus courses (NEA Higher Education Research Center, 2000). In Africa, each credit can cost between $200-300 USD at the African Virtual University (Guttman, 2000). The disadvantaged groups who could not afford higher education before are still at a disadvantage.

4 Whose Knowledge?

The Internet has increased the possibilities for collaboration between universities across the national boundaries. But the implications on local curricular and accreditation policies from such collaborations are complex.

On their off-shore campus in Singapore and Malaysia, British and Australian universities provided all the teaching staff, textbooks and curricula for the local students who can afford such off-shore degrees in the 'twinning programs' (Blight et al, 2000). In Africa, at the World-Bank-funded African Virtual University (AVU), which connects universities in six African countries to universities in Europe and North America, lectures are all pre-recorded from the universities in the United States, Ireland and Canada first and then delivered to the African students via the use of satellite and Internet technologies (AVU, 2001). Local higher educational systems are under erosion in such 'collaborations' since local needs, local knowledge and local expertise are neglected in the curricula and instructional design.

The accreditation policy carries a similar print of intellectual imperialism. Several years ago, representatives from 30 European countries signed the Bologna Declaration, agreeing to develop inter-institutional and international standards. The institutions involved agreed to move toward the Anglo-Saxon model of B.A. and M.A. degrees (Johnston, 2001: 20). The primary intention of this decision was to enable credit transfer among the higher education institutions of the European Union. However, given the current world power structure, the actions taken in Europe will have critical implications for the administrators and students everywhere who want to be considered as belonging to 'world class' universities. The definition of 'university' will likely be determined not by local residents and authorities based on local needs, but by the experts living in Europe and the U.S., based on their visions of future needs for their countries. Not all these decisions are being made on the basis of what is needed for economic gain, but surely these decisions undermine the importance of local concerns, needs, and knowledge.

Any education course offered through the new technologies is culturally laden. New education networks might increase access to courses, but also threaten the local institutions of higher education (Harry & Perraton, 1999: 5). This may or may not be a concern of multinational corporations interested in expanding educational markets. The corporate giants in the U.S., many of which have created the hardware, software, and Internet routers, are often more interested in exporting equipment and information to other countries than in receiving and sharing knowledge from other parts of the world (Schwab & Pollis, 2000: 211).

In addition to the threats coming from intellectual imperialism and technology giants, the content of the present online curricula continues to be gendered. On the one hand, many of the sexist characteristics in traditional higher education have been transferred to today's higher education online (Blum, 1999). (For example, men students in online courses continue to ignore more of the topics raised by women in their online classes; this has been a classroom problem for decades, of course, as is explained in more detail by Wetzel, this volume). On the other hand, the kind of knowledge associated with global education and computers is increasingly that of abstraction, rationality, theory, with a focus on 'universal' methods of diagnosing problems and framing solutions. 'High status knowledge' is what is usually considered important to digitalize and disseminate as education. 'Low status knowledge,' the kind of knowledge associated with local experience, within an ecological context (Bowers, 2000: 74-75), is seldom digitalized as part of higher education materials. Women are, of course, most closely associated with experiential, local, ecological knowledge. Their knowledge may become even more disregarded in this millennium than in the past.

5 Critical Questions for Designing Women's Worldwide Online Education

We suggest that teachers, students and administrators planning for online education consider critical questions related to women's experiences. Among them are the following.

5.1 What Are the Particular Local Implications of Globalization for Women's Higher Education?

While critics and theorists are defining globalization as a complex process involving political, economic, and cultural issues, as capital is increasingly controlled by transnational banks and multinational corporations, too few people are paying attention to the ways that these processes are affecting education. And even fewer are paying attention to the special local and regional impact of globalization on women's education. Online education can cross geographical boundaries, but the women who might be able to take advantage of such courses and degrees are often highly constrained by their situations in the family and the local economic and cultural situation.

The impact of globalization on women in their home life has been mixed. Recent statistics show that in many places women's unemployment rates are higher than men's, even as the women are having to assume extra activities to help their families survive the higher prices that have come with many globalization policies. In other places women have more of the jobs than the men, because the women are considered cheaper labor by multinational corporations. Women in most localities are disproportionately involved in temporary, part-time, and home-based work. Often the women are still responsible for the children and the elderly but social services are usually poor or unavailable. That is, many of the changes in many countries have made life more difficult for women.

On the other hand, in the world-market factories many women are working in the jobs which allow them to break away from the patriarchal structures of their cultures (Moghadam, 1999; Young, 2001). In recent years the concepts of women's rights and the growth of a global women's movement have created important alliances across nation-state borders. Some studies suggest that the growth of transnational feminist networks can be explained in part by women's growing educational attainment and participation in paid labor forces. Clearly we need to pay more attention to the ways that women's higher education is affected by globalization in order to help plan successful online educational programs.

5.2 What Are Women Saying about Their Higher Education Needs and Possibilities?

A clarification of the barriers and the educational needs of the women can be the first step toward redesigning online education for women. The *Future of Education* project at *ifu* is one of the attempts in organizing such information based on the perspectives of women from different parts of the world.[1] As many of the *ifu* participants in The *Future of Education* project have made clear in our discussions, privilege is often invisible to those who have it.[2] Many of the people most involved in making decisions that will have enormous impact on women and their educational opportunities world-wide are not very knowledgeable about women's knowledge or educational needs and wishes.

In a study designed to gather information on women's interest in and experiences with online education (Kramarae, 2001), women from 32 countries responded to interview or online questions about their goals and assessments. Tuition costs for online programs was the central concern for almost all. Additional major problems listed by many were difficulty getting access to computers and to the Internet, unreliable electrical sources, difficulty of finding good online programs in their own culture/language (when that language is not English), and difficulty of obtaining academic-related journals and books in nearby libraries. These women all had some (if often limited) access to computers and the Internet. Thus their experiences are not necessarily representative of other women in their countries.

However, there are many other sources of information about the online educational access and barriers of women that can be drawn on. For example, the well documented history of women participating in distance education in the South Pacific provides data not only about the types of courses that have been successful, but also about the links between women's health, standard of living, social networks, available communication facilities, educational backgrounds,

---

1   Visit 'Women's Higher Education Resource Space' at: http://www.ifu.uni-hamburg.de/
    webspace/education/
2   These questions are based on those suggested by Barbara Sutton (2001) in a paper written to aid in the general improvement of international women's education. She noted large global structural barriers to equality (with the 'developed' world dictating much of what is considered 'research' and 'academic').

and women's ability to access online educational opportunities (University Extension, 1995).

5.3 What Is the Role of Women in Designing Online Learning for Women?

A check on the involvement of women in every level of decision-making is critical to the success of online learning for women. In addition to voicing their needs for higher education online, women should also play a major role in deciding the goals, the content, as well as the style of learning in the actual design process.

There is a growing body of literature on using the principles of participatory design in developing technological and organizational systems (CPSR 1999; Druin et al, 1997) and on applying constructivist learning theories in designing online learning environments (Jonassen, Peck & Wilson, 1999; Wilson, 1996; Hannafin, Land & Oliver, 1999). According to these theories and practices, meaningful learning necessitates that users/learners are active agents in designing and constructing online education that work for themselves. This process requires a close collaboration between planners, designers, educators and learners in the design process, including women!

However, we would also caution planners not to assume that such collaboration will automatically lead to the desired results. Our experience with the *Future of Education* project group at *ifu* suggests that the success of such collaboration requires all parties in the collaboration to reexamine their assumptions of learning by reflecting upon their prior teaching/designing/learning experiences, to redefine their roles as planners, designers, educators and learners as they experience role shifts in the collaborating process, and to negotiate the communication patterns between all participants in the collaboration.

In addition to the above concerns, there are other critical questions that we should consider in planning online education for women. As one *ifu* participant suggested in another project: How do we create organizational structures that do not reproduce and reinforce existing stifling hierarchies? How is it possible to create a truly democratic educational system when the views of the participants are not only different but often contradictory? [3] We all have customary ways of doing things. If they are embedded in deeply rooted hierarchical power structures, they are not only familiar systems but also highly resistant to change. And

3   In her valuable critique of *ifu*, Barbara Sutton (2001) also writes of the aspects that made it such a rich experience for so many: the lack of a competitive atmosphere, the encouragement to see research and knowledge-making through a gender lens, the self-organizing, the stress on democratic actions, the supportive women's space, and the international community.

yet if online education is to become more equitable and democratic, we need to ask and try to answer these critical questions, no matter what approaches the on-line education takes.

6 Concluding Comments

As the editors of the journal *Gender and Development* point out, "Globalization has been associated with human exploitation and environmental degradation, as well as the creation of new opportunities" (Editorial, 2000: 3). The changes in the world economy and the growth of the Internet and of the online education industry are affecting gender relations and shaping women's and men's choices and chances in very different ways.

In 2000, the Director-General of the United Nations Educational, Scientific and Cultural Organization (UNESCO) pointed out that it is not technology itself that is widening a knowledge gap, but, rather, the globalized market economy (of which technology is the driving force) that is widening the gap. This market does not usually value such intangible aspects of education as those relating to human dignity, personal fulfillment, or the sharing of and access to knowledge (Mayor, 2000).

The new technologies make access to education a possibility for students who because of geographical location have not been able to find or afford the programs or courses they need at a campus. A global student body can provide a diversity and a cultural richness that is otherwise nearly impossible to represent in an on-campus course (unless it is as well planned and financially supported as the on-campus International Women's University was – a most unusual experience especially for women).

However, this diversity and richness is only possible if student expertise and understandings are considered a part of the course material. A young Fulbright scholar from Russia, studying in the U.S., suggested in an interview with us that effective global education "can only come from knowing about other cultures." She suggested that courses would ideally be co-developed by teachers from several countries (as was the case at *ifu*), pointing out, for example, that foreign students studying in the U.S. often find that professors "ignore what isn't immediate to them."

Not all education comes from educational agencies. Women are, of course, using electronic networking successfully in many ways (see the chapter by Harcourt in this volume). For example, the United Nations Fourth World Conference on Women, held in Beijing, was a huge educational event, organized in good part on the Internet, which was also used to publicize the NGO (Non-governmental Organizations) Forum far more widely than any earlier global conferences. Such events illustrate some of the possibilities that the Internet and related technologies hold for women in many countries. However, they are not in themselves cures for socio-economic ills and educational divisions, as we can see by the fact that throughout the world the majority of the illiterate, cut off from formal education, are women.

Women's education, online or on campus, cannot be effective without the continual (and legitimized and honored) monitoring, analysis, and planning of women. To make our education succeed, we need to first ask critical questions and look to women's ideas and experiences for our answers.

Acknowledgement

We are greatly appreciative for the discussion of many of these issues with the women from the *Future of Education* Project at *ifu*. Our sense of hope comes from the continuing work they are doing in their countries.

References

An Atlas of Cyberspace (2001). Source: http://www.cybergeography.org/atlas/geographic. htm; accessed May 9, 2001.

AVU (African Virtual University) (2001). Source: http://www.avu.org/section/about/ index.htm; accessed May 12, 2001.

Blight, Denis; Davis, Dorothy & Olsen, Alan (1999). The Internationalization of Higher Education. In: Harry, Keith (ed.). *Higher Education Through Open and Distance Learning*. London: Routledge, pp.15-31.

Blum, Kimberly Dawn (1999). *Gender Differences in Asynchronous Learning in Higher Education: Learning Styles, Participation Barriers and Communication Patterns*. JALN, vol. 3, no. 1.

Bolabola, Cema & Wah, Richard (1995). *South Pacific Women in Distance Education: Studies from Countries of the USP*. Vancouver, Canada: University Extension of University of the South Pacific, Suva, Fiji and The Commonwealth of Learning.

Bowers, C.A. (2000). *Let Them Eat Data*. Athens, Georgia: University of Georgia Press.

CNNIC Statistics (2001). Source: http://www.cnnic.net.cn/develst/cnnic200101.shtml; accessed May 17, 2001.

CPSR (Computer Professionals for Social Responsibility) (1999). *Participatory Design Bibliography*. Source: http://www.cpsr.org/conferences/pdc98/bibliography.html; accessed May 20, 2001.

Druin, Allison; Stewart, Jason; Proft, David; Bederson, Ben & Hollan, Jim (1997). *KidPad: A Design Collaboration Between Children, Technologists, and Educators*. Source: http://www.cs.umd.edu/hcil/jazz/learn/papers/chi-97-kidpad/KidPad.html; accessed February 22, 2002.

Editorial (2000). *Gender and Development*. 8:1, March 2000, pp. 2-9.

Faigley, Lester (1999). Beyond imagination: The Internet and Global Digital Literacy. In: Hawisher, Gail E. & Selfe, Cynthis L. (eds.) *Passions, Pedagogies, and 21ˢᵗ Century Technologies*. Logan, Utah: Utah State University Press.

Global Reach (2001). Source: http://www.euromktg.com/globstats/index.php3; accessed May 15, 2001.

Guttman, Cynthis (2000) Offshore threats. Interview in: *The UNESCO Courier; 53,* 11, 2000. Source: http://unesdoc.unesco.org/ulis/; accessed May 12, 2001.

Hannafin, Michael; Land, Susan & Oliver, Kevin (1999). Open Learning Environments: Foundations, Methods, and Models. In: Reigeluth, Charles M. (ed.). *Instructional-design Theories and Models: A New Paradigm of Instructional Theory*. Mahwah: Lawrence Erlbaum Associates.

Harry, Keith & Perraton, Hilary (1999). Open and Distance Learning for the New Society. In: Harry, Keith (ed.). *Higher Education through Open and Distance Learning*. London: Routledge, vol. 1, pp. 1-12.

International Data Corp. (2001). Source: http://cyberatlas.internet.com/markets/education/article/0,,5951_737341,00.html; accessed May 20, 2001.

Johnston, Sally M. (2001). Inspiration from Abroad. *Syllabus* (14:9) April, 20.

Jonassen, David; Peck, Kyle & Wilson, Brent (1999). *Learning With Technology: A Constructivist Perspective*. Upper Saddle River, New Jersey: Prentice Hall.

Kramarae, Cheris (2001). *The Third Shift: Women Learning Online*. Washington, D.C.: American Association of University Women.

Mayor, Federico (2000). *The Information Age: A Triumph of Knowledge, Not Just a Triumph of Technology*. Source: http://www.techknowlogia.org/TKL_active_pages2/Archives/main.asp; accessed February 22, 2002.

Moghadam, Valentine M. (1999). *Gender and Globalization: Female Labor and Women's Mobilization*. Journal of World-Systems Research, vol. V, 2, 1999, pp. 367-388. Source: http://csf.colorado.edu/jwsr/archive/vol5/vol5_number2/html/moghadam/

NEA Higher Education Research Center (2000). Distance Education at Postsecondary Education Institutions: 1997-98. *Update* 6:2, April 2000. Source: http://www.nea.org/he/heupdate/; accessed May 12, 2001.

Nielsen//NetRatings (2001). *Web Remains a Man's World Outside US*. Source: http://cyberatlas.internet.com/big_picture/demographics/article/0,,5901_409541,00.html; accessed May 12, 2001.

Schwab, Peter & Pollis, Adamantia (2000). Globalization's Impact on Human Rights. In Pollis, Adamantia & Schwab, Peter (eds.). *Human Rights: New Perspectives, New Realities*. London: Lynne Rienner, pp. 209-223.

Sutton, Barbara (2001). *Women's Empowerment, New Experiments, Old Dilemmas: Experiences from the International Women's University*. Paper given in the Women and Higher Education: Transnational Perspectives panel at the Feminism Unbound Conference. University of Oregon, USA, May 11-12, 2001.

United States General Accounting Office (2001). Characteristics and Choices of Internet Users. Source: http://www.access.gpo.gov/su_docs/aces/aces160.shtml; accessed May 12, 2001.

Wilson, Brent (1996). *Constructivist Learning Environments: Case Studies in Instructional Design*. Englewood Cliffs: Educational Technology Publications.

World Map of Internet Users (1999). Source: http://www.cybergeography.org/atlas/geographic.htm; accessed May 9, 2001)

Young, Brigitte (2001). Globalization and Gender: A European Perspective. In: Kelly, Rita Mae; Bayes, Jane H.; Hawkesworth, Mary & Young, Brigitte (eds.) *Gender, Globalization, and Democratization*. Lanham, MD: Rowman & Littlefield, pp. 27-47.

Part 5:
Networking for Community Development

Communities are formed by people interacting permanently or for a certain period because they live close to one another or share common concerns. Though communities are heterogeneous and marked by internal conflicts amongst individuals and groups, the building and developing of communities is one of the most important paradigms for social transformation and the improvement of living conditions. This holds for 'real' communities interacting bodily in a physical place as well as for 'virtual' ones, consisting of people communicating over distances through telecommunication networks. The chapters in this part of the book examine from various angles the role of information and communication technologies for community development with a focus on the advancement of women.

The project on *Virtual Communities* at *ifu*, described by Karolyn Kerr and Elke Mätschke, aimed at understanding the idea of virtual communities and on building technical resources for enabling a virtual community. They cooperated with the South Pacific Telehealth Project in Fiji attempting to improve medical service for underserved population groups. The *ifu* women contributed by carrying out a gendered analysis of the information requirements of health professionals, and produced a prototypical interactive website for the use of this virtual community.

Mona Dahms and Edla Faust-Ramos give a comprehensive analysis of the relationship between development, gender and information technology in countries of the South. Community development is constituted by learning processes, for which information is a crucial resource, and which should be the basis for assessing the potential of information and communication technologies. Transformational participatory processes, engaging women in active decision-making, are the key to enable community development from within.

The topic of Lena Trojer is the evaluation of community development projects, focussing in particular on how they affect women, an issue she discusses with reference to a case study. The Blekinge region in Sweden participated in a special E.U. development program in the emerging information and communication society. Looking in detail at the intricate web of processes of this specific community development, she stresses the need to contextualize/situate all knowledge and technology production, which is at the heart of gender research ambitions.

An innovative attempt of using the Internet for community development is reported by Tanja Carstensen, Sabine Issa-Beuster, and Liane Melzer, who have conducted a project 'Times of the City' on behalf of the Hamburg Senate for Equal Opportunities. Time structures are not geared to the needs of working mothers. Time-related information is hard to find. Through cooperation with all parties concerned in a pilot district of Hamburg, they have succeeded in making time stuctures more flexible and information more accessible to the women in that part of the city.

Wendy Harcourt discusses her experience with 'Women on the Net', set up by the Society for International Development to encourage women, in particular from the South and from marginal groups in the North, to use the Internet more easily. Here, the Internet is seen as a resource for groups, such as non governmental organizations or women's group to promote their causes. The strategies of empowerment developed by women in this forum in the course of several years gave rise to lively discussions in the international community of *ifu*.

The International Women's University itself was an excellent example for how social and technical networking, face-to-face meeting and communication over distances all come into play and interact in community development. One of *ifu*'s most interesting results is the continued communication of the alumnae over the net: keeping up their spirit of belonging, feeling enriched by receiving news from all over the world, exchanging information on scientific events, discussing important political themes, forming initiatives of solidarity, and setting up an international conference. Thus networking leads to intricate meshes and webs of mutual sharing on a local and global scale.

Christiane Floyd

Karolyn Kerr & Elke Mätschke
With*: Elaine Maria Barth, Suzanne Belton, Annemarie Gustava Bütow, Anne Eickenberg, Aradhana Gupta, Asmita Jayendra, Sora Kang, Kerima Kostka, , Nai Li, Angelika Möser, Katerina Sedova, Mirela Skenderi, Esther Williams*

Building Virtual Communities: The Case of a Telehealth Project from the South Pacific

Abstract
Fifteen women from eleven countries participated in the *Virtual Communities* project at *ifu*. After learning the theory behind the social and technical meanings of a virtual community the team developed their idea of a telehealth website for the use of health care staff in the South Pacific. A prototype of the website was realized by members of the group in order to offer suggestions to the proposers of the South Pacific telehealth website. The project group made further recommendations on operational and strategic issues relating to the development and implementation of the project.

1   Introduction

This chapter is the outcome of the *Virtual Communities* project directed by Esther Williams from Fiji in the international context of *ifu* (International Women's University, here: *ifu's* Project Area INFORMATION). The contributors were fifteen women from eleven countries; representatives of Pacific, Asia, Africa, Australia, Europe and South America. We share diverse disciplinary, personal and cultural backgrounds and have not worked together on any previous projects, all adding to the challenge of working as a team. Most of us had never been in contact with a virtual community. In looking to find answers to our main objective we worked on definitions for virtual communities as well as for the conditions in which they take place. Of main interest was the question how we could participate and build a virtual community to be a sustainable, dynamic place.

Our divergent interests played a vital role in the project. Whereas some of us wanted to develop the technical skills for creating a virtual community, others struggled with its social dimensions. The five subgroups of the project each consisted of four to six women with varying disciplinary backgrounds: health, computing, linguistics, social sciences, visual communication and communications research, women's studies, management information systems, educational psychology, geography of industry, transport and trade as well as the theory of music. This made working in subgroups an interdisciplinary and challenging experience.

Individual members of the group all had different expectations and aims for the three months at the International Women's University. Even though each member of the group wanted to work in the project *Virtual Communities*, our individual understanding of the concepts differed. The group was able to find a basis for debating the theories as well as defining the goals for the project outcome. Working towards 'a real product' and knowing that our contribution would be appreciated by the South Pacific Telehealth Project was always a motivating factor. The group made positive use of the diversity of its members and found that the contribution of the different experts in our group helped to compile a product that covers many angles and meets our expectations of an interdisciplinary approach.

2 Working Towards an Understanding of Virtual Communities

The two main areas to explore are the social and technical concepts of virtual communities. Subgroups researched and shared findings on the following issues:

* Conceptualization of virtual communities;
* Online/virtual communities – how do they operate and who controls them?
* The character of virtual communities: real, phony, or just elitist?
* Cooperation and conflicts in virtual computer-mediated communities;
* Cyberspace and disadvantaged groups;
* Socialization in the virtual community.

Each subgroup selected an issue to present and lead a discussion for the group as a whole. Recommended reading included *Communities in Cyberspace* by Smith & Kollock (1999), parts one and two of FEED's dialogue, titled *Virtual Communities*, by Harold Rheingold (2001). The readings helped us to broaden our understanding of virtual communities and clarify our own expectation of 'our virtual community.' The group members said that they wanted to share their experiences of participating in virtual communities in practice. To experience belonging to a virtual community we made use of the whole range of options from using e-mails, USENET, chat rooms, conference systems, to becoming members of MUDs (multi-user domain, multi-user dungeon, or multi-user dimension). These tend to provide an environment where people log on to interact with each other (cf. http://www.mudconnect.com).

Our main virtual means of communication was the web-based system CommSy, developed for *ifu* and still in the growing phase. The group experienced team project work as a challenging and successful way of learning through an online communication system.

In the later phase of the project some subgroups concentrated on developing the technical structure of our website and the discussion forum for health professionals, a part of the telehealth project. Other subgroups concentrated on delivering the content for the pages and researched relevant web page URL links. Throughout the process of managing the technical and theoretical requirements the group worked on contributions to the project from a feministic intercultural perspective.

3 Defining Virtual Communities

Humans live in communities for survival and social reasons. Communities can be in the same geographical location or may share common interests but be dispersed. The advent of modern telecommunication technology has allowed people to form communities in new ways. It is now possible to discuss shared topics and meet in 'cyberspace' and be geographically far apart. It is simply a matter of having the computer systems, Internet access, electricity and the knowledge to work the system.

This new phenomenon has been subject to research. Smith (1999; p. 2) states that "a virtual community is a set of on-going many-sided interactions that occur predominantly in and through computers linked via telecommunication networks." A computer conferencing system enables people around the world to carry on public conversations and exchange private electronic mail (cf. http://www.well.com). Virtual communities are "social aggregations that emerge from the [Internet] when enough people carry on those public discussions long enough, with sufficient human feeling, to form webs of personal relationships in cyberspace on the Internet" (Rheingold, 2001: Introduction).

Virtual communities can be seen as a modern form of committees, composed of groups brought together by a common interest and separated by great distances, and limited to the speed of the computers and network links. They can take the form of bulletin boards, newsgroups, computer conferences, e-mail communication, interactive websites, or games.

Little research has been undertaken on the structure of virtual communities and how they are formed, but the literature suggests that virtual communities can be built in a number of ways. Units, partners and individuals can come together voluntarily to advance a technology-based community. The members of such a community tend to influence each other through social actions. They are independent of the roles and status they hold in the organizations they work for and use electronic mail to share information and coordinate work. They assume well-defined roles and status relationships within the context of the virtual group. Virtual communities can be utilized for both social and work-related interactions.

Nonetheless, social interaction is not sufficient for a collection of individuals to be viewed as a group. Groups must have permanence, structure and a sense of belonging. It is possible for virtual communities to come about unplanned and to be then fostered and maintained by meetings, workshops or face-to-face discussions at different intervals that are decided on by the group. They may or may not share a physical setting and can be dispersed across different organizations, types of organizations and individuals. Sometimes, there is shared government and shared property and they can be bound by common interests and goals. E-mail can take various forms: it can be posted individually, to the group, or on a bulletin board for discussion. This system can be used for feedback, support, ideas and stimulation.

Virtual communities will be able to govern and organize themselves if certain principles are established. These include:

- Group boundaries should be clearly defined;
- Members can participate in modifying the rules;
- The rights of individual members to modify the rules are respected by all members;
- A system for monitoring members' behavior exists; and
- the size of the membership is defined.

4 Developing a Virtual Community: the South Pacific Telehealth Project

The project group was given the task of looking at a telehealth system as a form of a virtual community and to offer recommendations for its development.

The Fiji School of Medicine wanted a telehealth service that could meet the need for specialist medical advice, thereby improving the quality of health care to underserved populations. It would also provide up-to-date medical information via the Internet, and ongoing medical education using distance education materials sent via the Internet, CD-ROM or traditional mail services. Professional isolation is a significant problem for health care workers in the South Pacific. For example, the northern group of the Cook Islands is a four-hour plane ride away from the main island of Rarotonga. There is often only one health worker on each island, who could be a doctor or a registered nurse covering a population of around 1,000 people. This, among other issues, such as low pay rates and political instability, has caused a severe problem with recruitment and retention of qualified and experienced staff throughout the South Pacific. It is hoped that a telehealth service could go some way towards solving this issue. The Fiji School of Medicine has been working on this project with the Secretariat of the Pacific Community and the Pacific Basin Medical Association and plans to set up the Fiji School of Medicine's Telehealth Unit. Funding for a service has been sought from the New Zealand Overseas Development Assistance, which is part of the New Zealand Ministry of Foreign Affairs and Trade.

The Fiji School of Medicine proposes to have eight staff working within the Fiji School of Medicine Telehealth Unit. They will be responsible for the initial development of the telehealth service, training and ongoing support.

Telehealth may be defined as the use of electronic information and tele-communications technologies to support long distance clinical health care, patient and professional health-related distance education, public health, health administration and access to information via the Internet.

This process usually involves the sharing of information between health care providers and is often directed by either distance consulting or distance learning (Pryor, 2000:2).

The development of a telehealth service is expected to produce extensive health benefits to the South Pacific in the form of an increased awareness of current overseas health care practices, current research findings, and improved diagnosis. But there are of course limitations, particularly where there are currently no health professionals on an island. The telehealth service could offer a virtual village square, a virtual conference room, a virtual school and a virtual open forum for health professionals, key individuals and organizations to interact, discuss, debate, learn and create better health for the people of the South Pacific. Teleprevention, using the telehealth service to promote wellness and disease prevention by public health methods, has the potential to significantly raise the level of health care in remote areas.

Those using the service would ideally be from all health disciplines. Therefore nurses, doctors, physiotherapists, radiographers, administration staff and all other health care workers should be able to access the site and make use of the facilities. All require up-to-date information about their specialty in order to provide the best health care possible. Discussion groups via e-mail or web pages allow for relatively inexpensive synchronous (real time) discussion among professionals within the South Pacific, giving them the opportunity to support each other.

The South Pacific Telehealth Project fits with the concept of a virtual community. The Fiji School of Medicine, Telehealth Unit needs to consider its vision and begin building a functional virtual health community that is inclusive and welcoming to a diversity of people. Ideally, there could be many different health professionals contributing to the website, rather than just employees of the Fiji School of Medicine, Telehealth Unit. The dissemination of local research, however, should be encouraged. The contribution of a variety of health information that is pertinent to the South Pacific would add to the wider interests of all health professionals encouraging a 'community' perception of the site along with shared ownership of such knowledge.

5 Website Development

A website was developed by members of the group in order to offer suggestions over and above a page for distance consultation, keeping in mind the requirements of the South Pacific Telehealth Project. The requirements for such a website were adapted from the already existing telemedicine design used by the Tripler Army Medical Center in Hawaii. The group was requested not to change the design of the existing Tripler website. Buttons were added to link to the new pages that copied the original layout. Figure 1 is a description of the web pages and some recommendations for the future.

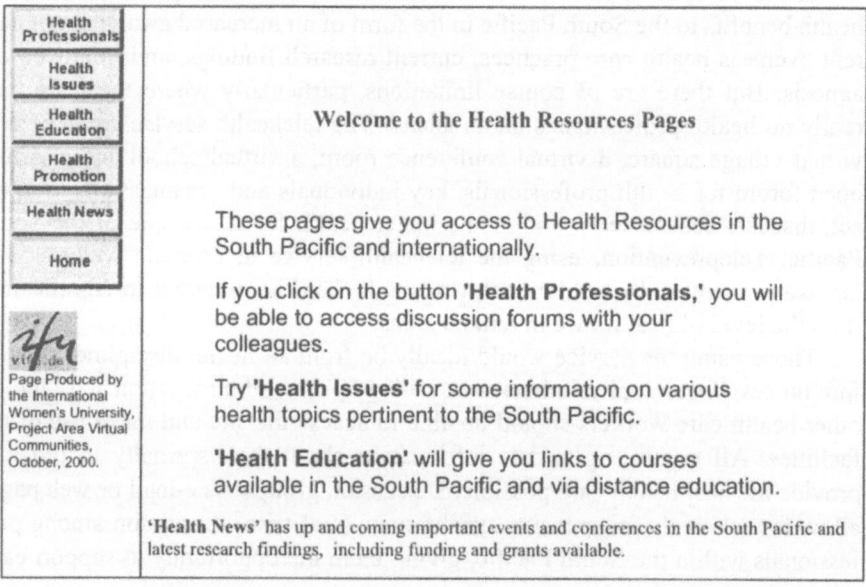

Figure 1: Screenshot of the concept of welcome to the Health Resources page

The Health Issues Page: Adding Women's Issues

The emphasis on this page is on health issues that directly or indirectly affect women in the South Pacific, including organizations that support women, but the page does include sites also relevant to men. Mental health website addresses have been added, as this is currently a major issue in the South Pacific, with few staff qualified in Mental Health. As shown in Figure 2, communicable diseases and in particular HIV/AIDS links have been added to provide up-to-date information.

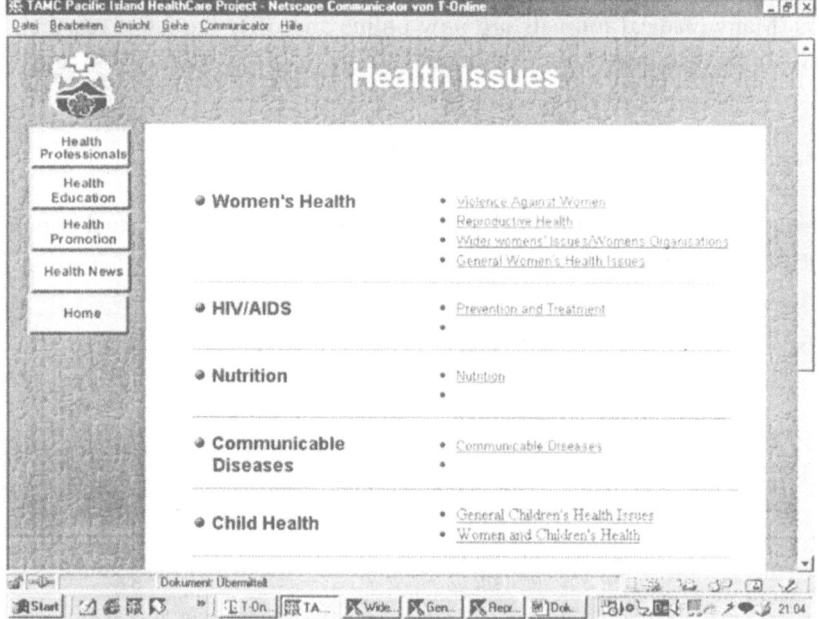

Figure 2: Screenshot of a detail of the Health Issues page

The Health Promotion Page

There is a large amount of information on the Internet about the prevention of disease through public education and health promotion strategies. Many common diseases in the South Pacific could be prevented through effective health promotion strategies, i.e. the promotion of immunization programs. Health staff may also find the information useful as patient education tools by printing it out from the website to make it available to their patients.

The Health News Page

They are provided for those practitioners who may wish to attend conferences, find out the latest health news in the region, or attend meetings of interest.

The Health Education Page

There are huge numbers of distance education courses available, and it may be possible for the Fiji School of Medicine to form links with other education centers. Many medical journals are now online and offer the latest research information; links to these have been included.

The Health Professionals Page

This page (as shown in Figure 3) was created to add to the 'virtual community' concept of the site.

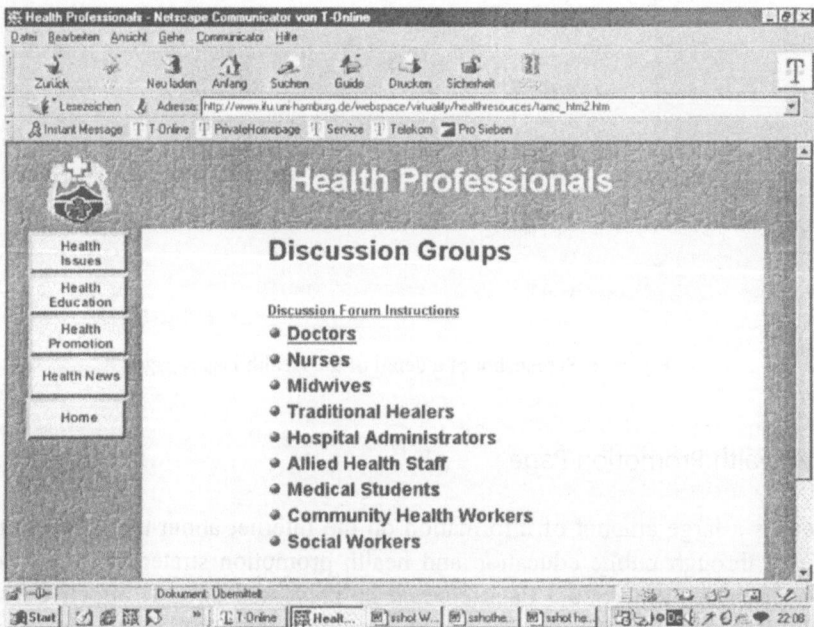

Figure 3: Screenshot of the Health Professionals – Discussion Groups page

For practitioners on remote islands an informal discussion group may help to keep each other informed. Or they may wish to discuss an interesting case, but do not consider a consultation with a specialist is required. The discussion forum may also be used as a support network. Multidisciplinary discussion forums on particular health related topics might be added later.

6 Group Recommendations for the Website

When developing the website, the group discussed options for maintaining its relevance over time. The following recommendations were made for the future of the website content:

- The Health News page would need to be updated on a regular basis by someone in the South Pacific.
- It may be possible in the future to add links that provide further patient education material to the Education page, it may also be possible for the Fiji School of Medicine to form links with other education centers, to enable the school to expand the number of courses on offer.
- Multidisciplinary discussion forums on particular health-related topics may be added later to the Health Professionals pages.
- Ideally there could be an extra page with open access for non-professionals, patients and patient support groups to encourage patient participation and networking.

The project group then made further recommendations on operational and strategic issues relating to the development and implementation of the project:

- It is necessary to identify and establish a coordinating unit for membership together with objectives and a working mandate.
- The steering committee should be gender-balanced with more input from women in their fields.
- The steering committee should be more diverse and interdisciplinary with experts from a variety of fields.
- Small teams should be established to direct the three approaches of consultation, education, and information.
- A variety of communication media should be used where these are available and not be limited by lack of access. This is responding to the need to expand the target groups and not limit the service to doctors and professionals.
- An innovation section needs to be established within the coordinating unit to keep abreast with developments and research that is being undertaken in telehealth in other parts of the world.

- Related to this are concerns over costs of equipment and telecommunication lines and space. The steering committee has all the CEOs of the telecommunication companies of participating countries as members, and they should have the power to decide on the cost of telecommunication links for all aspects of health.
- The employment of a person with health informatics skills would be beneficial.
- The employment of a person with community development skills would be beneficial.
- We suggest that before patient information is sent via the telehealth site the patient should give her/his informed consent so that the commonly understood ethics of medicine are not compromised.
- A code of practice needs to be developed that protects patients' rights during telehealth consultations.
- A review of currently available distance health education programs should be conducted to see whether these are suitable to the needs of health professionals in the South Pacific.
- Memorandums of Understanding should be obtained from organizations willing to work collaboratively with the telehealth project.
- Not only professional women who are experts in their fields should be included to assist in the development of the telehealth project, but also women who represent the potential patients and female community leaders.
- A broader view of health needs to be taken in the telehealth project specifically with regard to gender and health. Issues such as sexuality or sexual orientation, family planning, maternal mortality and abortion as well as violence against women need to have representation within the telehealth site.

7 The Continuing Interest

At the end of the project, the group handed over all results to the Project Leaders of the South Pacific Telehealth Project, Dr. Wame Bravalia and Dr. Jan Prior.

Karolyn Kerr is now studying the South Pacific Telehealth Project as a Masters thesis topic. The study involves a needs assessment, using qualitative methods to examine the needs of the users and beneficiaries. Karolyn felt that the top-down approach used in so many telehealth projects could be detrimental to the smooth implementation and utilization of the South Pacific Telehealth Project. The aims of this study and needs assessments in general are to

- identify positive aspects of telehealth that would enable implementation;
- look for concerns that might pose obstacles to implementation; and

• develop goodwill and a sense of inclusion in the final design process through stakeholder participation in the needs assessment.

The single most important step in starting a telemedicine program is conducting a needs assessment. This is the basic foundation on which all clinical and educational applications, technology selections and purchases, and operational decisions should be made (Yadava, 2000). Siden (1998: 225) states that "needs assessment is a critical part of the design and implementation of a telehealth project". The needs assessment process creates a sense of ownership amongst the participants, referring and consulting personnel that helps to improve system satisfaction and utilization. A needs assessment should take a holistic view of the community beyond an overall appraisal of the health needs of the community. It must take into account the economic and educational status of the community and any other local factors that will impact on the introduction of a telehealth system. Planning for the active input of communities and their health workers must be an integral component at all stages in the planning and implementation process for telehealth (Cardno, 2000: 7).

The telehealth service is planned to be implemented within the next year and it is hoped that the recommendations from the *Virtual Communities* project will be taken into account alongside with other pre-implementation assessment findings. The Fiji School of Medicine is considering the idea of a virtual community or 'one-stop shop' for all health professionals in the South Pacific but no final decisions have been made. It does appear, from the funding proposal made, that the needs of nurses and allied health professionals will not be considered in the initial development of the site. This is severely restricting the potential benefits of the service. McGee & Tangalos (1994: 1134) note in their assessment of potential contributions of telecommunications technology to the delivery of health care to underserved populations that

> effective telemedicine will dramatically improve the ability of midlevel providers (for example, physician's assistants and nurse-practitioners) to participate in health care delivery in underserved populations. Midlevel practitioners are an important resource for improving access to medical care with a low health care cost.

The group at *ifu* gained an extensive understanding of the concept of a virtual community, both in theory and in practice. The team was able to build the dimensions of a virtual community. The development of a telehealth project in the South Pacific, the group believes, will be enhanced by basing the site on the virtual community concept of shared governance and inclusion of all those affected by health care in the South Pacific.

The team's most valuable lesson, however, was learning to take time to listen to all members of the team. Attempting to understand the cultural and disciplinary background of all members of the team and valuing the contributions each woman can make is a skill we will be able to use throughout our careers and in our personal lives. Building a new intercultural study group, negotiating working procedures and keeping a positive communicative climate was equally important to creating the real end product. The firm friendships made from taking part in this project are what all group members first and foremost received from *ifu*.

The group is especially pleased about the fact that Karolyn Kerr is continuing our work. Her further commitment allows us to feed back on the acceptance of the work within the South Pacific Telehealth Project one year after *ifu*.

References

Cardno, E. Jayne (2000). Managing the Fit of Information and Communication Technology in Community Health: A Framework for Decision Making. In: *Journal of Telemedicine and Telecare*, vol. 6, suppl. 2 (12), pp. 6-8.

Introduction to MUD (2001). *The Mud Connector*, pp. 225-35. Source: http://www.mudconnect.com/mud_intro.html; accessed October 4, 2001.

McGee, Richard & Tangalos, Eric (1994). Delivery of health care to the underserved: Potential contributors of telecommunications technology. In: *Mayo Clinic Proceedings*, vol. 69, pp. 1131-36.

Pryor, Jan (2000). *NZODA Narrative Version 2*. Suva: Fiji School of Medicine.

Rheingold, Harold (2001). *The Virtual Community Online Book*. Source: http://www.rheingold.com/vc/book/; accessed October 4, 2001.

Siden, Harold (1998). A Qualitative Approach to Community and Provider Needs Assessment in a Telehealth Project. In: *Telemedicine Journal*, vol. 4.

Smith, Marc & Kollock, Peter (eds.) (1999). *Communities in Cyberspace*. London: Routledge.

Yadava, O. P. (2001). An Introduction to Telemedicine. Health4India Ltd. Source: http://health4india.com/new/Hospital-Update/telemedicine.asp; accessed October 4, 2001.

Mona Dahms & Edla Faust-Ramos

Development from Within:
Community Development, Gender and ICTs

Abstract
This chapter discusses definitions of and relations between community development, gender and information and communication technologies (ICTs). The relation between gender and development is examined from a historical point of view. In assessing ICTs for development, the emphasis is on revealing the underlying causes of the fervor of the current debate and on the learning processes and knowledge involved. The discussion on the relationship between gender and technology, especially ICTs, focusses on the reasons for the low representation of women in these areas. The overall aim is to analyze reasons for the apparent gaps which exist in all three relations. Based on the analysis, solutions to bridge the gaps – in the form of participatory processes which ensure 'development from within' – are sketched in the concluding section.

1 Introduction

It is a sad fact that in the world of today, where more wealth is being produced than ever before, there are also more people going hungry than ever before, more children are malnourished than ever before, and the gap between rich and poor countries and between rich and poor people within countries is widening. This happens in spite of more than half a century of development assistance to the so-called 'developing countries.'[1] Recently, there has been much hype and fervor about the role of ICTs in development but more than anecdotal evidence of the beneficial developmental impacts still remains to be documented. In this chapter we will take a closer look at the relations between the three key concepts: development, gender, and ICTs, in an attempt to answer the following question:

---

1   The authors strongly reject the notion of 'developed' and 'developing' countries. This terminology hails from the period of 'modernization theory,' where the assumption was that 'development' was equivalent to 'becoming like the industrialized countries,' an assumption which we do not adhere to.

How – if at all – can information and communication technologies be applied to support and enhance equitable and gender-inclusive participatory community development in countries of the South, as well as in countries of the North?

Our claim is that the continuous neglect of women's crucial contributions is a great obstacle to bringing about development. The two concepts of 'participatory development' and 'participatory design,' suggested as useful approaches to gender-inclusion, have some interesting similarities and both have gender connotations which will be elaborated here.

This chapter has been inspired and very much influenced by the work carried out in two of the *ifu* (International Women's University, here: *ifu's* Project Area INFORMATION) project groups: *Information Kiosk*, of which Edla was the director and Mona the facilitator, and *Community Development through Information*, of which Mona was the facilitator. The women in both of these groups came from different continents, with different cultural, educational and professional backgrounds and were of different ages. In spite of their differences they shared one fundamental idea: Development must come from within through a process of autonomous and critical learning while co-operating within a group.

Some participants of the *Community* group came from Sudan, Congo, Sri Lanka and South Africa, countries presently or previously torn by internal strife, so to them issues of conflict and conflict resolution were crucial. The *Kiosk* group included women working with participatory design of ICT systems. Both groups included community development workers who had many years of experience with participatory development. The discussion in this chapter owes much to the work of these women.

2 Development

The important concept of 'development,' a word much used and abused, will be used here mainly to describe processes of human, social and economic change in countries of the South. We will discuss different paradigms within development research, as well as different strategies for development assistance. In the conclusion, we give a definition of 'development' for the purposes of this chapter.

Since the end of the Second World War several development paradigms have formed the basis of research and of strategies for intervention. The *modernization* paradigm of the 1950s, framed in the North, perceived 'development' as a phased process of change, with traditional backward societies of the South becoming like modern industrialized societies of the North, and focussed on massive technology transfer and urban industrialization. As will be shown in section 4, today's discourse on ICTs for development strongly resembles the discourse of this paradigm.

The *dependency* paradigm of the late 1960s was a reaction from critical development researchers, especially from the South, against the modernization paradigm. It explained the underdevelopment of poor countries of the South (the 'periphery') as a dynamic process taking place concurrently with the development of rich countries of the North (the 'center'), both being a result of the capitalist world order and the global power imbalance. Obviously, this paradigm never formed the basis of any development assistance strategies, but it did contribute to a more general acknowledgement of the complexity of the processes of development.

In the 1970s it became clear that the expected development in the form of improved living conditions for poor people did not happen. At the same time experience from socialist oriented countries indicated that direct investment in basic needs gave visible and quick results. This brought about a shift in development assistance to the *basic needs* strategy focussing on shelter, food, clothes, health and education, mainly in rural areas. At that time, the first approaches to 'participatory development' were launched, mainly by non-governmental organizations (NGOs) of the North.

Gradually it was realized that the basic needs strategy did not succeed either in bringing about eradication of poverty. Thus, during the 1980s the *sustainability* strategy came into focus as a set of guiding principles for development assistance. Emphasis was once again on technology transfer, but this time operation and maintenance were also seen as important aspects, and institutional and human resources development, aimed at creating local capacity, were included.

Around the same time a *neo-liberal* paradigm emerged, emphasizing the role of the free market as a means of promoting development. The adjoining strategy was called 'structural adjustment,' and the introduction of structural adjustment programs (SAP), dictated by the World Bank (WB) and the International Monetary Foundation (IMF), became a condition for obtaining loans from these institutions. Such programs focus upon downscaling or privatization of public institutions, introduction of user payment for social services, increased export and de-regulation, and liberalization of trade and markets.

The neo-liberal paradigm and the structural adjustment programs have had a major detrimental impact in many of the countries of the South. At the macro level countries have 'sold out' of their economic independence by adhering to these programs in order to be eligible to borrow from WB and from IMF. At the micro level, poor people, among them women and children in particular, have been hit hard by SAP initiatives such as user payment for health services and schooling. Attempts to introduce structural adjustment programs with a 'human face' have not proven effective in resolving the underlying problems of economic dependency of nation states and impoverished living conditions for the poor. Even so, many technicians and economists from WB and IMF still argue that the suffering caused by SAP is the bitter but necessary remedy that will eventually bring the 'cure' that countries of the South become part of the global market economy and that people in these countries become consumers.

A very different view is taken by what might be termed the post-development school of researchers and writers, who contend that the whole body of theory and practice associated with 'development' is based on a discourse that maintains and perpetuates the global power imbalance between the powerful North and the subjugated South. While this critique is very useful in looking beneath the surface, in formulating critical questions to development issues and practices often taken for granted and in making explicit the assumptions (too) often underlying development interventions, it does not offer any simple answers to the question of how to improve the life of the poor people of the South.

Presently, at the beginning of the 21st century, the picture in development research as well as in development assistance is a complex and mixed one, with modernization, basic needs, structural adjustment and neo-liberal theories, strategies and practices co-existing side by side and influencing each other, while also being influenced by critical voices from the South.

One of the writers from the South who has written on the subject is the late president of the United Republic of Tanzania, Julius K. Nyerere, who has given the following definition:

> Development brings freedom, provided it is a development of people. But people cannot be developed, they can only develop themselves. ..He[2] develops himself by what he does; he develops himself by making his own decisions, by increasing his understanding of what he is doing and why; by increasing his own knowledge and ability, and by his own full participation – as an equal – in the life of the community he lives in. ..Development of a man can, in fact, only be effected by that man; development of the people can only be affected by the people." (Nyerere, 1973: 60)

Another definition in line with the above is given by Nobel Prize winner Amartya Sen:

> The analysis of development presented in this book treats the freedom of individuals as the basic building blocks. Attention is thus paid particularly to the expansion of the 'capabilities' of persons to lead the kind of lives they value – and have reason to value. (Sen, 1999: 18)

Two common characteristics of these definitions are, firstly, emphasis on 'development from within,' i.e. on development as a personal process of change taking place within the individual human being and under the control of this in-

---

2   In fairness it should be mentioned that President Nyerere was very much aware of women's crucial role in development. The original book was written in Kiswahili, where the third person singular pronoun (*mtu* = 'person') is neutral as far as gender is concerned, but in the translation to English *mtu* has been rendered as 'he.'

dividual; secondly, emphasis on freedom as a necessary prerequisite for this change process to take place. Thus, development can be likened to a learning process increasing and expanding the knowledge and capabilities of a person and allowing this person the freedom to be in control of her or his own life.

In Latin America, the discussion on development and learning draws on the concept of *autonomy*, where "autonomy is the capacity that the human being has to transform the world or environment in which he or she lives" (Faust-Ramos, 1999: 6), and development is the process through which the subject achieves this autonomy. In order to be able to transform the world it is necessary to have the cognitive ability to think about and critically reflect upon the transformations intended and therefore – as a first necessity – to understand the world and the reality that is to be changed. It is, however, not enough to conceive the transformation; the freedom and the means to accomplish this new reality in communion with others are equally important (Freire, 1993). Here, too, we find the emphasis on 'development from within' and on the freedom to accomplish change.

It is important to notice that transformation does not take place without crisis and anxiety, and this anxiety can be overcome only through co-operation with others. Therefore the above definition of development, which focusses upon individual learning, has to be expanded to include 'community development,' which is the emphasis of this chapter.

A definition of 'community' was given by Gyekye:

> A community is a group of persons linked by interpersonal bonds – which are not necessarily biological – who share common values, interests and goals. What distinguishes a community from a mere association of individual persons is the sharing of an overall way of life. (Gyekye, 1998: 35-36)

This definition is useful because it establishes the community[3] as a socio-economic unit of analysis; it does, however, conceal power imbalance, inequalities, oppressive social hierarchies and discrimination, often found within a community and based upon social categories such as gender, class, ethnicity, age, religion etc. In other words: the definition is "suffering from 'HBS', the 'homogenous blob syndrome'" (Guijt & Shah, 1998: 8). Specifically, the definition hides any gender differences in values, interests and goals occurring because of the different tasks and roles of women and men. To be realistic, the imagery of homogeneity and harmony needs to be replaced by a recognition of conflicts of interest within communities and attempts to deal with such conflicts in a positive and constructive way (Guijt & Shah, 1998).

---

3   See Kerr & Mätschke, this volume, for a discussion extending the concept of 'community' so as to include virtual communities enabled through interaction via the Internet.

Holding on to the similarity between development and learning, 'community development' can be likened to the concept of organizational or collective learning, defined as follows:

> ... the intentional use of learning processes at the individual, group and system level to continuously transform the organisation in a direction that is increasingly satisfying to its stakeholders. (Dixon, 1994: 5)

Replacing 'organization' with 'community' and 'stakeholders' with 'members,' this definition also holds for community development. It does, however, also suffer from 'HBS,' since stakeholders within an organization do not necessarily all have the same values, interests and goals. Thus, when dealing with community development it is necessary to accept conflict as an unavoidable aspect, and the concept of autonomy of learning must be expanded to include the ability to overcome conflicts of interest, to jointly define goals and strategies for transformation, and to co-operatively establish and maintain relationships based on mutual respect (Faust-Ramos, 1999).

In conclusion, development is a process of autonomous and critical learning, whether at individual or at community level. Learning processes expand the knowledge and capabilities of individuals and communities, and at the same time increase the freedom to be in control of one's own life. At the community level, conflicts of interest have to be dealt with in a constructive way in order to establish co-operation and mutual respect.

3 Gender and Development

'Gender' has been firmly established as a concept in the language of development agencies, government departments and NGOs since the UN Decade for Women from 1975 to 1985. Yet, it is still questionable to which extent it has had an impact on the lives of poor women in the South. In this section we will first discuss a definition of the concept of 'gender' and then provide a survey of how the discourse of gender and development has changed over the years, in line with changes of development strategies.

While the word *sex* refers to the biologically determined characteristics of the female and the male, *gender* is the term used to describe the socio-culturally constructed roles and characteristics associated with being female or male. In all societies of the world women and men differ in the activities they undertake, in their access to and control over resources and in their participation in decision-making processes. These differences are not biologically determined, but rather a result of practices and norms prevailing over centuries and perpetuated by socio-cultural institutions and culturally determined stereotypes. While we are not arguing that all women are worse off than all men, the existing gender differences are accompanied by gender inequalities, with women's work consistently being valued lower than that of men, a fact which is illustrated by the UNDP Human Development Report 2001, which states that "for all countries the GDI (Gender-related Development Index) is lower than the HDI (Human Development Index), indicating the presence of gender inequality everywhere" (UNDP 2001: 15).

The question of women's roles in development efforts is not a new one. In the earliest years of development assistance, i.e. in the 1950s, women were mainly seen in their role as mothers, and social welfare initiatives focussing on nutrition, food aid and family planning, were undertaken in order to make them better mothers. This approach was a residual model of social welfare during colonial administration, closely linked to the modernization strategy and based upon (implicit) assumptions about the man being the breadwinner and the woman being the housewife.

In the mid-1970s the so-called *equity* approach was introduced in response to the failure of the modernization strategy to provide sustainable development. This was the first Women-in-Development (WID) approach and it saw women as active participants in development processes, emphasizing the inequalities between women and men by attempting to gain equity for women through direct state intervention. The approach was challenging the gender inequalities; it was criticized as 'Western feminism' and was not popular, neither with development agencies nor within governments of the South.

An alternative was the *anti-poverty* approach – the second WID-approach – connected to the basic needs strategy. Its emphasis was on small-scale income-generating activities for poor women, thus recognizing that women play a productive role in society. This approach enjoyed limited popularity with development agencies and with governments in the South because it did not challenge the existing gender inequalities.

In the wake of the debt crisis of the late 1980s came the *efficiency* approach to gender and development. The emphasis of this approach – termed the third WID-approach – was to ensure that development interventions were more efficient and effective through the economic contribution of women, drawing upon the elasticity of women's time. This approach, which is linked to structural adjustment strategies, is still very popular with development agencies, governments and NGOs because it does not challenge existing gender inequalities.

A more recent and more radical approach – the *empowerment* or *Gender And Development* (GAD) approach – has arisen during the late 1980s and 1990s out of feminist grassroots organizations of the South. It seeks to create sustainable and equitable development for women and men by challenging and changing gender relations and by empowering women. The GAD approach is based on bottom-up mobilization around practical issues and problems while at the same time striving to increase the self-reliance and internal strength of women. In spite of much lip service to women's empowerment, it is not particularly popular with development agencies and governments of the South (Moser, 1993).

Based on the GAD approach a number of different frameworks for gender analysis have been developed, which "aims to break the MAMU syndrome, i.e. interpretations of society monopolized by Middle Aged Men with University Training!" (Mikkelsen, 1995: 157) by incorporating women's work, values and views into development work. Tools for gender analysis vary between the different frameworks and include, for example, gendered activity profiles, gendered profiles of access to and control over resources, gender roles identification and gender needs assessment. There are, however, still many questions as to how to translate the theoretical frameworks and tools of gender analysis into practical implementation in development initiatives. Problems identified are, among others:

- Gender analysis is difficult to carry out in practice and tends to impose an agenda from the outside, the purpose of which is often not understood by the people involved.
- Gender analysis does not account for the fact that questioning gender relations in many parts of the world is a sensitive issue which one does not approach easily.

The most recent approach to gender and development – termed *engendering development* – responds to some of the problems identified with practical implementation of gender analysis. While the overall aims do not differ from the GAD approach, engendering development is based on participatory processes and takes its point of departure in the gendered realities rather than in an imposed agenda of gender analysis.

In communities of the South, women are the ones who strive to meet the daily needs of families and communities by carrying the triple responsibility of economic production, social reproduction in the household, and community management. These efforts of women are well respected within the family and in the community, but are often not acknowledged by governmental institutions and development agencies and therefore overlooked in development interventions. The engendering development approach is based on partnership, dialogue and mutual learning. The diverse practical experiences of women are seen as important inputs to the development process and women themselves are seen as active participants in development efforts. This approach is closely linked to the concept of 'participatory development,' which will be discussed in section 6.

4 ICTs and Development

In order to understand the hype and fervor about the role of modern ICTs in development assistance we will take a closer look at concepts of 'information' and 'communication' and their role in community development. Further, we will discuss the relationship between information and knowledge in the form of learning processes. Also, the relationship between knowledge and power will be discussed in order to understand the current dominant discourse on the 'knowledge-based society.'

In phrases such as 'information society,' 'information highway,' etc., the word *information* is used to denote a physical quantity which can be stored, processed and transmitted. A more precise word for this physical quantity would be *data*, and the use of the word information should be reserved to denote meaning. This qualitative difference is brought out in 'the value chain of information':

$$\text{Data -> Information -> Knowledge -> Wisdom}$$

where value is added from one step to the next (Fuchs, 1997). The process of adding value between data and information is based on the '4 A's' model: data must be accessible, assessed and adapted in order to be transformed into meaningful information. Based on the information gained, the person can start acting (Heeks, 1999).

The value adding from information to *knowledge* comes through learning processes to which information constitutes the input. Given the definition in section 2, these are equivalent to development processes that lead to increased and expanded knowledge. In the context of autonomous and participatory development, information becomes a very important social resource.

Information becomes accessible to the individual as well as to the community via communication, which in this context can be seen as mainly fulfilling an informative function. In the process of dealing with conflicts in community development, communication also serves other important functions, such as negotiation, cooperation and the establishment of relationships.

According to Maturana (1999) we construct ourselves as human beings in the interactive process of communication, thus we can say that communities construct themselves through communication. Language and interaction bring forth human nature; therefore, the more intense, supported and free these processes are, the more development will occur. In this view development is proportional to the ability and possibility to communicate. This implies social relationships based on mutual respect and acceptance of the legitimate participation of others.

Thus, information and communication are indeed crucial for community development. However, it is the information exchange and the interactive communication processes which are important, not the technical means of accessing and producing information or of mediating communication.

ICTs for development are often implicitly taken to be computer based technologies providing access to the Internet. But ICTs encompass any kind of technology that allows the production, processing and transmission of information, for example, the telephone, telefax and telegram; radio, television, and recorded audio and video material on tape or on CD-ROMS; books, newspapers and other printed material; indigenous folklore, popular theatre and proverbs. Finally and most importantly in this context, the production, processing and transmission of information that takes place within and between human beings (without ever being recorded explicitly) is the most important information and communication system in most rural communities of the South (Dahms, 2001).

When discussing knowledge, the question of power relations is important. The following quote illustrates the relationship between knowledge and power:

> This is maybe the single most important characteristic about the rationality of power..not that power seeks knowledge because knowledge is power, as Francis Bacon said, but that power defines what counts as knowledge and thereby what counts as reality. (Flyvbjerg, 1992: 424; our translation)

In this connection the global power imbalance is important: "The real power of the West is not located in its economic muscle and technological might. Rather, it resides in its power to define" (Sardar, 1999: 53; here quoted from Müller & Bertelsen, 2001:3). Therefore the articulated and formalized types of knowledge so highly valued in the North come to form the basis of the dominant discourse about the global 'knowledge-based society,' while tacit knowledge – which may be tacit simply because it is not perceived as knowledge, neither by the authorities of power nor by the holders of the knowledge themselves (Freire, 1993) – by its very nature is excluded from this discourse, although this may be assumed to be the dominant form of knowledge held by large parts of the populations in most countries of the South[4].

By excluding tacit knowledge we risk loosing a valuable body of knowledge developed by people of different cultures through knowledge production methods unknown to and therefore not validated by Northern science. We also run the risk of decreasing the social value of those who hold this knowledge – in other words: The more articulate culture of the North may eventually exterminate the more tacit cultures of the South.

---

4   See also the chapter by Floyd in this volume, where 'knowledge flowers' visualizing the conceptions of knowledge of participants from different cultural backgrounds are discussed.

Discourse analysis of documents discussing the 'knowledge-based society' and ' ICTs for development' reveals a strong resemblance to the modernization discourse of the 1950s and 1960s. As also pointed out by Akande and by Williams in this volume, the discourse on the 'digital divide' creates categories such as the 'information rich' and the 'information poor' and the 'knows' and the 'know nots' which tend to reinforce the divide between North and South. Like the modernization paradigm, the 'digital divide' model is based on technological determinism, while overlooking complex social factors influencing underdevelopment and poverty, such as power imbalances and inequalities at global, national and local levels (Wilson, 2001). It also overlooks simple factors such as the lack of electricity and telecommunication facilities in many of the poorest rural communities in countries of the South. This barrier is not technical, but rather economic, and can be overcome only by massive investment and political commitment.

Analysis of implemented ICT projects, such as telecenters for community use in countries of the South, provides rather disappointing lessons to be learned. For example, about a third of 65 telecenters, established during 1998-2001 by the Universal Service Agency, a governmental agency in South Africa, were not operating at all in early 2001, although the communities had been carefully selected among a large number of applicants, and one of the selection criteria had been that the applying organization should be a respected community organization with some idea of how they would use the equipment (Benjamin, 2001). Analysis of the impact of telecenters that were operating revealed that access to ICTs often reinforced existing social relations and inequalities. The focus was more on giving computer skills to individuals, of whom a fortunate few would find jobs outside the community, than on improving the standards of living of the many remaining in the community (Benjamin, 2001).

An important issue here is the propagation of computer literacy. From the point of view of an industry in search of a consumer market, users with basic computer skills are sufficient. But from our point of view much more is needed: freedom to decide what users want to use the ICTs for; guaranteed access to materials of interest; the possibility of writing about their own experiences and their own world, and the right to have their writings published and read. Only then does the user become the actor and the delegation of power to the specialist can be minimized.

We want to draw attention to two important points when considering ICTs for development. The first point is that development must take its point of departure from existing knowledge in societies, because it is a process of adapting new information into existing knowledge structures. The second point is that when designing ICT projects for community development, the focus should be on information and communication services needed in the community, rather than on the technical means to deliver such services. Identified need should determine the choice of technical tools. In many cases this may lead to the necessity of designing and implementing information systems with specific purposes and characteristics different from existing technical solutions. Therefore, the transfer of ready-made technical solutions developed for a different context is not sufficient. Instead, a participatory approach should be applied, allowing users a say in the design of the systems. We will return to this discussion in section 6.

5 Gender and ICTs

Like gender, technology is socially constructed and has in the North become stereotypically associated with men and male activities, thus excluding women's activities as non-technical. This exclusion happens in spite of the fact that technology is regarded as one of the means by which human beings reproduce and expand their living conditions, coping with needs for food, shelter, health, clothing etc. – practical activities which in most societies fall into the sphere of women's work. The perceived relationship between masculinity and technology also tends to exclude women from education and occupation within all areas of technology, a fact which is illustrated by the low percentage of women participating in technical study programs and technical jobs in most countries of the world.

Concerning the more specific field of gender and computer-based ICTs, the situation in many countries of the world is such that although the number of women using ICTs for information search and for communication is increasing, the number of women involved in research and development of these technologies, whether on the hardware side or on the software side, is still depressingly low.

According to a survey made at the Department of Computer Science, Norway Institute of Technology, one of the major reasons for low female participation was that the institutional culture at the department was dominated by the values of the so-called 'hackers.' These values, which are characterized by machine fascination, work addiction and a playful attitude towards computers, are reinforced by professors, teachers and dedicated male students and therefore become dominant at the department. They are, however, in opposition to the values of women students, who therefore become marginalized and feel alienated. In conclusion the researchers note that there is a need for a change in contents of computer science courses towards a greater interest in the needs of users and more emphasis on the complex and diverse contexts in which computer applications take place (Rasmussen & Håpness, 1991; Wetzel, this volume).

Another reason, argued by Sherry Turkle, why many women (and some men) are alienated from computers is that the present social constructions of computer culture and programming styles impose a particular formal, analytical, top-down deductive mode of thinking and working with computers, which is predominantly male, Northern and middle-class. Turkle does, however, point to another, more concrete approach, which she calls 'bricolage,' a term borrowed from anthropology, where it is used to describe ways of tinkering in traditional societies of the South[5]. Based on this approach to computing, she suggests that women should reject the formal top-down approach and instead search for ways in which the social constructions of computing can be modified and changed in order to make the computer a convivial tool in the hands of women (Turkle, 1990; in Kirkup, 1992).

In conclusion, two main points stand out. The first is that research on and development of ICTs is a male dominated field where women opt out and women's perspectives therefore are missing. This is a problem for the industry because it results in a lack of professional personnel, but it is an even greater problem for society because women might bring different ideas and interests to the development and use of computers (Bratteteig, this volume). The second point is that a shift in computing culture and curriculum contents towards 'softer' and more user-oriented approaches might bring more women into computing (Woodbury, this volume). This supports the statement that women would bring other ideas and perspectives to computing than men, and thereby contribute to making computers and computer systems more useful for larger parts of the population.

6 Learning and Participation – the Key Concepts

In this last section we will draw together the different strands of the discussion and propose a conclusion.

The definition of development outlined in section 2 stated that development is synonymous with autonomous and critical learning processes, individual as well as collective. Comparing this definition with the fundamental meaning of 'participation,' i.e. people's right to decide over their own lives, it seems obvious that no development can be sustainable unless it is participatory; people cannot and will not learn unless they are motivated to do so by a prospect of improving the lives of themselves, their families and their communities.

The concept of *participatory development* refers to the distribution of roles and responsibilities between 'outsiders,' i.e. government officials, development workers, NGO representatives etc., and 'insiders,' i.e. local community members.

---

5   See also the chapter by Weber in this volume, who described the group process in her *ifu* project, which involved theorizing, action and creative computer work as 'tinkering.'

Common use of the term 'participation' does, however, conceal very divergent views about its aims and practices. Two major alternative uses can be distinguished: *transformational* participation, where participation is an end in itself, and *instrumental* participation, where participation is a means to development. While the former entails empowerment of the local population and focusses on political strategies to achieve that goal, the latter aims at achieving more efficient project management and thus applies pragmatic public management strategies through which the state attempts to mobilize local resources. Transformational participation tends to predominate in project documents, while instrumental participation predominates in real project situations (Mikkelsen, 1995).

Needless to say, we are proposing transformational participation, which aims at empowering local community members while acknowledging and building upon their skills, experiences, creativity and knowledge. We thus see community members as active agents of transformation and change, based on autonomous and critical learning processes that allow people to develop capabilities and freedom.

A very important question to ask in connection with participation is: Who are the community members to participate, i.e. who are the 'insiders'? Who wants to participate? What makes their participation possible? What do they stand to gain from participating? All too often the use of the term 'participation' – as indeed the term 'community' – has suffered from 'HBS,' i.e. has glossed over internal power imbalance and conflicts of interest among 'insiders' within the community.

Tools for participatory development are legion and include, for example, temporal tools, such as historical profiles and trend lines; spatial tools such as community maps and mobility maps showing contacts with the 'outside' world; socio-economic tools such as daily calendars, Venn diagrams reflecting institutional relationships, transects, i.e. walks through the study area and preference ranking and scoring. Once community specific data has been gathered using the most relevant tools, possibly adapted to the given context, a Community Action Plan (CAP) can be prepared that will then guide further development activities. In the process of gathering and analyzing data for the CAP, development workers and community members should cooperate and learn from each other – the process being characterized by mutual learning and information exchange.

A very interesting observation is that – despite shared goals of empowerment and social change – the two fields of 'gender and development' and 'participatory development' have existed side by side for quite a long time and have begun to merge only during the mid 1990s. The reasons for this apparent gap are several, the main ones being:

- Participatory development practices have overemphasized community cohesion and consensus at the cost of ignoring, among others, gender differences.
- Gender and development practices have tended to impose 'top-down' conceptions of gender and presented ideas of desirable gender relations which have often conflicted with views of local community members, female as well as male.

In practice the group of 'insiders' has to be redefined away from the harmonious conglomerate of 'community members' to different social groups determined by gender and by economic, political, ethnic, religious and age characteristics. Different social groups very often will have different needs and interests, and changes resulting from participatory development processes are not always win-win situations. Areas of conflict have to be identified, discussed and analyzed and participants need to develop proposals for solutions. Therefore, participatory development is inherently linked to dealing with conflict, and active and explicit management of change, power relations and conflict resolution need to be an integral part of the development process:

> ... equitable participatory development requires explicit attention to gender relations. This, in turn, can only be effective if based on a sound understanding of the dynamics of power, the nature of conflicts and conflict resolution, and the process of social change. (Guijt & Shah, 1998: 13)

In summary, gender issues should be an integral part of any development effort using equitable and gender-inclusive participatory development processes.

Participatory design is a generic term for a broad set of ideas, organizational means, methods and tools for design and development of ICT systems that takes the user and her or his specific context as the point of departure for design of such systems. Systems development is here seen as a process of social and organizational change where one of the most important changes has to do with the introduction of ICT systems. Obviously, the participation of future users of such systems in the design process is of great importance in order to fit the systems into a given context. On the other hand, user participation changes the design and development process into an evolutionary process of mutual learning and co-operation between designers and users about technical possibilities and useful deployment of these possibilities.

There are normally three reasons for involving future users in the systems development process:

- It may improve the knowledge upon which the system is built and therefore make it fit better to the given context.
- It may enable the users to develop realistic expectations of the system and may reduce their resistance to change.

- It may increase the local democracy by giving future users the right to participate in decisions that are likely to affect them.

The first two reasons, which are 'instrumental' in nature, may be found in other systems development approaches, while the third reason is transformational and has empowerment as the end goal. Thus, issues of power and control are of major importance in connection with participatory design, as are the conflicts of interest that may arise when involving users in decision-making processes.

Tools and techniques for participatory design include, among others, search conferences, future workshops, design workshops and the use of paper-based prototypes, so-called 'mock-ups.' Differences in language, competence and experience have to be overcome in the cooperation between designers and users.

Gender aspects in participatory design are often implicit, since the risk of the 'homogenous blob syndrome' is also present in this field. Nonetheless, we would assert that the inclination to involve users in ICT systems design will be more marked with female than with male systems designers and that the inclusion of participatory design approaches in curricula of computer science study programs might attract more women, resulting in more women computer scientists with more emphasis on user involvement – thus, a positive circle could be set in motion.

Comparing 'participatory development' and 'participatory design,' the most striking similarity is the fundamental idea of people having the right to be involved in making decisions affecting their lives. Other similarities are the overall aims of empowerment of community members, respectively ICT systems' users and the enhanced democracy, including the recognition and acceptance of social conflicts linked to shifting power balance. The differences between the two approaches are mainly due to the fact that participatory development is rooted in a social science background while participatory design has its origin in a technical scientific background. Therefore also the methods and tools used in the two fields differ, but when used together, synergy effects might develop which could lead to enhanced impact of the use of these participatory methods.

Having closed the gap between gender and development by the use of gender-inclusive participatory development processes and the gap between gender and ICTs by the introduction of gender-inclusive participatory design processes we would finally like to close the gap between ICTs and development by asserting that gender-inclusive participatory development processes should be employed in the identification of and the needs analysis for ICT development projects. Once needs are identified, gender-inclusive participatory design processes should be applied to the design, implementation, monitoring and evaluation of the ICT systems while remembering that ICT does encompass a broad range of traditional and modern technologies – choice of technical means should be second to and based upon identified user needs. Throughout the process focus should be on mutual, autonomous and critical learning and co-operating. By building on the strengths and potentials of the poor people themselves, by enhancing the individual and collective learning processes that are synonymous to development and by respecting people's right to decide for themselves, it may be possible to achieve 'development from within' for the poor people of this world.

Acknowledgements

We would like to express our gratitude to the two *ifu* project groups *Community Development through Information* – Astrid Binda Matiaba, Daya Ekanayake, Somaya El Bashir El Tayeb, Fidensia Lado, Faith Nebo Legoabe, Pretty Lilly Majola, Asita Molotii, Hanan Satti, Merridy Wilson – and *Information Kiosk* – Dwi Astharini, Meryem Atam, Lynda Awasum, Yolisa Faith Bomela, Carol Delgado, Violet Kabarenzi, Sarah Yonjo Kibaalya, Florence Muinde, Josephina Paul, Maria Rossal Lins, Nina Rutakyamirwa, Kutoma Wakuñuma – for all the inspiration and fruitful discussions we have had within the two project groups. A great THANK YOU to all of you, wherever you are! We would also like to thank Govind Kelkar, director of the *Community Development through Information* project and Yvonne Dittrich, facilitator of *the Curiosity and Intuition: Becoming Comfortable with Technology* project, of which Edla was the director, for the exchange of many useful ideas throughout the *ifu* period. Further thanks go to Christiane Floyd for very sensible and useful suggestions to early drafts of this chapter and last but not least to Gudrun Parsons for careful proofreading and finishing off the chapter.

References

Benjamin, Peter (2001). *Telecentres and Universal Capability. A Study of South Africa's Policy on Universal Access to ICTs and the Telecentre Programme of the Universal Service Agency, 1996-2000.* Unpublished PhD. thesis at Aalborg University.
Dixon, Nancy (1999). *The Organisational Learning Cycle. How We Can Learn Collectively.* 2nd ed. London: McGraw-Hill.
Faust-Ramos, Edla (1999). *Autonomy and Emancipatory Ways of Learning and using Information Technologies. Research Report of Departamento de Informática e Estatística,* Universidade Federal de Santa Catarina. Florianópolis.
Flyvbjerg, Bent (1992). *Rationalitet og Magt,* vol. II. Odense: Akademisk Forlag.
Freire, Paulo (1993). *Pedagogy of the Oppressed.* Harmondsworth: Penguin Books.
Fuchs, Richard (1997). *If you Have a Lemon, Make Lemonade: A Guide to the Start-up of the African Multipurpose Community Telecentre Pilot Projects.* Paper submitted to the In-

ternational Development Research Centre. Source: http://www.idrc.ca/acacia/outputs/lemonade/lemon.html; accessed February, 16 2002.

Guijt, Irene and Shah, Meera Kaul (eds.) (1999). *The Myth of Community. Gender Issues in Participatory Development.* London: Intermediate Technology Publications.

Gyekye, Kwame (1996). *African Cultural Values.* Accra: Sankofa Publishing Company.

Heeks, Richard (1999). *Information and Communication Technologies, Poverty and Development. Development Informatics.* Working Paper Series, No. 5/1999. Institute for Development Policy and Management, University of Manchester. Source: http://www.man.ac.uk/idpm/; accessed February16, 2002.

Kirkup, Gill (1992). The Social Construction of Computers: Hammers or Harpsichords? In: Kirkup, Gill & Smith Keller, Laurie (eds.). *Inventing Women. Science, Technology and Gender.* Cambridge: Polity Press & The Open University, pp. 267-281.

Maturana, Humberto (1999). *Emocões e linguagem na educacão e na politica.* Belo Horizonte: Editora da UFMG.

Mikkelsen, Britha (1995). *Methods for Development Work and Research. A Guide for Practitioners.* New Delhi: Sage Publications.

Moser, Caroline (1993). *Gender Planning and Development. Theory, Practice and Training.* London: Routledge.

Müller, Jens & Bertelsen, Pernille (2001). *Changing the Outlook. Reconciling the Indigenous and the Exogenous Systems of Innovation in Tanzania.* Paper presented in the International Workshop on African Innovation Systems and Competence-building in the Era of Globalisation, Aalborg University.

Nyerere, Julius K. (1973). *Freedom and Development – Uhuru na Maendeleo.* Dar es Salaam: Oxford University Press.

Rasmussen, Bente & Håpnes, Tove (1991). Excluding Women from the Technologies of the Future? A Case Study of the Culture of Computer Science. In: *Futures,* pp. 1107-1119.

Sardar, Ziauddin (1999). Development and the Locations of Eurocentrism. In: Munck, R. & O'Hearn, D. (eds.). *Critical Development Theory – Contributions to a New Paradigm.* London: Zed Books, pp. 44-62.

Sen, Amartya (1999). *Development as Freedom.* Oxford: Oxford University Press.

Turkle, Sherry & Papert, Seymour (1990). Epistemological Pluralism: Styles and Voices within the Computer Culture. In: *Signs: Journal of Women in Culture and Society,* vol.16, no.1, pp. 128-157.

UNDP (2001). *Making New Technologies Work for Human Development. Human Development report 2001.* United Nations Development Programme. New York: Oxford University Press.

Wilson, Merridy (2001). *Information and Communication Technology, Development and the production of "Information Poverty".* Unpublished thesis submitted for the Degree of Master of Philosophy in Development Studies, Oxford University.

Lena Trojer

Rhetoric and Realities:
Evaluation of IT Projects

Abstract
A discussion of complex information technology development processes is presented by means of an evaluation of a major development project in the county of Blekinge, Sweden.
The public image of the Blekinge region in southern Sweden has changed during the last five to ten years from a region in deep crisis to a dynamic region with special attention on information technology. In an E.U. context Blekinge has been successful in launching the region as a full-scale laboratory, which was aided by a closed structure of the region and by its smallness (150,000 inhabitants), in order to develop and change the society.
A number of competencies are necessary to evolve complex understandings and make them a suitable basis for different kinds of strategy decisions and further development. Gender research has relevant expertise to contribute in various fields. The Blekinge case study illustrates the importance of carefully selecting evaluation tools and methods to be able to assess how IT projects affect community development, as was proposed by the author as part of a more general strategy for implementing the visions created at *ifu*.

1 Introduction

The background for this chapter comes from my engagement in the very last phase of the study program at *ifu* (International Women's University, here: *ifu*'s Project Area INFORMATION). I was asked to join the strategy team and contribute with experiences from evaluation of a regional initiative about telecottages outside urban areas. My concern in gender research perspectives of process evaluation and development of information technology as part of a regional innovation system brought me to Hamburg and *ifu* – an opportunity for which I am most grateful.

This chapter presents a discussion of complex IT development processes by means of an evaluation of a major development project in the county of

Blekinge. Its aim was to create jobs and enhance dynamism in the region based on a platform of information and communication technology.[1]

A number of competencies are necessary to evolve complex understandings and make them a suitable basis for different kinds of strategy decisions and further development. Gender research has relevant expertise to contribute in various fields. The first one is research about situated knowledge and situated technology development. The work of Donna J. Haraway is particularly important in this context (Haraway, 1991 and 1997). Secondly, the understandings within gender research concerning the knowledge production of our time bear transformative potentials (Gulbrandsen, 1995; Trojer et al, 2000). Alliances exist in epistemological thinking with researchers stressing contemporary distributed, non-linear research and technology development processes (Gibbons et al, 1994; Nowotny et al, 2001). In Sweden we find contributions to more modulated, varied and integrated knowledge about innovation and innovation systems associated with late modern forms of universities (Uhlin & Johansen, 2001; Fernvall, 2000). Thirdly, the interest among gender researchers for IT policy and dominating and alternative IT discourses can be utilized (Elovaara, 2001). Finally, it is critical in the IT region Blekinge to consider the serious limitations that oppose affirmative action for decreasing the gender gap in production of IT and IT politics.

The public image of the Blekinge region in southern Sweden has changed during the last five to ten years from a region in deep crisis to a dynamic region with special attention to information technology. This changed view (rhetoric) of Blekinge is particularly palpable in the eastern part of the region. In the indicated situation of regional development it is in the interest of Blekinge to evolve a comprehensive understanding of the complex processes contributing to the ongoing change. This transformation can be described as a regional experiment of interpreting a rising information society and putting it into practice. In the context of the European Union Blekinge has been successful in launching the region as a full-scale laboratory, a step which was aided by the complete structure of the region and by its smallness (150,000 inhabitants) in order to develop and change the society.

There is a technical university, Blekinge Institute of Technology (BIT), in the region. This university is nationally unique in its profile in that it combines a focus on applied IT with developing a practice for distributed knowledge production, with three chief actors – the university, regional authorities, and indus-

---

1   Blekinge became one of the 22 regions that participated in a special E.U. development program called RISI (Regional Information Society Initiative) in 1997/98, the aim of which was to study how the regions could make continued and increased use of the unique possibilities afforded by the emerging information and communication society while at the same time avoiding the problems that frequently result from such development.

try. The profile integrates research, education and development. The technical faculty of Blekinge Institute of Technology includes a division aimed at technoscience studies from gender research perspectives. The scientists at the division are committed to developing complex understandings of IT as a reality producing technology and of the dominating transformations following in its footsteps.

2 Background of the BIT Houses Project

The region of Blekinge underwent a tremendous change in its economical structure during the 90s. The dependence on heavy industry and military authorities changed dramatically in favor of telecommunications and software industry. The whole region is emerging into the information society. Three closely cooperating regional actors have been, and still are important for this process, namely the university, industry and local/regional political authorities. As an example of the economical development in the region, 1,600 new jobs were created, predominantly in the IT sector, between 1994 and 1996. A professor for strategic social planning, Jan-Evert Nilsson, states (BIT 1999, p.76) that Blekinge is the best example of a transformation from an old industrial society to an information society in Europe.

When Sweden joined the European Union, four of the five municipalities in Blekinge were classified as 'objective 2 regions' and were thus eligible for support from the structural fund for regional development. IT Blekinge, as a non-profit organization,[2] was responsible for running the E.U.-funded development program IT-Blekinge, within the framework of which there were several different projects. One of these was the telecottages project 'BIT -Världshus i Blekinges tätorter' (BIT houses in the villages of Blekinge), running from Nov 1, 1997 to May 30, 1999.

It was decided to set up nine BIT houses, spread geographically across the county. IT Blekinge entered into agreements with nine independent legal entities, each of which was made responsible for one telecottage for the duration of the project.

An organization was then established for the BIT houses project, with a central project management team responsible for co-ordination. Contracts were signed with Telia for the provision of an Intranet between the BIT houses and a common Internet connection. Sun Microsystems provided servers and network

---

2   IT Blekinge consisted of representatives from the county administration in Blekinge, the Blekinge Association of Local Authorities, Blekinge County Council, Blekinge Institute of Technology, the Southern Sweden chamber of commerce and various representatives of the local business community.

terminals, and Jämshög Folk High School provided training and technical support in connection with the project.

IT Blekinge's main aim of the project was for the actors involved to work together to enable a broad sector of the public and small local companies in the small communities outside the main towns in the county to grasp the possibilities afforded by the new information technology for both individual people and small businesses. By means of the users' activities in the BIT houses, the new technology was supposed to be made tangible and accessible to larger number of people in the region.

IT Blekinge wanted the BIT houses project to be evaluated and commissioned a group of gender researchers – headed by the author of this paper – to follow the project throughout its entire duration. The expectation from this thorough evaluation was to contribute to further initiatives in the regional IT development process.

3 Evaluation: Why and How?

One crucial outcome of evaluating IT projects might be to develop an understanding of the complex prerequisites and contexts in which the projects try to give shape and substance to ongoing transformations in society. Research about evaluation (Baklien, 1993) suggests that – besides observing functions of mapping consequences and giving feedback – an evaluation also means 1) to legitimize the project; 2) to justify the use of state financial resources; 3) a control function from which the participants in the project can learn something; 4) to give other actors outside the project opportunities to gain access to experiences from the project; 5) of providing a knowledge base for further decisions.

In a pilot study (SNS 1998) it was stated that we have a couple of decades of international experience concerning the evaluation of technical and industrial renewal policies. Just as in any field of research there are borderlines within evaluation research. One borderline divides those who advocate some kind of 'steering approach,' where mostly quantitative methods are used to measure the impact of programs and policies (often in the form of a cost-benefit analysis), and those who believe that individual projects and set goals are insufficient and inexpedient as units of analysis. In addition there are different expectations and understandings of what an evaluation of a program or a policy can provide. When the impact and relative usefulness of a policy is to be assessed, strong arguments from the latest decades of evaluation research suggest a starting point from a broad evaluation perspective like 'an adaptive learning approach.' Out of such an approach the evaluation will deliver not only the necessary feedback based on set standards, but also more well-founded knowledge that can be used for decisions to continue support or phase out a policy.

The pilot study also emphasizes that the reference frame out of which the evaluation is developed should be explicitly presented when the evaluation is used in a 'learning policy process' where the feedback aims at providing policymakers with bases for supporting or stopping projects. The reason is to make it possible for different partners to easily assess how balanced the evaluation is. In case one single evaluation perspective does not satisfy all the needs or provide answers to all relevant questions, it is of course better to evaluate as many dimensions of a policy as possible. Such a 'mixed assessment' seems to be the best one can achieve when there are no absolute truths.

3.1 The Experience of LOCREGIS

As the BIT Houses project was an integral part of the RISI project of IT Blekinge, evaluation approaches in similar E.U. projects were considered. LOCREGIS (Local and Regional Information Society) started in the summer of 1996. One of its aims was to make an inventory and analysis of IS (information society) projects fostering competitiveness within less favored or scarcely populated regions by innovative uses of IT. As part of LOCREGIS an evaluation tool was produced.

The LOCREGIS evaluation tool was called 'Best practice criteria for the information society and regional development' and was supposed to be used for evaluating local and regional IT (IS) projects primarily concerning the impact on regional development.

To give an example of the somewhat limited way of thinking involved, the tool states "a discussion between the evaluator and the project coordinator has shown to be the most sufficient way to assess projects. However, the evaluator ought to have knowledge about the case in order to be able to make the evaluation as objective as possible. This concerns particular the criteria of relative values as innovation."

The criteria used in the evaluation tool were *power of attraction, innovation, partnership, strategic planning, leverage* and *reproducibility.*

Judgements were made for all criteria and subcriteria and quantified on a scale from 1 to 5. The average value was calculated for each head criterion and put in a radial graph. This evaluation tool is not sufficient to show the processes necessary to understand valuable experiences from a project. The evaluation team found the view of evaluation within LOCREGIS to be too uncritical and too unsophisticated to use for the BIT houses project.

3.2 Evaluation of the BIT Houses Project

The evaluation team defined its task as an overall process evaluation of the 'BIT houses in the villages of Blekinge' project and adopted the following understanding as the starting point for the assessment:

> The major structural transformations, the works mentality, the strong traditions of low self-esteem ("It'll never work.") that are to be found in Blekinge make it extremely difficult for people to find the new life patterns that are needed to maintain their society and culture. The only solution is to expose their life conditions to previously untried ideas. For this reason, we should try to circumvent the established structures to ensure that the process of change is not hampered by previously defined goals. Of course, this is a demanding task – for the actors in the IT Blekinge project, since their role as experts will be queried, and for the people who live in Blekinge. If the latter are to be allowed to take part on their own terms, their skills can be employed and their wishes can be satisfied, but in a different way to what may have appeared possible at first glance. The goal for IT Blekinge – to develop democratic structures and give the people an opportunity to exert an influence – should be reconcilable with the idea of giving people the opportunity to shape their own lives, in new and as yet unrealized ways. (Ekdahl et al, 1999: 8)

The BIT houses project brought with it major challenges with regard to realizing the visions that are formed in an emerging information society – visions that seek points of balance between rhetoric and various different realities in a pluralistic society. Paul Cilliers (1998: 9) claims that

> ...it is not possible to tell a single and exclusive story about something that is really complex". During the project period, the BIT houses project revealed itself to be an increasingly complex experiment, which could only be broached with complex descriptions and commentaries. It was not possible to make generalizations and give simple interpretations, and this complexity was also reflected in the evaluation report. (Ekdahl et al, 1999: 8)

The evaluation project tried to go beyond an instrumental, linear, quantitative evaluation model, all too common in European Union IS contexts[3]. The evaluation project focussed on processes in order to develop complex understandings of why things happened as they did. A multicontextual approach was used. When trying to understand the BIT houses project from a regional strategic view expressed in different documents and from dialogues with regional actors, a number of questions were discussed, namely:

- How can IT strengthen democracy?
- How is it possible to create a virtual meeting place giving the inhabitants an increased insight into the work of societal institutions/authorities which influence the inhabitants' lives?

---

3   See Dahms & Faust-Ramos, this volume, for a distinction between instrumental and transformative strategies for participatory community development.

- How will the work of organizations and associations be affected by new digital meeting places?
- How can the need for interactive distance learning be provided for?
- How can new job opportunities be created that are traditionally missing in heavy industry regions?
- How can financial support be found for high risk projects?

The evaluation team understood the answers to the how-questions as growing in an open and continuing process. What is needed for a working process is: staff with the requisite knowledge about the field; flexible premises; techniques for creating learning environments to fulfill goals and aims; techniques that can be used in professional IT projects; opportunities for inspiration and development; qualified help for education and consultation in certain phases; time and room for continuing evaluation, reflection, analysis and feedback.

The evaluation team was inspired by Baklien and SNS and their views on evaluation. Particularly the evaluation attempt focussing on processes was guiding the team. The reasoning of Baklien about the relation between ideal and reality was brought together with the interest of the evaluation team to problematize the ideal and dominating IT discourses. After this extended introduction of knowledge and experiences of project evaluation, I want to present some of the results of the BIT houses project itself and comment the dominant parts of the IT rhetoric.

4 Rhetoric and Realities

The BIT houses project was initiated and carried out on the basis of a number of strong visions expressed on several different levels – ranging from the level of the European Union to the local level. The rhetoric in the visions tried to find a way into various different realities in order to be able to manifest itself in concrete results and at the same time to help create new and different realities. It is a quest for balancing points that can never be fixed, but which place themselves somewhere between rhetoric and the currently existing realities.

In order to be able to visualize the encounter between rhetoric and reality, it may be useful to study the experiences reaped from the BIT houses project, which I believe express core questions regarding the processes that took place and developed in the project.

Time, Space and Trust

Knowledge organizations have some fundamental requirements: Time is a positive quality when you have it, and an enemy when you do not. This may sound banal, but any project of change using a digital infrastructure as the main and consuming element necessarily takes twice as long as planned. Other aspects of time as a weak link in the project include the relationship between time and trust, and the relationship between time and the necessary scope for failure and mistakes – an absolute must in real-life transformation projects. The shorter the project period, the greater is the need for tight project management and transparency in the project. Space – the project space, i.e. the figurative space in which the project exists and unfolds, should be built on a foundation of openness and the ability to listen. There must also be room for mistakes (see also the discussion of knowledge projects by Floyd, this volume).

The Role of Technology

The evaluation demonstrates two diametrically opposed ways of relating to technology. IT Blekinge expressed a relatively strong linear, instrumental implementation philosophy. The other approach was the process-focussed and catalytic one, which was represented by other actors in the project, including Jämshög Folk High School, where people's dynamism, ideas and creative wishes were in focus and IT was a supporting, albeit changeable, function.

Processes of Change

Here, too, different points of view were in conflict – between those held by IT Blekinge and those of the support functions that Jämshög Folk High School was supposed to provide – causing confusion and misunderstandings, according to many of the BIT houses. The BIT houses provided examples of both approaches.

The Project Period

In the beginning in particular, it was clear that the BIT houses project had been planned as a pan-regional project implemented during the time span available for the project within the framework of RISI. It is important to bear in mind that the RISI projects in other countries used the entire 18 months of the project period solely to plan the various IT-related projects. It is unrealistic to believe the period allotted to the project would be sufficient to initiate, establish and create activities that were to be commercially viable or supported by various authorities. To this end, a project would reasonably have needed at least three years.

New Arenas for IT Development

One of the ideas behind the BIT houses project was to create a new space and new arenas in which established actors would not have the opportunity to dominate and demand 'more of the same,' but where innovation and creativity would be nurtured and allowed to bear fruits. However, the financial partners behind the BIT houses were conventional, established actors, such as the *Federation of Educational Associations*. This caused an unavoidable divide and constituted a major paradox, as a development rooted in local conditions must start with good local knowledge and be based in local organizations.

Setting a Good Example

The goal of setting up Blekinge as a full-scale laboratory for IT-related experiments was also carried by the wish to set a good example. The experience gained in this case would suggest that a good example in the sense of finding a shortcut for other interested parties does not work in local realities. Each local transformation project by definition works from the starting point of its own specific conditions and presuppositions. There are no shortcuts. The task will be as strenuous and time-consuming for each new undertaking. The sum of knowledge and experience gained may lead to a short list of tested strategies, which are thought to be relevant in the dynamic development of systems that characterize an emerging information society. These tested strategies may provide inspiration for new projects, but they will never constitute a straightforward template.

The Role of IT Manufacturing Companies

Here the evaluation team found three factors constituting interesting observations. The first was the rivalry between *Sun* and *Microsoft*; the second was the way in which *Sun*'s network terminals were presented as a well-functioning system easy to integrate – in stark contrast to the users' actual experience of using these computers.

The third interesting observation was the way in which the BIT houses understood and viewed the computer systems. They were almost completely focussed on PC environments. There was a great deal of external pressure at the time when the BIT houses project was starting up from local inhabitants with personal computers at their work places. No other than PC environments had even been considered, which of course exerted an influence on the education programs offered and the demand for service at the telecottages.

Closeness Versus Distance

This element can be likened to a balancing act. In order to have a sufficient overview, the project management needs a certain amount of distance, but in order to communicate with the participants in the project in a useful multilateral discourse, they also need a degree of closeness.

Transparency, Accessibility and Simplicity

The project management should strive to make the project process as transparent as possible to the participants in the project. This entails all aspects of the project to be open and accessible. Simplicity was always sought for – in respect of information, communication and technology.

5 The Rhetoric of Regional Development

The experience gained from the RISI work, in which the BIT houses project constituted a major part, suggests three priority aspects for regional development. If we regard these aspects as three parts of the dominant rhetoric, the issue then becomes: how has this rhetoric interacted with the realities in the region?

The 'Everyone Perspective'

The first part of the rhetoric is an approach that has become known as the 'everyone perspective.' Many of the preconceptions dominating the BIT houses project can be summarized like this: the technology already exists; the challenge is to make it accessible to everyone. IT as something to be discovered, to be recognized as useful and to be used, is one of the basic ideas in the broad implementation philosophy that persists. However, what this 'everyone' is supposed to mean was not analyzed at all and appears to include only the traditional preconceptions. The BIT houses' interpretation of the 'everyone perspective' was clearly demonstrated by the predominant activity of the project: traditional educational activities, often in collaboration with established educational associations. This makes it far too easy to drag out the old, familiar structures and thereby limit the 'everyone perspective.'

However, there were some other movements in the BIT houses opening up the concept somewhat, namely the people: the local population, women, tourists, young people, parents, children, pensioners, immigrants, home-owners, farmers and many other categories of people who came to the telecottages to use e-mail, surf the net to find information (or just for fun), to play games (via the Internet), try new things and learn, to taste the new technology and either swallow it or spit it out. The local ties seemed to motivate the BIT houses to experiment and work with the 'everyone perspective' in order to give it meaning and develop plurality.

The 'everyone perspective' also encompasses the explicit objective of promoting the opportunities of women. Some BIT houses devoted special attention to fulfilling this objective. There were special measures taken to reach the target group 'women' at five BIT houses.

Vandana Shiva once said "*New technologies travel on old social relations*"[4]. Experiences reveal that new technologies simply reinforce old social structures rather than transforming them. The concern to understand the underlying cognitive structures, which are reality producing in the evolving information society, has been and still is comprehensive in gender research.

Christina Mörtberg (Trojer et al, 2000: 3) holds that equal access to ICT ought to be a basic principle, when the slogans are no longer 'technology in a democratic society' but 'democracy in an information society'. She problematizes the discourse of equal access by showing that the limitations of equal access are rendered visible by a multiplicity of variables such as gender, class, race, region, etc.. There are no automatic links between the political goal of equal access and the opportunities that are opened up by information technology.

The Bottom-up Approach

The second part of the rhetoric is the bottom-up approach. This perspective can only be understood in the light of its opposite – the top-down approach. If we assume change, and in particular sustainable change, requiring reciprocity, it is more logical to relate horizontally (as equals) than vertically (hierarchically). This also applies to our interaction with people in connection with IT-related

---

4   Vandana Shiva, lecture focussing on biotechnology, Lulea University of Technology, March 5, 1998.

development. Some BIT houses struggled to maintain some minimum of equality in their interactions. With respect to services provided by the authorities, we are all too prone to slip back into a top-down approach. This will happen for as long as we fail to recognize clearly the average citizen's motives for seeking out information, forms and the like so ardently that s/he can be bothered to attempt to overcome all the obstacles posed by complicated and trying technical systems – and is willing to leave the comfort of the home to go to a telecottage.

Jämshög Folk High School believed it had failed in its role as a support function with regard to its goal of providing a counterbalance to and possibly overcoming the top-down approach. For reasons both beyond and within their control, it was impossible for all the BIT houses to attend a sufficient number of meetings together to make much progress in the more fundamental discussions regarding the motives for implementing the IT project. If this had been achieved, it seems likely that more of the people involved would have started to consider other ways of developing activities than those provided by traditional computer education and to define the possibilities afforded by as well as the consequences of the information society. This in turn would yield new ideas regarding what IT can mean and what it can be used for – absolute prerequisites for the generation of innovative activities and new areas of employment.

A Regional Development Laboratory for Full-scale Experiments with IT

The third part of the rhetoric considers Blekinge a regional development laboratory for full-scale experiments within the field of IT. The county of Blekinge was considered suitable as a testing ground for the development of technology and new IT-based services. This kind of reasoning has been offered as the strongest argument in the various talks regarding allocation of resources. The work at the BIT houses demonstrated this kind of rhetoric not to be subject to any kind of noticeable reflection or the motive behind any special undertakings. Each telecottage was simply concerned with starting up activities in its own location.

There was an explicit understanding at some of the BIT houses about 'you have to know what you want,' i.e. develop a profile, before linking up with the other telecottages to constitute a functional and unified network (a laboratory). The regional coverage in Blekinge for BIT house activities was satisfactory. For coordinated regional networks it is crucial to build a firm foundation first by gathering a wide range of knowledge and experience from local projects. Once the local bases have been established, there is a certain degree of stability and the profile can be recognized; then the foundation has been laid and it is possible to start testing different types of IT -based applications.

6 Conclusion

The rhetoric I have discussed has not really had much of an opportunity to en-counter and interact with reality. At the end of the BIT houses project, this en-counter was still a long way off in the future. It must be remembered that the evaluation was only a stage in the development and changes will continue be-yond its completion in May 1999. The focus of the evaluation was on the poten-tial significance of IT in specific local circumstances.

It is fair to state that the BIT houses project proved it was possible to:

- mobilize great force, energy and patience for a far-reaching and complex project;
- find new arenas that provide people with the opportunity to try new things;
- unite people from the whole region and overcome the old conflicts and dif-ferences between Eastern and Western Blekinge;
- create expectations outside Blekinge regarding the development of exciting new IT-related activities; and
- test the limitations and possibilities provided by IT in a number of different (local) conditions.

It is also fair to state that it was not possible to find or implement a simple dis-course in the nine BIT houses – a discourse that could unify all forms of under-standing and practices of IT. I use a thinking similar to Cilliers' (1998: 114), whose opinion is that "we have to cope with a multiplicity of discourses, many different language games – all of which are determined locally, not legitimated externally. Different institutions and different contexts produce different narra-tives which are not reproducible to each other."

If we look at the BIT houses project as a part of a regional innovation system, Uhlin and Johansen (2001: 16) show how such a system must be recognized as a complex system and needs to be "managed by complex resources, and in par-ticular that the governance system within an innovation system is always com-plex in itself." One of the definitions of innovation presented by Uhlin and Jo-hansen (2001: 17) sums up the overarching situation of the BIT house project, namely that

> ...innovation is not random; it is shaped by history and institutions and nurtured (or the reverse) by a wide range of societal, cultural, political and economic arrangements. In this cross-cutting combination of investment strategies, of scientific and technological talent and skills, tax incentives, government regulation (or de-regulation), company start-ups (and failures) and the dynamics of innovation process itself, the contextualization of scientific knowledge production thrives.

This last comment brings us back to the heart of gender research ambitions – the urgent need to contextualize/to situate all knowledge and technology production.

The straightforward guidebook for community development that also promotes gender issues is not just there to be found or written. The realities are far too complex and context-dependent to be formulated as generalized strategies. I have tried to contribute some threads in the web that constitute regional development out of IT implementation and integration processes. One framework in particular helps me not to fall into a too narrow and poor process of understanding and thus limited strategy development. That is gender research theory linked to technical progress. The consequence is an implicit position of gender issues and gender research, which is nonetheless important in the overall reasoning.

Acknowledgements

I want to convey my sincere thanks to my colleagues at the evaluation team – Peter Ekdahl, Elisabeth Gulbrandsen, Gro Hanne Aas and Christina Mörtberg. A special thanks to Peter Ekdahl for commenting on this text and to Svante Ingemarsson for never-ending support and interest.

References

Baklien, Bergljot (1993). Evalueringsforskning i Norge. *Tidskrift for samfunnsforskning,* vol. 34, pp. 261-274.

Blekinge Institute of Technology (BIT) (1999). *Tioårskrönika 1989-1999 Högskolan som sticker upp.* Karlskrona: Högskolan i Karlskrona/Ronneby.

Cilliers, Paul (1998). *Complexity & Postmodernism, Understanding Complex Systems.* London & New York: Routledge.

Ekdahl, Peter; Gulbrandsen, Elisabeth; Mörtberg, Christina; Trojer, Lena & Aas, Gro Hanne (1999). *The Encounter between Rhetoric and Realities.* Ronneby, University of Karlskrona/Ronneby Press.

Elovaara, Pirjo (2001). *Heterogeneous Hybrids. Information Technology in Texts and Practices.* Ronneby: Blekinge Institute of Technology Press.

Fernvall, Lars (2000). *Forskningsfinansiering i samverkan.* Report from the Organisation Committee for the New Organisation Authority for Research Financing, Stockholm: VINNOVA, pp. 38-53.

Gibbons, Michael; Limoge Camille; Nowotny, Helga; Schwartzman, Simon; Scott, Peter & Trow, Martin (1994). *The New Production of Knowledge.* London: Thousand Oaks; New Dehli: SAGE Publications.

Gulbrandsen, Elisabeth (1995). *The Reality of Our Fictions: Notes towards Accountabiltiy in (Techno)science.* Luleå: Luleå University of Technology Press.

Haraway, Donna J. (1991). *Simians, Cyborgs, and Women. The Reinvention of Nature*. New York: Routledge.

Haraway, Donna J. (1997). *Modest_Witness@Second_Millennium*. New York & London: Routledge.

LOCREGIS (2000). *Best Practice Criteria for the Information Society and Regional Development*. Source: http://www.locregis.net/Doc2/handbook.html; accessed January 20, 2001.

Nowotny, Helga; Scott, Peter & Gibbons, Michael (2001). *Re-Thinking Science. Knowledge and the Public in an Age of Uncertainty*. Cambridge: Polity Press.

SNS Förstudie (1998). *Förstudie inför utvärderingen av KK-stiftelsens program för kunskapsöverföring*. Umeå:, Centre for Business and Policy Studies, UCER, Umeå Centre for Evaluation Research.

Trojer, Lena; Eduards, Maud; Glass, Marianne; Gulbrandsen, Elisabeth; Gustafsson, Bengt; Björlig, Sofie; Leman, Gunnar; Bergman, Erland; Runesson, Ingegerd; Roemer Christensen, Hilda; Sandahl, Ingrid & Westerholm, Barbro (2000). *Genusforskningens Relevans*. Report from the expert group of the Swedish research councils for integration of gender research. Stockholm, Sweden.

Uhlin, Åke & Johansen, Ragnar (2001). *Innovation and the Post-academic Condition*. Nordregio, paper presented at the 2nd Research Conference on University and Society Cooperation, Halmstad University, Sweden.

Tanja Carstensen, Sabine Issa-Beuster, Liane Melzer

Times of the City:
The Use of ICTs in Timesaving

Abstract
This chapter gives an overview of the project 'Times of the City' conducted by the authors for the Hamburg Senate for Equal Opportunities. It brings out the main problems concerning time structures in metropolitan cities as well as gender relations. It also focusses on our ideas and visions of using the Internet to save time. Although there is a lack of everyday life topics on the Internet, this new technology offers a lot of possibilities to ease concomitant tasks women have to fulfill. When the project was presented in an *ifu* course, it led to stimulating discussions on an international level about time, cities, gender relations and the possible benefits of the Internet.

1 Introduction

Since 1995 the Hamburg Senate for Equal Opportunities conducts research for a model project called 'Times of the City.' The idea for researching time policy emerged in Italy in the 1980s. The Hamburg project focusses on urban *time structures* with special consideration of working mothers. At first we determined both the women's demands on time and the available time structures in Hamburg's Barmbek-Uhlenhorst region. In a second step we developed ideas for timesaving possibilities. We succeeded in changing opening hours of 'time suppliers' (public services, child care, doctors' offices). The new information and communication technologies (ICTs) provide one possible perspective for the future of the project. Since 2000 we developed several basic ideas for using ICTs for timesaving purposes. These were discussed in a weeklong course at *ifu* (International Women's University, here: *ifu*'s Project Area INFORMATION), which was also named 'Times of the City.'

In politics and society, as well as in everyday life, we are experiencing the changes brought about by ICTs. Telebanking, teleshopping, e-commerce, e-magazines, e-newspapers, and electronic communication are just a few of its many manifestations in Germany. They are changing our actions, routines, work, communications, as well as our thoughts. During the last few years, especially in the public sphere and in scientific communities, this process has received special attention. It is now uncontested that the ICTs have massively altered our lives.

More and more cities and communities are going online and present themselves on the Internet with the help of different electronic news services. Usually the services cover information for tourists, but information about the city's public and private services is also provided for citizens – from the opening hours of the civic centers to the announcement of events at cultural centers for youths.

These city information systems provided an interesting starting point for our project 'Times of the City,' which focusses on the time structures in cities and their relevance for women in particular. Time at work, scheduling visits to supermarkets and kindergarten, doctors' appointments – all these time-consuming activities influence our everyday life. A lot of people are dissatisfied with the time structures of the city. The work distribution between women and men and the division of roles play an important role in this context. 'Times of the City' is an attempt to find new arrangements for achieving more quality of life for women and men in the cities. In one neighborhood in Hamburg we even succeeded in changing opening hours in cooperation with the corresponding institutions.

2 'Times of the City' – An Equality Issue

In modern industrial cities, and particularly in metropolitan cities, there is a multitude of various time structures for employment and work. Most public and private services operate on the assumption of so called 'normal' work hours and leisure time. They are also still based on the old-fashioned norm of work distribution between women and men: on the one hand you have the 'working man,' who is away from home for eight, ten or more hours a day, and on the other hand, the woman – economically dependant on him – taking care of the children, household and maybe with additional part-time employment. The latter actually means that she also has to cope with all the concomitant tasks which have to be taken care of outside the domestic sphere. To put it differently: she must accomplish the shopping, make visits to the doctor, ferry children between kindergarten or school, music or sports lessons, and make visits to government agencies during normal work hours when most services are also open.

In Germany the problem of meeting the regular, but often short opening hours is intensified by the fact that there are no reliable school hours. Children usually return from school at about 1:00 p.m. in the afternoon at the latest. If a lesson is cancelled, the children have to go home earlier. No meals are offered at schools either. This implies that somebody has to cook for the children and to be flexible if the timetable suddenly changes. These circumstances create tough situations and definite restrictions regarding women's possibilities of employment outside the home.

Surprisingly there has been little change in gender division of roles. Yet participation in the employment of women, especially mothers, has increased steadily in many countries in the past 30 years. Today one in three employed women has children under 18 in her care in Germany. This double or triple role of combining a job, a household and children represents an enormous burden on women.

Mothers in the labor market are hit harder by the demands of synchronizing different time patterns than other working people or women who exclusively work at home. For this reason the Senate Office for Equal Opportunities in Hamburg has focussed its project 'Times of the City' on working mothers (Issa, 1998).

3 An Investigation of Time Patterns and Possible Changes

When we conceived this project, we were aware that time policy would only be successful for all participants in the long term if it were to be organized in a non-bureaucratic and decentralized way and included all those affected by time regulation, companies, employees, etc. Time policy must be tailored to take into consideration economic interests as well as social compatibility and responsibility.

The investigation was divided into three areas: Analysis and compilation of the existing time structures in services and the demands on time; development of a concept of new time structures, and implementation of a new time concept through a model project.

To determine what time structures were available, the first task was to document all the services and institutions in the area. We sent a questionnaire to 1,500 service establishments. We asked about the existing opening times, but also about the busiest and least busy times, the client or customer structure, waiting times, specific rules for special groups of people, and about changes in opening hours which had already been carried out or were planned for the future.

To determine the demands on opening times and analyze them, a written survey was carried out on a cross-section of 4,000 women in the 18 to 65 years age range. The detailed questionnaire covered seven key topics: questions about the participant's personal life, on her family/household situation, occupation or otherwise, about opening times and availability of appointments, travel routes and about reconciling family, work and leisure times.

Interestingly women did not only want better coordinated opening times, but also timesaving facilities, such as a warm mid-day meal and transportation for their younger children.

In cooperation with the corresponding institutions it was possible to change the following times:

- times of the doctors;
- times of the public service;
- warm mid-day meal for schoolchildren;
- time schedule for care of the children, e.g. fathers look after their children on Saturday mornings;
- child care in difficult situations, e.g. an information network ensuring that when children get ill, elder volunteers take care of them during their mothers absence.

4 Discussion at *ifu*: Times of Cities in Other Countries

While discussing our project with the *ifu* women we were surprised to note that the problems with time structures do not differ that much all over the world. There are different opening and shopping hours, but women's situation concerning the care for children in most countries is very similar; and it is the women's responsibility. But the solutions according to the *ifu* participants vary. For example in Togo many girls are prevented from going to school because they care for other – richer – people's children, and in Brazil a lot of money is paid for services which working parents can call up to take care of their children.

In many countries it is a problem for women to find a job, so the problem of combining non-domestic work with family duties does not exist. Further, women often worry about leaving the children with men because they do not trust men's competence in regard to the children's education and proper care.

5 Present Content and Options through the Internet

Considering these problems we developed several ideas for using the Internet to improve the time structures in the cities. We thought that it must be possible to create means for timesaving on the Internet. Some problems remain: as much as the Internet booms and expands, many social classes still have no access. Even if access exists, the use is frequently limited to private contact by e-mail and information searches on the World Wide Web. Many people, who are under intense time pressure, hardly use the Internet for private business. On the other hand, content deficits also lie with the provider. We need a new perspective of the Internet as a technology that can facilitate women's special concerns in their everyday life.

If we look precisely at the contents on the Internet we can see that they are really one-sided. Most people use the Internet to get information for research, news and product information. There is a great amount of commercial offers made by banks, firms and advertising. And there is also a lot of content regarding the Internet itself, computers, cars, sports, music and movies. Even worse is the flood of pornographic material. Topics of everyday life and information, which could make dealing with daily tasks easier, are significantly underrepresented. The reason is clear. The stereotype of the typical internet-user is: male, 30 years old, a computer freak, and he puts corresponding contents on the Internet.

The cities' information is likewise biased. The urban information systems do not take into account the women's infrastructures existing in their respective cities. The center for lesbians, the women-only sauna, the women's work group of the trade unions, advice for pregnant women, are not adequately represented in the online guides posted by councils. There are few or no references or links to these institutions. Perhaps you manage to find the opening hours of the responsible council if you are searching for a kindergarten place, but the information is often so limited that placing a phone call simply seems to be much quicker. At the same time it is significant that there are a lot of feminist projects in big cities which provide information on women's interests and centers. The sites are attractive and easy to find, but accessed frequently only by a small group of women – so this offer does not change the underrepresentation of women.

6 Use of the Internet for Timesaving Purposes

The introduction of a new technology provides potential for change in everyday life. The way technology is used depends on the participants involved. Certain ways of using a technology will be accepted and become part of normal everyday life; others will not be developed further and may disappear. The Internet as a new technology is still somewhat open in its development. Therefore it is important for women to make the new technology appropriate for their needs.

Our key question was: How can the new information and communication technologies be used to promote saving time for the group with limited time, i.e. the working mothers? Several aspects are important:

- *Access to the Internet*: Women have limited Internet access, use the Internet differently and want an easy handling of the Internet. Connected net systems for household could improve access: While at work people have easy access to the Internet, this is not the case in the private sphere. Gabriele Winker, Spokeswoman of the expert group *Women in the Information Society*, demands consideration of the following aspect: how can connected systems contribute to the households' economizing of time? We have to make an effective move in the direction of teleshopping, and in the direction of an electronic time management system to coordinate heterogeneous time requirements. We can imagine software which can manage several calendars for one person, e.g. one for the user's own professional dates, and another one for the user's children's activities (Winker, 1999).
- *Content of the Internet*: Required Internet contents should be useful for everyday life, related to problems of arranging family and employment demands and coping with day-to-day situations. Further, contents need to be actual, transparent and easily searchable. We must work for a structure on the Web that supports information exchange and networking about relevant topics of our everyday life. We also need links and connections which make it possible to find existing information easily and fast. We must fill this male dominated medium with women's contents and make them visible and accessible for all. Urban information must be linked in creative ways and search engines must be devised according to their keywords and search mechanisms. Moreover, the information needs to be promoted outside the Internet in creative ways.
- *Local Concerns on the Internet*: One of the results of our project 'Times of the City' was that the information posted by cities like Hamburg (for example, see http://www.hamburg.de) is a good starting point for our consideration. The actions and problems of our everyday life refer to the cities where we are living and not to the whole world. Although we can surf globally, many of our questions arise in the local area and context. So the Internet postings which refer to our own city are very telling. We looked for perspectives to use city information systems on the Internet for improving women's quality of life and for creating more time availability in the city.

We developed the vision of an Internet information supply that includes all important information for women, structured to provide fast and clear answers and connected with an interactive service supply. A start page would cover all important topics, i.e. kindergarten, doctors, offices, stores etc. Thus we can achieve some regularity in the organizational work, and also complete work at home faster. We would not need to sit in waiting lines for hours. Also, an interactive emergency program could offer assistance, for example for childcare. Furthermore, an electronic purchase note could be filled out in the morning before office work and the purchased goods be delivered in the evening.

7 Reorganization of Urban Time Structures

An important task of our project was to find better time arrangements for women and to make time-related information on services available in a convenient way.

- *Adapting services to time related demand*: The shopping hours in large cities still are not optimally adapted to the needs of the population. The consequences are 'time bottlenecks.' Our project achieved that different services changed their opening hours.
- *Providing time-related information:* We assume that some services are not only frequented according to their place, but also because of their opening-hours. Thus these must be also considered as a search criterion in city information systems. For example, an employed mother, working until 6 p.m., is looking for a kindergarten for her daughter and is perhaps willing to drive into a distant neighborhood if a kindergarten has opening hours until 7 p.m.. At present she would have to go through the complete list of kindergartens listed at http://www.hamburg.de.
- *Extending Doctors' Office Hours*: In the project, we cooperated with 35 doctors who were willing to extend their opening hours in the early morning, the late evening and Saturdays in an experiment to reorganize urban time structures. This experiment proved that a visit at the doctor's is less stressful for both doctors and patients outside the time frame of 8 a.m. to 6 p.m..
- *Cooperating with the Doctors' Union*: The cooperation with the doctors was very satisfying and convincing. We saw a chance for more publicity for these new times. The Hamburg doctors union also saw this chance, so we soon arrived at a cooperation. The union developed an Internet site for searching doctors and took time as a search criterion into consideration. If you are looking for a doctor, you can select the search criteria *name, street, neighborhood, working hours* and *specialization*. You can select one, two or all criteria. If you are looking for a doctor who has working hours on Saturdays, no matter if she or he is far away from your home, you will find her/him easily now.

One thing is clear: Mothers hard pressed for time will not stream into the Internet just because they can search a kindergarten not only for its location but for its opening hours. But it is a beginning to remodel the Internet in a way that it can be of help for many women.

8 The *ifu* Perspective on the Use of the Internet to Save Time

We plan to go on developing these ideas together with the *ifu* participants. Therefore we draw on the different ways of using the Internet in their countries. The following statements describe the diversity of their personal impressions concerning the importance of this new technology in their countries.

Some remarks referred to specific situations in certain countries:

- The Turkish participants told us that in Turkey the equipment often is very bad and the Internet is slow. Internet cafés are part of a new lifestyle ('explore the world'). Nobody knows how to use the Internet in a useful way, although ordering food via Internet is already common. People also have a culture strongly based on face-to-face-contact. If you want to know something, you ask the person directly. Likewise it is not even common to consult a telephone book, so the Internet would perhaps not be used for dealing with daily questions.
- A Korean participant said that the Internet, especially using Internet shops, is very popular too. Women sites boom and there is free Internet training for women.
- In Australia the Internet is attractive mainly because of its ability to bridge great distances on this continent, as stated by a participant.
- In Brazil there are special programs for Internet access for very poor people, but there are no special programs to support women's Internet learning.
- According to a participant from Togo, personally owned computers are rare, because they are very expensive. Using Internet cafés is the norm. Togo does not provide special programs for Internet use by women – they are still struggling for girls' access to schools.

Other remarks addressed general issues:

- Many women think e-mail cannot be trusted; that is why they do not want to use it in emergency situations. There are also others expressing some fear regarding password security and confidentiality of inquiries.

- Some participants felt that there are questions, e.g. referring to health, for which women would not have to go to the doctor, if they could consult the Internet instead.
- Some stated that the Internet wastes time rather than saving it. In their view, using the phone is faster.

It becomes clear that cultural aspects determine Internet use considerably. Apart from economic conditions cultural differences have to be taken into consideration to create Internet services which are able to save time. Also, it is not useful and sensible to replace most daily personal interactions by contact over the Internet – no matter how much time they take – since personal interaction and socializing add to the quality of life.

9 Conclusion

Time structures in metropolitan cities are an important topic today. Our everyday life depends on work time, opening hours and a lot of other time issues. As soon as we have to coordinate work times, visit the doctor, buy food and care for children, the times of a city prove to be unsatisfactory. That is why women, who still have most of the responsibility for children and household in many countries, are burdened with homogeneous structures of opening times. In our project 'Times of the City' we tried to change time structures according to the needs of women and men within some areas of Hamburg. In cooperation with the corresponding institutions it was possible to change the opening times of doctors, public services and childcare.

We developed the idea to use the Internet for timesaving, too. We thought of several ways of using the new technologies to provide better information about opening hours and to supply organizational services. We discussed these ideas with *ifu* participants. The opinions were quite different here and very interesting for us. It further showed that above all we have to take cultural conditions into consideration when we design ways of using new technologies for improving our time of the cities and our quality of life. The Internet will not solve all our time problems. Face-to-face-culture for example is considered to be very important.

Therefore, technological solutions of social problems are not to be overestimated. However, at the same time we should not stop thinking about using technology for easing our everyday life. It could take some tedious work from us. It is our hope that the project 'Times of the City' and its gender specific approach – also referring to the new information and communication technologies – will stimulate public debate of time problems and the resulting need for changes in time structures. Time crises and time conflicts should be recognized as a general social problem and not just as an individual one that particularly affects working mothers.

References

Adam, Barbara (1998). *Timescapes of Modernity. The Environment and Invisible Hazards.* London/New York: Routledge.
Bonfiglioli, Sandra & Mareggi, Marco (eds.) (1997). *Il tempo e la città fra natura e storia. Atlante di progetti sui tempi della città.* Rom: Urbanistica Quaderni 12. Collana dell' Istituto Nazionale di Urbanistica.
Boulin, Jean-Yves & Mückenberger, Ulrich (1999). Times of the City and Quality of Life. In: *European Studies on Time,* No. 1. Dublin: European Foundation for the Improvement of Living and Working Conditions.
Friberg, T. (1993). Everyday life: Women's Adaptive Strategies in Time and Space. In: *Lund Studies in Geography Series.* Bd. 55. Stockholm: Byggforskningsrådet.
Harvey, Andrew S. & Michalos, Alex C. (1993). Time Use Research – An International and Interdisciplinary Journal for Quality-of-Life Measurement. In: *Social Indicators Research.* Vol. 30, Nos. 2-3. Halifax: Kluwer Academic Publishers.
Issa, Sabine (1998). Zeiten der Stadt – Forschungs- und Modellprojekt des Senatsamtes für die Gleichstellung Hamburg. In: Mückenberger, Ulrich (eds.) (1998). *Zeiten der Stadt. Reflexionen und Materialien zu einem neuen gesellschaftlichen Gestaltungsfeld.* Bremen: Verlag Edition Temmen, pp.163-168.
Rotenberg, Robert (1992). *Time and Order in Metropolitan Vienna. A Seizure of Schedules.* Washington/London: Smithsonian Institution Press.
Winker, Gabriele (1999). Geschlechterverhältnisse und vernetzte Systeme. In: *Zeitschrift für Frauenforschung.* Bielefeld: Kleine Verlag, 17. Jg., Heft 1+2, pp. 9-25.

Further Readings

Davey, Brian (2001). *Pathologies and Policies of Time.* Source: http://www.sharelynx.net/A_Strategy_For_Losers/Pathologies.htm
Zeiten der Stadt. *Website created as a contribution to the European 'Times of the Cities' project organized in the context of EXPO 2000,* Germany. Sources:
http://www.zeiten-der-stadt.de
http://www.wow-conference.de/download/winker-e-08-03.pdf
http://www.europaforum.or.at/HomepageITECHwomen/documents/Winkeren.pdf

Wendy Harcourt

Strategies for Empowering Women on the Internet

Abstract
This chapter is based on the experiences of 'Women on the Net' (WON) as an example of the different geopolitical and cultural responses of women in their use of the Internet. The focus of the paper will be on how women are building on their strengths – particularly networking and lobbying for women's rights – through the Internet. The chapter explores the use of Internet as a globally accessible tool to create a new politics for women based on their every day life realities, their current questionings of hierarchies, resistance to male domination and confidence in their own creativity. Specifically it looks at how this thinking was very dynamically applied during the *ifu* experience.

1 Introduction

The central question that the course *Women on the Net* at *ifu* (International Women's University, here: *ifu's* Project Area INFORMATION) addressed was how the Internet is opening up spaces for the empowerment of women. The discussion focussed on concrete examples from the organization 'Women on the Net' (WON) as well as encouraging participants to use their experience at *ifu* to challenge their own empowerment process using information and communication technologies (ICTs). As well the lecturers invited participants to take the opportunity at *ifu* to build links that will allow them to continue connections beyond the course. A particular focus of concern was how to make women's politics in the North and South more effective in terms of Internet exchange in order to strengthen personal and collective action.

The women in the course worked in small team groups to build up their own empowerment agenda using the Internet and learning from the discussions raised by the joint leaders of the course, Fatma Alloo from Tanzania and Wendy Harcourt from Australia. The resources for the discussion were principally drawn from the book *Women@Internet: Creating New Cultures in Cyberspace* (Harcourt, 1999) that gathered together the initial work and experiences of the 'Women on the Net' project of which the two lecturers were founding members.

The weeklong course provided an important exchange among the participants about the changing nature of women's empowerment agenda with the use of ICTs. The participants together with the lecturers raised some key issues both analytical and practical about the use of the Internet in places as diverse as Germany, where the course was taking place and rural Sudan, where one of the participants was a lecturer at a women's university. The WON experience was seen as an important experiment that opened up possibilities to examine how organizations in women's movements employ the Internet as a tool for social activism. The course examined this potential in the context of the *ifu* asking:

- How is information communicated on-line helpful in framing shared values and in facilitating consensus among women (feminists)?
- What and how have strategies been developed for Internet activism by women, and how do they differ across the cultures?
- How does the Internet facilitate organizations in women's movements to communicate with their members, manage information, and network with other organizations?

The discussion was wide-ranging, beginning with a case study of the Women on the Net (WON) project. The participants had copies of the book and the lecturers were very candid in their sharing of this particular experiment of using ICTs to promote North-South feminist ideology.

2 A History of Women on the Net (WON)

The project 'Women on the Net' (WON) was set up in 1997 by the Society for International Development (SID) with UNESCO funding. WON aimed to do several things. Firstly, to encourage women, particularly in the South and in marginal groups in the North (and Central and East Europe) to use the Internet more easily as their space in an effort to 'empower' women to use technology as a political tool. Secondly, to open up and contribute to the new culture that was emerging on the Internet from a gender perspective that is at once local and global. Thirdly, to bring together individual women and men working from different institutional bases (women NGOs, IT networks, academia, women's movement activists) to explore a transnational women's movement agenda in response to evolving telecommunication policies. And fourthly, to create a resource (community and support) base which different women's groups could use to assist their analysis, knowledge and skills for navigating the Internet.

The group is made up of individuals (mainly women), many with strong institutional affiliations, who dialogued with one another intensively from 1997 to 1999 using a listserv as the main mechanism for communication. The group met twice, initially at the SID World Conference in Spain in 1997 and at a second meeting at a Conference on Gender and Globalization in March 1998 at the University of California, Berkeley. There have also been two WON training workshops held in Kenya and Tanzania, a book Women@internet, two Internet guides for women, a stream of articles in books and journals. Further, SID has provided resources (people and material) for several UN meetings, higher learning courses and NGO workshops on the topic. Based in NGOs, resource centers, academic institutes, UN agencies and homes in rural and urban Europe, Asia, the Pacific, the Middle East, North America, Latin America and Africa, and connecting intellectual and visionary migrants on the move, WON provides an eclectic mix of people who are involved in women's issues in different ways – as migrant and indigenous rights activists, policy lobbyists, (women) development researchers, journalists, technical communication experts, ecologists, anthropologists and policy makers. They were all brought together because from their local positions – as they try to fight for change, build their political analyses and skills, sort through the maze of information, the types of knowledge required and the potential allies – they have recognized the power of the Internet. The Internet has become an increasingly accessible learning space, a place to network, and to gain power and strength. They introduce their local needs into the global space of the Internet in order to help them with their local battles but also to understand the process and transform cyberspace so that it reflects theirs and other women's needs in the creation of a 'glocality.'

3 The WON Dynamic

The participants in the *ifu* course were particularly interested in the dynamic that evolved through the WON experience as a model for how their own Internet discussions and network building could function, particularly how to cope with the merging of the personal, political and professional aspects. At *ifu* as with Women on the Net it seems that discussions have been intense over the crossing of academic and activist knowledge terrain, over language and meanings, over concepts of place and identity.

The WON experience recorded different geo-political and cultural responses and use of the Internet revealed how women are building on their strengths – particularly networking and lobbying for women's rights – through the Internet. As with the *ifu* experience, WON suggests that women are creating and managing new knowledge systems. What is important, and what came out of the *ifu* discussions is that for ICT to have political meaning women have to be deeply conscious of the different realities of women from marginalized communities. Therefore it is important not to take up cyberspeak, analytic jargon and assumptions that a wonderful new world will open at the touch of a button. The *ifu* participants were fully aware that screen-to-screen contact can never replace face-to-face. The maleness and the elitism of the tools – the exclusivity, the language barriers, the high costs, the Western biases and the divides – were all issues the participants wondered about as issues that did not require just more information and skills. The participants asked how to overcome the divides, how to combine face-to-face with cyber discussions and in what way, if any, were ICTs new. The fact that so many of the examples of WON come from the South was seen as positive and opened up different issues for the participants from the North, who felt overloaded with information. All of the participants took a great deal of interest in being able to link South-South and South-North.

4 Crossing of Boundaries

A major discussion was what type of boundaries could be crossed and in what way the *ifu* experience had helped to cross them. In the discussion of the crossing of time, place, space, gender, the participants were fascinated to understand how real place and cyberplace were blending in such networks as WON. How did the group interact in cyberspace, and how did that virtual reality fit with the allure of the Zanzibari breeze, the heat of Rome summer, the deep winter snow of Toronto, the buzz of the people around the clatter of the keyboards? But the questions that the participants were keenest to explore was how to embed and to root virtual discussions in the political reality being fought every day; how to anchor the happenings of the real life community to the virtual global discourse in order for the cyber communication space to have meaning.

The participants focussed those questions on their own experience at *ifu*. What sort of political community did they wish to form after the *ifu* experience? Where is that community to be located? In space – which space? Whose space? How will *ifu* participants locate themselves as people logging in around the world to discuss *what*? Were there equivalent happenings as in the WON that *ifu* participants could follow? Could such a virtual community exist to provide knowledge, solidarity, support, services to build another kind of women's politics that is both global and locally relevant? How can participants who may never meet again share their lives and professional concerns, support each other's valuable strategic knowledge, engage in a debate that each will use in different contexts enriched by what they have exchanged?

Whereas it was clear for participants that the personal can be shared, and that e-mail communication and listserv lend themselves to those exchanges, it was less clear what they all could share beyond *ifu*, something they agreed to consider beyond the week long course. The discussion also looked at the difficulties of resolving differences of sexuality, class and ethnicity and race, and the prejudices and difficulties they were facing within the course – in and outside the university (see the chapter by Mihelj, this volume, for a detailed discussion of identities and differences at *ifu*).

WON provided examples of how women were using the ICTs to open up new political spaces. Nevertheless the participants did not think that this was enough. They asked the difficult questions of whether we are truly connected or just scratching the surface of a fast changing world that is evolving without our design or needs in mind. How can intercultural differences be resolved largely in the English language? What about issues of who has the resources and who has the control of the technology, and the context in which it was largely developed (for the military, and global economic markets)? The attempts by some members of WON, for example Sophia Huyer and Nidhi Tandon, to venture into the world of decision-making and policy agenda-setting on telecommunications and other areas affecting access and use of the Net and Web were of interest. Nevertheless it was clear that the world of Microsoft, high finance and telecommunications business are not the spaces in which women or those pushing for an alternative agenda easily find a voice.

5 A Sense of Identity

Although WON never found its true institutional identity, members continue to interact because of their interest in political activism. The question for the participants was if and how *ifu* would provide a similar platform for them to use the Internet as a global tool for local political needs (see, for example, the chapter by Williams, this volume). To go a little further, perhaps what was of most interest was the relationship between the local and the global or 'global delocalization.' The experience of WON suggests women and men activists are seeking not to be trapped in the excitement and hype around the cyberworld but are trying to map out virtual reality as closely as possible to their place-based politics. And in this resides some sort of identity in cyberculture, one in which the challenge was for the participants to locate themselves.

6 The Politics of Place

A core discussion of the lectures was the meaning of place and gender in relation to cyberculture on several levels. This was explained by the lecturers in order to support the participants' search to define how they could use the *ifu* experience back home to help support their local activities as feminists. The participants were keen to have new analytical concepts to help put into context their
own work and to situate the whole *ifu* experiment. The politics of place was one
such potentially useful concept that the WON project had developed.

Owing to the gender bias of social and cultural processes, women's bodies
are their first environment or place. It is the female body in all cultures that defines women as the other, as the reproductive being, the mother, as the sexually
desired. It is the body through which women are primarily to mediate all gendered interactions including those from which they defend and evolve their
identity. The cyborg woman has evolved an identity which on the one hand
breaks this notion of biological body by extending communication of self
through the sexless machine of the computer and modem. And on the other
hand, cyberculture offers the possibility to celebrate and share the feminine
space with other women from many diverse situations, giving credibility to
women's bodily experience through a medium which encourages a more open
personal discourse – if the safe space can be nurtured. It also, in its darkest interface, allows for manipulation and misuse of women's bodies – another area for
women to fight against in their struggle against bodily violence.

A second level is the domestic space of the home that for many women still
defines their primary social and cultural identity and lived domain. The home
and immediate community are the safe places for women to express themselves,
and it is here that the terminals in the home, the personal and political exchanges
this potentially facilitates, could change women's political lives. Women, calling
on long traditions of flexibility between reproductive and productive work,
could weave new political spaces while maintaining their reproductive work
space. Already Northern women are increasingly working from home, raising on
the one side the problems of exploitative work conditions but on the other the
potential of new feminine spaces from which to launch plans for change.

The third place is that outside the home – the political and social public
place – the male dominated domain to which some women still have no access,
and where many women find themselves silenced and few women rule. The
women's movement for many years now has been creating diverse avenues for
entry into that space, even if marginal to the pulse of political power. The cyberculture now being created in this public domain is a new type of political space
which has power and impact in the public domain. Its current accessibility for
women suggests a possible opening that could promote women's public political

battles and link these three different levels of place: the body, the home, and political and social public space. The critical point is that women have to ensure that they are part of the design and crafting of the cyberculture in order to produce new types of gendered communication spaces throughout the Internet. They need to craft a process where their voices are heard in ways that can mediate through and radically change the public political domain.

The vision of WON is to use the potentially globally accessible tool of the Internet to open out the corridors of power and create a new politics emanating from place. Such a place-based strategy is being mapped out and defined by women based on their sense of the feminine, their everyday life realities, their current questioning of hierarchies, resistance to male domination and confidence in their own creativity. The proposal of the lecturers to the participants was to take this up in moving with and beyond the *ifu* experience as one that could empower them in new and exciting ways in their different political places.

8 Reflections

The WON experiment and the sketch of the politics of place are useful examples of how to approach the Internet as a tool for empowerment by women's political groups. ICTs in this approach can be seen as an important medium that allows women to go beyond traditional cultural experiences, allows for new types of gender relations, and new types of development. As the WON experience showed, women are setting up safe cyberspaces where they can converse across geo-political divides.

The response and interest of the participants in the Women on the Net approach focussed on how women in the South were using the Internet creatively and, it seemed, often differently from women in the North. This led to lively discussions about how the *ifu* experience can help cultural understanding and encourage greater participation of women in development at the different levels of place. The greatest challenge it seemed was to acknowledge and respect those differences and how the specific places where feminist politics are practiced can come together in a safe space on the Internet. The possibility of collaboration, networking and support was mapped out during the course using the Women on the Net experiences, but relying on the participants' own knowledge of their places. The enthusiasm of the participants and the experience in cyberspace, the course itself and the links it forged show how the Internet is stretching out experiences on all three levels of place and moving forward the political terrain for gendered social and political change.

Reference

Harcourt, Wendy (ed.) (1999). *Women@Internet: Creating New Cultures in Cyberspace*. London: Zed Books.

Further Readings

Arizpe, Lourdes (ed.) (1998). *World Culture Report: Culture, Creativity, Markets*. Paris: UNESCO.

Castells, Manuel (1996). *The Rise of the Network Society*. Oxford: Blackwell.

Dirlik, Arif (1998). Globalism and the Politics of Place. In: *Development 41* (2), pp. 7-14.

Escobar, Arturo (1999). *Gender, Place and Networks: A Political Ecology of Cyberculture*. In: Harcourt (1999), pp. 31-54.

Escobar, Arturo (1998). Creating 'Glocality.' Editorial (with Wendy Harcourt). In: *Development*, vol. 41, no 2.

Gibson-Graham, J.K. (1996). *The End of Capitalism (As We Knew It)*. Oxford: Basil Blackwell.

Harcourt, Wendy (1999). Women and the Politics of Place. Rethinking Cultural Diversity, Equality and Difference in Response to Globalization. In: Arizpe, L. (ed.). *World Culture Report II*. Paris: UNESCO.

Harcourt, Wendy (2000). World Wide Women and the Web. In: Gauntlett, David (ed.). *Web. Studies: Rewiring Media Studies for the Digital Age*. London: Arnold.

Latour, Bruno (1993). *We Have Never Been Modern*. Cambridge: Harvard University Press.

Massey, Doreen (1998). Spaces of Politics. In: Massey, Doreen; Allen, John & Sarre, Philip. *Human Geography Today*. Oxford: Polity Press.

Rocheleau, Diane; Thomas-Slate, Barbara & Wangari, Esther (eds.) (1996). *Feminist Political Ecology*. New York: Routledge.

Part 6: Fostering Democracy

In the present age of globalization, more countries attempt to implement democracy than ever before. But what democracy means and to whom, which factors are present or denied, varies. From its very origin in Greece, democracy did not apply equally to all population groups: it defined rights for free Greek men, thus marginalizing women, poor people and foreigners. In spite of many efforts, these problems have not been eradicated in history and take a new form in the age of globalization. Now, the possibility of participating depends not only on political conditions but also on education, income, access to technology and to the benefits of civilization. Also, new developments, such as mass media and the internet, come with new hopes and risks for democracy. The chapters in this section examine this situation as it affects women worldwide.

The project *Visions of Citizenship* at *ifu*, reported by Carina Keskitalo and Cirila P. Limpangog, was concerned with what they called 'full' citizenship. Taking a gendered point of view, the group examined the political and civil, economic, and cultural dimensions of citizenship. In an inquiry conducted with the participants at *ifu*, they established the obstacles women experienced in countries all over the globe to living their citizenship. Due to dependency relations in families, lack of education and freedom of movement, women can often not fully participate. This points to the need of empowerment to be able to transcend existing constraints.

Aleida Calleja tells about the profound changes brought about by a community radio station in the Cuetzalan region in Mexico. The Nahua and Totonaca ethnic groups live in isolated places in a culture strictly based on the spoken word in a language understood only by themselves. Women, doubly marginalized, are completely tied to traditional family settings, many of them not even being registered and having no legal status at all. But high technology brings change: women, accustomed to silence, gain voice through their work in the radio station, and see their status in the community transformed.

Adopting an information rights and a feminist point of view, Irma Ávila Pietrasanta looks at the paradigms of the developing globalized societies and at the interaction between politics, the economy, and the media in providing information for citizens. The more mass media get tied up with economic interests, the more the selection of news is geared to maximize profits rather than to best inform the population, amounting to private censorship. Solutions are community-based information channels breaking the monopoly of the unique view and the monocultural Western way of seeing the world propagated through the mass media.

By reference to the recent uprising in Fiji, Esther Batiri Williams discusses the potential of the Internet for promoting democratic processes. The population can now follow developments as they happen. The open structure of the Internet makes censorship impossible, thus counteracting developments of political or private censorship in other media. But the Internet can also be used for disinformation, allowing political radicals to communicate with equal ease. To use the potential of the Internet, women must be empowered through education and better access, security and privacy must be guaranteed so that the trust in the new media is justified.

Drawing on the wealth of her experience in working for the United Nations High Commissioners of Refugees, Luise Druke views information technology as one means to promote the cause of people in distress, in particular of women and children. Specialized and modern it can be used, on one hand, to enable refugees to take a proactive initiative in aiming for local integration, on the other hand, to aid the logistics of refugee protection, and even to prevent the causes for refugees in countries of origin. However, the conditions for it use, both in terms of costs and of security, must be drastically improved. Also, special education is necessary for empowering people, in particular women, to make use of these possibilities.

Thus, at the end of this book, we are lead back to the beginning: In order to foster democracy, we need to build international learning communities for women, enabling them to gain voice and listen to each others' perspectives, to make explicit their dreams and wishes, and to find the courage to work for them in their own, often constrained circumstances. This mutual empowerment was at the core of the *ifu* idea. May all participants feel lasting benefits and pass on this spirit to others.

Christiane Floyd

Carina Keskitalo & Cirila Limpangog
With: Delphine Djiraibe, Melanie Dunn, Ulrike Ebeling,
Stephania Evboikuokha, Irem Inceoglu, Margaret Nyambura
Ndung'u, Kateryna Pishchikova, Terri Sundin, Esther Wil-
liams, Lubomira Zaloudkova, Isabel Zorn

Visions of Citizenship:
Women, Democracy and Information

Abstract
People's empowerment relies strongly on their right to self-determination, as individuals and
in groups of their choice. As a democratic right, citizenship is made up of political, civil,
cultural and economic dimensions, which need to be fulfilled in order for full political participation to be possible. This chapter investigates understandings of citizenship among participants at *ifu*, which were examined by the project group *Visions of Citizenship*. It indicates
how even relatively privileged women from a variety of countries are limited in their practice
of full citizenship rights by formal and informal constraints.
On the basis of an historical and conceptual survey of the concept of citizenship, the project
utilized questionnaire survey and focus group interview techniques to gain an understanding of
citizenship in the context of women's experiences in their own countries. Mechanisms were
identified in which information and information technologies assist as well as hinder women
from pursuing democratic participation. Women's preferences of traditional and new information technologies, and their means of optimization to generate greater political participation, are
taken as offering grounds for new visions of alternative citizenship to germinate.

1 Introduction

Look beyond the legal definitions and the global status quo. But beware. Looking more proximately can usually cause blindness. Then it is best to examine
one's own experience as basic grounding as well as road map: What does it
mean to be a citizen in the information age? This chapter provides a collage of
citizenship as felt and seen by women at *ifu*, Project Area INFORMATION, resulting from an inquiry conducted by the project group *Visions of Citizenship*. A
self-mediating group, the project was co-moderated by Esther Williams as director, and Cirila Limpangog as facilitator. Our project group provided a unique
setting for discussing problems of citizenship on an international scale, as it was
composed of twelve women of diverse discipline and generation coming from
Asia and the Pacific, the Americas, Europe and the African continent.

Intertwined with our aim at exploring the full participation of women as a means to enhance democracy, we also examined the potentials of the mass media and the information technology as they support education and interactivity. As it stands today, woman's participation, thus, her capacity to acquire, exercise and enjoy the benefits of full citizenship is obstructed by several factors. To magnify the various discourses of women's citizenship from the French Revolution, the fall of the Berlin wall, up until the age of globalization, the inquiry took off with a street theater dubbed as 'Citizenship through Her Lenses.' Here, snapshots of women seeking identity as they cross the borders, give birth to and bring up an offspring without paternal acknowledgement, enter marriage, amongst others, demonstrate inferiorized positions across cultures and ages. At the foreground, we drew reflections on the work of visionary thinkers, philosophers, scientists and artists using our feminist perspective.

Our present political system remains flawed by its neglect in treating citizenship as a gendered concept. Embarking on full participation of women as a vision, we postulate that they should be capacitated to exercise the political, civil, cultural and economic dimensions of citizenship. Without these, women can remain largely subordinated, underrepresented, invisible and less capable in fully harnessing their situation. The chapter of Druke in this volume shows an example on how even refugee women, when given the opportunity to voice can identify survival needs and re-integration tactics that otherwise are blurred or insufficiently handled.

In this chapter, we provide a four-pronged illustration. First, a universal progression of citizenship; second, a gendered analysis of citizenship vis-à-vis its various dimensions; third, the results of inquiry on women's citizenship and democratic rights at *ifu* that vividly accounts our experiences and viewpoints; and fourth, our futuristic approaches and gleanings to re-invent women's position.

2 The Future of Citizenship

The future of citizenship and democracy in both the developed and developing world seems uncertain. While the Western world faces the forces of internal factionalism on one hand, and the economic market pressures toward globalization on the other, many countries struggle to define themselves in terms of democracy. The contradictions are so great and powerful that the future of citizenship in many countries is somewhat blurred.

In addition to these developments, we see the many mergers and the power of big business and the information industry dominating our lives and the market. These may bring pressures of homogenization and a new way of controlling people's lives. In such situations, many questions are being raised about the decline in political participation and the growing mistrust in political institutions as the people who control the markets also control the governments and individuals.

These state-society relations raise important questions about the participatory and organizational underpinnings of democracy. Clearly, there is a need to look beyond constitution to practice: not to evaluate democracy as a unified system, as the 'end of history' but to look at the broader political situation. Rather than focussing only on the legal or constitutional constraints, it is preferable to examine the constraints inherent in informal systems and practices. While democracy has swept some parts of the globe, changes are still resonating, and there is no indication in which direction these will continue. As one woman in our research phrased the importance of social organization: "the right to communicate is closely related to the right to association and organization in the society".

The jigsaw pieces of revelations do not necessarily conform with generalizations that only women from the South, the so-called 'Third World' countries suffer invisibility or inferior status. There is also generally an indifference in women's claiming of their rights to full citizenship. Superimposed on threats of cultural homogenization, women tell of the dire need for basic literacy and political will to overcome cultural sanctions for their inferiorized position, as in the case at least of India and some Latin American countries. Moreover, their right to reveal their experiences of violence and marginalization through the mass media is crippled by a lack of serious attention from the media and the public, even in supposedly IT leading countries like Germany. Much more, migration and consequent 'displacement phenomena' create information barriers by way of media exclusion, as in the case of Turkish people in Germany, and African-Americans in the USA. Views of these politically and socially engaged women show up the problems they have had in accessing mechanisms and public resources that will help them participate fully as active citizens, and provide an illustration of the multiplicity of democratic practices, problems and new possibilities.

3 A Gendered View of Citizenship

Citizenship is a contested concept and can mean different things to different people, shifting in meaning throughout history. Historically, citizenship is very much a gendered concept; the Greek philosopher Aristotle's citizen in his *Politics* was a 'free man.' This practice was justified by ideas about the nature of men and women, related to positivistic beliefs about rationality, and the separation of emotion or value and ascribed rationality. These differentiated thought worlds have been used to exclude groups other than relatively resource-independent male non-immigrants, from ancient Greece right up to the present century, and influencing public discourse, government and academia.

Up until the first world war, citizenship discourse was not in many countries seen as including women. The guarantee of equal political, civil and social rights to all citizens can be seen as a prerequisite for democracy. This is the democratic component of citizenship:

> Citizenship is a status bestowed on those who are full members of a community. All who possess the status are equal with respect to the rights and duties with which the status is endowed. (T. H. Marshall, 1950: 28-29)

3.1 The Political and Civil Dimensions of Citizenship

Although every country has its own laws on citizenship, the concept can generally be divided into two main categories. The first is the territorial principle, *jus solis*, where anyone born in a spatially delimited area automatically becomes a citizen of its state. The second principle is the principle of 'blood,' *jus sanguinis*, based on the origin of the parents (Friedman, 1999: 155). The understanding of citizenship has evolved over time and includes political, civil, cultural and economic components.

The origin of the modern understanding of citizenship is based on the concept of the rights of man proclaimed by the French Revolution, whose proponents argued that in civil society, all individuals had a God-given right to equality of respect. The concept of the individual was, however, limited to *men of property*: women's interests were to be represented by their husbands and fathers. T.H. Marshall (1949) shows that the modern models of citizenship have been consistently evolving to the 19th century citizenship, which includes the right to political participation and concerned access to the parliamentary process. *Political citizenship* for women in 'democratic' countries was only gained after the turn of the 20th century, when suffragettes after defeating the view that women were not to be seen as 'persons' in a legal sense, gained the right to vote for women.

This development also ushered a few significant others, such as access to education and employment, and civil rights. This was the basis from which to exercise rights of *civil citizenship*, usually thought of as related to individual freedoms – such as freedom of speech, the right to own property, and the right to justice; and, for example, women's right to obtain justice against violence, which of course is not yet fully obtained. Political citizenship is related to civil citizenship in that only someone seen as a person in a legal sense will be able to own property and independent development. Today, *universal suffrage* is largely accepted as a principle, including all adults who are 'citizens' within the state, and allowing choice by voting, to be governed through majority rule (CCLA, accessed June 15, 2000).

3.2 The Cultural Dimension of Citizenship

However, membership of social structures, such as the state, could not be restricted in legal terms alone. Citizenship also denotes, among other things, a sense of belonging to a group, including contributions to and benefits from that membership. In the process of globalization, arguments about virtual membership have arisen to question bordered societies, whereupon *cultural citizenship* has been critically discussed. Cultural citizenship can be seen as the extent to which society provides for commonly available semiotic material cultures that are necessary in order to make social life meaningful. It appraises the practices of domination, as well as recognizes people's cultural differences under conditions of tolerance and mutual respect (CCLA accessed June 15, 2000).

As there exist differences between socio-cultural groups, a democracy needs to provide mechanisms for the effective representation and recognition of disadvantaged groups. This implies institutional mechanisms and public resources for: (1) self-organization among individuals towards collective empowerment, in accordance with any shared experience and interests they may have; (2) the possibility to voice views on the effect of social policies, and promote alternative ones; and (3) a veto of policies that affect the group directly (Young, 1995).

There are, however, many obstacles to equal representation and recognition of different individuals and groups. The inclusion of women in the democratization process is faced with several barriers. Among them, according to Ashworth (1996), is the absence from media and opinion polls, through both deliberate and inadvertent censorship, of women's political voices, views, demands and leadership with which others can identify and through which they can find a legitimacy for their own views.

3.3 The Economic Dimension of Citizenship

Further, concepts of political, civil and cultural citizenship are not extensive. The concept of citizenship has largely focussed on the public sphere. Thereby, for example women's work at home often remains expected although other definitions of work, and the possibilities for women to gain equally paid employment (through, e.g. child care and maternity health schemes) are limited. Thus, a further focus on *economic citizenship* centers on the non-acknowledgement of much of women's work. If an economic analysis of what constitutes work ignores women's experiences, then their rights and opportunities are also limited as a consequence (CCLA, accessed June 15, 2000). This results in economic dependency and limited access for women and non-acknowledgement of systemic factors of exclusion.

Together, the requirements of political, civil, cultural, and economic citizenship need to be fulfilled to promote equal rights for women.

4 An Inquiry on Citizenship and Democratic Rights at *ifu*

The impact of discrepancies in citizenship and democratic rights is felt differently by different groups. To sample women's perceptions of citizenship and democratic rights, a survey and interviews were conducted at *ifu*. While relatively privileged (all holding at least first degrees), these women from a diversity of countries nevertheless recognized powerful obstacles to their democratic rights. The survey was conducted by handing out the questionnaires mentioned earlier to all participants and staff, about 150 women, with a return of 72 responses. Supplementing the survey, focus group discussions were held with *ifu* participants, in four groups of two to six interviewees. The focus group interviews comprised women volunteering for participation on themes of information technology, health, media, and studentship.

The participant group comprises women from more than fifty countries, with the greatest numbers from India and the African continent. To judge from the responses, the participants are educated young women, mostly active in the public life of their societies, who feel they have a considerable degree of influence in their respective professional spheres. The responses indicate some of the problems, and spread of problems, felt in such a wide variety of national contexts and cases.

4.1 The Focus Group's Citizenship and Demography

Most of the women present in the focus group interviews stated that citizenship to them meant something granted by birth in a country or to anyone born of parents with this citizenship, and being able to vote in democratic elections. Some differences were found to the attribution of citizenship according to Friedman's (1999: 155) definition, with the USA exercising the *jus solis*, territorial principle, and Germany having long represented the *jus sanguinis*, the principle of blood. As a German woman stated:

> In Germany it was until recently that you could get citizenship only when both of your parents were Germans by blood and not just by being born in Germany. To be born in Germany did not give one an automatic right to acquire German citizenship.

Differences could also be seen on matters of citizenship acquired through marriage: a foreign man marrying an Egyptian woman does not necessarily gain Egyptian citizenship, while the reverse is true.

Out of the 72 women who completed the questionnaire, 50% were aged between 20 and 30, 33% between 31 and 40, and only 17% were older than 40. Altogether, more than half of the participants were unmarried – they were either single (24%) or lived in partnerships (28%), while only 19% were married, and 29% divorced or separated. 50% of the women did not have children, 33% had one or two children, and 17% had from 3 to 5 children. Over 50% of the women came from cities of more than 100,000 inhabitants, while the other half of the sample came from small (2,000-5,000 inhabitants – 33%) and very small towns of under 2,000 inhabitants (17%). All *ifu* women (as a prerequisite for the course) held a Bachelor's degree, 61% held a Master's degree, and 13% had already obtained their PhD. As many as 50% of the women believed they had a great deal of freedom of decision in their places of work. Thirty percent were members of a social movement or organization, 20% of a political movement or organization, and 10% of a political party.

Of the 87.5% of the participants who worked, 50% stated that they were free to make decisions at work, 33% that they did not have much freedom, and 17% that they had no freedom to make decisions at work. Those who were free to make decisions were mainly employed in academia or in a business company. A high percentage of 40% did not belong to any political party, while only 10% did. This did not correspond to the high number of *ifu* participants (50%) who wished to exercise fully their interest in or right to run for an office. A smaller percentage, 36%, indicated their wish to run for a political office as a priority. This response is further confirmed by a question on how interested the participants were in politics, with 30% very interested, and 40% somewhat interested.

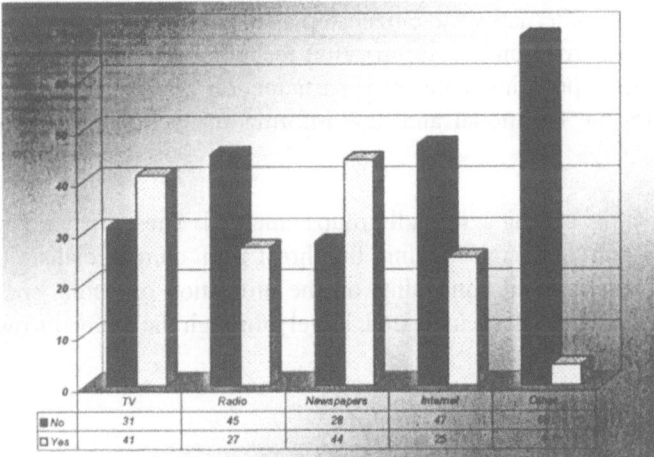

Figure 1: Women's media choices. A high preference for newspapers for keeping track of local events and women's issues validates the dominance of traditional mass media despite the surge of new information technology.

4.2 The Focus Group's Practice of Citizenship

While *ifu* participants were interested in politics, most did not regularly take part in political campaigns or meetings. About 30% never attended a political campaign, and 40% did occasionally. Only 10% regularly attended political campaigns and meetings. However, a high percentage did not listen to political debates on the radio and television.

ifu participants obtained information about their legal rights in their countries from different sources, listed as important to them: educational establishments, media, parents, books, and friends. Table 1 indicates that they still preferred newspapers as the best source of information and local events (61%), followed by television with 56% Women's newspapers were felt to provide the best source of information. Almost 70% of the women at *ifu* felt that they had the same rights as men, as far as citizenship is concerned.

Regarding basic human rights, the two most important ones identified are *freedom of opinion and expression*, and *education*. Moreover, the basic human right that is least fully exercised is *protection in case of unemployment*.

5 Problem Areas of Citizenship Identified at *ifu*

The focus group interviews were structured around five theme areas:

- What does it mean to be a citizen?
- What can be alternatives to citizenship as it exists now?
- How do information and information technologies assist as well as hinder women from pursuing democratic participation?
- What are the traditional and new information technologies they prefer to use?

Several concerns cutting across all groups emerged. These include: the informal constraints upon democratic voting; the threat from commercialism to information access; the implicit constraints on the utilization of public space. Below, these problem areas will be indicated, largely through the women's own voices.

5.1 Informal Pressures in the Ballot

Many informal pressures were felt to be imposed upon the citizens' right to vote Taking on the situation of the indigenous people in her country, a Brazilian woman related :

> Women in the traditional Indian community are not treated as citizens. They are not allowed to vote.

Similarly, an Indian woman stated that men more easily gained formal recognition, while those considered property-less can lose their citizenship rights.

> Citizenship actually means representation. This is the difference between women and men I would make. Men have more representation rights in running the government, and in participating in all tiers of decision-making. In effect, women are not only able to exercise their civil rights, but also lose the opportunity to articulate their needs.

This also pertains to segregated groups: it was reported that, in spite of legislation, the lives of the 'untouchables' are threatened if they go out and vote.

Another Indian woman illustrated a case:

> There are still rural places in India where religious leaders impose 'you have to vote for this person.' Then, everybody, regardless of gender, will vote for that 'anointed' one.

An Egyptian woman agreed that men and women may have equal rights, but as fewer girls are able to access education, then there lies a large deficiency in exercising their rights:

> ... in some rural areas, men are more obliged to be citizens and women are not considered as full citizens.

A Brazilian woman stated the complexity of the problem at length:

> Putting democracy into practice has been a problem, even if our laws provide for it. You can vote. But then, you don't know how and whom to vote. When a candidate gives you some salt or sugar, then you go out to vote. In Brazil, where 'democracy' remains only in paper, we are restricted from participating even in the primary level of the community affairs. What is then the value of voting?

Similar examples came up throughout the interviews:

> In Kenya, the majority of the rural population and especially women, are not educated.

So during election campaigns, when somebody offers sugar in exchange for votes, these women lose their independent voices.

A Congolese woman volunteered:

> During election campaigns, when somebody comes with a gift, then the woman will go and vote, or the husband will instruct her in advance : 'you will vote for that man.'

To counter such practices, certain women's organizations conduct voters' education by performing dramas that critically lampoon the politicians. Videos are shown to illustrate proper voting, highlighting the evils of vote-buying, as well as the ideal profile of candidates.

Furthermore, the Congolese woman said:

By means of education, we can change the mentality of our women. Because, at times, they don't even want to vote! They think that casting the ballot is the work of men and young people, or maybe, of some women who don't have something to do at home.

Another Indian woman spoke about how

... still human rights [or in particular, women's human rights] are being violated ... women [are seen] as property.

A Bulgarian woman related how in post-communist societies, informal means of control could be more or less clearly seen, as in the killing of a Bulgarian journalist.

A German woman emphasized these informal pressure problems from another perspective:

The problem is more than the right to communicate. The right to communicate for women is there, but women have not claimed this, so they remain marginalized.

Consequently, women's needs are not known to the public, even the magnitude of their problems range from domestic violence to sexual harassment at work. It remains difficult to find a public forum to take up these issues in the public at large or as a sector. In the focus groups, as in the survey many of the women also highlighted the link between access to education and ability to exercise citizenship rights.

5.2 Citizen Education and Information

An Indian woman examined a core obstacle women met in exercising their citizenship rights:

The lack of education or illiteracy is probably the biggest stumbling block women are faced with in claiming their space for participation in a democracy. Because if you cannot understand what it means to vote or get elected, if you have not been educated – how does somebody explain to you the concept of democratization?

As a prerequisite, education must take place as a first level intervention, to promote the democratic process in the villages. The Indian woman further suggested:

If women literacy level is elevated to a certain degree, it will be like achieving 10 steps forward.

An Egyptian woman offered:

As long as the woman remains illiterate or semi-educated, how will she appreciate and even challenge the concept of democracy, and be interested to share in that process.

Women need to have access to education in order to gain access to political positions in order to influence women's issues, and be freed from the vicious circle. Today, well-educated women, even in small pockets, are actively involved in the democratic process and in politics. They have gained the power to voice their opinion and be heard.

Several women cautioned that information per se, and not necessarily information technology, is the imperative for citizens to achieve democracy. It is the quality and availability of information, and the participatory process required, that will enable us to deal with our handicaps in democracy (see also the chapter by Dahms & Faust-Ramos in this volume).

This indicates that even if access to new technology is a necessity in everyday work, it exists and is used on the basis of social networking, and in expanding if not enriching one's options to expedite communication. As a Turkish journalist stated: "the phonebook is the resource." Rather than searching for official information, the informal contacts were what mattered. The phonebook, electronic or otherwise, serves as a menu of contacts – it is used to systematize mails, and in the process, deepen rather than diminish personal relations.

5.3 Blocks in the Social Spread of Information

Another major issue centered on the extent these relatively well-educated women working in the media or involved in activism perceive their access to information and use of IT. Related to this is the problem of unequal media access and their own possibilities to reach out. A Turkish woman stated:

> This question of access to information varies according to the level of education, social status, and place of birth.

An Indian woman working with information portals saw her occupation as an elitist activity. Despite the pressures of commercialism and restrictions, the space provides incentives for feminist and social development organizations to publicize their advocacy work and gain support. The women's portal has effectively spread information on legal matters, such as the process of litigation, which is otherwise not easy to obtain.

Another Indian woman, a television journalist, stated:

> Ours is not an elite media at all because we're catering to the rural children of India who belongs to the rock-bottom of the society.

In some rural areas, the absence of electricity and television poses basic technical problems, compounded by the lack of educated teachers. She has observed the dearth of children educational program, as Indian commercial and cable channels do not make special efforts to promote children's programs. To promote acceptance of children's education through media, people's attitude and not only government policies need critical change. In this instance, the informal, socio-cultural setting and its impact upon use and access to new media can be gleaned (see the chapter by Calleja in this volume). The new media, as such, do not necessarily facilitate information access change of people's attitudes. In societies in transition, these informal constraints are, of course, of even larger impact.

Fast societal transformation by way of democratic processes imposes a major cognitive change. A Bulgarian journalist noted:

> People's consciousness is still tied up with the past, which is hard for us because the old people are comparing the past with the present condition. Everybody then had a job, salary was equal even if it was absolutely low. But since the country's doors were closed, we couldn't go abroad and exchange experiences in every context of life. Now we have again the possibility to be an active neighbor, but the other countries put the borders. So it is really not so easy to put this democratic orientation in the mind of the people. A lot of people are thinking that the state or somebody else is responsible but not themselves, and it is not so easy to become aware of it.

With the large differences in systems come the difficulties in adjusting to different logics – and to the exclusion of another kind.

5.4 Commercialism as a Constraint

Commercialism as a constraint was mentioned independently in all of the focus group interviews. An Indian woman saw the basis of citizen information in commercializing societies as a risk for jeopardizing information access: commercial interests waver, and do not necessarily present a continuous and reliable information supply. In her experience, language choices became increasingly stratified. For example, the language of the Internet is becoming predominantly English, to cater to those who use largely the medium, thereby excluding those less internationalized. A Brazilian woman mentioned the risks of globalization where citizenship rights are much more diminished rather than becoming inclusive.

An African-American woman challenged this eloquently:

> Does democracy just automatically assume a capitalist market economy or is there any alternative to it? Is there a crisis in terms of global capitalism in the supposed notions of democracy that we view? What does it mean that I have the right to vote? Is that really my voice? Or do I feel comfortable being able to run for office? Do I think I am qualified? Do I believe that my involvement with the media, and especially, community media, is influenced by my notion of democracy and citizenship? Am I being able to participate within a larger realm beyond my sphere of experience? Am I able to get my voice and other voices out there in the public, challenge other positions that are in oppressive positions by way in which people hold and operate communication equipment?

The fundamental purpose of a free media, notwithstanding the various commercial constraints, has to be preserved. This is strongly proposed in the Pietrasanta chapter in this volume against the backdrop of globalization. The potentials of media should be exploited beyond hygienic news dissemination, but towards one having an impact – through the images that are being seen, the voices that are being heard, the music that is played, the culture that is lived throughout society via television, via radio or through print media.

5.5 Empowerment Deficits

What emerged as a strong issue in all interviews was the primacy of empowerment in the face of limited access. An African-American woman stressed the need for personally becoming involved with matters of migration and for understanding its impact upon different citizens and their citizenship rights. Referring to her experiences in southern California and with Mexican-origin Americans, she shared

> the whole notion of citizenship really hits home, as well as the whole notion of immigration, citizenship, basic human rights, affirmative action.

She also emphasized the link of information access and education to an understanding of rights – that often, resources for education are scarce in areas where people's rights are grossly violated.

A Brazilian woman stated the complexity of the social parameters of democracy at length:

> The so-called citizenship endowments just don't mean anything, because we don't discuss the significance of people's participation in schools. Yes, we talk about democracy, but we're not democratic. We need to learn to be democratic, to be autonomous, to be citizens and to exercise it. Today in Brazil, there is a strong movement that tries to spur 'democracy' in schools. It influences the administration to having the communities participate in decision-making. We also have some cities that are being led by people from the workers' party. Then, we establish committees in the quarters to participate in the affairs of the community level and not only in the parliament. The people are in contact with the parliament in these cities where democracy is somehow practiced. It is a good exercise.

Empowerment, guided by the principle of the right to people's self-determination is always a long, tedious process. An African-American woman stated:

> It is almost like learning how to write or to speak a foreign language. You have different vocabularies and different tools in getting your message to a larger group of people. Individually, you are able to develop more self-esteem, but [as a group] you also grow politically and more socially conscious about your surroundings and your situation, and [finally] being able to articulate your situation.

One discussion focussed on the use of different information technologies, emphasizing the role of mass media , and the integrated use of several mass media, i.e. radio, in conjunction with the Internet. It saw the merits of marrying the 'old' and new technologies. A German woman reported a South African example, where the Internet had been used at a radio station to get reports from a feminist journalist. News stories are published on the net so that community radio stations in South Africa could download and broadcast them. However, one problem among these practitioners was the question of social spread. She confronted the input-output-feedback dynamics. With most of the women's radio and media groups we know, we are left with asking: who are listening and viewing us? We had the impression that more or less only our friends are viewing us. This is not really where we want to go. But then, there is no concrete research on the audience and impact of our programs.

In Northern Germany, there is a different model for citizens' participation in each federal state, by amongst others, allotting a prime time slot in the radio. It had started as promising for people to air their views. But the commercial programs could not attract sponsors as they were aired in dead slots. After a dispute on schedules, the commercial program won the upper hand with the argument that nobody anyway will listen to a talk show of socio-political issues.

An African-American woman compared this problem of spreading information with the problem any actor faces in spreading citizenship information:

> How are people producing these radio and television media programs informed by their notions of citizenship and democracy? Again, when you think about being a citizen – that you can vote – but how many people actually exercise their rights of suffrage especially in American elections? Whom will you vote for? Being an African-American, I try to vote during election. But it seems that a lot of people in my community do not feel it is necessary since their platform and the people they want to vote for are not running for office, anyway. No one is representing them, so what is the use? People could be listening, for example in the radio, but most of the time they remain passive. So there is a necessity for the radio to produce a program solely dedicated to a special sector.

From the basis of understanding democratic citizenship as a developing concept with formal and informal components (including political, civil, cultural and economic), we can view the interlocking constraints keeping people, and particularly women, from fully exercising, and thereby, fully enjoying their rights. The constellation of deficiencies, whether pressures in the ballot, clout of the commercial sector, illiteracy, cultural sanctions for women's inferiorized position, or the people's passiveness from claiming their rights, point to three core issues: information, education, and informed participation. The empowerment process happens when people themselves choose for it. The rhetoric of democratic citizenship is often cloaked by the electoral contests alone. But in the bottom-line, there is so much neglect in real issues concerning immigration, disenfranchisement of women by cultural defaults, and the like.

6 Where Next? Future Directions

In the age of globalization, a major focus is placed on the need for governance structures that can extend and support democratic processes. A Bulgarian woman observed the discrepancies in implementation of a democratic system which is often attributed to the principle of democracy rather than the embodied implementation itself: "Our new government didn't manage to fight corruption", something that frustrates the electorate in search of a 'cure-all' solution and perhaps felt more secure under socialism.

> It is very difficult to choose because even if the democratic power is making mistakes now, it is better to support it. But seeing the harrowing rate of unemployment in contrast to picture of politicians becoming richer and richer, can only harbor further pessimism. People say 'I don't care about freedom when I don't have anything to eat.'

An Indian woman highlighted the constraints related to capitalism and democracy in countries in transition, claiming that capitalism is not democratic. She asked:

> Can you really call a country – such as the United States, where only fifty percent of the population vote – democratic?

There is a necessity for equal distribution of wealth, opportunities, and space for participation. Right now, resources are concentrated to a few. We cannot altogether claim that the deficiency for this is caused by population explosion.

Though non-governmental organizations (NGOs) are often seen as a possibility to alleviate this problem, several participants spontaneously mentioned the problem of cooperation between NGOs and traditional governments. Stating that non-profit organizations today work as an industry, an Indian participant proposed that NGOs must focus more on "investing rights in local communities in line with the principles of democracy," where government efforts are often inadequate. This, however, should not assume that NGOs should fulfill the roles of government, but that a healthy, even critical balance between the responsibilities of the government and civil society must be promoted. While non-governmental organizations are often highlighted as a complement to traditional governance structures, NGOs are not free from, for example commercial constraints, nor do they operate outside society. NGOs also have a very limited accountability.

Citizenship rights entail extensive and substantive participation in defining the nature of society, while the reverse is likewise true. In countries where political leaderships neglected people's rights to voice, and had abused in the first instance the soul of the constitutions, direct participation was triggered. Such is the case, for example, of the Philippines' bloodless people's power revolutions in 1986 and 2001, which respectively unseated two corrupt presidents. But even so, elites in the country and many political observers abroad dismissed this display of direct democracy as a mob rule, believing that they are best educated to make government decisions and the citizens at large should believe in their well-meant intention.

This standpoint should be contested, as citizenship must seek remedy in allowing both the critical mass as well as the excluded members of the population, e.g. indigenous peoples and marginalized women, to acquire full participatory rights. In multi-cultural societies, re-defining and broadening the concepts of citizenship may be necessary, to make it even more inclusive. In the Philippine example, the free and independent press combined with people's cohesive communication via Internet, telecast polls and text messages made a significant difference in forming public opinion that eventually led to the staging of people's power revolution.

7 Conclusion

While everyday activity in civil society has to a large extent been disregarded by the hard politics at the higher levels – without linking this level to the factors crucial in supplying the possibilities for an equal representation – the study undertaken at *ifu* supports a broader view on the citizenship problem. The study especially highlights a focus on education and informal rights as important factors toward equal women's citizenship rights. While tied to the functioning of the general political system, women's rights are nevertheless especially vulnerable, suffering not only from the general limitations of the democratic system in practice, but also from politicians' inattention to a gendered perspective. What is needed is a multi-factor model for women's empowerment, focusing on education and access to resources – including information, possibilities of organization, as well as formal representation. This requires a redirection of political science studies, which have generally focussed on the lack of representation of women in formal politics.

As some thinkers in democratic theory have stated, the only antidote to faults in democracy is more democracy. In recent times, with the fall of communism on a large scale, and the struggle among earlier colonies for self-sufficiency, various forms of principles of democracy have, with a few (if very important) exceptions, come to span the globe. However, its formal application does not equal its principles, or unify the diversity of practices under its heading.

References

Ashworth, Georgina (March 1996). *Gendered Governance: An Agenda for Change.* Source: http://www.panasia.org.sg/nird/rrdl100.htm; accessed April 28, 2001.

Friedman, Lawrence M. (1999). *The Horizontal Society.* New Haven: Yale University, chapter 6.

Fukuyama, Francis (1992). *The End of History and the Last Man.* Harmondsworth: Penguin.

Marshall T. H. (1949). *Citizenship and Social Class.* Lecture. Source: http://www.sfi.dk/summaries-of-reports/wprp_show.php3?request=38&open=3; accessed April 5, 2002.

Marshall T. H. (1950). The Centre for Citizenship Learning and Action Internet Module. In: *Citizenship, Democracy and Women.* Source: http://www.ccla.org.uk/aecd/mod3/frame1.htm; accessed June 15, 2000.

Women and Citizenship Research Group (1995). *Women and Citizenship: Power, Participation and Choice.* Belfast: Women and Citizenship Research Group.

Young, Iris Marion (1995). Polity and Group Difference: A Critique of the Ideal of Universal Citizenship. In *Theorizing Citizenship.* Ronald Beiner (ed.). Albany: State University of New York Press.

Aleida Calleja

Indigenous Women and Empowerment

> We speak to the moon
> We walk through the streets and open spaces
> And we cannot forget those wombs open to the sun
> She climbs the mountains
> She is silent, cries, laughs, shouts
> Until she almost goes mad
> The wind carries
> The weeping of orphans
> Your petition for peace
> Who would deny that your spirit is that of a woman?
> *Concepción Suárez*

Abstract
This chapter deals with the way in which the concept of 'new technologies' reaches nebulous boundaries when applied to rural social and cultural contexts. In the case of Cuetzalan, in the Northern Mountain Range of Puebla, Mexico, the introduction of a radio station that broadcasts programs produced in the indigenous languages helped the empowerment of indigenous women of the Nahua and Totonaca peoples. This chapter explores the experience of two young women who redefined their positions as women within their communities and their families, owing to their participation in a medium that gave them a voice and a presence in the public sphere of life. The experiences reported here were shared with the participants at *ifu*'s project *Identities and Globalization*.

1 The Meaning of High Technology in an Indigenous Society

This chapter refers to the radio because the experience I am going to share about women and high technology is about how the indigenous radio system in Mexico has helped to empower some indigenous women in our country. This was also the topic of the project *Identities and Globalization*, where I was involved as group facilitator and of the courses in which I participated at the International Women's University (*ifu*), Project Area INFORMATION.

Imagine living on an island where there is no electricity, nor telephone; imagine living in a single-room home that you share with six other persons. Cars cannot get there because there is no road that leads to your home. If you want to reach the islands around yours, you have to swim because there are no means of transportation available.

Imagine that you speak a language that only the people living on your island can speak. No one else can. Imagine that from time to time you have news about what happens in other places because you only have a small radio that works with batteries. You receive the information in a language that you can barely understand. Imagine that you do not have the chance to be heard, except for the words that you share with the ones that also inhabit your island.

Imagine now that one day someone comes and constructs a radio station on your island. That person is going to give you information in your native language, and will let you use the microphone so others can hear you. You can even be heard on the islands in the vicinity, so you will not have to swim through the sea to exchange information. I think definitely that this would be a new technology for you.

I would like to pose some questions. What do *we* understand when we talk about high technology or new technologies? Are *we* talking about the same thing within different cultural patterns and in different socio-economic conditions and realities? Who are those 'we' that even have the power to pose these questions?

In order to understand why a chapter like this deserves a space in this volume, I would like to begin by giving some figures that could help *us* understand why a radio station in this place offers the opportunity to construct an educational tool for women.

In Mexico, only 3.2 persons in every 1,000 inhabitants have access to the Internet. According to official surveys, of a total population of 100 million, 40 million live in extreme poverty, that is, on less than one dollar per day. The poorest among the poor are the people who inhabit an indigenous zone in the country.

The case presented in this chapter is located in Cuetzalan, in the Puebla's Northern Mountain Range, in the central part of Mexico.

Cuetzalan is the municipal capital, made up of 100 small communities. Of the total population, 42% are illiterate (most of them women), and 25% are monolingual, that is, they do not speak Spanish. 75% of the houses do not have drainage, and 59% do not have electricity. Furthermore, 53% do not have access to running water, and 92% of households have a single-room house. 85% of the families use firewood, because gas is not available in the villages. The average family income is only 2 dollars a day for an eight-hour working day.

Besides, most villages are isolated because of a lack of roads. People normally have to walk six or eight hours to reach other villages, a fact that reinforces the segregation and marginalization of the communities.

None of these communities have a writing system in their own language. Although efforts have been made to develop writing systems corresponding to the various mother tongues, such systems are still inadequate, and only a few members know how to read and write in their own languages. This means that oral tradition is still the most efficient method for transmitting knowledge. Traditional medicine and systems of justice, among others, are still governed by the words passed on from generation to generation.

When I worked in that place, I had to go deeper into the concept of 'word,' because communities without a writing system assign great value to the spoken word, while paper is meaningless to them. If one gives one's word, one has to keep it. It was hard for me to understand such codes, considering that I come from a culture that envisions paper as law, and where words that are not written down are insignificant or even (conveniently) forgotten.

In this context of complete isolation and marginalization, radio becomes a high-tech resource. Although radio has become very common or even obsolete as a means of communication elsewhere, it represents an opportunity of seizing what are otherwise 'means of cultural colonization' for these indigenous communities. It becomes a tool for education, communication and development that complements their ancestral strategy for cultural survival: the spoken word.

Before describing my concrete experience, I would like to make some remarks that I consider useful for a thorough understanding of the case.

Mexico has extensive, well-known credentials regarding anthropological studies of indigenous communities. This is not surprising, considering that in Mexico there are 62 identified ethnic groups distributed over the territory. However, there are scarce possibilities for carrying out studies and publications that can reflect the complex and diverse dynamics of these communities in depth. This is especially problematic when considering the situation of the indigenous women in the geographical region of this case study. It was not until recently that female researchers and scholars interested in gender perspectives set foot in this area. This does not mean that there is a total absence of previous works on gender perspective. In fact, some non-indigenous women have developed a series of projects with indigenous women from a gender perspective for over 20 years. The problem is posed by the material itself and by financial limitations to systematizing and publishing this broad experience.

I would also like to emphasize the difficulties encountered by both researchers and promoters who work in this region in encouraging gender perspective in their work with indigenous women. Other anthropologists have even accused them of threatening the family and community structures. This 'threat' refers to the conflicts that the consciousness of their rights as women brings, and the possibility to defend their rights, refusing to accept 'traditional' or 'historical' roles of subordination to men. They have been accused of attacking traditions and customs.

This situation has created a wide discussion on the contradictory roles of 'traditional culture' and 'universal human rights.' I am convinced that, beyond a respect for cultural diversity and 'otherness,' it is our duty to contribute to human development, and this is impossible to achieve without empowering the women.[1]

2 Radio for Gender and Ethnicity Issues in Cuetzalan

Before going deeper into reflection, I shall briefly describe some geographical and cultural aspects that form the context that surrounded the creation of the indigenous radio station in Cuetzalan, which was later to constitute a tool of empowerment for some indigenous women of the zone.

Cuetzalan is the municipal capital of 143 indigenous communities. The inhabitants belong mainly to the Nahua ethnic group, but there is an important Totonaca population as well. These communities are distributed over an area of 135.2 km^2. According to the official census, Cuetzalan has a population of 35,676. 72% of them are Nahua and speak the Nahuatl language. Life conditions are considered highly marginal, and most of the population do not have access to public services such as drinking water, electricity, schools and hospitals.

75% of the population are devoted to farming activities, predominantly those related to the cultivation of corn and coffee. Corn is produced for private consumption, while coffee is commercialized. However, since the international crisis of 1989 caused a dramatic drop in prices, it has ceased to be an interesting alternative to subsistence farming.

The social structure and the inter-ethnic power relations, as well as class relations are extremely polarized. Being the municipal capital, the political and administrative control in Cuetzalan is in the hands of the *mestizo* population or 'coyome,' which is the name for non-indigenous people. Most of the indigenous population live in the surrounding areas. They live in extreme poverty and are dependent on the goods and services that belong to the *mestizo* population. Concerning this situation, Luisa Paré states that

> The small and big commercial bourgeoisie maintain strong exploitative relations with the *masehuales* [indigenous people], which are, however, concealed by other dependencies, such as *compadrazgos*, loans, etc. However, they have also resorted to violence to maintain their control over the zone. (Paré 1979: 20; my translation)

In Mexico there is a complex system of social relationships constructed around the *compadrazgo*.[2] The godfather is a moral authority to whom both godson (or

---

1   We see empowerment as a multi-dimensional social process that helps people gain control over their lives. It is a process that fosters power in people for use in their own lives, their communities, and the society by acting on issues that they define as important. (Page & Czuba 1999: 14)

2   *Compadrazgo:* Literally, the *compadre* is the godfather seen from the point of view of the child's godmother or parent. Thus, if I am the child's godmother, my *compadre* is

goddaughter) and his/her parents owe special respect. The godfather, in return, gives them protection, money and special treatment. The *compadrazgo* establishes a hierarchical relationship between both parts. The hierarchies based on culture are very strong. However, this does not mean that there is no open confrontation between groups. In fact, the indigenous communities keep close community links as a strategy of resistance to this cultural, political and economic hegemony. Nonetheless, if the indigenous population in general is subordinated, women exist under worse conditions of subordination.

Women suffer double discrimination: besides being subordinated as indigenous, they are also lowered for being women. In many cases, women do not even have the possibility of being considered citizens, because their parents did not register them in the Civil Records Office at birth. Thus, for the state, they simply do not exist. Without being registered, it is impossible to enter into any official procedure (see also the chapter by Keskitalo & Limpangog in this volume).

Women's role is to bear children and do the housework. They do not go to school because it is 'unnecessary' for them to learn how to read and write if their sole function is to get married and have children. They virtually never participate in domestic and community decisions; they do not have a voice or right to vote, and constantly suffer situations of domestic violence, and even community violence. These societies are very permissive with respect to aggression against women (Martinez & Mejía, 1997: 4).

The barriers imposed on them for participating in the public spheres of the community cause women to be withdrawn and unwilling to express their thoughts. This prevents them from claiming their rights from the authorities or persons with higher hierarchical status.

In other cases, some women have had the opportunity to receive elementary education and have gained a wider experience of participation and decision-making within their communities. However, they are still subject to subordination within this highly patriarchal society, and they are frequently stigmatized as 'women of the streets' because they do not play their allotted parts as housewives. In other words, these women are considered 'subversive.'

The social situation of this region is not very different from most of the indigenous zones of Mexico: extreme poverty is rife, and there is a high rate of child and female mortality. Malnutrition, underemployment and farming crises are also common. There is also the extreme isolation from the rest of the country. This means that community events rarely get known outside the zone, and that any information is passed on orally on market-days or in community assemblies. In this sense, the radio broadcasting system has filled a considerable in-

---

'my fellow godparent' and, if I am the child's parent, my *compadre* (or *comadre*) is 'my child's godfather' (or godmother).

formation gap. In general terms, the community structure is very solid, and they have fixed rules of coexistence, with rigidly defined roles for both men and women. Many internal problems are solved according to conventions and customs, i.e. according to the rules that the community has followed for over 500 years. Thus, for example, if one man kills another, instead of being imprisoned, he is obliged to pay all expenses of the widow and the orphans of his victim for the rest of their lives.

In the context of isolation and exclusion that characterizes these communities, the *Instituto Nacional Indigenista* (National Institute for Indigenous Concerns) decided to open an indigenous cultural radio station in 1992. The Institute is a governmental agency that promotes policies to encourage the development of indigenous communities all over the country, and this radio station was created as a tool for achieving its goals in this zone. The main objective was to give access to information that might be useful to the indigenous people in their own language, that is, Nahuatl and Totonaco. The radio station's aim was also to create appropriate conditions for cultural strengthening, and the encouragement of alternatives in farming development, human rights, women's rights, and other matters.

This radio station is part of a broadcasting network that comprises 20 radio stations distributed in different indigenous zones of Mexico. The financial support for carrying out this project is provided by the *Instituto Nacional Indigenista*. The programs are produced both in Spanish and the indigenous languages spoken in each region. These programs are mainly characterized by the important communication services offered to the communities, and produced generally by persons living within the area of broadcast coverage, so that between 80 and 90% of the programs are produced locally. This is very important, because cultural models are instrumental for transmitting information. Thus, for example, there is no translation for 'East' and 'West'; such concepts are expressed as 'where the sun rises' or 'where the sun hides.' A similar situation occurs around morning's greetings: people do not say something like 'good morning'; rather, they have different expressions for different hours of the morning.

2.1 La Voz de la Sierra Norte de Puebla

This radio station (The Voice of the Puebla Northern Mountain Range) devotes 80% of its programs to news and educational programs related to farming, health, human rights, women's situation, and to children. These programs are designed to appeal to the cultural and linguistic framework of the target group. With its focus on their particular problems and culture, the radio has become the point of reference for many social groups that listen to its programs. At the same time, it is an important vehicle of communication in a context characterized by a lack of basic services such as roads, telephone and electricity. The section devoted to 'messages' allows people from different communities to exchange short announcements through the radio. In this way, they announce community assemblies, saving an enormous amount of time and money that would have to be invested if they were to walk to each community to relay the message.

But beyond this practical function, one of the great merits of the radio station is the possibility of redefining identity in positive terms. It means assuming with pride their identity as indigenous peoples and, in the case of women, accepting the challenge of redefining the value of being an indigenous woman. When we talk about identity, we refer to a social location, a place within a hierarchic system but, at the same time, we are concerned with our way of life and how we see and understand ourselves. Being within a given location (privileged or subordinate) is not an inherent characteristic of the self: one always sees, feels or assumes oneself as superior or inferior in relation to others. Identity is a deeply political matter, because each person determines the boundaries of her/his identity within given structures of power that affect them in the most intimate part of the self, defining their being-in-the-world.

The creation of a radio station for and with the active participation of the indigenous communities, and not in the service of the *mestizo* population, represented an extraordinary opportunity for many women and men to locate themselves within the power hierarchy of the zone. Above all, the fact that indigenous women were able to represent their interests for the first time and play a crucial role in the production of the messages, brought important changes. Those changes were evident not only in relation to the *mestizo* social structure, but also within the indigenous social organization.

In this world governed by globalization, where huge corporations dominate the production of messages, the community radio stations and local stations play a key role in focussing specific problems of local women and men. These radio stations are part of a strategy to give voice to the subordinate groups, locating them in new spaces of the hierarchical structure to express their will and their demands, their dreams and realities. They represent an opportunity of human development and empowerment of the weakest:

> The development of communication abilities and the acquisition of tools for the encouragement of the possibilities of organization for uttering a message, demand a process of self-valorization of the group as cultural subject, as a corpus able to create culture and articulate interesting and important proposals for the whole society. (Charles 1995: 173)

2.2 The Process of Creation

When I started to talk to the people about the possibility of opening a radio station that would broadcast programs in their own language, that would play their own music and create messages concerning their particular problems, they stared at me and smiled incredulously, astonished. Because to give a name to people means to put an end to anonymous existence, and to give them something to hold on to for existing – maybe rescuing them from the place of those who have no name.

Moreover, when we organized a workshop with women to discuss the possibility of their having a thorough participation in the production of programs and becoming reporters of the events of their community, there was an incident that moved me deeply. When the discussion ended, a woman came to me with tear-filled eyes. She said she would not be able to participate in the project because she could not write nor read. However, she was willing to learn and then work with the team of the radio. She nearly broke my heart. Those small steps were part of the achievements of the radio, a means of communication that began to be seen as the possibility of becoming visible, of having presence.

3 The Sierra Norte Women's Testimonies

Within this framework, the experience of two indigenous women is presented through their work with the radio station. It highlights the way they have been empowered, helped other women to be empowered, and ultimately, redefine the role of women within and outside their communities.

One of them, Ocotlán, was born in San Miguel Tzinacapan and belongs to the Nahua society. The second one, Alelí, was born in Zapotitlán de Méndez and belongs to the Totonaca ethnic group. I have chosen these two cases because, to some extent, throughout my work at the radio station they showed clear attitudes of leadership within the team (five men and five women). Besides, they demonstrated more self-confidence in their work with local women's organizations.

Ocotlán Pinahuis started working for the radio station when she was 18 years old. She is 24 now and single. She lives with her grandmother and has been a member of a music group since she was fourteen.

Alelí began to work for the radio station when she was 20 years old. She is now 26 and has a son. Before working for the radio station she lived with her parents, being their only daughter.

I asked them to answer the following questions:

How did you decide to look for a job at the radio station? How did you feel when you started working? Do you think that working for the radio station has made any special change to your life? Did your relationship with your family change when you began to work for the radio station? How did your community treat you before working for the radio station? Which is the most significant change you experienced during all these years of working for the radio station?

The following are extracts from their testimonies.

3.1 The Testimony of Ocotlán

"I have three sisters, but since I was a child I have lived with my grandmother and my aunt, who are artisans. I have always loved music, and when I was very young I joined the church choir. I learned to play the guitar and to sing there. Later, some young boys from the community organized a group that played modern music, or tropical music, as they call it. They invited me to play the guitar and I have been with them since that time. We play at parties.

"When I knew that they were taking on people to work at the radio station, the first thing I thought was that maybe I could enter. First of all because I know something about music, and also because they asked for people who spoke Spanish and Nahuatl. Thus, I went for the voice test, and I passed. I was very surprised to know how much I had to learn to work in the radio station. I felt that I would never make it... it seemed incredibly difficult to me. When I was in front of the microphone for the first time, my tongue was completely stiff... it didn't want to move... All the words seemed to have gone from my mind. I felt like a fool, but my need to find a job that would increase my family's income was stronger.

"At the beginning I felt a little like a blockhead, because the rest of the team knew more than I did. Men have greater opportunities to go out from home and even from the community, and they know more and are less afraid of facing new things. When I started working for the radio station, for example, I didn't even know the discs, nor how to talk over the microphone and the rest of the equipment. When I entered the radio station, I began to know many things that I didn't know before, because they were things that didn't occur in the everyday conversations at home..., or simply because I didn't know they existed. For example, I learned for the first time about women's health, a subject we normally don't talk about. They say that those are bad things, and that the 'women of their homes' never speak about them... Or women's rights, for example, the right to have access to information.

"I do believe that radio has changed my life, because without this experience I would never have had the opportunity to have so much information and training. I used to think that speaking my own language would never be useful in my life. However, it was a very good point for having the job here. It also changed the relationship with my family, mainly because I could take money to my home and that gave me a different place. I also gained their respect, because my mother and my sisters frequently heard people telling them that I spoke on the radio. Sometimes they looked for me and asked for information: the price of coffee, or some information about services or institutions. The same happened within the whole community... Before that, I had no hope of being listened to and nobody bothered to know my opinion. But since I have worked in the radio, people sometimes listen to me. This doesn't happen to the rest of the women, who normally remain unheard.

"Well... it's not always the same, because, you know, some men accuse me of being a rebel because I say on the radio that we women have rights.

"Nowadays there are many women who follow us. They speak to us. But there are also many men who cannot take us for what we say on the radio. They say that we're only inciting women... but for good or for bad, they always listen to us.

"Sometimes I have to talk with women that tell me to say this or that, because their husbands listen to what the radio says. I believe that it would never have been possible without the radio.

"In the days when I went to other communities for a concert with my group mates, people said that I was a whore because I traveled with many men, and that only God knew what I was doing with all of them. My grandmother didn't say a word, because she has always trusted me, but my relationship with the community was very complicated. My relationship with some *mestizos* was not very different.

"I remember that when I was a child they didn't want me to go to school because I didn't wear shoes and because I dressed like a *maseual*.[3] I really tried hard to go to school dressed like that. If I was an indigenous girl... why should I dress like a *coyome*? I was not ashamed of being an Indian, as they say. Now that I work at the radio station, I don't think that all those people respect me, but at least we talk on more equal terms. I know they still look down on me because I'm indigenous, but they don't dare to tell me many things because they know we can denounce them on the radio... I mean, not directly, but we can say what's going on.

"I remember that once I was walking down the street, and a woman came to me and asked me if I wanted to work as a maid at her home. The *mestizos* believe that indigenous people are only useful to work as servants. At that moment I didn't know whether I should get angry or what to feel and I only told her that I couldn't because I was very busy being a radio producer. The woman smiled slightly and apologized because she didn't know I worked for the radio station.

"But it was not only talking on the radio that has changed my position as a woman. When the rest of the team or some other people see that I can operate the equipment, they also feel a little more respect for me. I have demonstrated

---

3   *Maseual* is the term used by the indigenous people to refer to their own group. It means 'indigenous' or 'indigena' in Spanish.

that it is possible to do things, that we are not fools. We only need a chance to prove that we can do other things than having children and take care of our husbands.

"I haven't got married because I can't see a good man who wants me to keep on working. The problem is that, if you get married, they want you to stay at home. If there is a man who would accept me, he would also have to accept that I work... I mean, that's the way they know me and that's how I am.

"We women are afraid of many things. We're afraid of talking, we're afraid of machines or the equipment that only men can operate; we're afraid of giving our opinion and saying what we think... and what they would say about us, and we're also afraid of being alone. Now that I can speak and be heard I am not afraid anymore. I am also not afraid of being alone... they say it's better to be alone than in bad company... I don't need a man who will treat me badly or who won't let me go to work. I prefer to remain like this.

"I think that if I hadn't had the chance to work at the radio station, I wouldn't have the place I gained within my family and my community... maybe I wouldn't even think like this. But you can never know... I've been a rebel my whole life."

3.2 The Testimony of Alelí

"I am the only child of my parents, and never had problems or fights with my brothers or sisters ... you know, as a woman, here you have to serve them and obey them. I never saw my father treat my mother badly, but I had seen many men beat their women. Those women have no right to go out or do something different from housework.

"I studied at High School, and I was thinking about going to the capital city of Puebla, because there are not many job opportunities here. But the chance to work at the radio station came, and they took me because I can speak the Totonaco language. When I speak Totonaco I feel like an indigenous woman, although I don't dress as an indigenous girl. Since I was a child I was dressed like other *mestizas* because my parents didn't want me to be discriminated like the other indigenous girls who are dressed in the traditional costume. I'm already used to dressing like this, but I think that dress doesn't make you an indigenous woman, but what you think and what you do.

"I have always been a person that talks a lot, but when I was in front of the microphone for the first time, it seemed that a mouse had come and eaten my tongue. I said things I didn't want to say, but they went out of my mouth just like that. Later, with practice, things went easier, but it was a long way. It was also difficult to learn how to operate the equipment. But I had no option: I had to learn. This was very good because I didn't have to show my 'good girl's face' anymore to ask them to please operate the equipment. That made me more independent.

"After many years, I have a different role within my community now. I can sit down with men and talk with them as an equal. Firstly, because now I have much more information, and secondly because they listen to me a little bit more because I work on the radio. This doesn't happen to the rest of the women, who remain unheard. For many years I had produced a series of programs devoted to women where we talk about women's rights, reproductive health and things like that. One day, a man of the community, a mature man, came to me very angrily and told me that I was only inciting the other women. He said that if I didn't stop, the problem would have catastrophic consequences, because women would eventually abandon their husbands and their children, and I don't remember what else.

"At the beginning I was scared. I thought that maybe one day they would beat me or they would throw stones at me for my work. Although many men are willing to do that, I later realized that the men's strategy to keep women under control is to threaten them. But since I work at the radio station and people know me, they wouldn't dare to hurt me. Besides, many men are scared themselves when they know we are in contact with institutions that work for our human rights and things like that.

"This work has helped me to know many communities, to know my people better and those that come from outside and have different ways of thinking.

"Now I have a daughter because I decided to have her, and have her alone. This is not common among the indigenous women, because you always have to get married. But until now I haven't found a man who can accept me as I am and who wants to live with me... although frankly speaking, I prefer to be like this. Nobody bothers me, and I don't bother anyone.

"If I hadn't worked in this environment, I think that I would never have had the chance to be like this, enjoying the opportunity of being heard and having my opinion considered. Although in the *mestizo* context it is not really heard – after all, for them we're only indigenous and they don't take into consideration what we think – the radio changes some things. For good or for bad, they have to talk with us, because that's their only possibility of having their messages on the air.

"If women were given access to this kind of space for talking, learning and getting information, things would be totally different. We would have more tools to defend ourselves. It is true that if I hadn't had this chance, I would surely be working as a secretary in some place in the city. Maybe I would be married, bearing I don't know how many children and taking care of my husband. Not now. I am Alelí, and I have my own place, my own image and my own voice. These things make me what I am."

4 Transforming Cultural Structures and Gender Relations

Both Ocotlán and Alelí produce a radio magazine for women in three languages: Nahuatl, Totonaco and Spanish. They also train other women and teach them to produce their own programs. During the time I worked with them, I could observe how other members of the group warned them to moderate the tone of their discourses because it was dangerous: some men had already shown their disapproval. When the weaker talk about their rights, the stronger invariably become angry – in any case, men would never stop speaking up, because if they kept quiet, then the rest of the team would have to do so, too. After all, talking about the rights of the indigenous people always bothers the *mestizos*.

Naming, rendering visible other ways of being a woman has a deep impact on our society because it allows us to understand ourselves better, and to understand how valuable we are. However, the punishment of society is loneliness. Like other women who exert leadership in other women's organizations, we are often lonely women. Nobody forgives us for our choice. Men prefer women that submit to the patriarchal power. We do not affirm this because we think that a woman without a man is automatically alone. But the fact is that in such communities, where the rule is that a woman should be married and bear children, single women are seen as abnormal and treated with some reserve. They are respected, but with reserve. They are under a great deal of social pressure to play the parts they are supposed to play. Otherwise, they have little possibility of meeting other women and develop closer relationships with others:

> When we look through the feminist and gender perspective, we name in a different way the things we already know, making evident hidden facts and giving new meanings. This way of looking at things includes the aim to create a revolution in the order of power among genders, and with it, a revolution in the whole daily life, the relationships, the roles and the statutes of both men and women. It comprises, in a concomitant way, changing the society, the norms and the beliefs, as well as the State, and this can cause distress to more rigid and conservative persons and institutions, more assimilated and in agreement with patriarchal order. (Lagarde 1998: 20; my translation)

To resist deeply rooted traditions and the governing social system always leads to conflict. When the radio started transmitting its messages, representatives of the *mestizo* society visited us immediately. They wanted to advertise their stores or products, and we had to explain that ours was not a commercial radio station and that its main objective was the participation of the people, as well as the creation of a special forum for the expression of indigenous organizations. At that moment they stopped being interested in the project. We were proposing the vindication of the communities, an issue that makes the *mestizos* feel uneasy because it challenges their privileges as a political, commercial and administrative oligarchy.[4] A dialogue in a context where even different *mestizo* groups collide[5] is complex and needs much effort to overcome deeper structural problems, such as social inequality, racism and corruption, for example. Furthermore, the radio cannot be considered as a possible solution for gender inequality and power struggles between indigenous and *mestizo* groups. It would be naïve to think that it could work as a peaceful and democratic forum for negotiations between two peoples that fought in complex and violent scenarios for centuries. Women, for their part, have much to do in terms of everyday struggle if they want to achieve an equal position with the men. Real battles are not won through new technologies, but through committed and combative proposals against oppression exerted both by individuals and the system. Radio could, however, play a very important role in giving voice to the otherwise unnoticed indigenous communities. It could help to make their problems visible, and promote reflection and debate about their situation as an indigenous people.

Moreover, the importance of radio cannot be neglected in a context where access to other technologies is extremely restricted. Internet cafes do not exist because it would be unaffordable to pay a long-distance call only to be connected to the nearest server. The cost of about one dollar per minute is sometimes covered by certain organizations, but only on very specific occasions. At this moment, only one of the women's organizations has Internet access, and their members are learning how to use it. This organization is in very close contact with the radio station, and it will be interesting to see how Internet and radio work together as a means of empowering women.

Young people have slightly easier access to the Internet, but they represent only the very privileged group that has gone to high school. In any case, their access to information is limited, because most of the information is written in languages different from Spanish.

5 Bringing the *ifu* Experience to the Mountains?

Women's movements, especially those devoted to communication as a means in enabling women to participate, must be committed to finding effective strategies to strengthen our right to information and communication. We need to participate in scientific and technological decisions. Technology alone cannot con-

---

4   Most of them belong to the political party that has governed the country for seventy years. Despite having a mainly indigenous population, Cuetzalan has never had indigenous municipal authorities, which have always been *mestizos*.

5   Other visitors to the radio station were *mestizos* that work with social organizations. These are persons normally not Cuetzalan by birth, but men and women who have decided to work with the indigenous communities of the place.

struct a critical society; a solid concept of democracy and participation is the most important tool to attach a political meaning to the new technologies.

The right to communication and information is particularly important to those who suffer from violence, poverty and social exclusion. The possibility to exert this right still seems too far away. For this reason, having access to the new technologies of communication represents an invaluable tool for those who have to fill the gap between high technology and the simplest strategies for survival.

My experience at *ifu* confirms that the new technologies hold great potential for bringing together our projects and our struggles. However, each day I wondered how I could possibly apply some learning in the present reality at home, and above all, how I could transfer this experience to the indigenous women of Mexico.

I encountered marvelous media projects that enriched my knowledge enormously. This experience deepened my understanding of the internationalization process of civil rights movements. I had the chance to share my experience... but I always felt I was an intermediary for the women I have been talking about. It was not the same when I narrated the experience. It was lacking in, precisely, the voice of the women that the radio had made heard for the first time.

The experience also made me think about how we could develop a joint project to carry our dreams and struggles elsewhere. Most of the time I listened to proposals related to new technologies, and I always came back to the same basic question: how can we do it if these women don't have the infrastructure for it? How can we overcome the language barrier? How can illiterate women be part of this worldwide connection?

I still cannot find the answers, but it is now clear to me that projects such as *ifu* can help us to outline our tasks. I can see the huge challenges we must face so that more and more women can join in the struggle against oppression. The first step will be to make accessible to them the same benefits that industrialized countries have, where it is possible to reach a person in a distant country by only making a local phone call.

The experience at *ifu* also made me realize how strong the impact of homogenization is that moves global capitalism. In this context, small communities' shared experiences and media are more necessary than ever to resist this onslaught and vindicate our struggles. The diversity among women, cultures and projects at *ifu* showed me again that the common basis of our struggles as women is the nature of our work. Communication and information have become the center of our economic, social and political interactions, and this situation urges women's participation in every sphere of social action. Younger feminist communicators who are introduced to the new technologies should turn around and look at the important social processes behind technology itself. The important thing is not knowledge in itself, but how we are going to use that knowledge to build a more equitable world.

6 Conclusion

This chapter tried to show how the radio can be instrumental in making indigenous women visible, and of course, heard, and how it can help them to reassess their identities as indigenous women in a society that most of the time did not bother to look at them. Much has been said about the mass media's impact on modern, urban societies. This chapter shows, in a nutshell, how a medium can be used to attain cultural vindication by democratizing the word. This results in having women access to information and knowledge. There are no worse or better media technologies. We can only put a moral value on the ideas and purposes that move them.

I do not doubt that women find special challenges within society and the communication arena: we need to keep on working for women's empowerment, and for a representation that does justice to what we are and to what we can contribute to the world. We cannot postpone the construction of an identity that would enable us to understand ourselves and that liberates us each time that we appeal to it in order to overcome barriers. We have to keep on working to ensure that the community communication incorporates a strong feminine presence. Then the right to communicate and express ourselves, the right to know, to be informed, the right to render ourselves visible and develop leadership, may one day become a reality.

In this globalized world, the means of communication are, more than ever, an extremely effective political tool for subordinate sectors, and especially to achieve the goals of women's struggle.

Acknowledgements

I would like to thank my dearest *comadre* Yolanda Muñoz for her support in correcting and translating this chapter, and Irma Ávila Pietrasanta because she opened my horizons through the contact with *ifu*.

And, above all, I would like to thank the indigenous women who inspired all these ideas. Without them, all this knowledge would simply never have been accessible to me; and to many others who are still looking for new, unbeaten tracks.

References

Aldana, Celia (1998). Los medios y las identidades de género. In: *Chasqui, revista latino-americana de comunicación*. Quito, Ecuador: Ed. Chasqui, pp. 20-24.

Charles, Mercedes (1995). *Educación para la recepción ciudadana*. Lima, Perú: Ed. Calandria.

Garcia Lourdes, Rubio Blanca, Alberti Pilar & Pérez Elia (2001). *El desarrollo rural. Un camino desde las mujeres. Género, poder y sustentabilidad*. Ciudad de México, México: Ed. Red Nacional de Promotoras y Asesoras Rurales.

Hernández, Rosalva Aida (1998). *La otra palabra*. Chiapas, México: Ed. Ciesas.

Lagarde, Marcela (1998). *Género y feminismo*. Ciudad de México, México: Ed. Moras.

Martínez, Beatriz & Mejía, Susana (1997). *Ideología y práctica en delitos cometidos contra mujeres. El sistema judicial y la violencia en una región indígena de Puebla*. Puebla. México: Ed. Colegio de Postgraduados, Campus Puebla.

Page, Nanette & Czuba, Cheryl E. (1999). Empowerment. What Is It? In: *Journal of Extension*, vol. 37, no. 5, pp.10-20.

Paré, Luisa (1979). *Caciquismo y estructura de poder en la Sierra Norte de Puebla*. Ciudad de México, México: Ed. siglo XXI.

Irma Ávila Pietrasanta

Information Rights and Media Democracy in Times of Globalization.
A Women's and Civil Society's Perspective

> Everyone has the right to freedom of opinion and expression; this right includes freedom to hold opinions without interference and to seek, receive and impart information and ideas through any media and regardless of borders.
> *United Nations: Universal Declaration of Human Rights, Article 19, 1948*

> The main way the powerful make their voices heard is via electronic means, radio and television. With no one questioning them, they become the dominant voice. Electronic communication does not disseminate news, but creates it, feeds into it, makes it grow and annihilates news. Mass media can build parallel realities, it takes sides, and attacks social movements, while society stands by and observes, almost in silence.
> *Subcommandante Marcos 2002*

Abstract
Information rights are fundamental human rights: the right to know and the freedom of speech are part of the people's rights. But these rights which originated from the French Revolution took too many years to being realized, being exercised in diverse ways with more or less success in different regions of the world. They are, like other human rights, in danger of extinction. Social rights are rarely discussed in times of globalization. In this chapter, as in the projects and courses I held at *ifu*, I attempt to show how the economic globalization process affects the people's information rights, and how markets can distort the fundamental purpose of the media and the primacy of information and social needs, by converting them into merchandise. This in effect also distorts democracy and social life. This chapter explores the multiple ways the new society, or more aptly, the 'emerging horizontal society,' struggles to recover the rights it is losing.

1 The Right to Communicate is Not the Speaker's Corner

Discussing information rights today implies relating their actual exercise to the access that the various social groups have to the media and the new information and communication technologies (ICTs). Information right is a fundamental human right and is an indispensable tool for each social group to fulfill their goals. Thus, information access ought to be translated into a right to know, a right to demand good quality information, and a right to communicate. As a matter of fact, the right to information access became one of the key issues addressed by me at *ifu* (International Women's University, here: *ifu's* Project Area INFORMATION), where I was the director of the projects *Identities and Globalization* and

Media Industries and Democracy, and taught a course. on *Cultural Identity and Globalization*.

The possibility to have good quality information is yet to become a reality in today's world, despite official declarations that world information networks will help us to have closer communication than before by having unlimited access to information – more so than ever seen before in the history of mankind. And of course we will also have many more channels than previously through which to express ourselves. This is a byproduct of technological breakthroughs and economic globalization.

The usefulness of information has to be defined in terms of social needs and goals, concerning such issues as health, politics, environment, human rights, as well as the right to communicate. As it stands today, the enjoyment of such rights has been rather limited. Women as well as other social groups, e.g. environmentalists, indigenous peoples, trade unions, human rights organizations and others, face serious problems of invisibility and lack of access to information (see also the chapter by Calleja in this volume). Concerning women, the 1995 Beijing Declaration, which was endorsed by international organizations, governments and the civil society organizations, contains the following:

> Ensure women's equal access to economic resources, including land, credit, science and technology, vocational training, information, communication and markets, as a means to further the advancement and empowerment of women and girls (Fourth World Conference on Women, Beijing Declaration, September, 1995, United Nations).

> Strategic objective J.1: 'Increase the participation and access of women to expression and decision-making in and through the media and new technologies of communication.'

> Strategic objective J.2: 'Promote a balanced and non-stereotyped portrayal of women in the media.' (FWCW Platform for Action Women and the Media, 1995, United Nations).

Five years after the Beijing Conference, assessments indicate that the two strategic points are not easily realized. Both the objectives then proposed as well as the efforts made have not been sufficient in solving the problems that result from the complex relationship between women and media.

Various reports from around the world have acknowledged the important progress in women's enrolment in universities, creation of spaces for women journalists, a growth in number of women media managers, and a few educational programs stressing a gender perspective. However, such advancements are related to sustained monitoring of women's image in media through a network of efforts, and an intense lobbying with governments, political groups and media by women's organizations. Nevertheless, there are recent cases of the use of a negative female stereotype, which is probably due to the non-implementation or simply non-existence of a code of ethics for national media. Moreover, women continue to have limited access to, as well as limited participation in the decision-making in government, and in supervisory bodies of the formulation and implementation of communication policies. Women working in the media still face gender discrimination, including sexual harassment at work. Hence, the power to influence and shape the media is still elusive for women.

> Yet the booming communications industry – the fastest growing sector of the economy – is becoming increasingly concentrated in national and transnational monopolies, which are driven overridingly by profit. Information becomes a commodity and the function of media as a public service is swept aside. Under the sway of the mass media, women are portrayed to the public view in a highly selective and disempowering manner, and a majority of the world's women are simply invisible. Their viewpoints and concerns are grossly underrepresented. [...]

> Meanwhile, international communications regulation and policy are concentrated in bodies such as the World Trade Organization and International Telecommunications Union, which are dominated by business interests. Women's access to the means of communication is not represented in their decisions and is given little weight. (Declaration to UNGASS, (United Nations General Assembly) from the Caucus of NGOs on Women and Media (2000).

They also state that:

> Any serious review of Section J (Women and Media) of the Beijing Platform for Action has to address the emerging scenario at the global, regional, national, and local level. It must recognize the strategic weakness of Section J, which failed to articulate the structural constraints and impediments that women and other marginal groups face due to commercialization and globalization of media and the concomitant decline of public broadcasting media in societies with democratic and pluralistic traditions.

2 Unique Thought

Global processes have a double face that affects women as well as other social actors, particularly in Third World countries. This process is related to 'modernity,' i.e. a modernity apparently lacking ideology, but which actually closes the door to pluralism in thought; a modernity which points to economics as the only way to rational decision-making; a modernity that demands everyone to adapt to. This is related to what journalist Ignacio Ramonet (1997) calls "unique thought."

> And it has been handed down to us as a unique reasonable ideology. We are living in an ideological totalitarianism which attempts to convince us, with all the resources of the big money, that our mission is to serve to the market.

Following Fidel Castro's words, "Everything through the Revolution, nothing against it" we could say "Everything through the free market, nothing without it".

This process has produced not only billionaires and some changes in the production of goods, but has also changed the forms of human life around the planet. In addition, it has transformed social concepts and political subjects, creating new global and ethnic identities. According to Ignacio Ramonet (1997)[1], editor of *Le Monde Diplomatique*, two ideas about social organization are considered old-fashioned: progress and social cohesion. This is due to two revolutions: First, the technological revolution. In general terms, this means the transfer of human work to machines, which not only replaces human muscles but many of the brain's functions as well. Secondly, the digital revolution. To date, human beings have communicated among themselves using sign systems: words, images, sounds, and texts. Each one of them had its own way of communicating, but with the digitalization process, most of them are using the same means of transmitting sound, images and text messages at the speed of light around the world.

However, both of these aspects – the substitution of the brain's functions and the digitalization process – opened up new possibilities for people to come together on a planetary scale. This is the third big revolution. Communication and information technologies have encouraged financial activities and transfers of currencies, leading to economic globalization. This form of production has been reflected in power relationships, displacing the authoritarian perspective in favor of a consensual one.

On the other hand, whereas in the past the two biggest sociological paradigms were the ideas of progress and social cohesiveness, these have been replaced today by the communication and free market paradigms.

In the twentieth century the idea of progress for all people was proposed as a way to avoid social conflicts between the poor and the rich in societies of liberal regimes. The social cohesiveness paradigm stated that in a modern democratic structure society must function as a machine in which all pieces are important and necessary for its general functioning. Therefore, society must be in solidarity with each of its members. This paradigm does not function today, and there is not even a national cohesiveness anymore.

It was not until the 1980s that the idea of progress was questioned as the origin of social welfare, and it was replaced by the idea that social welfare, paradoxically, leads to social backwardness. Twenty years later, many of us understand that this is not true, but it is still maintained as a truth according to the neo-liberal way of thinking.

Today the communication paradigm fulfills the mission played before by the progress paradigm; that is, to maintain societies in peace. It rests on the idea of a

---

1   These ideas were taken from an unpublished conference witten by Ignacio Ramonet for the Encuentro Internacional de la Radio, Santiago de Chile, Universidad Católica and Radio Netherlands, in October 1997.

free market around which a society is organized. The free market not only rules the exchange of goods, but all activities in society. There is no major activity outside free market rules. The free market legitimizes everything. The vocation of free markets is to organize all our activities under its rules.

The consequence of these changes is that political power does not rule anymore. Before today, any political power had the ability to intervene in development and social cohesiveness issues, and society was organized to cover this, but with the new paradigms, political leaders do not have too much say anymore.

We are undergoing the second big capitalist revolution, economic globalization, which has led to political, economic and social consequences like a decrease in political power. This process has created new owners of the world.

Ramonet tells us that if we look at the list of the ten most powerful and influential men of the world, we can see that none of them are politicians, none of them have been elected by the people – they are entrepreneurs, most of whom own huge media corporations. The U.S. President is not on the list, and he is considered the leader of the world's most powerful country. Power hierarchies have changed, the current main trend is economic power; the second one is mass media; and the last in line is political power.

All of these changes endanger democracy. The problem is that the average citizen has only two ways of influencing society, by voting in elections and participating in public meetings, or through freedom of speech. But if we exercise these two rights, the only thing that can be modified is political power, and today politicians cannot change the rules which determine our daily life.

Neither Ted Turner of CNN, nor Robert Murdoch of News Corporation, nor Bill Gates of Microsoft, nor Robert Allen of AT&T, nor dozens of new owners of the world media have submitted their projects to the will of the people yet, although these are projects which transform the lives of hundreds of millions of people. Democracy is denied.

As Ramonet (1997) points out, we have impotent democracies, and it is for this very reason that we see the emergence of groups that deny democracy and its legitimacy as a self-governing regime. Financial markets are today the main subjects of international political life and nobody has influence over them.

This is a 'Democracy of Low Intensity' (Robinson, 1996: 4) and the one which is now ruling most parts of the world. In keeping with these ideas, many social projects have disappeared in Mexico as well as in many other countries of the world during the last few years.

3 Communication and Democracy

How does globalization, which would not be possible without a modern communication system, impact every-day information?

Before the 1980s, mass media were considered to be a social service for society, and in many countries, thanks to the rules established for their operation, strong and competitive public mass media developed. After the fall of the Berlin Wall and the end of the Cold War however, most mass media had to 'adapt' to free market rules. They were involved in mergers and the integration of market rules, just like other industries, and very soon lowered production costs and offered a poorer quality of information to the people. This is what large alliances represent, and this model became a unique way for mass media to survive.

Alger (1998) shows how mass media merged with commercial corporations, and in exchange sacrificed their initial and true reason for existing – they have ceased to be service-oriented but instead turned into being merely business ventures. Citizens' freedom of speech and the right to know set forth in Article 1948 of the Universal Declaration of Human Rights, are no longer mass media priorities. Information empires have largely controlled the playing field, and consequently the message. Records reveal that multi-national mergers have assumed power over media's fundamental use: Disney Capital Cities – ABC, Time Warner – Turner, News Corporation, Bertelsmann, General Electric – NBC, Westinghouse – CBS, Newhouse Advanced Publications, Viacom, Microsoft, Matra Hahette, Gannet, TCI Telecommunications Inc., and so on.

The news media are absolutely central to the functioning of democracy today, and entertainment and other features and programs in the mass media, in the aggregate, have powerful effects on society in a more general way Alger (1998: 2). We all rely on information, an exchange of ideas and basic images are fundamental in determining whether the democratic process works as intended, or whether it falters or is subverted. This is why the First Amendment to the United States Constitution – the prime pillar of the Bill of Rights – has as its cornerstone in freedom of the press and speech.

The essence of the First Amendment's central provision is to ensure that the principal sources of information and ideas for 'us the people' are genuinely independent and that we hear diverse voices for the 'conversation of democracy'. Democracy is a 'marketplace of ideas', where a wide range of people and organizations have a real opportunity to pass on information and ideas for all of us to ponder. Correspondingly, we should be greatly concerned if much or most of the main media increasingly fall under the control of a small number of giant corporations and extremely wealthy and willful people, especially when such people are inclined to use the powerful media of mass communication for their own political and economic ends.

Many of the U.S. newspapers and magazines are falling under the control of media corporations, which do not have any commitment to society, democracy or social dialogue at all, and seem interested only, or principally, in milking their media properties for as much money as possible (Alger, 1998: 12, 44-50).

These changes forced some journalists to quit. For example, Gerry Solomon, who after seventeen years working for NBC, explained: 'Quality definition has changed since General Electric arrived. It is not the quality of a reporter which matters today, but the quality of profits.' (Alger, 1998: 14). Wright speaks of costs, journalists speak of things like credibility, vocation and professional news quality, which are not quantifiable for General Electric. Wright said that

> News is a very expensive product for us and NBC is a dinosaur. Its budget is two hundred million dollars per year, but we do not go out with you as partners to spend two million dollars on something you think is good, but we think it is not a priority. (Alger, 1998: 24)

Many correspondents and other information sources and resources of mass media companies disappeared; the capacity of news coverage decreased, and news programs were replaced by cheaper stories about crime, scandal and celebrities. The coverage of public issues dramatically decreased. These changes are especially dangerous for any society, not only in the way they impact on democracy, but because they lead us back to the logic of the Unique Thought, which means that we must comply with our last goal in life, to serve the free market.

According to Alger (1998: 19), many studies carried out in the United States show that mass media have a powerful impact on political processes, and many other studies show that the role mass media are playing in providing information and analysis of political processes is a very poor one, because news in mass media are focussed only on political games, conflicts and scandal issues, violating in doing so a fundamental human right, the right to know.

Political Scientist Robert Dahl (cited in Alger, 1998: 20), emphasizes two primary elements of the democratic process, i.e. effective participation, and enlightened understanding. With regard to the 'enlightened understanding' element, the *Supreme Court of Justice* in Florida in the United States stated that

> The right of citizens to know all the elements of a controversy in order to make a wise choice about it, is becoming endangered by the increasing concentration of mass media in a few hands, which often results in a private censure. (In Alger, 1998: 20)

Communications Scientist George Gerbner (cited in Alger, 1998: 23) points out that

> The fabric of popular culture that relates elements of exercise to each other and structures the common consciousness of what is, what is important, what is right, is now largely a manufactured product. A change in that ability transforms the nature of human affairs. We are in the midst of such a transformation. It stems from the mass production of symbols and messages, a new industrial revolution in the field of culture.

Philosopher Iovanni Sartori (1998: 43) goes beyond that and states that this phenomenon is changing human nature, from *homo sapiens* to *homo videns*, that is, human beings whose reflexive capacity and understanding of social complexity have been radically reduced. Lee Bollinguer (cited in Alger, 1998: 153), Dean of the Michigan University Law School, said that

> The press can exclude important points of view, operating as bottleneck in the marketplace of ideas. It can distort knowledge of public issues, not just by omission but also through active misrepresentations. It can also exert an adverse influence over the tone and character of public debate in subtle ways, by playing to personal biases or by making people fearful... It can fuel ignorance and pettiness by avoiding serious issues altogether favoring simple-minded fare of cheap entertainment over serious discussion, of course, all these concerns become more serious as the number of those who control the press becomes fewer.

On the other hand, we can add to this situation the fact that many advertisers are attempting to have more influence on TV contents. Some huge corporations such as Chrysler have even demanded a preview of the programs sponsored by them. CBS and ABC sent TV programs to sponsors like Procter and & Gamble, and Westinghouse, among others, before showing them.

The assets of many mega-media empires not only include radio and TV corporations, but also computers, video games, direct TV, entertainment, telephones, films, newspapers, magazines and publishing houses, household appliances, airlines, auto financing, travel agencies, fast food, plastics, resorts, hotels, cruises, sports, and participation in many mass media in countries such as Austria, Australia, Brazil, Finland, Germany, Great Britain, Hong Kong, Hungary, India, New Zealand and Mexico. Their impact is not only on a local level, but also at a global one.

For most people, mass media are the only source of information on which to form their own opinions on public issues. Mass media corporations have determined that entertainment is more profitable than news. Disney Corporation, which directly reaches more than one hundred million homes in 160 countries around the world, is a very good example of a profitable and successful entertainment corporation. According to Alger (1998: 195-216), the former president of the NBC news section, Larry Grossman, points out that 'corporations do not have any direct responsibility with the people, but they exert an extraordinary power on ideas and information that people receive.'

Alger (1998: 19, 115) tells us about the most important impacts of megamedia:

- Unfair economic competition and distortion of market principles;
- Unfair competition in the fields of information and ideas of generalized dominance of a few corporations, as well as the elimination of alternate sources;

- Deterioration of news items and matters regarding public issues; deterioration of information, reports, articles and entertainment shows.

4 The Role of Society

Meanwhile, what role does society play in this process?

- Information is seen more as merchandise and not as a service to society as it used to be seen; society becomes a consumer and is treated as such.
- Society has drastically decreasing access to a good quantity and quality of information.
- Large companies with the capacity to impact media decide what is information in social terms and what is not.
- Society and its needs do not even have a minimum impact on the decisions made by the owners of mega-media.
- Society is sold, via rating studies, to the advertiser. We are sold as brains open to the advertisers' needs who do what they want us to do, without care, to keep us in front of the TV.
- Society pays for the whole process out of its pocket, be it through pay TV or by means of additional costs to the products we buy or through taxes. We pay the final tab of the whole mass media production, like it or not, watch it nor not.

Something is wrong, something is not working at all. We pay while others benefit. And meanwhile, in the U.S. and Canada, we see the start right now of polemics regarding how much these changes have affected people's rights to free expression and access to information. International agreements contribute to this process, first the North American Free Trade Agreement (NAFTA), and now the Free Trade Agreement of the Americas (FTAA) which is trying to cast aside local laws with a social or national content that are an obstacle to the strengthening of the mega-media. Also, the lack of some social communication laws, as in the case of Mexico, has led not only to discretionary impunity of the media and the government, which to date is under no obligation whatsoever to inform the citizens of its acts and omissions.

5 Displacing Traditional Cultures and Women

This situation only points to another thorny issue related to the globalization of different social realities. While we are barely able to fight for including the exercise of these rights and freedom of expression in countries like Mexico, international agreements even propose to eliminate part of the legislation in these areas, especially social content of matters related to democracy and national concerns, since they get in the way of free development of the media market. Researcher Ramonet (1997) points out that 90 percent of broadcasting time is taken up by programs produced in Japan, the U.S. and Western Europe, which means that most countries are simply consumers.

But this situation is very favorable in economic terms for the media industries, and adds a new dimension to the already existing problems, since it is not only a matter of democracy, but also a matter of attributing more importance to a certain vision of the first world countries, to a certain culture, a certain outlook in life, with all the biases possible, and dominating the rest of cultural wealth on our planet.

In the face of this reality, in our countries there is an ongoing debate about whether or not this media reality removes people from the media who do not reflect the way the people are or, on the contrary, if they develop a process of acculturation to these new electronic totems.

In the face of a lack of legal security, we have begun to work with the peoples' organizations who do not believe in market globalization and who would be strong and capable of facing new challenges: women, social organizations, and community-based groups. They are likely to demand political accountability from the media and fight for the exercise of freedom of and access to information.

Far removed from the newspapers and from electronic news, Subcommandante Marcos (2000) from the Zapatista National Liberation Army (EZLN) argues that the hope of the people of Mexico lies in the resistance. With the globalization of the economy, cultures also have become globalized; however, this almighty globalization seems to have fissures. Marcos further stated that

> In spite of globalization across the planet or perhaps due to it, homogeneity is very far from being characteristic of changes in this century or millennium – this unique globalized issue is really the proliferation of heterogeneity. (*La Jornada*, February 25, 2000)

Agreeing with the analysis of Subcommandante Marcos, sociologist Manuel Castells (1998: 395, Spanish Edition) says:

> We have experienced an emergence of vigorous expressions of collective identity that challenges globalization and cosmopolitanism on behalf of the cultural singularity, and of people's control over their lives and their environment.

These cultural expressions are manifold and include movements that seek to transform human relationships at their most fundamental levels: feminism, ecology, ethnic groups, family and religion.

New and powerful technological communication media, such as world nets, are used by some social movements, broadening their struggles, and transforming the Internet into an instrument of international environmentalists, Mexican Zapatistas, or the American militia, who respond with the same weapons of computerized globalization and the information process. Castells (1998: 25, Spanish Edition) states that

> The process of techno-economic globalization is that of modeling our world. It is being challenged and will end up being transformed, from a great diversity of sources of all types, ideological current trends and perspectives.

Castells (1998: 395, Spanish edition), tells us that at the beginning of the information age, a crisis of genuineness will void traditional institutions of their original meanings. It is an irony that when most of the countries of the world have achieved liberal democracy, this is far from true for the social processes of real-life importance.

We are facing the formation of new historical subjects, which contradicts the logic of geographical society networks. Information technology goes beyond physical boundaries, and brings to the fore the phenomenon of horizontal communication. This new power resides in the codes of information and in the representation images around which societies organize their institutions, and people build their lives and decide on what patterns of behavior to follow. The seat of this power is in people's minds. Those who win the battle of people's minds will govern, and this will be lasting if it starts from identities and is not built on the ephemeral aspects of media images.

These horizontal nets are something more than organizing activities and sharing information. They are the producers and real distributors of cultural codes. Subcommandante Marcos (La Jornada, March 25, 2000) says:

> ... social movements of resistance or of protest in the face of power, in this case in the face of globalization and neo-liberalism, must still travel a long road to achieve their ends, or at least to consolidate themselves as organization alternatives for others. Transformation of reality is not a single actor's task, no matter how strong, intelligent, creative and visionary he may be.

Despite these hopeful realities in formation, neither women's movements nor other civil society organizations will be able to optimize the media for their goals until globalization and concentration of power are swept aside. They fight by any means against a unique way of thinking which jeopardizes the very principles of democracy and its achievements is shared throughout the world.

6 Moving Forward

Nevertheless it is necessary to develop strategies at the global, national and local levels. For instance, world organizations such as WIN-AMARC (the Women's International Network of the World Association of Community Radio, 1999), which has the job at world level for

- women's right to communicate as a basic human right expressed trough community radio;
- supporting women's empowerment, gender equality, and general improvement in the conditions and positions of women world-wide;
- promoting women's access to all levels of community radio, including decision-making;
- supporting women's efforts to express themselves within and beyond their communities with training programs and production exchanges;
- changing negative images of both women and men in the media to challenge stereotypes.

As we can see, among other things, WIN's work aims at impacting on the local media. It also includes a global activity which might lead to international legislation on this issue. It is necessary to develop national strategies which lead governments to support women's actions in the media, develop legal frameworks that limit private firms when trying to convey derogatory stereotypes and clichés of women. More importantly, it is necessary that women and other social actors, particularly minorities, take the media into their hands, that is, small media, communal media for social uses, contributing to the task from below.

Locally, a few distinctive examples can be cited. Sometimes small media can make big changes in the people's life, such as the establishment of a community-based radio in Cuetzalan, Mexico, chronicled by Aleida Calleja in this volume. Confronted with severe drawbacks, such as illiteracy as well as the culturally entrenched subordination of indigenous women, the radio serves as their voice through which they can re-assess their identity, which is also eclipsed by the dominant *mestizo* culture.

There remains the need for a legal framework to check stereotypes and the derogatory portrayal of women. More important, it is necessary that women and other social actors – particularly national minorities and indigenous peoples – take the media into their hands and obtain community-based radio, television and Internet access.

In conclusion, this is a collective task with work on many fronts, the use of technology for human beings, and not for markets.

References

Alger, Dean (1998). *MEGAMEDIA, How Giant Corporations Dominate Mass Media, Distort Competition, and Endanger Democracy*. Lanham, MD: Rowman and Littlefields.

AMARC and WIN-AMARC. For more information see: http://www.amarc.org; acc.essed May 17, 2002

Beijing Declaration (1995). *Conference on Women*. United Nations. September 1995. Source: http://www.un.org/womenwatch/daw/beijing/platform/media.htm; accessed May 17, 2002

Castells, Manuel (1998). The Information Age, Economy, Society and Culture, vol. ii. In: *The Power of the Identity*. Oxford: Blackwell.

Declaration to UNGASS of the NGO *Caucus on Women and Media (2000)*. New York, June 7, 2000. Source: http://www.womenaction.org/ungass/caucus/media.html; accessed May 17, 2002

Marcos, Subcommandante Insurgente (2000). *La Jornada,* Feb 25, 2000. Source: http://www.jornada.unam.mx/2000/feb00/000225/comunicado1.html; accessed May 17, 2002

Marcos, Subcommandante Insurgente (2000). *La Jornada*. March 25, 2000. Source: http://www.jornada.unam.mx/2000/mar00/000325/impugna.html; accessed May 17, 2002

Marcos, Subcommandante Insurgente (2000). *La Jornada*. June 23, 2000. Source: http://www.jornada.unam.mx/2000/jun00/000623/comunicado.html; accessed May 17, 2002

Ramonet, Ignacio (1997). *Conferencia Magistral, Encuentro Internacional de la Radio*. Santiago de Chile: Universidad Católica and Radio Nederlands.

Ramonet, Ignacio (1999). *Un Mundo sin Rumbo*. Madrid: Debate.

Robinson, William (1996). *Promoting Polyarchy. Globalization, US Intervention, and Hegemony*. Cambridge, UK: Cambridge University Press.

Sartori, Iovanni (1998). *Homo Videns*. Mexico: Juan Pablos.

United Nations (1948). *Universal Declaration of Human Rights*. United Nations. December 10, 1948. Source: http://www.un.org/Overview/rights.html; accessed May 17, 2002.

Esther Batiri Williams

The Internet in the Service of Democracy

Abstract
The Internet is one of the most powerful tools to facilitate and promote democratic values and principles in the world today. It will also become one of the most powerful tools in promoting the democratic process in the future. The potentials of virtual communities to build and revitalize real life democracies and electronic democracy look promising. But the Internet can also be the most destructive tool for democracy in a number of ways. Despite the advantages and disadvantages of the Internet, its unavailability and inaccessibility to many people in developing countries, particularly women, make the Internet as a service to democracy limiting in the countries that may need this tool most. Whichever way one looks at this medium of information and communication, there is no doubt that its penetration into all continents and many countries, developing and developed, is having profound effects on the lives of many people. These points are illustrated here in the case of the recent upheaval in Fiji. Beyond the individual case the author postulates the multi-faceted discourses that enable women in a developing country to shape democracy with the help of IT, which was her main contribution to *ifu*.

1 Introduction

I was preparing for a sabbatical to join *ifu* (International Women's University, here: *ifu*'s Project Area INFORMATION) as director of two curricular projects, *Visions of Citizenship* (see Keskitalo & Limpangog, this volume) and *Virtual Communities* (see Kerr & Mätschke in this volume) at the time of the coup in Fiji. The Internet enabled me to continue communicating with the *ifu* organizers without major disruption while being trapped inside the campus of the University of South Pacific in Suva for days.

At about 11:20 a.m. on Friday, May 19, 2000, a group of seven armed men illegally took over the Parliament of the Republic of the Fiji Islands in the South Pacific. They also took over thirty people hostage, including the Prime Minister of Fiji, government ministers and a few civil servants. At about 11:40 a.m. the same day the news of the illegal takeover or civilian coup was announced by the local media, and a few minutes later it was on the local Internet address *fi-jilive.com*. Immediately after this, the news was on various Internet addresses throughout the world. People were able to contact friends abroad and locally through e-mail services to get the latest news on the hostage situation. A few days later a number of ministers and civil servants were released. In the period that followed, negotiations and meetings took place between the rebels and the Great Council of Chiefs, a traditional political body charged with protecting the rights and interests of indigenous Fijians, for the release of the remaining hostages. As talks failed and law and order broke down, the army stepped in, placed the country under martial law, and took over the running of the country on Monday, May 29, 2000, to maintain peace and order and to protect the well-being of the people of Fiji. The rebels then started negotiations with the army. On June 4, 2000 – 17 days after the takeover – talks with the army also broke down and thirty ministers were still being held hostage in the Parliament Complex. On Sunday, June 25, the women ministers held hostage were released on humanitarian grounds, according to the rebel leader who wished to be known as the crusader of Fijian rights. On Thursday, July 13, the remaining hostages were released.

During this period, both local and foreign media kept the public overseas informed of all the happenings. There was no news blackout. On the contrary, there was too much media coverage, and in many cases, conflicting reports. The media had too close a relationship with the rebels, reporting heavily on them, which led to many questioning the media's role and support of someone widely denounced abroad. Apart from the media, there was e-mail and, most importantly, there was now the Internet, a channel through which those who have Internet access could maintain all links to the outside world. Through the Internet, people were kept updated and informed about developments concerning themselves as well as about what the outside world was thinking of the situation in Fiji. The various chat groups on the Internet enabled people in Fiji and throughout the world to voice their views on the takeover of a democratically elected government. A number of people of Fiji had Internet access, including the army and the rebel group. They drew some courage from the people's support that appeared on some sites on the Internet. The rebel group had used the media effectively, including the Internet, to publicize its cause. But to many rural people the Internet was a thing unknown and their main source of information was the radio and what is called the coconut wireless, or informal communication within the communities.

This was the third coup that had taken place in Fiji in the past fourteen years. The first two were in 1987, May and September. In 1987, there was a news blackout for a period and people were kept in the dark. There was no television and no Internet in Fiji at the time. Indeed, there was no other means of communication than the local news and short-wave radio through which news could be obtained. In 2000, the situation was entirely different. The people had various other sources of information and the Internet played a central role in this political chaos.

This case study highlights a number of crucial issues on the Internet in the service of (or disservice to) democracy. It raises important questions:

- What role can the Internet play in building and sustaining democracy in developing countries?
- How can women take advantage of this tool for political development and promotion of free speech? What educational role can it play in the promotion of democracy?
- What are the possibilities of using the Internet to topple a democratically elected government? What role can or will the Internet play in political negotiations of the future?
- Can the Internet, as a new mass medium, make a contribution toward keeping the press free?

None of these questions will be easy to answer, as there are very few studies on the subject so far. Neither is it easy to generalize the role of the Internet in democratic development or its breakdown, as I am only able to get the information needed to make an assessment of this kind for Fiji. But in two countries at least, China and Russia, recent Internet regulations, the content of sites, and the imprisonment of a Chinese website owner and a freelance journalist in June 2000, have brought to the fore the question of universal access to the Internet. and human rights. Other countries have also tried to control their citizens' access to the Internet for political reasons, but usually with limited success.

It has been suggested that it was because of access to information through the Internet and through the various media outlets and coverage, and the consequent support received from the rural sectors of the community, that the coup leader was encouraged to make more demands. Apart from this, the accessibility of new information technology and the mobile phone made negotiations to free the hostages difficult as the coup leader was able to obtain advice from many external sources.

2 Defining Democracy

But before continuing, it is necessary that we look at the definition of democracy used here. The literature on democracy is massive and continues to grow. The concept is not easy to define and remains highly contested (Galie, 1956). Democracy means different things to different people in different societies with different structures and values.

I have chosen Dahl's (1971a) definition of democracy as the basis for this paper. Dahl has defined democracy as a political system with three essential conditions: competition, political participation, and civil and political liberties. In such a political system all citizens have the right to vote and be elected in regular free and fair elections. The main characteristic is the continuing responsiveness of the government to the preferences and choice of all its citizens. All citizens, including the minority groups in a country, have freedom of speech, information, worship, and assembly and are equal before the law. There is also freedom of the press.

According to Dahl, the application of this definition may not be easy. Not all societies will be able to fulfill these conditions. This is the reason why Dahl prefers to call them 'polyarchies.' Countries that try to meet these criteria do so to different degrees. This makes it difficult sometimes to categorize countries as democratic or non-democratic. This ambiguity is further complicated by constraints on free access to information and free expression that may make a country less democratic even though there are free and fair elections on a regular basis; Malaysia, Sri Lanka, and Turkey are examples. For governments that cannot fulfill the criteria laid down for democracy, political mechanisms should be in place to replace them when they no longer respond to the needs of the citizens (regarding this issue, see also the chapter by Keskitalo & Limpangog, this volume).

3 Democracy on Trial

Some observers argue that Fiji at its current stage of development lacks the necessary attributes and prerequisites to make a democratic system work. Its middle class is small, its business group is still largely apolitical, and if political, it is still disorganized; the rural population is still very much under authoritarian rule, and while the working class as a whole is active in union activities, many of its members still do not want to risk jobs by engaging in political and union activity. It has also been argued that it is difficult to practice democracy in a multi-ethnic society, and that the constitutional crisis in 1987 was largely due to the Fijians' non-acceptance of a non-Fijian government and the government's inability to cope with ethnic and religious issues. This happened again in May 2000. If this is correct, then it could mean that democracy would have a tough going in Fiji. This view should be seen against the fact that the people of Fiji today are far better educated, better informed, and more politically aware than in

May 1987. It may not be democracy they understand, but they would know their rights.

Developments would seem positive or negative depending on the view one takes in viewing the whole saga of the civilian coup. If one were a nationalist, then it would seem wrong for the people of Fiji to pursue democracy, a foreign concept. If one is more in favor of open and good government, then it is the road to democracy that one would choose to follow. Certainly, there has been a strong show of support for greater participation and openness in the political process. In determining the outcome of the elections and the road to recovery, the caliber of our leaders and their ability, or lack of it, to set aside their differences, personal rivalries and narrow interests and to work together in the interest of the nation, will be of the greatest importance.

In the 1960s it was widely assumed that democracy was a consequence of socio-economic development, not a condition of it (Lipset, 1960). Democracy would result if the following existed: high-level literacy; communication and education; an established and secure middle class; a vibrant civil society; relatively limited forms of material and social inequality (Dahl, 1971b). Arguments tended to link democracy to economic and social factors. It has been argued that a well-organized working class is important for promoting and defending democracy. The struggle for democracy was seen as the struggle for power (Rueschemeyer, 1992).

There are other preconditions but it is not my intention to go into them. One main precondition which I see as important in the emergence of democracy is access to and the availability and use of information for democratic purposes. There is no one path to democracy, but one could possibly argue that with increased access to information brought about by improved technology and the Internet, and more open government legislation on information, people will demand to have more say in government decision-making and accountability of government officers.

4 Building and Sustaining Democracy through the Internet

It can be said that Internet technology is the fastest growing technology ever developed in history. In just over three decades, the Internet has evolved from a secret, closed technology used by academic and military communities to an open, uncontrolled, horizontal system all over the world. It is now an academic tool, a popular tool, an economic tool, and also growing into a political tool.

The Internet is proving to be one of the most powerful tools for free speech, for providing information to many users world-wide, for education online, for commerce, and a growing new mass medium. Even though only 7% of the world's population can access the Internet and its advantages, it is foreseen that in about 20 years' time or less, about 25% of the world's estimated population will be on the Internet, i.e. about 1.5 billion people.[1]

As shown in Figure 1, the Nua Surveys give the following numbers as of December 2000:

World Total	418.59 million
Africa	3.11 million
Asia/Pacific	104.88 million
Europe	113.97 million
Middle East	2.40 million
Canada and the U.S.	177.78 million
South America	16.45 million

Figure 1: Estimated number of people online: The World, December 2000.

5 Current Status of ICT in the South Pacific Region

While developments in ICT have moved on ahead, many developing countries are still lagging behind technically and in terms of human resources and skills. This digital divide[2] has had some negative as well as positive impacts on development in the developing countries.

For the South Pacific region, while some of the new ICTs are penetrating the region and adopted for use for various purposes, there are many sections of the community –women, the rural populations and the urban poor in particular – who do not and cannot have access to computers and other forms of ICT because they do not have electricity to begin with. In some areas, there are no phone lines, nor roads. In these situations, the development priorities would seem to be in developing the basic necessities of life. ICTs and their use become a low priority in this competition (see also Dahms & Faust-Ramos, this volume).

It is not that the technology is not available for communication and education. The issue is to ensure that ICTs are available in the region and can be accessed by women for education and development. This would also mean that to make better and more effective use of ICTs, users must be computer-literate and have skills in using the technologies. If we accept that the Internet has the po-

---

1   The world population in 1996 was 5.8 billion. It is estimated that in 2047 it will be 11.5 billion. Estimates provided by Internet Society and Nua Surveys. Source: http://www.nua.ie/surveys/ (This site is regularly updated and may be consulted for the latest numbers.)

2   'Digital divide' refers to the gap between those with and those without access to information and communication technologies, such as the technologies used to access the Internet and engage in e-commerce (cf. Paltridge, 2000).

tential to be accessed by everyone, it can facilitate democratic practices in many and different ways. In Fiji, the fact that the Internet kept people well informed of the daily happenings confirmed the direction the country was moving with democracy. It also enabled people to think more deeply about this 'foreign flower' called democracy and its application in this country. But perhaps the most useful part of the medium was the fact that people who were afraid and unhappy with all that had happened were able to take solace in the encouragement and comments received from the international community.

In promoting democratic principles in general, the Internet can be used for the purpose of democratic activities now. For instance, in countries that have greater access to the Internet, voting in the national elections can be done through the Internet. On the other hand, there are some downsides. Membership system is voluntary, and intended to represent diverse groups, interests, and people around Internet Governance. But those registered were predominantly from the North, commercial, and male. Because of this, a Civil Society Forum, a group of non-government organizations (NGOs) promoting the participation of individuals and NGOs in the governance of the Internet had been set up on July 16, 2000.

On the personal and professional levels, the Internet is indubitably enabling many people to communicate with each other easily, regularly and without fear. It is like a big repository where all our thoughts, emotions, likes and dislikes are stored. We forge a close link with whomever we are communicating with, and this does a lot to our own person and emotions. Therefore we must be careful as to what we commit to e-mail as messages may turn up in unexpected places (see the general discussion of women on the net by Harcourt, this volume).

6 The Internet: Not Yet a Tool for Women in Developing Democracy

Too much confidence is being placed in the Internet as leveling the playing-fields in the different regions and countries of the world and bringing about more equality, freedom, increased knowledge, understanding, tolerance, peace and development – social, political, and economic. Despite many positive comments and promises, there are a number of social scientists, e.g. Sussman (1989), Castells (1996), and Mowlana (1994: 202-232) who caution us against these views. To them, the Internet will only widen the gap between those who have and those who have not: the rich will grow richer and the poor poorer.

For the women in developing countries, three main questions arise: How can women in developing countries be connected to the Internet? How can women take advantage of this tool for political development, and the promotion of free speech? What educational role can the Internet play for women in the promotion of democracy?

According to the Nua surveys (2001), the number of women in developing countries that are now online has grown considerably in the past five years. In the Asian-Pacific region women account for 36% of users as compared to 50.4% in the whole world; the respective figure for Africa is approximately 15%. In Latin America, close to 25% of women have access to the Internet. A number of organizations use the Internet to connect women, to inform women of various and specific activities and information, to communicate with women in their respective communities, and to seek support for ideas and strategies (an example can be found in the chapter by Carstensen et al, this volume). Women's groups have created and maintained many websites, particularly for their own members. These users in turn represent women at the grassroots level who have limited or no access to computers and the Internet. Nevertheless, there are still serious problems related to access by women for whatever purpose.

In a so far unpublished study about women in the Pacific using information and communication technologies for distance and open learning, I found that while new ICTs have emerged and are being used to improve the delivery of education programs, many barriers have to be faced. These are technical, economic, social, cultural, organizational, and political.

The findings showed that almost 90% of female students would prefer to use new technologies, particularly computers and multimedia, for their studies rather than traditional methods. The major barrier is access. While technologies are widespread in the region, about 85% of participants indicated that they did not have access to computers as and when needed, and close to 98% did not have access to computers at home (the access problem is stressed by Woodbury, this volume). Apart from the inconvenience and high cost of transportation, access is made difficult by other factors. There are strict control policies and only a limited number of functioning computers. The low bandwidth and the slow response time for weekly online discussions are major obstacles. Downloading one week's tutorial material usually took more than two weeks owing to some links being timed out. Associated with access and equipment is the low level of expertise available for maintenance.

A serious barrier is the clear lack of computer literacy and training programs for women users of the Internet. This has far-reaching consequences. (Wetzel, this volume, discusses pedagogical concerns with a view to overcoming this barrier).

Above all, the Internet generally is expensive. For women in rural areas, print packages are still the best way of learning. Radio delivery methods also provide a viable alternative. Therefore, if we are to make the Internet more accessible to people, particularly to women, for the development and maintenance of democracy, we will need to do a number of things. These include:

6.1 Making the Internet Affordable

The Internet is supposed to be for everyone but it cannot be if it is too expensive and not affordable by many people. We will need to look at reducing the cost of equipment, supplies and communication links world-wide.

6.2 Free and Universal Access

The Internet needs to be able to be accessed by everyone, irrespective of social, political and economic status. Government restrictions and regulations should not be accepted. We must have the freedom to speak and the freedom to be heard. This is important for the growth of equality and peace in the world now and in future. The Internet must be available to everyone, in every country in the world, in every school and university, in every institution and government department, and in every language.

6.3 Sustainability of the Internet Is Vital

Here, both the technical standards and funding to keep the system going, particularly in developing countries, will be necessary. The Internet is ever changing technically and in its use expanding more and more into various futuristic areas. It will be an evolution and revolution and we, as women, must be prepared for the changes and the knowledge required to master the system and its changes.

6.4 Internet Legislation

This is a growing area of development and one that will work for and against democracy, for and against the people. Legislation must ensure that growth in electronic commerce and freedom of expression are made possible, and protect intellectual property rights. Also, privacy on the Internet and the confidentiality of communications and transactions need to be protected. There is the need for trust and the need for support. If privacy is lost, the use of the Internet will be restricted. Laws will have to be developed that work across national boundaries to ensure that the Internet retains the value it currently has (see also Druke, this volume, on how this problem affects the Internet's use).

6.5 Responsible Use and Sharing

It is important that we take responsibility for the use of the Internet. This tool is powerful and we should use it with care and consideration for democratic purposes. We should not, for instance, use it as a tool to support or take down a government through political publicity. We should also not use it as a tool for unethical purposes, like passing on false information or inciting people to do wrong. And we should not use the system to promote political propaganda – much of this is happening in developing countries, Fiji is an example.

A particularly important issue for the promotion of democracy is the education and empowerment of women through the Internet. During the 55-day captivity of the Fiji Members of Parliament, many Fijian people voiced verbal support for the 'Fijian cause,' the desire and the need to take responsibility for their own future and development without others interfering and having a say in the running of the country and government. But many people did not support or agree with the method of taking hostages. There were legal avenues that could have been followed and used to ensure that the rights of the Fijian people were protected. A large group of supporters consisted of Fijian women. Many believed that their rights to their land and their country were being taken away. There was a great deal of false information and propaganda.

It has also been argued that the use of propaganda over the different forms of media, particularly the radio and also the Internet, has created an upsurge of dangerous nationalistic feelings. Many women felt quite justified in helping and supporting the rebels in the Parliament building by cooking and caring for them. Many people asked whatever went wrong with education itself and the continuing educational programs for women in rural areas. The happenings seemed to confirm a number of things. The women were not aware of the contents of the new 1997 Constitution. Rural education programs have not reached them to enable them to distinguish between simple right and wrong. So much is still to be done to educate women and empower them to seek and obtain information to help them decide on what actions to take over issues that are personal to them and affect their livelihood in every way. While the Internet is not accessible to many rural women, what seems possible is to empower women to access more information, to require more education and to explain the law to them so that they may make wise and better decisions for themselves.

The Human Rights World Report (1999) indicates that although progress has been made by the women's international human rights movement, there were threats of a go-slow. And women's rights were challenged almost at every turn. For instance, governments would claim their commitment to women's rights but pursue policies that ignored or even undermined them. Despite this, there continues to be a strong lobby and support for taking international responsibility for ending the violation of women's human rights in the areas of violence against women, rape, enforced prostitution, women and war, and to promote their access to justice. While some governments and institutions were beginning to integrate women's movements into mainstream development, there was no inclusion of the right to information by women, for women and on women. Perhaps this is an area that is not known and one that cannot be seen as having an impact. On the contrary, it can be argued that because women cannot have free access to information and are, in most cases, not informed of anything happening in a community, that the right to information for women becomes absolutely important. If this is so, some structure will have to be developed to allow women to become information literate, and in the short and long term, able to make informed decisions on matters that affect them directly, including the ability to vote for the best person without being influenced (see Keskitalo & Limpangog, this volume).

In 1998, many governments around the world acknowledged that the Internet promotes participation in civil and political life and democracy within and between countries. Despite this acknowledgement, there is the fear that countries will attempt to introduce legislation that will threaten free speech. Originally, the Internet was developed to promote free speech and enable people all over the world to be able to take advantage of this new medium and opportunity to create better understanding and a more peaceful and tolerant world. It would seem now that the trend is to extend the censorship more broadly and this will have many repercussions. Online content providers may have to regulate and rate their content, or have material blocked from public access and use. What limitations to free speech would undoubtedly do is to limit the diversity of expression on the Internet, where content is as diverse as human thought.

There are many websites developed by, for, and on women. In Fiji, *Fijiwoman.com* was launched in 2000 as the major website for the Fiji Women's Crisis Center. Women have taken advantage of this site to communicate on various subjects. Again, the big problem with this site is that only those women who have access to a computer and Internet services can access it. So again, it can be regarded an elitist service but one that is fulfilling a need. The idea is that modern service needs to complement the traditional to ensure that all women are informed and a large section of the community is not excluded.

7 Regulation of the Internet

At the present time, no one can completely own the Internet or control it. Each network in the collection of interconnected networks is responsible for its own areas, each is owned by different stakeholders, and all work together according to certain rules and regulations they set themselves and agree on. No-one is forced to connect but there is a great advantage for people who share interests to link up and enjoy global communication.

Also, no central body governs the Internet. However, a number of organizations exist that work cooperatively to establish standards and quality if necessary, such as the Internet Society. For control, there are two major aspects which I would like to cover: control of access and control of content, both have everything to do with democracy.

7.1 Control of Access

In recent months, there has been a push to control access as well as content over the Internet. A number of countries have tried to introduce controls on the Internet. In Singapore, local industry was required to label websites, which meant that unrated sites would be automatically blocked. While this system was only adopted in Singapore, what it means is that all unrated websites around the world will be blocked.

Thailand already has a draft Internet law that will require Caller-IDs to gather information about each user logging into the network. In China, the use of the Internet was encouraged in 1998. The number of users rose from a few thousand in 1995 to 16.9 million in July 2000, and this trend is continuing. The Chinese Government has created an office to regulate news on the Internet to ensure that harmful information is excluded and to establish copyright standards. There was also a view that some service providers were giving false and untrue reports on China. The office would also police online pornography and gambling. Recently, China launched the new website for women in Beijing, designed to attract female users of the Internet. It includes many services including information on life, work, entertainment, and personal feelings, aimed at single women and mothers. In the year 2000, 25% of Chinese users were women and the number is growing (see Freedom Forum, 2000).

In Singapore part of the plan is to relax regulating the Internet as Singapore plans to become an international center for global electronic commerce. Service providers, however, will be expected to prevent access to any site that has been banned by the government. So while the Internet is growing in its use, measures to control its accessibility and use are creeping in. The Internet Democracy Project (2001) is one of the projects that has been developed to enable a critical mass of non-governmental organizations to work on creating Internet governance structures that sustain and promote the principles of a civil society.

7.2 Control of Content

Controlling access to Internet content is not easy as the Internet was designed to allow easy access to all information. To control access to content may require funds and a number of new technologies. There are technically two basic ways to limit access to content: blocking requests for identified unacceptable content in certain sites, and filtering of content. This is very expensive to implement and may lead to delays and inefficiencies in network performance. In the end, it is the quality of the content that will be important and of interest to the users and we will have to leave the decision to Internet users whether they wish to see a particular site.

8 The Mediating and Negotiating Role of the Internet

As noted in the Fiji case study, the rebel group used the different communication media including the Internet to promote their cause and succeeded. Thus with the Internet, mobile phones and other technology, negotiation styles have and will become more sophisticated and advanced. The pool of people inputting and making decisions on a deal is suddenly enlarged, and this can become problematic. On one hand, this new technology may be a hindering factor in any negotiation forum as people at the table will always 'check back' at headquarters before accepting any deal. On the other, the technology can speed up negotiations. There is little doubt that the Internet will continue to greatly impact on negotiation styles and culture.

8.1 The Internet as a New Mass Medium: Keeping the People Informed and the Press Free

It was through the Internet that many Fiji people living abroad received news about Fiji. In many cases the news on the Internet would be more up-to-date and accurate than in other media. In addition, the news was constantly changing as events unfolded. The newspapers were not able to do this as they published once daily. In a state of emergency such as Fiji was in, people who had access to the Internet were always trying to get up-to-date with the news.

For the journalists in Fiji, the situation was different than for journalists covering stories in, e.g. Sierra Leone, Indonesia or Serbia. Ibrahim Seaga Shaw, publisher of the award-winning *Expo Times*, launched *expotimes.net* after fleeing Sierra Leone more than two years ago. The online paper operates from London and Paris and enjoys a very wide readership. There are other newspapers online for a number of countries where journalists send in stories and these are included in the online edition. Another example is *free92.net*, a website and webcasting service which has been operating since the independent Radio B92 of Serbia was shut down. The government continues to try to shut this down, but the Internet technology is such that the system resumes after a few hours.

Indeed, these examples show clearly that the Internet is a system that can enable radio stations, newspapers, and other news forums to function "even in the circumstances of total repression."[3] The other important development that has assisted journalists in troubled areas is the use of e-mail, which enables reporters to send in reports immediately to the papers. This has revolutionized journalism but more importantly, the Internet has enabled free reporting and keeping democratic principles alive in many of the trouble spots in the world.

8.2 The Internet as a Medium of Disinformation

We have looked at the Internet as a tool for promoting democracy, but it can also be used as a tool to promote anarchy and trouble, and undemocratic messages. This was the case in Fiji, where the rebel leader was often seen on television and on the Internet propounding his views of the takeover and also his propaganda. Indeed, there was more reporting on his views and cause, and of his supporters, than on the attempts by the army to keep law and order in the country. But disinformation on the Internet is only successful if the people are less educated and believe what is reported. Disinformation normally refers to a lack of objectivity, it is propaganda, there is a lack of completeness and a lack of pluralism. Through the Internet we are able to be informed wholly, partially, or not at all. We are dependent on what we receive from the writer of the article, report, or the message. But with the increased convergence of the mass media, the level of disinformation may grow. Also, the more people there are on the net, the greater will be the likelihood of disinformation from one user to the other. The Internet can be seen as a unidirectional mass medium and can be very powerful. It is when information is mishandled and manipulated that the Internet becomes a carrier of disinformation, which is hard to police. It is important that some direction is established and some guidance given to the use of the Internet for information providers and information users.

Disinformation will be difficult to police in the future as the number of users increases. It will be very difficult to check on the authenticity of a story. Furthermore, the people who are using the Internet now can be considered the

---

3   Veran Matič, founder of Radio B92 and now editor in chief of *free92.net*, Serbia. Matič was honored in 2000 as one of the 50 press heroes of the 20th century.

'elite' of society and already will be aware of the disinformation that may be provided.

All said and done, in the case of Fiji, people were selective in their acceptance of information. Some people would ignore the truth and only believe what their minds wanted them to believe – the information that mattered to them and their colleagues. The Internet is only a technology that is there to help people access information and be informed. The more powerful influences will be social, cultural, educational and political, where the desire for political power is central to the acquisition and the use of information and the Internet.

9 Conclusion

In presenting some answers, a number of points come out clearly. First, that there may be a need to look more closely, and in more detail, at the law and regulation dealing with the Internet. On the one hand, there is a need for freedom to access and use information and the corresponding medium to relay messages to promote democracy, and on the other, there is a need to limit the physical means of distribution for anti-democratic messages. In the end, we may have to protect the individual's right to use the Internet even though we do not agree with the purpose and the messages. But the control over the physical technology of a virtual space is no guarantee of the social actions and messages channeled within it.

Second, it is clear that the Internet as a medium is not the only important consideration in understanding a political crisis and democracy. The cultural context of the message and an understanding of the local situation are also significant. In other words, information is situational and cultural, and the process of imparting information to the people may be undertaken in a number of ways reflecting cultural and social practices. The medium is not the message. However, it does shape and channel the messages it carries.

Third, through the chat groups on the Internet, it is possible for different people, including women, to hold a discussion on the wrong that has been committed, on the overthrow of a democratically elected government, and find suggestions as to the way to steer the country back to democracy. Women are always ill-informed about their rights, political situation, their needs and their security. In the case of Fiji, it could be argued that the overwhelming support of the rebels and the 'cause' by women with little regard and concern for what is right or wrong, good or bad behavior, confirms the lack of awareness and education. The discussion can also influence decisions and actions of international organizations and individuals with regard to Fiji in some way. What this highlights is that no country, big or small, in this new information society can be isolated from the new international social order. It is not possible to commit a 'crime' and get away with it without almost immediate international repercussions. This raises the question of the unique opportunities offered by virtual interaction and the virtual community. In this case, the Internet can be considered as a service of democracy.

Fourth, the case study shows the potential of the Internet becoming a powerful means of information in support of democracy but also to provide disinformation, a new mass medium. This disinformation engendered via the Internet differs in some way from other forms of disinformation, spread via the newspapers and the radio, but it can be considered more effective as it can be updated and changed almost every minute, and accessed right away. If the Internet can become a powerful means of disinformation, then the question that should be asked is whether there is anything that can be done to avoid this problem or to solve it? It is not easy to regulate Internet use in a country in terms of cost, time and democratic principles.

"The Internet is for everyone." It is the most democratic innovation of all times, and despite the controls and questions of its influence in the future, it should continue to be for everyone.

References

Castells, Manuel (1996). *The Rise of the Network Society.* Oxford: Blackwell.

Dahl, Robert Alan (1971a). *Modern Political Analysis.* Englewood Cliffs, NJ: Prentice Hall.

Dahl, Robert Alan (1971b). *Polyarchy, Participation and Opposition.* New Haven, CT: Yale University Press.

Freedom Forum (2000). Source: http://www.freedomforum.org/; accessed March 18, 2002.

Gallie,W.B. (1956). Essentially Contested Concepts. In: *Aristotelian Society,* 56, pp. 167-198.

Internet Democracy Project (2001). Source: http://www.internetdemocracyproject.org; accessed March 18, 2002.

Lipset, Seymour Martin (1960). *Political Man.* London: Heinemann.

Mowlana, Hamid (1994). Civil Society, Information Society, and Islamic Society: A Comparative Perspective. In: Splichal, Slavko; Calabrese, Andrew & Sparks, Colin (eds). *Information Society and Civil Society.* West Lafayette: Purdue University Press, pp. 208-232.

Nua Surveys (2001). Source: http://www.nua.ie/surveys/; accessed March 18, 2002.

Paltridge, Sam (March 2000). *Local Access Pricing and the International Digital Divide.* Source: http://www.isoc.org/oti/articles/1000/paltridge.html; accessed March 18, 2002.

Rueschemeyer, Dietrich; Huber Stephens, Evelyne; Stephens, John D. (1992). *Capitalist Development and Democracy.* Cambridge: Polity Press.

Sussman, L. R. (1989). The Information Revolution. *Encounter* 73 (4), pp. 60-65.

World Human Rights Report (1999). Source: http://www.hrw.org/hrw/worldreport99/women/index.html; accessed March 18, 2002.

Luise Druke

Information Technology and Protection of Refugees

Abstract
Information technology (IT) not only brings benefits and challenges to the general human development, but has also become indispensable for managing and solving refugee problems
around the world. The growing number of refugees, with more than 50% women and children, who are the most vulnerable in conflicts that force them to flee, require adapted and
new, more modern IT as one means of dealing with their drama as well as for finding solutions. However, access to and funding of IT will determine where and how these new means
will actually be contributing as an effective tool in refugee protection. Based on the author's
experience of working for the United Nations High Commissioner for Refugees, these questions were discussed from a feminist perspective at *ifu.*

1 Introduction

In between changing assignments for the United Nations High Commissioner
for Refugees (UNHCR) in summer 2000, the author delivered a lecture at *ifu* (International Women's University, here: *ifu*'s Project Area INFORMATION), which
is reflected in this chapter.

Today, most non-governmental refugee and human rights organizations
(NGOs) are online for fund raising, advocacy and management. In many instances they allow asylum seekers and refugees to seek and maintain contact
with loved ones elsewhere. They can also look for work, housing and contacts
as part of their own efforts to find a solution to their problem through local integration, or start to explore options for voluntary return to their homeland. This
has two significant advantages: first, it enables refugees to play a proactive role
in helping themselves, which is always a more dignified way of ceasing to be a
refugee. Secondly, it frees up refugee-assisting NGOs and the governmental
refugee authorities and, where locally available, the UNHCR from spending time
on these issues.

Costs involved depend on location and access to the Internet. To give an example, the cost of transmitting a trillion bits of information, e.g. from Boston to Los Angeles, has fallen from U.S. $150,000 in 1970 to 12 cents today. It is, however, the public sector which usually provides the telephone system that is required to go online, which is causing great disparities between the developing and the developed world. Nevertheless, it is the private sector that has taken the lead in IT development and access. Refugees are rarely a priority on governments' and donors' agendas. Therefore, more global initiatives, such as those of the UNHCR, are taken in order to lobby for more adequate support for IT development, funding and application in the field of refugee protection, also through IT initiatives in cooperation with international, regional and local networks of the media and public policy.

Economic growth contributes to stronger social stability (with advances in medicine, communications, agriculture, energy and manufacturing). It also contributes to the stabilizing of political conditions, allowing for the rule of law and the establishment of democratic institutions. This in turn can promote further technological change, especially if resources are put aside for technology development, in particular for affordable and simple technologies in poor countries, such as hand-held devices with touch screens, Internet connections and translations. Therefore, IT might be able to assist in dealing with existing refugee situations, and help to prevent new ones from occurring, as prevention is always better than cure.[1]

This chapter brings up the issues arising in connection with IT and the problems of refugees while arguing for the adoption of a feminist perspective. Using Bulgaria as a case study about the protection of refugees, it discusses the implication of IT in the context of globalization. By way of conclusion, the connection between IT and refugee questions, in particular relating to women and children, is established as a topical focus to be taken up both by organizations helping refugees and by institutions providing education in this area.

2 IT for Refugee Protection and Management

As we have seen, IT has become indispensable for the survival and management of today's refugee problems around the world. However, access to and funding of IT are serious problems which will determine where and how these new means will actually be contributing as an effective tool in refugee protection and management, especially in massive operations. These operations occur in war-

---

1   For further references see, among others, the websites of the UNHCR headquarters in Geneva (http://www.unhcr.ch) and of the UNHCR branch office Sofia at http://www.unhcr.bg

torn areas where the local infrastructure is non-existent or destroyed. The author was involved in several operations where UNHCR installed IT and independently operating communication technology that proved life-saving for refugees and staff alike.

In Singapore (1978-81) she was head of the office during the Vietnamese boat people operation, where tracing of missing refugees was made feasible by specialized IT.

In Angola (1989) she was coordinator of the repatriation of Namibian refugees. Armed conflicts had been going on there for decades. Thus, UNHCR needed to bring in and install the entire IT system for communication within the country and with neighboring countries. The aim was to connect, amongst others, the places from where refugees transited en route to Namibia, the UNHCR office in Luanda, the Land Rovers, the airport, the refugee and the transit camps.

In Honduras (1985-86) she was acting representative in one of the poorest countries in Latin America with refugees from all three neighboring countries as a result of armed conflicts since 1979. Repeatedly, military attacks on refugee camps occurred and such plans could be communicated over the internal UNHCR radio. Even so, severe crises, as for example in August 1985, when three refugees were killed and 10 abducted, could not be prevented. Therefore, IT was introduced to give early warning to field staff and ensure that such crises could be handled in a better way.

In Kazakhstan (1997-99) she was head of the country office. Cross border operations within the region (in Kyrgystan, Tajikistan, Turkmenistan and Uzbekistan) required communication possibilities which UNHCR operated from the Land Rovers. This was crucial especially during winter temperatures of up to minus 50° C to ensure the survival of arriving refugees and to support logistics coordination.

Other major operations with crucial IT support included those in Iraq in 1991, Bosnia and Herzegovina from 1992 and onwards, Mozambique and Rwanda in 1994, East Timor and Kosovo in 1999-2000. IT support was severely needed again in the neighboring countries of Afghanistan after the attacks in the U.S. on September 11, 2001.

While all these cases illustrate the use of IT when crises have already arisen, there is increasing concern with prevention nowadays.

3 IT for the Prevention of Refugee-producing Situations

Since the end of the Cold War, when political will became more flexible, it has also become possible to consider activities to prevent the emergence of refugees within their countries of origin. Several papers have already been published on this subject, including one by the author (Druke, 1990). The manifestation of such political will goes back to consensus forged in, e.g. the Agenda for Peace of 1991, one of the first meetings in which Heads of State, also represented in the UN Security Council, spoke of the need for prevention. Almost ten years later, the world leaders at the Summit of 2000 adopted the Millennium Declaration[2] in recognition of their "collective responsibility to uphold the principles of human dignity, equality and equity at the global level." In more concrete terms, the UN Development Program in its Global Development Report (GHDR) of 2001 included the human development indicator (HDI), which measures a country's achievements in three areas of human development, namely longevity, knowledge, and a decent standard of living. It likewise focusses on human, not economic outcomes with a special emphasis on developing countries.

It is in the developing world, where most of the refugee situations occur, that the cost of IT is still very high. Great disparities between the developing and the developed worlds in getting online access result from the latter's public sector's small capacity in providing the services. In addition, in developed countries it is increasingly the private sector that is leading in the creation of technology.

This complex situation requires managing the risks of IT worldwide, through legislative and applied means of personal data protection. For UNHCR and its partners, it is a principal rule not to disclose data on individual refugees both in asylum and in home countries. 50 years of experience of UNHCR since its establishment have shown that the protection of refugees must start by protecting their identity. With only one click, IT can massively copy and channel lists of names and other details of entire refugee populations into the wrong hands. Such risk must be carefully managed and avoided, as it can cost human lives. Global and quick information transfer can contribute both to producing refugees and to mitigating the causes that might force people to flee. The CNN effect is just one of those elements.

Global initiatives for distance learning through virtual programs and universities will be an important tool for human development in general and for the prevention of refugee-producing situations. The human rights movements have taken such advantage and will need more support through distance learning and online connections in order to consolidate the rule of law, establish and enable democratic institutions. This in turn can promote further technological change, especially if resources for technology development are limited. In particular, affordable and simple technologies in poor countries, such as hand-held devices with touch screens and Internet connections and translations can be used.

---

2   Resolution adopted by the General Assembly (A/55/L.2) 552, on September 8, 2000.

4 What Can a Feminist Perspective Provide?

Refugee women and girls often live in particularly vulnerable conditions. They are exposed to the risks of sexual exploitation, especially when they are not accompanied by male family members and when they have children to feed in massive refugee camp situations. In spite of these risks, experience has shown that women are usually more resilient and strong in surviving serious hardships. For example, El Salvadorian women in Honduran refugee camps have raised the issue of balanced attention between technological innovations and basic socio-economic needs to include food, health, nutrition, participation, employment and economic activities. On one hand, refugee women and girls are more active in self-help, but on the other, they suffer the same phenomena experienced by women in society in general, in having to work twice as hard to achieve the social standing of men. Though millions of people can now access the Internet at a lower cost, this is neither the case for women in the developing world nor in refugee camps. It is known that while in late 1995 fewer than 20 million users had access to the Internet, there will be more than 1 billion users in 2005, and that in mid-1993 there were fewer than 200 websites, while by late 2000 there were 20 million websites.

A feminist perspective can place a special emphasis on the needs of refugee women in all parts of the world and especially in places, where IT is still very difficult to acquire. It will help encourage women to be more daring in learning and applying IT, as skills matter more than ever for survival, advancement and gender equity. Companies are starting to converge into new global hubs of innovation in dynamic and opportunity-driven environments. There are about 50 companies moving into this trend, many of which are in the U.S. (e.g. Silicon Valley), Hong Kong, France (e.g. Antipolis) and perhaps soon in Bulgaria. IT has important repercussions also in terms of women's income-generating opportunities for the present and the future. Women in developing countries are not provided with equal opportunities to generate income comparable to that in developed countries. Experience has shown that Internet users in general are primarily:

- urban and located in certain regions;
- better educated and wealthier;
- young, i.e. in average younger than 35 years;
- male (except in the U.S., where there are more than 51% female users).

Refugees who were fortunate enough not to have spent too much time in refugee camps have similar demographic characteristics. Those refugees, especially refugee women – though still few in the category mentioned above – are usually in a privileged situation. They manage better to proactively find a solution to their particular situation.

5 Digital Divide Impacts Refugees

Globalization has to first and foremost start at home and in the backyard of the poorer villages, cities, countries and regions before it can truly claim to be inclusive. As matters stand today, IT and globalization are reserved for the wealthier in society and mostly men. By virtue of their status, resources and opportunities, they manage to achieve some degree of participation and enjoyment of the benefits of globalization.

Refugee protection has some prospects for benefiting a globalized world. On one hand, information about new refugee-producing situations is transmitted much faster via means of IT. Thus, financial, diplomatic, as well as humanitarian means might be shared and found faster than before. On the other hand, at times refugee problems attract international media exposure, which results in both risks and opportunities for the refugees.

Aside from being more vulnerable, refugee women and girls encounter protection problems. They also have less access to and protection through IT. Consequently, they are even more impacted by the digital divide. They have prior disadvantages compared with the generations to come, also for mostly being in the poorer regions of this world. Despite the adoption of the *1989 Convention on the Rights of the Child*, millions of the world's dispossessed boys and girls, including huge numbers of refugee children, still suffer violation of their rights.

In 2001, there are approximately 50 million uprooted people around the world who have sought safety and refuge in another country or region after having been displaced within their own. About half of these displaced people are children. Many organizations, including the United Nations High Commissioner for Refugees (UNHCR), UNICEF, Save the Children, help many of these refugees. At least 10 million of the refugees are children under the age of 18, and about 50% are girls. They are often abused as child soldiers, kept in sexual slavery and left in the absence of adequate welfare support. The majority of people flee their homes because of war. As a result, it is estimated that more than two million children were killed in conflicts in the last decade. Another six million are believed to have been wounded, and one million orphaned. In recent decades the proportion of war victims who are civilians rather than combatants has leaped from 5% to more than 90%.

Children in 87 countries live among 60 million land mines. As many as 10,000 children per year continue to become victims of mines. More than 300,000 youths (including girls) are currently serving as child soldiers around the world. Many are less than 10 years old. Many girl soldiers are forced into different forms of sexual slavery. An estimated 1.2 billion people worldwide survive on less than $ 1 per day. Half of them are children. Ten million children under the age of 5 die each year; the majority from preventable diseases and malnutrition. Each year around 40 million children are not registered at birth, depriving them of a nationality and a legal name.

In conclusion, given the destitution and marginalization of refugee women and girls, IT with gender perspective should be used to educate them about their rights. This will enhance their ability to help and protect themselves and create better chances for equal treatment in their post-refugee condition. Refugee-assisting organizations of governments, UN and NGOs alike, should take advantage of the drive and ability of refugee women to proactively seek to improve socio-economic conditions, as in the case of Bulgaria.

6   IT for Refugee Protection and Assistance: the Case of Bulgaria

Even though IT has not yet reached all refugee women and girls in Bulgaria, where the gender and digital divide is also visible, small concrete steps are being implemented. For example, with the assistance of the Bulgarian *Red Cross*, the refugee women and the refugee workers of government agencies are establishing a data base of skills and assets. Refugees, and in particular refugee women, are assisted in finding useful occupations.

This is the result of discussions at the UNHCR branch office of Sofia, where the regional employment service of the government and the refugee women were represented. To promote integration possibilities for recognized refugees in Bulgaria, regional focal points for training and skill development, including in IT and computer programs, are being established. Subsequently, the government, through the *Agency for Refugees* and *Caritas*, a non-government organization, jointly implement projects geared to job deployment of refugees.

UNHCR Sofia has developed the website http://www.unhcr.bg in Bulgarian and English. It aims to inform asylum seekers and refugees about their rights and obligations through the different international, European and national refugee and refugee-related texts published. More importantly, the information available through this website is intended to achieve a better understanding of refugee issues in general, and of those in Bulgaria in particular. Thus, it maintains a positive image of refugees with the public at large, and a favorable political position with the Bulgarian government decision makers. The government of Bulgaria has implemented the *1951 Geneva Refugee Convention*, article 22, that prescribes free primary level education for refugee children despite economic constraints. However, in view of scarce government resources available in the public administration and public schooling system, access of refugee children to IT education and use of computers is still limited, especially in the countryside. Means permitting, plans are under discussion for creating modest IT centers with the assistance of governmental structures and NGO capacities for refugee women and children to study and develop IT skills, also in the framework of the Bulgarian EU integration.

7 Education on IT and Refugee Questions

The objective of a special course on IT and refugee questions is to give students an insight into using modern methods and approaches of communication, technology and methods for advocacy, training, teaching, cooperation, negotiation and mediation in law and politics at the international, regional and national level.

Topics might include technological infrastructure, access to the Internet and web-based data bases for international legal and policy instruments and texts; modern means of training and teaching with distance learning and conference transmissions/presentations in consultation with professors with expertise in this field and in democracy issues[3]; multicultural challenges, ethical and diplomacy issues in co-operation, negotiation and mediation.

Assignments might include keeping a journal to record learning in class through an interactive process, such as debates and website investigation of issues for analysis.

Readings available on websites include:

- http://www.unhcr.ch.refworld/; Office of the UN High Commissioner for Refugees (UNHCR);
- http://www.unhchr.ch/; Office of the UN High Commissioner for Human Rights (UNHCHR), Bill on Human Rights European Convention on Human Rights;
- http://www.icrc.org/; International Committee of the Red Cross (ICRC) Geneva Conventions of 1949 on humanitarian law and Protocols of 1977;
- http://www.un.org/; United Nations, Agenda for Peace and the work of the UN Security Council and humanitarian intervention.

---

3   See, for example, the website of Professor Pippa Norris, Lecturer at the Kennedy School of Government of Harvard University: http://www.ksg.harvard.edu.people-pnorris/; or http://www.pippanorris.com/

8 Conclusion

Based on the author's experience of working for the United Nations High Commissioner for Refugees, the following suggestions for improving the situation conclusions can be made.

IT with a Gender Perspective

...is a *conditio sine qua non* in order to secure an understanding of issues at stake when analyzing IT. It will bring out the particular problems of the female segment of the population in any given country, in particular the ones of the developing world. The continued efforts among the destitute and marginalized female segments of populations worldwide, of empowering women and eliminating gender disparities, are necessary in order to improve the situation, especially at the primary and secondary education level for future generations.

IT for Refugee Protection and Management...

...has become an indispensable tool for the survival and management of today's refugee problems around the world, especially in war-torn areas where the local infrastructure is inexistent or destroyed, as illustrated earlier on the basis of the author's personal experience in Singapore, Honduras, Angola, Kazakhstan and the UNHCR's experience in Rwanda, Bosnia, Kosovo, East Timor and in the 2001 Afghanistan Crisis following the events of September 11, 2001 in the U.S.

In addition, refugee-assisting organizations, including non-governmental refugee and human rights organizations, are online for fund-raising, advocacy and management. As has been discussed in this chapter, IT is very important for refugees to find solutions to their problems, but infrastructure has remained inadequate. Therefore, access to and funding of IT must be addressed by donor agencies.

IT for Prevention of Refugee-producing Situations...

...is necessary, since prevention is better than cure. Even though there may be more political will today to consider and take preventive action within potential refugees' countries of origin much more must be done about causes of flight and to achieve more dignified living conditions. The use of IT in public education and in shaping policies are proactive measures.

IT and Managing the Risks for Personal and Other Data Protection...

..., including that of refugees through legislative and applied means of personal data protection laws in general, and for refugees in particular. UNHCR and its partners must be even more careful in applying IT not to disclose data on individual refugees both in asylum and home countries, and to prevent that massive IT distribution channels lists of names and other details of entire refugee populations fall into the wrong hands, for example through e-mail, as this can cost human lives.

IT and the Feminist Perspective...

...can provide a special emphasis for the needs of women in all parts of the world and especially those countries, where IT is still very difficult to access, in order to advance today's and tomorrow's issues, but also to avoid neglect of the very basic needs of the human society, such as food and health, participation, co-organization and equal employment opportunities.

Global Distance Learning through Virtual Programs and Universities...

..., such as through *ifu*, a successful initiative in which nearly 1,000 women participated, among them many from the developing world and some from Central and Eastern European countries. Such initiatives are future-oriented and respond to the need and increasing interest of women and men to demystify IT by learning more about and actually using it for self-development and more gainful activities than was possible before. Distance learning has made progress in the human rights community and has proved to be also an important tool for human development in general and for the prevention of refugee producing situations.

As further readings on the questions addressed here, selected refugee-related books and articles authored, edited or co-edited by the author can be downloaded from http://www.unhcr.bg or http://www.luisedruke.com.

References

Druke, Luise (1990). *Preventive Action for Refugee Producing Situations.* With a foreword by Poul Hartling. Frankfurt, New York: Lang, 2nd ed. 1993.

UNDP (2001). Making New Technologies Work for Human Development. Human Development Report 2001. Published for the United Nations Development Program. New York: Oxford University Press.

Resolution

This book draws on the thoughts and actions of the participants, faculty, organizers, sponsors and supporters of the Project Area INFORMATION of the International Women's University (*ifu*), held at the University of Hamburg in summer 2000.

It is a book about communication and learning, as information is seen as a social resource in individual and community concerns for spreading knowledge and enabling development relevant to women. It is an attempt to integrate interdisciplinarity, interculturality, gender perspectives, theory and practice, and artistic approaches in several areas of concern around ICTs.

The *ifu* model, as developed in the Project Area INFORMATION, offers an important resource for the empowerment of women through education, paying attention to political, ideological and technological dimensions of women's struggles all over the world. Major features of the *ifu* program, as reflected in various chapters of this book, include:

- Respecting women's existing knowledge and skills;
- Co-constructing the educational processes and knowledges;
- Dealing with gendered structures of power across various cultures in North and South;
- Working towards an effective intercultural creation of knowledge;
- Emphasizing interdisciplinary cooperations and approaches;
- Focussing projects and courses on real problems in the information society – involving theoretical as well as practical aspects;
- Using intergenerational exchange as an important resource for learning.

Success occurs in increments, event after event. Keeping up educational efforts with innovative principles and practices is critical to bringing a change in women's lives – globally. We believe, therefore, that the continuation of *ifu*, with all the features highlighted above, is an important contribution to the empowerment of women in this era touted as the Information Age. Establishing an institution like *ifu* on a permanent basis will enable women to continue to raise challenges for themselves and everyone concerned with educational needs in this century.

The spirit of *ifu* is expressed beautifully in a poem by Mildred Kiconco Barya, a participant from Uganda[1]. She wrote it in Hamburg and read it at the closing session of the study program. Therefore, we as the editors would like to place this poem at the closing of this book. The common experience of *ifu* has changed our lives as well as the lives of all those involved.

Christiane Floyd, Govind Kelkar, Silvie Klein-Franke,
Cheris Kramarae, Cirila P. Limpangog

---

1   A collection of her lovely poems can be found in: *Men Love Chocolates But They Don't Say* by Mildred Kiconco Barya, printed in Uganda by The New Vision Publications, ISBN 9970 9888 0 8.

RESOLUTION

Cease living in the past
Make a new decision
Face the facts
Deep in your heart
Is the crux of the matter.
Stand up for realism
Challenge the status quo
And the system
Rise against irrelevancy
And legality
Live differently.
Don't be a mediocre.
Redirect the course
And the history flow,
Give it a name
Resolution.

Mildred Kiconco Barya

List of Authors

Dorcas Mofoluwake Akande, Nigeria; MA in English, Ph.D. in Literary Stylistics, specialization in gender perspectives to African literary text. Lecturer in the Dept. of English, Faculty of Arts, Obafemi Awolowo University, Ile-Ife. President of 'Soroptimist International', Ile-Ife Chapter. President of 'Fragrance of Literary Women in the Academia in Nigeria' (FLWAN). Fellow of the Center for Gender and Social Policy Studies, and of the British Council of Nigeria. Publicity secretary of 'Women against Rape, Sexual Harassment and Exploitation' (WARSHE). Member of the Association of Nigerian Authors, the Association of African Women for Research and Development, and the Reading Association of Nigeria (RAN).
At *ifu*: Facilitator for the Project *Cultural Modes, Self-Expression and New Media*

Mildred Kiconco Barya, Uganda, BA Literature; Author of poems and short stories; focus on writing women's documentaries, writing creativity, poetry. Engaged in women's networks, e.g. the Uganda Women Writers' Association (FEMRITE), writers networks and Christian projects.
At *ifu*: Participant in the Project *Identities and Globalization*

Tatjana Beer, Germany; Artist, Diploma in Visual Communication, Academy of Fine Arts, Hamburg. Besides artistic
work teacher of WenDo, self-defense and self-empowerment
for women and girls (www.wendo-hamburg.de). Former
work as an editor for the *NetzkunstWörterBuch* (NetArtGlos-
sary) and was engaged in various Internet art projects.
At *ifu*: Art Facilitator

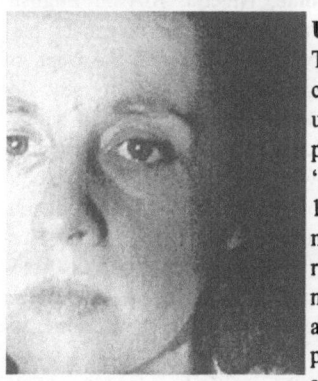

Ursula Biemann, Switzerland; graduated in Art and Cultural
Theory, in Mexico and the United States. Video artist and
curator focusing on gender relations in economy, media, and
urban space. Engagement in cross-cultural and collaborative
projects such as 'Kültür'; Istanbul/Zurich. Video essays:
'Performing the Border' on the U.S.-Mexico free trade zone,
1999; 'Writing Desire' on female sexuality and the bride
market in cyberspace, 2000; and 'Remote Sensing' a topog-
raphy of the global sex trade in the age of geographic information systems, 2001, shown at international festivals and
art exhibitions. Curator of exhibition on gender and geography at Generali Foundation in Vienna, 2002. Most recent
artist publication: 'been there and back to nowhere - gender
in transnational spaces', Berlin. Researches at the Institute
for Theory of Art and Design in Zurich and lectures internationally. (www.geobodies.org).
At *ifu*: Artist

Tone Bratteteig, Norway; Associate Professor, Dept. of Informatics, University of Oslo. Research interests concerned
with relations between design and use of IT: participatory design, systems development as social and technical change
processes. Current interest is global software outsourcing
where technical, social and cultural issues are equally important. Has a long standing interest in gender aspects of
technology / informatics. Norwegian representative in the
steering committee of the Nordic Association on Information
Systems Research in Scandinavia; Norwegian coordinator of
the Nordic/ Baltic research network 'Information Technology, Transnational Democracy and Gender'; member of the
International Federation for Information Processing (IFIP),
working group 9.1. (www.ifi.uio.no/~tone/).
At *ifu*: Lecturer, Director of the Project *Health Care Information*

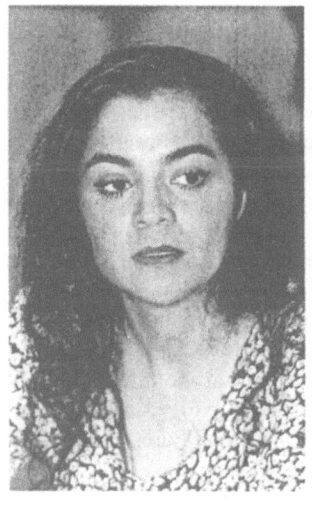

Aleida Calleja, Mexico; BA in Communication, NGO-journalist. Director-Founder of the first indigenous radio station in Puebla, Mexico. Coordinator of the Radio Project with Female Refugees from Guatemala in Chiapas, Mexico. Experience with the coordination and production of video and radio for indigenous children. Focus on: communication and democracy; alternative communication, rural development, indigenous cultural radio, narration, women and indigenous autonomy. Currently, she is the president and co-founder of first center for Citizens' Communication in Mexico and the Mexican representative to the World Community Broadcasters Association (AMARC). She is the co-author of legislation concerning electronic media and citizens' right to participation.
At *ifu*: Facilitator for the Project *Identities and Globalization*

Tanja Carstensen, Germany; MA in Sociology. Assistant of the project 'Times of the City' at the Senate Office for Equal Opportunities of the Free and Hanseatic City of Hamburg, Department 'Arrangements Between Work and Family, Social Networks'. Research areas: the relation between technology and gender; women, new information technologies, time, and electronic urban information systems.
At *ifu*: Lecturer

Mona Dahms, Denmark; MS in Electronic Engineering; Associate Professor, Department of Development and Planning; Aalborg University. Formal education in International Development and Adult Education. Present research on ICT for development: impact of a Multipurpose Community Telecentre in Tanzania. Seven years in Tanzania: teacher at Dar es Salaam Technical College, Dept. of Electronics and Telecommunications, later as technical expert at Staff College, Tanzania Posts & Telecommunications Corporation. Head of Electrical Department in a factory in Brazil. Cooperation with UNESCO/ Danida and the International Development Research Center, Canada. Chair of the international Gender and Science and Technology Association (GASAT).
At *ifu:* Lecturer, Facilitator for the Projects *Community Development through Information* and *Information Kiosks*

Luise Druke, Germany; LL.M Intl. Law, Brussels; MA Economics, Finance and Management, Webster; MA Public Administration, Ph.D. at Harvard. Lecturer at Boston University, the College of Europe and elsewhere (www.luisedruke.com). Engaged by the Office of the United Nations High Commissioner of Refugees (UNHCR) since 1977. Former Head of UNHCR offices in Kazakhstan, Portugal, Nordic countries, Angola, Europe Dept. Brussels with the EC/EU institutions, then Honduras, Chile, Singapore. Currently the UNHCR Representative and UN Resident Coordinator in Bulgaria. Research specializing in refugee law and policy. Works with the United Nations in conflict prevention, the EC/EU to standardize asylum and refugee law and policy, and various human rights and refugee institutions for the development of strategies in Central European countries and countries of the Former Soviet Union.
At *ifu*: Lecturer

Marlis Dürkop, Germany; Professor of Sociology; until 2001, Deputy Minister for Science and Research of the Free and Hanseatic City of Hamburg; former President of the Humboldt-University in Berlin; long standing engagement in promoting feminist research; initiated first German gender studies program at the Humboldt-University in 1995 and was a key promoter of the interdisciplinary gender studies program, realized through a cooperation of all higher schools of education in Hamburg.
At *ifu*: Political Representative in charge of the Project Area INFORMATION

Mona El Tobgui, Egypt; Ph.D., Assistant Professor of Child Health, Child Health Department Supervisor, Central Internet Unit, and member of International Relations Office, National Research Centre, Cairo. Supervisor at the Healthy Baby Clinic and of the NGO 'Egyptian Society for the Care of Children', Cairo. Research focus in conceptualizing and promoting preventative health care for adolescents. Member of the NGO 'Egyptian Society for the Prevention of Harmful Practices to Woman & Child.'
At *ifu*: Participant in the Project *Healthcare Information*

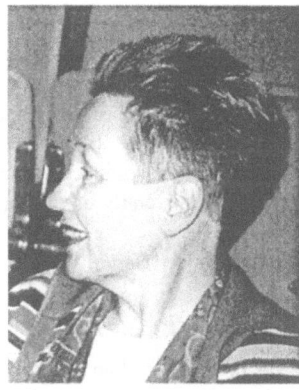

Antje Eske, Germany; Professor of Fine Arts; Academy of Fine Arts, Hamburg. Designs interactive, web-communication-projects, working with linked picture-files, conversatories, HyperCard-correspondences, electronic links and formed chats, connecting History of Art with Net-Art, long term network 'Urbino-chat' since 1988. Focus of activity: Circulating Arts. Former work with other artistically formed conversational media, e.g. social games, theatre-in-the-street, three-dimensional-caricatures or mutual conversational-drawings like visual notes, visual diaries, drawing-upside-down, blind- and automatic-drawings. Member of 'Data-Art-Movement'; engagement in Net Art, http://swiki.hfbk.uni-hamburg.de:8080/netzkunstwoerterbuchAt *ifu*: Artist

Edla Maria Faust-Ramos, Brazil; Professor of Mathematics and Education; University of St. Catarina (www.inf.ufsc.br/~edla). Studies focus on technologies and education, especially learning processes and techniques to support autonomous use of new technologies. Designs and promotes information services for cooperative organizations and communities.
At *ifu:* Lecturer, Director of the Projects *Curiosity, Intuition and Information Technology and Information Kiosks*

Christiane Floyd, Austria/Germany; Professor and Head of the Software Engineering Group at the Informatics Department, University of Hamburg. Long standing interest in human-centered software development, main author of STEPS (Software Technology for Participatory, Evolutionary Systems Design); interdisciplinary research into epistemological foundations of software development and on knowledge co-construction.
At *ifu*: Lecturer, Local Dean of the Project Area INFORMATION, Head of the Hamburg Local Team and of the Hamburg sub-project of virtual *ifu*

Judith Gregory, USA/Norway; Ph.D., Work Sociologist at the University of Oslo. Expert in field work methods particularly in the area of health care, gender perspectives on technology and work theories. Formerly researcher and member of faculty, Department of Science & Technology Studies Rensselaer Polytechnic Institute, NY and researcher at the Department of Communication, University of California.
At *ifu*: Lecturer, Facilitator for the Project *Health Care Information*

Wendy Harcourt, Australia; Ph.D. Australian National University. Focus on gender and development policy, culture and development, women's networking, research into health and globalization. Director of programs and editor of Development Journal at the international secretariat of the Society for International Development, an international NGO headquartered in Rome with a worldwide network of professionals working in development including the SID-WID network (www.sidint.org). Research focus: international policy and lobbying for gender and development, environment, and reproductive rights and sexual health, and alternatives to development. Author of books and articles on alternatives to development; sustainable development; power, gender relations and reproductive rights; and women and cyberculture.
At *ifu*: Lecturer

Sandra Harding, USA; philosopher and professor of Education and Women's Studies; UCLA .Director of the Center for the Study of Women. Co-editor of: the 'Interdisciplinary Journal of Feminist Research and Scholarship'; 'Signs'; Author or editor of several books and special journal issues. Visiting professor; University of Amsterdam, the University of Costa Rica, and the Swiss Federal Institute of Technology. Consultant to the Pan American Health Organization, the United Nations Development Fund for Women (UNIFEM), the United Nations Commission on Science and Technology for Development, and UNESCO's World Science Report 1996

Sabine Issa-Beuster, Germany; Sociologist. Manager of the project 'Times of the City' at the Senate Office for Equal Opportunities of the Free and Hanseatic City of Hamburg, Department 'Arrangements Between Work and Family, Social Networks.'
At *ifu*: Lecturer

Berta Jottar, Mexico/USA; Video-Artist from Mexico City, ABD in the Program of Performance Studies at Tisch School of the Arts, New York University. Currently Ph.D.-studies about exile Afro-Latin communities in their relationship to rumba music. Focus: Afro/Latin migration, diaspora, dance and music in/to the US. Member of the San Diego/Tijuana art collective 'Border Art Workshop/Taller de arte fronterizo,' from 1989-1991. One of the founding members of 'Las Comadres.'
At *ifu*: Artist

Govind Kelkar, India; Ph.D. in Political Economy, Professor of History and Gender and Development Studies, Consultant for the International Fund for Agricultural Development (IFAD) and the Food and Agriculture Organization (FAO). Formerly Head of Gender and Development Program, Asian Institute of Technology, Thailand. Expert on Gender and Technology and on Indigenous Knowledge; Editor of the journal 'Gender, Technology and Development'. Author of numerous articles and books.
At *ifu:* Lecturer, Director of the Projects *Community Development Through Information* and *Cultural Modes, Self-Expression and New Media*

Karolyn Kerr, New Zealand; Ph.D. candidate in Health Informatics. Background in nursing management at Wellington Hospital and medical research at the Wellington School of Medicine. Focus of study is Telehealth in the South Pacific as a form of a virtual community, introduced to this subject at *ifu*. Further research on health informatics and telehealth in the future of New Zealand health care.
At *ifu*: Participant in the Project *Virtual Communities*

Carina Keskitalo, Sweden; Ph.D. candidate in International Relations, Faculty of Social Sciences, University of Lapland, Finland. Research interest in participation in decision-making (Ph.D. work on agenda setting in the Arctic region). Formerly visiting fellow at the Institute of Arctic Studies at Dartmouth College, USA, and visiting scholar at Scott Polar Research Institute, Cambridge University, UK. Previous work as newspaper journalist and photographer with specialization in environmental issues.
At *ifu*: Participant in the Project *Visions of Citizenship*

Silvie Klein-Franke, Germany; Ph.D. Immunobiology/Biochemistry; further education in affirmative action. Program development, student affairs, fundraising and PR for the Centre for Tropical and Subtropical Agriculture and Forestry (CeTSAF, www.tropenzentrum.de), Göttingen. Former coordinator for central *ifu*, Hanover, and for Project Area INFORMATION, Hamburg: local and international coordination, curricular development, project management. Member of the German associations for the International Women's University and of the activist movement and association 'More Direct Democracy'.
At *ifu*: Coordinator of the Project Area INFORMATION

Cheris Kramarae, USA; Professor, Center for the Study of Women in Society, University of Oregon. Author and editor of numerous articles and books on women and technology, feminist scholarship; language and gender, women and on-line education, and global women's knowledges. Consultant and recipient of numerous teaching and scholarship awards.
At *ifu*: Lecturer, Director of the Projects *Future of Education* and *Reconstructing Gender on the Internet*, International Dean of the Project Area INFORMATION

Cirila P. Limpangog, Philippines; B.Sc. Mass Communication, Master in Public Administration, post graduate fellow in Germany on 'Gender and Corruption'. Presently specialist at Consuelo Zobel Alger Foundation, and consultant at the Roldan HRD Philippines. Also focused work on alternative communication, gender and development, good governance. Involved in capability-building and evaluation of programs on gender and development and sustainable development; Formerly technical consultant to the 'National Commission on the Role of Filipino Women'. Affiliation with 'Transparency International' (TI) and the 'International Association of Women in Radio and Television' (IAWRT).
At *ifu*: Facilitator for the Project *Visions of Citizenship*

Lisa Link, USA/Germany; BA (hons.) in Political Economy and German Language, Literature and Linguistics; Ph.D. Research at the University of Hildesheim, Germany, in the field of applied computer linguistics/e-learning. Research assistant and lecturer at the Flensburg University of Applied Sciences, Germany (http://www.wi.fh-flensburg.de/tue/link/). Affiliation with Tekom, a professional society for technical documentation and IT management, Board member of the Women's Centre Schleswig.
At *ifu*: Participant in the Project *Future of Education*

Elke Mätschke, Germany; graduated in Linguistics, Education and History. Project and personnel management in Training and Gender issues, 15 years experience in adult education with the focus on designing and implementing European training projects e.g. for women in ICTs. Currently working on career strategies for women scientists in medicine and natural sciences at the University Hospital Hamburg Eppendorf.
At *ifu*: Participant of the Project *Virtual Communities*

Liane Melzer, Germany; Lawyer. Former Head of the Department 'Women in Family and Social Environment' of the Senate for Equal Opportunities, Hamburg. Responsible for the project 'Times of the City', a support program for working and single mothers.
At *ifu*: Lecturer

Sabina Mihelj, Slovenia, BA in Comparative Literature, BA in Sociology of Culture, Ph.D. research and teaching assistant in Media Studies at Institutum Studiorum Humanitatis (www.ish.si). Regular participation/lecturing at the international course 'On Divided Societies', Inter-University Center, Dubrovnik, Croatia. Research focus on the role of media and media related rituals in the construction of imagined communities, especially in relation to nationalism, migration and manipulation of history in parts of former Yugoslavia. Affiliation to *ifu* alumnae network; managing editor of 'Monitor ISH - International Review of Humanities and Social Sciences'; participation in the project 'Changing Europe - Changing Media' (European Science Foundation).
At *ifu*: Participant in the Project *Identities and Globalization*

Therona Moodley; South Africa; M.Ed. in English from the University of Minnesota, USA; Lecturer at the Department of English at the University of South Africa (a distance education university). Research focus on English Language and Education, Cultural and Media Studies, Visual Literacy. Member of Women's University Forum and the Equity Committee of the University.
At *ifu*: Participant of the Project *Future of Education*

Heike Pienkoss, Germany; Engineer in Clothing Technology, MS in Clothing. Journalist and free-lance computer trainer (www.heikePienkoss.de). Research interest in women and technology.
At *ifu*: Participant in the Project *Future of Education*

Irma Ávila Pietrasanta, Mexico; Social Communication studies at the Universidad Iberoamericana; Videomaker in world-wide productions with national and international awards. Former professor of television and video at the Metropolitan Autonomous University. Video-Producer for the National Autonomous University of Mexico; Information rights activist.
At *ifu:* Lecturer, Director of the Projects *Identities and Globalization and Mass Media and Democracy*

Sara Sanchez Mera, Argentina; Diploma in Educational Administration, Diploma in Design of Social Development Projects. Teacher of Literature and coordinator of distance education programs at the University of Antafagasta in Chile. President of an NGO in Argentina.
At *ifu*: Participant of the Project *Future of Education*

Birgit Thies, Germany, Ph.D.-thesis on interactive models in the Internet at the Department of Ecological Modeling in Bayreuth (http://www.bitoek.uni-bayreuth.de).
At *ifu*: Participant in the Project *Future of Education*

Lena Trojer, Sweden; Ph.D. in Analytical Chemistry. Professor in Information Technology and Gender Research and Head of Department 'Human Work Science and Media Technology' at Blekinge Institute of Technology. Formerly associate professor in Gender and Technology at Luleå University of Technology. Member of the international research network 'Information Technology, Transnational Democracy and Gender', member of the research board of the Swedish International Development Cooperation Agency / 'Science of Anticipation, Recognition, Evaluation, Control of Health Risk' (SIDA /SAREC).
At *ifu*: Lecturer

Ina Wagner, Austria; Ph.D. in Physics, Professor and Chair of the Center for CSCW Research, Institute for Technology Design and Assessment; Vienna University of Technology, Austria (http://as15.iguw.tuwien.ac.at/). Pioneering research on a feminist perspective in science and technology, multi-disciplinary systems design and CSCW. Current European projects and international cooperation with researchers in Malmö School of Art and Communications, University of Milano-Biccocca, Oulu University of Technology, UC San Diego, IRESCO/Paris, Academy of Fine Arts in Vienna and the Danish IT University.
At *ifu*: Lecturer

Jutta Weber, Germany; Ph.D. in Cultural Science Studies; MA in Philosophy and Political Science. Senior Researcher at the Department of History of Science at the Technical University of Braunschweig in a research project on the concept of life in artificial life research.
At *ifu:* Facilitator for the Project *Reconstructing Gender on the Internet*

Ingrid Wetzel, Germany; Ph.D. in Informatics; former Assistant Professor of the Software Engineering Group of the Computer Science Department, University of Hamburg, Guest Professor at the Institute of Business Informatics, University of Linz, Austria. Software consultant for project management, object-oriented software construction, and developing interactive application systems in organizations. Projects in health information systems for hospitals. Long term interest in developing concepts for teaching computer skills to women students.
At *ifu*: Lecturer, Internet Training Advisor

Esther Williams, Fiji; Head Librarian of the Information and Library Studies Program, University of the South Pacific. Expert in long-distance education. Area of interest: The assessment of training needs for library and information studies; systematic surveys of democratic processes including elections. Cooperation with the Canadian International Development Assistance Agency (CIDA). Program on information society and informatics (UNESCO), needs assessment for libraries: maintains archives and ICT in the Pacific region. At *ifu*: Lecturer, Director of the Projects *Virtual Communities* and *Visions of Citizenship*

Marsha Woodbury, USA; Ph.D., Lecturer of Computer Science, University of Illinois at Urbana-Champaign, (http://www.cpsr.org/~marsha-w/). An active computer professional, she is involved in teaching, writing a computer ethics text book, 'Computer and Information Ethics', and working to encourage more women to study computing. Her research now focuses on how the disaster on September 11, 2001, has influenced the field of computer ethics in the United States. Former National Chair of the Computer Professionals for Social Responsibility (CPSR). Member of the national Association for Computing Machinery (ACM) and Institute of Electrical and Electronics Engineers (IEEE).
At *ifu*: Lecturer, Director of the Project *Knowledge Architectures*

Zhang Wei, China; Educationalist, Lecturer at the Department of English; Peking University on advanced English writing and speaking, the heart of computer, different approaches to teaching, language education at the turn of the century. Ph.D. on Developing a Web-based Course for Academic English Writing along with an Alternative Model of Assessment.
At *ifu*: Facilitator for the Project *Future of Education*

Index